Classics on Screen

CLASSICS ON SCREEN

Ancient Greece and Rome on Film

Alastair J.L. Blanshard
Kim Shahabudin

B L O O M S B U R Y

LONDON · NEW DELHI · NEW YORK · SYDNEY

Bloomsbury Academic
An imprint of Bloomsbury Publishing Plc

50 Bedford Square	1385 Broadway
London	New York
WC1B 3DP	NY 10018
UK	USA

www.bloomsbury.com

First published in 2011 by Bristol Classical Press
Reprinted by Bloomsbury Academic 2013

© 2011 by Alastair J.L. Blanshard and Kim Shahabudin

Alastair J.L. Blanshard and Kim Shahabudin have asserted
their right under the Copyright, Designs and Patents Act,
1988, to be identified as Authors of this work.

British Library Cataloguing-in-Publication Data
A catalogue record for this book is available from the
British Library.

ISBN: 978-0-7156-3724-1

Library of Congress Cataloging-in-Publication Data
A catalog record for this book is available from the
Library of Congress.

Typeset by Ray Davies

Contents

To Cressida, who currently reads my books.
And to Frankie, who may one day read mine.

List of Illustrations

All images provided courtesy of the William K. Zewadski archive.

Introduction

Few media can rival cinema for its ability to make the cultures of Greece and Rome accessible to the general audience. Film takes a world that is separated by space, time, and language and makes it comprehensible, entertaining, and intriguing. Its appeal transcends barriers of class, education, and ethnicity. Film stirs our emotions and fills our senses. Its impact is subtle, but effective. Its fictions become our realities. Rome may never have had regular orgies, saluted its emperors with raised arms, or condemned gladiators to die with a downward point of the thumb, yet thanks to cinema all of these have become absolute mainstays of popular conceptions about Roman culture. As one of the most potent forces for the transmission of knowledge about the ancient world, film demands our attention. As the playground where we enjoy the freedom to reassemble the fragments of the classical world as we see fit, it presents us with extraordinary intellectual opportunities. Importantly, it is a playground open to all, where access is not limited by disciplinary boundaries, educational experience, or conservative traditions. Cinema enables people to express a view about the classical world who might otherwise be prevented from doing so. Studying the cinematic output that depicts Greece and Rome (for which we have adopted the term 'cine-antiquity') provides an important vehicle for discussing the values, history, and cultural politics of the classical past. It demands that we think about what are the key elements that make the cultures of the ancient Mediterranean so distinctive and worthy of study.

At the same time, such study also makes us think about the nature of film and its place in cultural history. From the very beginning of cinema, filmmakers have routinely turned to the ancient world to provide them with inspiration for storylines, visual spectacles, and powerful metaphors. In doing so, cinema continues a long-standing practice of adaptation and appropriation of classical material. Rome's adoption of Greek culture started a trend that since the Renaissance has been one of the hallmarks of Western culture. The classical past has become the stuff of fantasy. It has many guises. It can be a lost golden age, a place where the arts reach their highest refinement. Alternatively, it has been represented as a world of pagan debauchery, one that for all its wealth and power, we are lucky to have escaped. All too often the stories that we project onto the past tell us more about ourselves than the ancient world. The past has proved a very useful vehicle for conveying lessons about the present.

Introduction

Visual and dramatic media have always been particularly attracted to antiquity. Both classical texts and objects exercised the minds of Renaissance artists. Painters and sculptors found inspiration in the Roman poet Ovid's retelling of Greek and Roman myth, or the architectural writings of Vitruvius, or Pliny's catalogue of ancient artworks. The rediscovery of so many pieces of ancient statuary in Rome acted as a catalyst for artists as they sought to imitate and (in their dreams) surpass the skill of the ancients. Roman copies of original Greek sculptures such as the Apollo Belvedere, the Medici Venus, or the Farnese Heracles became the highest examples of male and female beauty. By placing classical art at the centre of the western canon, these artists ensured that all subsequent generations had to wrestle with the classical legacy in order to establish their own aesthetic visions. From the seventeenth century onwards France demanded that its painters grapple with themes from the classical past (so-called 'history painting') before they could command the respect of their peers. Through such works artists could attain a reputation for greatness. Huge canvases depicting the great battles and events from Greco-Roman antiquity dominated the elite imagination. Their allegorical meanings educated numerous audiences about the nature of virtue and rulership. Historically significant moments and individuals became examples for imitation. Kings and Emperors learnt about how to be great rulers by reading about and seeing images of Alexander the Great or Julius Caesar.

The taste for the neo-classical spread throughout Europe. Archaeology fuelled this hunger. Eighteenth-century excavations in Pompeii and Herculaneum sponsored fashionable revolutions in interior design and the decorative arts. It became possible to travel through the grand houses of Europe and never leave a 'Pompeian-style' drawing room. This passion continued well into the nineteenth century where the classical world proved inspirational for artists such as Frederic Leighton and Lawrence Alma-Tadema.

Drama proved equally enthralled by the potential that the antique offered. One of the earliest forms of drama was the Renaissance masque and these often took the form of elaborate stagings of Greek myths. Authors such as Seneca proved popular with Renaissance audiences. Indeed, some plays such as *Hercules Furens* ('The Maddened Hercules') proved so popular that for a short period of time, it was rare to find a play without a mad character raving around in imitation of the Greek hero. Others found inspiration not so much in the plays of antiquity, but in the stories recounted in Greek and Roman history. So, for example, the biographer Plutarch proved inspirational to numerous playwrights; the most famous being Shakespeare who used Plutarch as the basis for most of his 'Roman' plays, *Julius Caesar, Antony and Cleopatra*, and *Coriolanus*. Greek drama could inspire a similarly dedicated following. During the nineteenth century, for example, special trains were put on from

2

London so that audiences could attend the Cambridge Greek play. This was aimed at an elite audience that knew (or liked to pretend it knew) classical Greek. However, it was not just high art that was attracted to antiquity. Popular nineteenth-century circus acts and burlesques often invoked the ancient world. Thus, a trip to the circus could involve such acts as *The Flying Mercury, Alexander the Great and Thalestris the Amazon,* the Ringling Brothers' *Cleopatra,* and the *Last Days of Pompeii.* However, the most elaborate of these classically-themed shows was *Nero, or the Destruction of Rome.* Staged in Olympia in London in 1888, this show boasted a cast of two thousand performers, one hundred massive golden chariots, wild beasts, and combined 'gladiatorial contests of the famed Coliseum and Circus Maximus with the Olympic Games of ancient Greece'. As if that weren't enough, the poster for the spectacle promised 'grand, bewitching dances' and 'gorgeous scenes of imperial orgies'.

It is no accident then that cinema, which combines elements of both the visual and the dramatic, should find itself drawn towards antiquity. Indeed, film has benefited from personnel drawn from both these traditions. Artists who trained in history painting in France ended up as some of the earliest set-designers in Europe and America. Both actors and directors who began their professional careers working with classical drama have made their transition to life behind or in front of the camera.

Cinema has benefited from coming at the end of such a long tradition of re-imaginings of the classical world. It has the advantage of not only being able to draw upon classical sources directly, but also the richness of the appropriation of the classical world by other post-antique art-forms. And cinema has shown itself only too happy to take advantage of this plethora of material. It is just as likely to turn to the French history-painter Gérôme's nineteenth-century depictions of the gladiatorial arena or Shakespeare's story of Julius Caesar as it is to read an archaeological report or the Roman biographer Suetonius.

Additionally, films involving the classical past represent the start of a new tradition. While cinema may look to the past, it also sets out a bold, original, and distinctive vision. A number of features make the study of cinematic version of antiquity particularly exciting. Cinema asks new questions about antiquity and offers new solutions to old problems. It has also proved the inspiration for other genres. The impact of cinematic versions of antiquity can be traced in spin-offs in TV programming and advertising as well as on-line and console gaming.

The representation of the classical world in cinema is important because no genre can match film in terms of breadth and depth of audience impact. It is both the most dominant and the most distinctive popular entertainment of the twentieth century. Moreover, it has the capacity to offer a vision that transcends national boundaries. *Gladiator* (2000) proved equally popular in places and cultures as diverse as Australia,

Germany, Japan, Korea, and the Czech Republic. Few art forms can command this degree of popularity.

Mainstream cinema is able to devote financial capital and technological resources to the recreation of antiquity that dwarfs the amount spent on similar academic endeavours. Even art-house films such as *Fellini-Satyricon* (1969) can command budgets of $3 million dollars. Directors are able (if they wish) to marshal teams of experts on everything from the fabrics worn by the women of Alexander's court to the strategy of his cavalry. Of course, such advice is always tempered by budgetary and narrative imperatives, but it is not hard to find its traces, if you know where to look.

The dynamic between the world of film and that of the academic study of antiquity is a complex one. Academics often like to imagine a large gap between the world of the ivory tower and the silver screen. Yet the gap is perhaps not as large as they would think. Cinema regularly brings into bold relief underlying assumptions about the operation of the ancient world shared by high and low culture. Set designers may constantly look to Pompeii for inspiration, but then so do the numerous academic studies that have elevated this provincial town into a model for domestic and civic arrangements throughout the Roman Empire. Pompeii dominates the academic and cinematic imagination for the same reason. It offers to fill gaps that no other source can.

Although it should be noted that cinema is far less tolerant of gaps than academic studies. Only a few directors are prepared to celebrate the fragmentary nature of the survival of elements from antiquity. Most prefer to plaster over the cracks in the pursuit of a seamless realism. One of the distinctive features of historical films set in the ancient world rather than the modern one is that the sources and evidence for the ancient world are far less complete than for other periods. There are significant absences in our knowledge. Films set in World War II or Revolutionary France (to take two popular cinematic historical periods) do not have to cope with large gaps (sometimes decades) when we know little or nothing about the activities of the principal characters, nor do they need to deal with often profound ignorance or contested theories about costuming, interior design, or props.

Watching films tackle these difficulties is revealing. For example, take the minor problem of depicting the ancient campaign tent. Owing to the nature of the construction of these shelters, none survive from antiquity, nor are they well documented in our ancient visual record. At best, we are presented with a few stylised exterior views. Yet, owing to the martial nature of so many films, they are important and necessary locations for preparatory scenes before large battle sequences. They provide a convenient location for explanatory dialogue and explanations of strategy. Cinematic imperatives pull in one direction whilst the limitations of our evidence pull in the other. Significantly, in such contests, the needs of cinema always win.

4

1. The image of Roman power. Interior of tent, *Herod the Great* (1958).

In such situations, films employ a variety of techniques to fill the gaps. They rely heavily on already well-established motifs so that the audience can recognise where they are. They import elements from other parallel traditions that seem appropriate to the situation. They ensure that such moments are, at the very least, thematically consistent with the rest of the film. Indeed, often so much effort is expended in filling in the gaps that the scene becomes over-determined, pregnant with all the potentiality of the film.

Compare the two tents depicted in *Herod the Great* (Italian title: *Erode il Grande*, 1958, US release 1960) and *The 300 Spartans* (1962). Both offer standard responses to the problem of filling the interior of the campaign tent. In *Herod the Great* [Fig. 1], we see the emperor Octavian/Augustus (Massimo Girotti) seated on the right. The basic structure of the tent interior is modelled upon eastern prototypes, however they have been given a classicising feel through the use of a key meander, a decorative motif most commonly found in Greek pottery and one synonymous with the classical world. Further classicising is done through the large number of props. Stools, jugs, and tables are all borrowed from Pompeian examples. In the corner rests a Roman standard. The placement is inappropriate (do you pick it up as you head out the door like an umbrella?), but few symbols are so identifiably Roman. Its only rival is the eagle and we see one of these adorning the frame displaying a campaign

5

map. This last element is curious. It is not a classical feature, but is one borrowed from modern warfare. Its origins lie in the 'war rooms' of twentieth-century campaigns. Through the repeated use of such maps in popular war films, audiences learnt to expect such elements as a feature of any campaign headquarters, even one set thousands of years in the past. Here preconception rather than archaeology populates the scene. The map is an object which can, in films, act as an easily-recognised signifier of antiquity: its fabrication from animal skins (as in this example), 'antique' fonts and primitive conceptualisation of the world outside, all cue us to our location. In each case, such elements help tell a story. Through the efficient deployment of staging and props (what is technically known as *mise-en-scène*), the audience of *Herod the Great* is presented with a visual shorthand of Rome's wealth (the exotic fruit and metallic drinking vessels), its power (the standard), its bureaucratic efficiency (scrolls), and its military strength (strategic map).

Contrast this with the depiction of the Persian king Xerxes' tent in *The 300 Spartans* [Fig. 2]. Again we are venturing into the realm of fantasy. The Greek historian Herodotus tells us that Persian tents were lavish in the extreme (*Histories* 9.80-2), but his description is light on interior details. He describes the plenitude of couches and cups and filmmakers have followed his cue, producing an opulent setting for the travelling

2. A sign of oriental excess. Life at Xerxes' court, *The 300 Spartans* (1962).

Persian court. Its size speaks volumes about Persian extravagance. Few cinematic tents can rival the tent of Xerxes. Rich carpets decorate the floor. There is space for a full troupe of dancing girls. In a film where Spartan austerity is pitted against Persian decadence, we need do more than look inside Xerxes' tent to see the character of the invader.

These are not isolated examples. It is possible to write a history of the depiction of campaign tents which would tell us much about the themes that flow through Greek and Roman films. Such a history would include the contrasting tents of *Spartacus* (1960), where Spartacus' egalitarian spirit and underdog status is expressed through the rustic simplicity of his accommodation in contrast to the splendour and magnificence of his Roman opponents. Place would certainly be found for Marcus Aurelius' headquarters in *Gladiator* (2000) which offer a particularly unique vision. The film abandons the simple, clean neo-classical aesthetic of many depictions in favour of a rich amalgam of textures, colours, and materials. The interior is almost baroque in its appearance. The headquarters is crammed with objects in a random assemblage of lamps, busts, diadems, armour and fabrics drawn from a variety of classical periods. It is the inventory of the British Museum rearranged as The Old Curiosity Shop. The audience can see the wealth and decadence of the late Roman Empire in every piece of overblown drapery. The dim lighting tells us that we are not witnessing the founding of a glorious future, but rather the last gasp of a world past its 'use-by' date.

We have dwelt on the image of the campaign tent because it provides a useful example of how consideration of even minor elements in a film can be rewarding. Students of the representation of antiquity in film need to pay attention to even the smallest details as sometimes these can be the most telling. The trick to studying film is knowing what questions to ask. In the following section, we present some of the issues that are worth bearing in mind when looking at cinematic Greece and Rome.

How to watch films: some preliminary considerations

The most important thing to remember when watching a film is that you are observing a carefully crafted product. Some films make this easier to remember than others. Many of the films in this book use a version of cinematic realism to portray their stories. The shots are composed to mimic the way we normally view the world, directorial interventions are minimised and hidden behind narrative imperatives (e.g. scenes change because the story demands that they do so), and there is no attempt to break the frame and remind the audience that they are watching a film. If stage drama often pretended that the audience was placed behind a glass 'fourth wall', then cinema tends to place the viewer in the position of an intangible ghost, transported from scene to scene, only able to view rather influence the action that surrounds you. These films encourage you to suspend your disbelief and imagine that you have been transported back to the age of Nero or the world of Greek mythology. Some prefer to make this act of transportation more self-conscious. DeMille's *Cleopatra* (1934) opens on an image of two immense blocks of stone. These slowly part to reveal a chained and semi-naked slave girl, holding smoking braziers of incense, and flanked by phallic columns and bestial statuary. The viewer is quite literally granted entry into the secret, forbidden, and exotic world of the Egyptian queen.

Other films deliberately remind you that what you are watching is a constructed artifice. Their directors show their hand and never let you forget that you are a witness to a very personal vision. Through editing, special effects, deliberate anachronism, and character addresses to the audience, they play up the artificiality of the cinematic experience. They show you their workings and invite you to appreciate their skill. Sometimes there is an opportunity to achieve both the aims of immediacy of audience presence and celebrate the artistry of the director through the use of cinematic effects. For example, in *Spartacus* (1960), the experience of gladiatorial combat is intensified through the decision to film the sequence through the slats of the arena's wooden fence. On the one hand, the viewer is placed in exactly the same position as the other slaves as they watch the fight. It is just like being there, standing next to them. On the other hand, we might understand the slaves to be figured as a cinema audience: witnessing only a controlled (and in this case 'widescreen') portion of the scene that is playing out on the other side of the fence. The double shift in perspective prompts the viewer to think about the 'naturalness' of shot composition. The obscuring of parts of the scene and the tight framing of the shot reminds you of the role of directing and editing. It demands that we think about how scenes are manufactured and makes us alert to the cinematographer's art.

The job of the critical viewer is to preserve a double-vision when watching all of these different types of films. We need both to appreciate the effects that films create and also the techniques by which those effects were created. Amongst other details, we must consider the study of camera angles, shot composition, the use of background music, lighting, props, and acting techniques. Hopefully this leads to a doubling of pleasure rather than a halving of it. Knowing that every sound of the arena in *Gladiator* (the roar of the beasts, the clang of metal against metal, the squelch of a body being sliced in two) was the result of meticulous sound engineering and design intended to create a complete soundscape can only increase one's appreciation of the total effect. Students should acquaint themselves with the various types of shots used in films and the basic techniques of cinematography. The list of suggested further reading at the end of this chapter will help you. In the following discussion, we raise some issues to consider when looking at the cinematic portrayal of antiquity.

One should never forget the industrial context when considering cinema. In some ways, this is true for all art forms. One gets a diminished sense of a painting if one examines it without considering the role of patrons, dealers, commissions, contemporary fashions, or the technical limitations of materials. Similarly, a full appreciation of the novel only comes with an understanding of the roles of editor, publisher, typesetter, and bookseller as well as the methods of its dissemination and circulation. The same idea applies only more so to cinema because more than any other art form, cinema is a collaborative activity. Naturally, one is drawn to the figure of the director, and some directors feature more than others in the story of a film's production. Yet even the most hands-on director cannot achieve their vision without the help, skills, and artistry of others. When one considers the roles of actors or screenwriters, this influence is often easy to see or trace. Less obvious, but equally crucial, are the huge number of ancillary figures (e.g. cinematographers, editors, sound technicians) that feature in a film's production. A director like Wolfgang Petersen may express a desire that his Helen in *Troy* (2004) is an 'unknown beauty'. Yet it is only through the skilled knowledge and negotiations of teams of casting agents and actors' agents that this desire can be translated into reality. Diane Kruger who played Helen in *Troy* was not magicked out of thin air, she was the product of a process. One should be wary of the fallacy of 'auteurism', the tendency to attribute every aspect of a film back to the director.

In addition, the film industry is a business. Films are expensive to produce and they need to make a profit. While some genres of film are more sensitive to cost/profit issues than others (and we will discuss these when looking at individual cases), it is worth bearing in mind that even the most avant-garde director will often have producers and funding bodies keeping an eye on expenditure and box-office receipts. Financial concerns impinge not only on production, but also on the way that film is sold. The director may intend one message, but advertising executives may play up another. The advertising for *Hercules* (1958) promised more action and spectacle than the film actually delivered. Similarly, the campaign for *Fellini-Satyricon* sold the sexuality of the film in a manner totally disproportionate to the film's contents. While most of the films that we examine don't suffer from the issue of sponsored product placement, almost all did enjoy a number of product tie-ins. Through examination of such products we can see refracted some of the key themes of the film. Roman bread may have been gritty, unprocessed, hard – and it certainly was not baked in a 'spotless, gleaming kitchen' – but Sunbeam Bread's advertisement on the back of *Quo Vadis* (1951) is less concerned about the type of bread that Marcus Vinicius would actually have offered his children than reinforcing Robert Taylor's portrayal as a trustworthy, wholesome father-figure [Fig. 3]. This advertisement ran in over 500 newspapers and helped maintain the public presence of the film. In relation to film advertising, students should keep an eye out for film

3. 'Bread beyond compare'. Quality Bakers' 'Quo Vadis' advertisement.

gimmicks. Cecil B. DeMille's reported decision to use solid gold cups in the barge scene in *Cleopatra* (1934) even though the film was shot in monochrome is not a story about directorial megalomania, but rather the story of a clever marketing ploy. What better way to sell a film about a world of excess than create a world of excess in its own right?

Throughout our discussion of films, we have favoured a very historicist form of analysis as we believe that once one begins to locate film productions within a particular set of industrial, collaborative and social conditions, one can appreciate the forces that operate upon a film to shape its form, style, and content. One needs to catalogue and understand the various environmental factors that surrounded a film's production. As we shall see, a tremendous variety of factors can impact upon production. These can include everything from personal relations between actors to the tax regimes that govern the distribution of a film's profits.

10

Introduction

One needs to appreciate the power and role of technology in film production. Over the period of time studied in this book, there are a number of revolutionary changes in film stock, projection techniques, and the ability to create special effects. Filmmakers responded accordingly. Indeed, new technology can even act as the spur to cinematic visions. Certain narratives play up the strengths of certain technologies, and one can understand the temptation to produce stories that take advantage of new advances in technology. Technicolour, Cinemascope, and CGI – to choose just three examples – have each in turn played important roles in making Rome come alive. Each technique promised a bigger, richer experience, and it is understandable that filmmakers deployed them in depicting the biggest, richest empire that the world has ever known – imperial Rome.

Appreciating film as an industrialised art form makes one see the ridiculousness of getting too hung up on 'historical errors' in a film. Filmmakers are not historians, and it is foolish to treat them as such or hold them accountable to the same standards. Films may claim in their publicity that they present events 'as they really happened', but such claims should be seen merely as another gambit in getting the audience to suspend their disbelief rather than a statement of fact. The fields of wheat that feature so prominently in *Gladiator* (2000) anachronistically show wrong strains of wheat and retroject monocropping practices onto ancient agriculture. However the Romans imagined the Elysian Fields, it wasn't like the ones shown in *Gladiator*. But so what? Spotting the error doesn't take us that far. It is a much more profitable use of time and effort to focus on the techniques by which a sense of 'authenticity' is instilled in the audience. Errors may be useful in bringing into relief certain narrative or directorial decisions, but a catalogue of 'mistakes' on its own misses the point of why one might watch films.

We should never forget that film production is only one half of the equation when assessing a film. The other half involves examining a film's reception and for this we need to consider the cinema audience. Audiences vary according to time and place. Watching a film today on DVD, or even on a cinema screen, is often a very different experience from watching a film at the time of its production. In order to appreciate the impact of a film, we need to appreciate the mindset of the audience that watched it. To do this, we need to consider what other films preceded their viewing of the film and so framed their expectations. Reviews and advertising colour an audience's experience. We need to look at the contemporary politics and social issues of the day. This all forms part of the baggage that the audience took with them when they went to the cinema. We ought to pay attention to the exhibition context as well. Watching a film in a drive-in is not the same as watching it in a darkened silent cinema. The disrupted, casual viewing environment of the drive-in favours an appreciation of the episodic and the spectacular far more than sustained narratives or complex character development. In addition, we should be wary of assuming a too monolithic notion of a film's audience. Different audience members take away different messages from a film and appreciate different aspects. One member of an audience may see Steve Reeves in *Hercules* (1958) as a symbol of healthy masculinity, another may see him as a figure of erotic camp. Some men may take the manipulative empress Cleopatra in DeMille's *Cleopatra* as a symbol of the dangerous liberated woman, whilst some women in the audience may see her as a symbol of power, an aspirational figure and the embodiment of style.

Finally, in focussing on the external factors of production context and audience expectation, we should not lose sight of the film itself. Films are not just a mechanistic product of certain environmental elements. These factors certainly shape the nature of the film and its reception, but we should not forget the individuality and innovativeness of the cinematic product. Each film has its own narrative pace, its own grammar and syntax. We need to look at a film and follow how it develops. Certain key moments are crucial. It always rewards to pay attention to the very opening sequence of a film to see how it establishes itself. This provides the entry point for all subsequent experience. The authoritative voice-over that begins so many Roman films may be a cliché, but it determines how audiences reacted to the central characters and themes of the film. Watching a film is a journey. Your point of departure, your method of transport, your guide, and your travelling companions all make a difference to the overall experience.

The format of this book

This book is arranged into ten chapters. Each chapter takes a particular film as a case study, and the films are arranged in chronological order by release date. Our films have been chosen not because of popularity (although almost all films were a success at the box-office), but because each film allows us to examine a different style of cinematic presentation or theme. In offering this selection of films we have aimed for breadth in genre, production technique, and narrative form.

Each chapter begins with a general introduction to the issues that such films raise for the representation of the ancient world. Particular focus is placed on issues of genre and style. A brief genealogy of the film is offered and the production considerations of each style of filmmaking are discussed.

After this broad contextualisation, there is a more detailed discussion of the individual case study. Each case study is introduced with essential background information, including the ancient narratives and figures which inspire the films, the social, political and production contexts of the film's manufacture, and their critical reception and afterlife. Issues addressed may include intra-cinematic notions like narrative, *mise-en-scène*, casting and performance, and extra-cinematic aspects like exhibition and promotion.

This background discussion is followed by textual analysis. This section begins with a plot summary and then examines a number of important themes in each film. Each theme includes examples of key scenes, set out in the boxes in the text, in which the themes are developed or fore-grounded.

Following this textual analysis, further examples of films in this style are briefly introduced. We have tried where possible to cite films that are readily available. There are notes at the end of the book that allow the reader to follow up more detailed points raised in the text of the book.

This book is designed for a variety of audiences. It emerges from a course first run by the authors in the Classics department at the University of Reading. As such, one of its principal aims has been to provide an accessible introduction to the undergraduate reader in the Humanities who would like to explore how the ancient world has been portrayed in cinema. However, we hope that a number of other users will find this book valuable. As a work of reception studies, we offer it as an example of what a study that places cinematic genre at the centre of its investigation might look like. In this, we hope to stimulate discussion about how reception studies might be taught and conducted. We hope that those working in the field of popular culture will also find this book useful. Classical source-material has been glossed so that those unfamiliar with the ancient world might better appreciate the extent to which cinema engages with issues fundamental to Greco-Roman civilisation. One should be wary about being too flippant about cinematic depictions of the past. Often a serious point lies beneath the cheap togas and plaster columns of popular films.

Further reading

On cinema and the ancient world generally:

Jon Solomon (2001), *The Ancient World in the Cinema* (New Haven: Yale University Press) is a comprehensive catalogue of films with Greek, Roman, and Biblical settings.

Martin M. Winkler (ed.) (2001), *Classical Myth and Culture in the Cinema* (Oxford: Oxford University Press) offers various articles demonstrating different approaches to films both set in, and inspired by, antiquity.

Maria Wyke (1997), *Projecting the Past* (London: Routledge) illustrates the historicist approach taken in this book, with a focus on films with Roman narratives.

Monica Cyrino (2005), *Big Screen Rome* (Malden: Blackwell) offers structured analyses of nine key re-presentations of ancient Rome in cinema.

On reading films critically:

James Monaco (2009), *How to Read a Film: Movies, Media and Beyond,*

4th edn (Oxford: Oxford University Press) is a thorough, accessible and comprehensively illustrated guide to almost everything you need to think about when analysing films.

David Bordwell, Janet Staiger, Kristin Thompson (1985), *The Classical Hollywood Cinema: Film Style and Mode of Production to 1960* (New York: Columbia University Press) focuses on the key features of Hollywood narrative cinema in its most influential period.

Graeme Turner (2006), *Film as Social Practice*, 4th edn (London: Routledge) shows how the social context of our viewing and understanding of films provides useful tools for analysis.

Acknowledgements

Numerous debts were accumulated in the writing of this book. Financial and resource support was provided by the UK's Arts and Humanities Research Board, the University of Sydney, and the Centre for Classical and Near Eastern Studies of Australia (CCANESA). The authors would especially like to thank the following for their help and friendship, without which this book would not have been possible: Maria Wyke (former colleague, former teacher, and constant inspiration), Garry Peirce, Dunstan Lowe, Nick Lowe, Joanna Paul, Peter Brennan, Olivia Kelley, Mark Ledbury, Murray Dahm, Tom Hillard, and Lea Beness. We are forever grateful for the extraordinary generosity and kindness of Bill Zewadski, a real visionary in understanding the importance of popular culture to the Classics. Finally our thanks go to our students at Reading and Sydney whose questions, ideas, and enthusiasm reminded us why books like this are worth writing.

Alastair J.L. Blanshard
The University of Sydney

Kim Shahabudin
The University of Reading

1

Establishing the Conventions:
Cleopatra (1934)

Introduction

Every cinematic version of antiquity owes something to the films that came before it. In this book, case studies are arranged chronologically to reflect that cultural genealogy. Our approach is to consider the choices that are made when films tell their stories about the ancient world within the social, historical, and cultural contexts of their production. One of the most important contexts will be the evolving discourse of representation created by the films themselves and their audiences. This chapter will focus on the early stages of this process: the introduction of cinematic conventions that make viewers feel that what they see on screen is a 'true' animation of antiquity – the ancient world brought to life.

The process to be described is a highly interactive one, as all evolutionary processes are. A number of factors are working together here, most notably cinema production processes and the preferences and social circumstances of cinema audiences. As commercially-orientated cultural products, the ways in which films depict and interpret narratives and characters are driven by the perceived tastes of their viewers at the time of release: what has proved popular in the past, what novelty can be introduced, and what audiences will not tolerate. This is not a new idea. It is now a commonplace to note that every kind of cultural text is in some way influenced by and reiterates earlier texts. However, the commercial nature of cinema tends to press down the accelerator pedal on this process. Films are expensive to make, and must recoup their costs. As a consequence, they tend towards conservatism in their representations, always seeking to re-use signs and imagery that audiences have responded favourably to. These features need to be highly familiar for the viewer, swiftly recognisable wherever possible. As a result, conventions can become established very quickly, through only a small number of texts. However, films also need to include something new, to pique the viewer's interest and distinguish them from their predecessors and competitors. This balance between conservatism and novelty drives the evolution of representational conventions in cinema.

To understand how these conventions might operate on the viewer's perceptions of the ancient world means considering the viewpoint of the contemporary audience at the time of a film's release. Of course, this

15

experience cannot be completely recovered: for instance, we can never hope for more than a degree of empathy with an audience that has recently lived through the catastrophic overturning of certainties that follow world-wide war. However, we can be conscious of the need to avoid anachronistic thinking, and take a broad and inclusive approach to the study of context. With these thoughts in mind, this section will illustrate some of the significant factors that shaped early cine-antiquity, before focusing in more detail on how these operated in one early sound example: Cecil B. DeMille's *Cleopatra* (1934).

Ancient Greece and Rome had been popular topics for cinema audiences, literally since the earliest days of movie-making. In early silent films, historical antiquity was useful to filmmakers because its characters and narratives were familiar to a broadly-constituted and popular (that is, non-elite) audience. With no synchronised sound, films could only tell their stories through images, with the occasional explanatory intertitle, and sometimes with interpretative background music provided by an in-house musician or on phonograph. The short lengths of film used for the earliest movies meant that the films themselves were also very brief, lasting from seconds to a few minutes. Audience expectations were cued by their identification with stories and figures from commonly-known narratives such as those of ancient mythology. Prior knowledge of characters and narratives meant a prompt engagement with the on-screen action.

The utility of the ancient world in engaging audiences can be seen in the example of *Cupid and Psyche,* a very short (28 seconds) film produced in 1897 by the Edison Manufacturing Company. The film itself showed little direct evidence of classical inspiration; it was without narrative and consisted of a single sequence filmed with a fixed camera of a young woman and child dancing on a stage at the Sutro Baths in San Francisco. However, through its title, the film elevates itself by playing upon mythic associations. The story of Cupid and Psyche is one of the world's great love stories. It has been a popular subject for artists, including paintings by Van Dyck (*c.* 1639-40), Gerard (1798), David (1817) and Burne-Jones (1865) and a sculpture by Antonio Canova (1796). In this visual tradition, the pair connoted both innocence and eroticism, with Cupid always depicted as a slim, hairless youth and Psyche always (partly if not fully) nude. These characteristics are well illustrated for example, in Canova's famous sculpture of the pair (1783-93), where Cupid cups Psyche's breast while she offers up her face for a kiss. The statue is simultaneously erotic and dignified; Canova's classicism and the sculpture's status as 'a work of art' validating its nudity and passion.

Such rich associations were useful to cinema. Very early cinema did not enjoy the status of 'art'. At this stage, it was still regarded as a novel demonstration of what modern invention could produce: a mechanical means of reproduction rather than a creative medium. Its appeal lay in the 'shock of the new'. However, film could play upon the cultural prestige accorded to the classical world. In the case of the Edison film, the mythological allusion is used to legitimise the display of a young woman, costumed in a short (to the knee) dress which she raises to show her petticoats as she dances; the child wears a frilled leotard with small wings attached. They are watched by an audience of male bathers, in various stages of dress or undress. The classical title diffuses any potential problems about this image. It also tells us that we are watching something special. Unlike other famous early titles (like the 1895 Lumière brothers' *Workers Leaving the Lumiere Factory in Lyon*) the film captures an event, something out of the ordinary, something not usually witnessed in everyday life. Thus even in this early and opaque allusion, ways that antiquity could be utilised by cinema begin to emerge: antiquity works as a signifier of exoticism, it legitimates display, it forms bonds of shared knowledge, and it adds cultural lustre.

Antiquity's historical distance and cultural otherness also made it an ideal location for spectacle and fantasy. In France, the showman Georges Méliès used stop-motion effects to turn the features of ancient myth into instruments for supernatural fantasies. In *Pygmalion and Galatea* (1898), stop-motion cinematography not only brings Pygmalion's statue to life, but thwarts the sculptor's attempts to embrace his creation by breaking it in two, with the top half floating across the room to mock its maker. In *The Oracle of Delphi* (1903), a thief enters the tomb of Delphi, intent on stealing a box of jewels. The ghost of the oracle appears and punishes the thief by giving him the head of a donkey: a mythological allusion to the story of king Midas who had his ears turned into the ears of a donkey by Apollo (the principal god of Delphi) for refusing to award him first prize in a musical contest. In these films, the ancient world provides a credible location for incredible events, being both historically and exotically far-removed. This use of antiquity as a site for spectacle in cinema continued traditions found in other popular spectacular forms of entertainment in the nineteenth century. For instance, the 'pyrodrama' was an outdoor entertainment, first staged in the UK, but later popular in the US. These acted out scenes from history or historical novels ending in destruction by fire, which would be represented by a spectacular firework display. Other examples included fairground displays by strongmen who drew on the Labours of Hercules for their acts; early physique displays by bodybuilders like Eugen Sandow (1867-1925), who borrowed poses from classical statues, and *tableaux vivants* in which subjects would pose, often nude or semi-nude, on stage or for photographs, in poses intended to copy paintings or sculptures or to illustrate vaguely classical scenes.

While such popular classicising entertainments were a widespread phenomenon, one country in particular was making great advances in the creation of cinematic entertainments based on the classical world. That nation was Italy, which from the beginning of its film industry had an intense focus on the production of historical films, drawing on local audience interests by featuring characters and narratives from ancient Rome. The success of the historical epic made Italy an international player in the developing film industry, reaching its apogee in the acclaimed *Cabiria* (1914), which is described in more detail at the end of this chapter. The film included many of the conventions and cues that would mark out the territory of cinematic antiquity, especially in epic films: excess and spectacle; the opposition of Westernism and orientalism; and the equation of strength and simplicity with morality. Features that started in Italy quickly spread to the rest of the world.

The Italian preference for (and success with) historical, rather than mythological, films draws attention to two shaping factors in the emerging discourse of cine-antiquity; namely the rise of nationalism and the impact of developments in technology. These are factors that we will see time and again influencing film development. As film historians have shown, the popularity of historical narratives with filmmakers and the public was influenced by Italy's own recent history. Following the unification of Italy in 1861 and the colonial war with Turkey in 1911-12, we see a new drive for national identity. Films that depicted the glory and power of imperial Rome helped to satisfy this new appetite. At the same time, such a desire could not have been satisfied had there not been corresponding developments in technology. Developments in film technology made the more complex narratives of historical films possible by enabling the production of longer films. For instance, one of the most successful early Italian historical films, *The Last Days of Pompeii* (original title: *Gli ultimi giorni di Pompei*, 1908) had only 366 metres of film (about 14 minutes of running time) in which to convey its narrative of desire, evil deeds, self-sacrifice, the arena, and an erupting volcano. Two years later *The Fall of Troy* (original title: *La caduta di Troia*, 1910) had more than twice the running time, and two years after that, *Quo Vadis?* (1912) had 2250 metres of film and 120 minutes of running time to tell its story.

A third factor was also responsible for the success of these historical films: their ability to piggy-back on the popularity of a pre-existing genre, namely the historical novel. Both *Quo Vadis?* and *The Last Days of Pompeii* were adapted from immensely popular historical novels. In *Quo Vadis* (discussed in Chapter 2) the personal desires and conflicts of two individuals, Marcus and Lygia, are set against the desires and conflicts of Nero's Rome and early Christianity. *The Last Days of Pompeii* also presented a narrative in which the pure desires of individuals (Glaucus for Ione, the blind slave-girl Nydia for Glaucus) are set against a background of decadence and destruction. In these narratives, the purity of individuals is presented as a microcosm of the purity of the Christian religion which is coming to overturn the decadence of Rome. As the historical film developed in the post-war era, this synecdochic mode, in which a small part stands for the whole, became the most common way to present ancient and modern history on screen: mapping the grand narratives of history onto intimate stories about individuals with which viewers might empathise.

The preference for fiction over historical writing as source-material indicates the limits of most films' historical ambitions. However, that did not mean that cinema was above using the high cultural status of ancient history to its advantage. The stories might have been fictional, but they always included some historical characters and authentic narratives in their settings, and a degree of research was undertaken to inform decisions about their depictions. Even the early historical films were prepared to boast of their pedagogic credentials, producing press releases that framed the films as educational, and sometimes suggesting activities for schoolchildren like essay competitions. Paramount, for example, produced a Study Guide to accompany *Cleopatra* (1934), including an essay competition with the prize of 'Cleopatra scholarships'. Publicists also emphasised, alongside the on-screen spectacles, the spectacle of the film's own production: the time taken in filming, vast numbers of extras, and authentic locations. From the earliest moment of the cinematic depictions of antiquity we witness the claims that these films were both 'outrageous spectacles in their own right' and 'true to life'. There is obviously a tension between these two claims, but that did not stop them being repeated endlessly over the next century in publicity for films about the ancient world.

By the mid-1920s, many of the conventions that would continue to characterise cine-antiquity throughout the twentieth century had already been established. Cinema faced only one more major challenge for the depiction of antiquity. This came with the advent of sound. How did characters speak in antiquity? What would the ancient world sound like? Sound technology developed swiftly following enthusiastic audience responses to *The Jazz Singer* in 1927, and by 1929 sound pictures were the norm. The transition has been described as 'from the movies to the talkies'. Certainly the need for scripted dialogue meant that new choices had to be made that had not been required for the brief lines provided in intertitles. For instance, what would the register of 'ancient' dialogue be? The high cultural status of classical literature indicated a high theatrical style, and so cinema turned to experienced stage actors to give the necessary gravitas to the characters, especially the historical figures (e.g. Charles Laughton as Nero and Ian Keith as Tigellinus in *Sign of the Cross* (1932), Warren William as Julius Caesar and Keith as Octavian in *Cleopatra*). These actors adopted a theatrical enunciation that more closely resembled an English accent (even if the actors themselves were American), and as the villains in these films tended to be the historical characters, a system of moral coding through accent began to develop. So in *Sign of the Cross*, the 'good, but unknown' Roman, Marcus (played by Frederic March), speaks with an American accent; the 'bad, but famous' Roman, Nero (Charles Laughton) is British. This practice of coding by accent persists even in recent films. For example, Celtic accents are used to indicate the Macedonians' outsider status in *Alexander* (2004). Sound in cinema also included music and sound effects. Jon Solomon (2001b) argues that musical scores for these early sound films set in the ancient world rarely aim to reference historical elements (as costumes and settings do), but rather seek to create a mood which will direct the viewer's interpretation of the onscreen action: romantic, orientalising, exotic, grandiose, or religious.

However, the coming of sound also saw a change in cinematic fashions more generally, turning the tide of fashion against portrayals of the ancient world. The inclusion of dialogue enabled a more naturalistic style of acting, which in its turn promoted contemporary narratives. There is a noticeable decrease in the production of films set in Rome during the 1930s and 1940s when compared to the volume of production for the preceding decades. It was not until after the Second World War that the ancient world on film would regain its widespread popularity. Once again developments in film technology would be crucial, with films like *Quo Vadis* (released in 1951) using spectacular effects made possible by new technology to tell stories of early Christianity, framing them as an allegory for more recent conflicts. In the meantime though, a few films set in antiquity continued to appear, including a number directed by that master of the grandiose, Cecil B. DeMille (1881-1959).

Background to case study

'How would you like to play the wickedest woman in history?' With this sensational question, the film director Cecil B. DeMille offered the part of Cleopatra to the actress Claudette Colbert. At least, that is the story which we as the audience have been encouraged to believe. Whether it is true or false is debatable: whether it is a good story, one that promotes interest in the film, is not. The very fact that it has become so widely known indicates the popularity of this vision of the Egyptian queen, and draws out the contradictory attractions of Cleopatra for filmmakers: simultaneously an historical figure and a fantasy figure; a focus both for escapism and for debate about the place of women in society.

Any account of Cleopatra's life must try to steer a course through a vast number of sources, ancient and modern, verbal and visual: and in doing so, must also attempt to untangle the desires and expectations that have been mapped onto her by successive authors. In order to understand DeMille's version, it will be helpful to start with some historical background.

Cleopatra VII Philopater was the last of the Pharaonic rulers of Egypt. She was of Macedonian Greek lineage, the descendent of Ptolemy I (one of Alexander the Great's generals, and himself a 'star' of later cine-antiquity in 2004 played by Anthony Hopkins as the narrator in Oliver Stone's *Alexander*). The early years of her reign were marked by internal politicking in favour of her brother, resulting in her absence from the court at

Alexandria for some time. Julius Caesar's arrival in Egypt gave her the opportunity to gain a useful ally in this local difficulty. She began an affair with Caesar and in 47 BC gave birth to a child named Ptolemy Caesar and nicknamed Caesarion to underline his mother's claims for his paternity, although Caesar never formally acknowledged him. After Caesar's death, Cleopatra avoided overt commitment to any side in the power struggles in Rome: a wise policy in her position as ruler of the wealthiest of the Eastern provinces. After 42 BC, power had settled jointly in the hands of Mark Antony (consul at the time of Caesar's death), Octavian (Caesar's adopted son, and the future emperor Augustus) and M. Aemilius Lepidus. Antony turned to Egypt in 41 BC, seeking funds for a military expedition against Parthia. He summoned Cleopatra to a meeting in Tarsus, and the two initiated a liaison. Antony returned to Rome, and married Octavia, the sister of Octavian (his third Roman wife), but in 36 BC, after his disastrous Parthian campaign, he retreated to Alexandria with Cleopatra. Of their three children, Alexander Helios and Cleopatra Selene had been born in 40 BC and Ptolemy Philadelphus in 36 BC. In 34 BC, in a ceremony that became known as the Donations of Alexandria, Antony 'gave' kingdoms to all three, in addition proclaiming Caesarion to be the legitimate heir of Julius Caesar. This was a direct threat to Octavian's claims to power in Rome, and in 31 BC the rivalry came to a climax, with the defeat of Antony and Cleopatra by Octavian's forces in a naval battle at Actium. Octavian reached Alexandria triumphant. Antony committed suicide. Cleopatra was taken prisoner, but also managed to commit suicide: the tradition being that she used the poison of an asp. Her children by Antony survived, but Caesarion paid the price for the claims for his paternity; Octavian had him put to death. Octavian himself went on to become Rome's first and most successful emperor under the name of Augustus.

Our sources for Cleopatra's life are always somewhat, and sometimes extremely, partial. Like other historical figures, she has been prey to the adage that 'history is written by the winners'. Most ancient sources follow Octavian's version of events, which painted Cleopatra as the undoubted villainess: both female and foreign, doubly 'Other'. In this version, she is a seductress who exercises an almost magical power over the infatuated Antony. The decadence which was rampant at her court turned him into an adulterer and a squanderer of wealth; addicted to luxury; a coward in battle; and lacking all civic responsibility. His defeat by Octavian and ultimately his death is no longer the result of a bitter power struggle; it is almost a kindness on Octavian's part to release him from the erotic bondage in which his Egyptian mistress has kept him. This spin on Cleopatra's history is very much the dominant one in our sources from the ancient world. Through the words of Plutarch, Suetonius, Dio Cassius and Appian, Octavian's preferred narrative glitters.

Lucy Hughes-Hallett (1990, 57) has pointed out that, ironically, Octavian's damning portrait of Cleopatra has probably kept her alive in cultural history where other less vividly drawn figures have vanished. The glamour that has attached to her as famed seductress and champion of luxury has prompted a constant stream of cultural re-figurings in art, literature, and, more recently, in cinema. As an icon of the emasculating potential of women, Cleopatra is an object of desire, and of horror. Her early appearances in cinema utilise both of these traits. In 1899, for instance, Georges Méliès produced a brief *Cléopâtre* in which Cleopatra's mummy is exhumed and brought back to life: it has become known as one of the first horror films. Later, Theda Bara played the eponymous heroine in *Cleopatra* (1917) as a 'vamp': the contemporarily popular notion of a female who functions like a vampire, in the sense that she uses her sexual allure to drain men of potency. The film is now lost, but Bara can still be seen playing a similar role in modern dress in the 1915 film, *A Fool There Was*. In stills for the 1917 *Cleopatra*, Bara wears heavy eye-make-up and risqué costumes, coupling strategically placed jewellery with transparent gauze. She is associated with exotic animals, perched on leopardskins, wearing a skirt of peacock feathers and snake jewellery: in perhaps the most notorious image, she wears both a snake headdress and breast cups formed from coiled snakes which barely cover her nipples. This film covers Cleopatra's relationships with both Caesar and Antony. Other film versions followed Shakespeare's lead in concentrating on her relationship with the latter. These included a slightly earlier film, *Cleopatra* (1912), produced by and starring the actor-manager Helen Gardner, which also drew Cleopatra as a vamp. Gardner's film was a six-reeler, playing at the unusual (for the time) length of about an hour at its original release. Especially interesting in the context of this book is the fact that it was promoted as an artistic piece, playing in theatres and opera houses rather than the more usual neighbourhood nickelodeons; an early example in US cinema of antiquity being used for cultural validation.

So the 'wicked' attributes an audience would expect to see in a cinematic Cleopatra were well established by the time DeMille offered the part to Colbert. However, there were starting to be limits to Cleopatra's wickedness. The shift which took film screenings in the US from the popular nickelodeon to the more respectable movie theatre also saw a shift in concerns about the kind of content that could be screened. *Cleopatra* was produced in a time when the film industry was under particularly heavy scrutiny. Stories about wild drug parties and sexual licentiousness among those involved in filmmaking prompted public outrage and created a popular notion of the film industry (and by extension, films) as decadent and a potentially corrupting influence. In an attempt to allay public concerns, the Motion Picture Producers and Distributors Association was established in 1922, led by a lawyer named Will Hays. The Association's explicit aim was to rehabilitate the public reputation of the movie industry by self-regulation: more pragmatically they also hoped to pre-empt censorship by local boards, which could result in expensive revisions to film prints. To this end, Hays produced a list of recommendations as to what should and should not be shown on screen. In 1930, Hays' guidelines were replaced by a more stringent set of restrictions that became known as the Production Code. They were governed by three principles that emphasised adherence to morality and the rule of law. More specific restrictions included the upholding of the 'sanctity of marriage and the home', and made it compulsory to only present adultery and illicit sex as activities that never lead to happy endings. By 1934 the Code was being rigorously enforced, and Hollywood cinema was no longer a place of infinite possibility. However between 1930 and 1934, studios were often successful in finding ways to circumvent these restrictions while acknowledging their existence, making films like Mae West's *She Done Him Wrong* and *I'm No Angel* (both 1933), both films that included racy storylines and risqué dialogue. Films made in this period which demonstrate the strategies used to avoid censorship have become known as 'Pre-Code' productions. They include DeMille's *Sign of the Cross* and *Cleopatra*, both of which used the high cultural status and exotic otherness of the ancient world to enable the screening of sequences that were far from the spirit of the Code – but close to the audience's viewing desires.

The influence of the Code on DeMille's *Cleopatra* will become clear in the analyses to follow. Certainly, this film wasn't DeMille's first foray into the delights of spectacle and on-screen immorality. DeMille started his career as an actor/director on the stage, but shifted his interest to cinema in 1913. He made a name with films that examined gender roles and marital relations, like *The Cheat* (1915), *Male and Female* (1919), *Don't Change Your Husband* (1919), and *Adam's Rib* (1923). However, his talent for putting spectacle on-screen became apparent with his biblical epics *The Ten Commandments* (1923) and *King of Kings* (1927). In 1932, DeMille advanced this use of religious topics for spectacular film with a highly successful version of Wilson Barrett's play, *The Sign of the Cross*. Set in the reign of Nero, the story focuses on a romance between a young Christian girl, Mercia (Elissa Landy) and a Roman patrician, Marcus Superbus (Frederic March). Marcus is also the object of the empress Poppaea's affections (played by Colbert), and is at first spurned by Mercia for his decadent lifestyle. The film included items that were certainly not encouraged by the Production Code, including a highly erotic lesbian dance sequence (later cut for a 1935 re-release); an extended arena sequence showing combats between women gladiators and dwarves, and lions eating Christians; and a plot that is firmly centred around the immorality and decadence of the imperial court. It redeems itself by ending with Marcus' conversion to Christianity, and marriage to Mercia, though this results in their sentence to death in the arena. A few years later, after failing at the box-office with *Four Frightened People* (1934), DeMille was casting around for his next project. Charles Higham's 1973 biography of DeMille quotes Paramount Pictures boss, Adolph Zukor's opinion; 'Better do another historical epic, Cecil, with plenty of sex.' The earlier success of Theda Bara's *Cleopatra* made the Egyptian queen a potentially profitable subject for such a film. DeMille took the hint and shooting on his *Cleopatra* commenced in 1934.

Apart from the aptitude of Cleopatra's story for validating erotic narrative on-screen, the oriental setting of the court at Alexandria also made it a good choice for the popular audience of the time. Early cinematic iconography, especially for historical films, was largely derived from nineteenth-century history painting. The influence of painters like Jean-Léon Gérôme, for instance, can be seen in a publicity still for the 1917 *Cleopatra* in which Theda Bara copies the exact pose of Gérôme's queen in his 1866 painting, *Cleopatra Before Caesar*. In this genre, the oriental (understood as any culture that originated in the East) was identified with the exotic. The perceived 'otherness' of oriental cultures prompted their use in art to present scenes of eroticism, luxury and sometimes cruelty – a world totally apart from the (allegedly) moral, restrained, ascetic West.

Cinema adapted this flawed but familiar iconographic schema for its own purposes. The discovery of Tutankhamun's tomb in 1922 by Howard Carter had additionally inspired great popular interest in everything Egyptian. This coincided with the growth of the Art Deco movement, which took many of its decorative motifs from Egyptian art. The two came together in the architecture of the dedicated 'movie palaces' that began to appear with the introduction of multi-reel 'feature' films like Helen Gardner's *Cleopatra*, and proliferated in the 1920s and 1930s as cinema audiences increased during the Great Depression. Audiences were perceived to be seeking a cheap escape from the drabness of everyday life; the movie palaces provided them with exotic glamour, both on and off the screen. Cinemas from Grauman's Egyptian Theatre in Los Angeles (opened in 1922) to the Plaza in Stockport, Cheshire (opened in 1932) were elaborately decorated, inside and out, with strikingly painted oriental motifs in bright green, red, blue and gold. Carved friezes of feathered canopies continued the theme, while frontages enticed audiences with their soaring sunray entrances to pleasure. With their luxurious seating and curtains, the movie palaces offered a luxurious environment in which to escape from the worries of everyday life: and, more specifically, they associated that Art Deco luxury with a popular understanding of ancient Egypt. DeMille would continue this trend on-screen. His *Cleopatra* combined ancient Egypt, Rome and modern Art Deco to create a luxury that Depression filmgoers could both identify with, and escape into. [Fig. 4]

Maria Wyke (1997a: 95) describes how the film's narrative is framed with a visual trope that literally invites the viewer to escape into antiquity. In the opening scene of the film, two enormous stones fill the screen, parting to reveal to the audience the world of cine-antiquity behind them – a backlit and nearly naked slave girl, chained and holding aloft two incense burners. The clear inference is that this ancient world will be

1. Establishing the Conventions: Cleopatra (1934)

4. Luxury, exoticism, spectacle. Cleopatra in Rome, *Cleopatra* (1934).

characterised by the erotic, the exotic, and the sadistic: a view hardly dispelled by the swiftly following first view of the young queen, also bound and gagged, or our first view of Caesar, dispassionately testing deadly new weapons of war. The same stones close again at the end of the film, obscuring our last view of Cleopatra, magnificently costumed and dead on her throne, fixing our idea of her as the image of glamour in death. The stones opening and closing restate the actions of the theatrical curtain used in cinemas of the time, opening and closing on the screen as the feature starts and finishes. As viewers, we are to be permitted access only to eavesdrop on a hidden world, while we sit in the dark, in silent isolation from our neighbouring audience members. The conceit showcases DeMille's own sophisticated understanding of how films operated as viewed texts.

The cinematic ancient world that the cinemagoers entered in *Cleopatra* was, in many ways, surprisingly like their own. Dialogue generally avoided the anachronistic use of an elevated register derived more from the classical stage than the classical world. Make-up and costume (designed by Travis Banton) also combined aspects of ancient dress with more

25

modern styles and silhouettes. Bias-cut dresses repeated the styles seen on contemporary fashion plates and in department stores. The overall impression was of a highly wearable antiquity – especially attractive to the female audience. By encouraging identification with Cleopatra's flawed femininity the film thus sold a vision of womanhood – and of the goods that could be associated with it.

Certainly, in centring on issues of femininity, the film involved itself in a live contemporary topic. Anxieties about gender roles were fuelled at the end of the nineteenth and start of the twentieth century by what seemed to be a rapid acceleration of changes in the roles women played, both within the family and domestic sphere and, with increasing numbers of women in paid employment, outside it. A further consequence of these changes was that women earning salaries of their own were now able to play a significant role in the retail economy as consumers of material goods in their own right. Merchandising began to be aimed more specifically at women and their particular concerns and desires. The fantasy identities of film characters and the star personae of cinema actresses played a significant part in this process. Marketing encouraged consumers to identify with actresses, on- and off-screen. This process was assisted in the case of *Cleopatra* by the fact that Egyptian decorative motifs were already considered the height of fashion. Among the products sold under the Cleopatra banner were dresses and hats, soap and hair treatments, jewellery and compacts – even cigarettes. The story of *Cleopatra* was being played out not just on the screen, but in billboards, newspaper advertisements, department stores, the home, and the wardrobe.

However, the film's usage of the notion of the 'New Woman' was two-handed. While its luxurious imagery enticed women to spend their money on goods that would make them more like the glamorous queen, the film's narrative simultaneously warned male viewers of the dangers of allowing women their independence. Despite the light touch of Colbert's accomplished comedy acting, Cleopatra remains the woman who used her sexuality to gain power, ruining two Roman generals in the process – and who still preferred suicide to seeing that power relinquished.

Plot summary

The film opens with Cleopatra (Claudette Colbert) and her tutor Apollodorus being dumped in the desert by Pothinus (Leonard Mudie), the country's scheming prime minister. Pothinus plans to barter Egypt's wealth for the support of Rome to keep him in power. The young queen is more concerned about missing her breakfast than the political consequences of the deed, but is persuaded by Apollodorus that for the good of Egypt she must return. In the meantime Julius Caesar (Warren William) has arrived at Alexandria. In order to get access to him and gain his support for her as queen, Cleopatra has herself delivered to him rolled up in a carpet. Caesar is at first exasperated, but then charmed by the young queen. After she discovers and kills Pothinus, who has been lying in wait in her chamber, Caesar begins to see that she might be more than just a foolish girl, and they begin an affair. Meanwhile, the affair becomes the topic for gossip among Roman society, who pity Caesar's wife Calpurnia (Gertrude Michael).

Caesar brings Cleopatra to Rome, but is assassinated as he arrives at the Senate. Cleopatra flees back to Egypt, and Rome is placed in the joint charge of Caesar's nephew Octavian (Ian Keith), and the soldier Mark Antony (Henry Wilcoxon). Antony travels to Tarsus and demands that Cleopatra meet him, but she fails to appear. He finds her on her elaborately decorated barge, hosting an extravagant feast in his honour with dancers, acrobats, and wild animals. He reluctantly joins her, and Cleopatra uses her charms to seduce Antony as she seduced Caesar. This time however, she tells Apollodorus that she will not make the mistake of falling in love as she did with Caesar, but will use Antony as a man would use a woman.

Antony settles in Alexandria, but Cleopatra's machinations continue. She is visited by king Herod (Joseph Schildkraut) who tells her that Octavian has declared Antony a traitor, and that her relations with Rome will improve if she kills him. Cleopatra determines to do the deed, and begins to test poisons on prisoners. She is about to administer the poison to Antony in a glass of wine when news arrives that Octavian has declared war on Egypt. Instantly regaining his fighting spirit, Antony leaps into action, and Cleopatra passionately declares her love for him as a woman, not a queen.

Antony's troops refuse to join battle against Rome, but he raises an Egyptian army who prove no match for the Roman soldiers and are defeated at Actium. Cleopatra goes to Octavian and offers him Egypt in return for Antony's life, but in vain. Antony returns to Alexandria and sees Cleopatra leaving the city. Believing her to have transferred her loyalties to Octavian, he stabs himself, but survives long enough to learn his mistake from his lover. Cleopatra now knows that Octavian's entry into Alexandria is inevitable. She settles herself on her throne, in all her royal finery, and is discovered there by the Roman troops, dead by the bite of an asp.

Key scenes and themes

The ancient world as the modern world

DeMille's *Cleopatra* was much criticised on its release for its anachronisms: in the colloquial language used in the dialogue and in the attitudes of its protagonists. One sequence that received special attention from the critics was the party hosted by Calpurnia in Rome. The reviewer in *Variety* describes it as 'like a modern bridge night', while the *New York Times* notes that it is 'done in the modern fashion'. DeMille's previous history as a director of marital comedies might suggest that this sequence defines his approach to historical film as, in Maria Wyke's phrase, 'a comedy of modern manners in fancy dress' (1997a: 91). In fact, the sequence performs a significant structural role in the narrative, and makes revealing comments on celebrity in contemporary society. By explicitly drawing out the similarities between Roman society and contemporary America, DeMille presents the viewer with a sequence which has something interesting to say rather than an accomplished, but ultimately meaningless, historical reconstruction.

Calpurnia's party

The scene opens on an elegant villa in Rome. A sophisticated group of Roman socialites are sitting around a table playing board games, sketching, and having a gossipy exchange about Caesar's absence in Egypt. They stop their gossip hurriedly as Calpurnia nears, and congratulate her on the success of the party. Calpurnia circulates among her guests, and similar sentiments are heard from other partygoers. As the camera pans across the room, Calpurnia is obscured behind a pillar and a more serious conversation is revealed in the foreground between three conspirators – Brutus, Cassius, and Casca. They fear that Caesar is to marry the Egyptian queen Cleopatra and adopt the title of king. Meanwhile Calpurnia speaks with Octavia (Antony's wife) and her brooding brother Octavian (Caesar's nephew), who asks why Caesar writes to Mark Antony and not him. A fanfare and great excitement heralds the arrival of Antony himself. He is surrounded by partygoers, but silences them to announce that Caesar is entering Rome. He asks Calpurnia to accompany Caesar but she refuses, saying she will wait for him at home. Antony and Octavian argue and are separated by Octavia before Calpurnia tells Antony, 'I know.'

This sequence is the audience's first introduction to DeMille's Rome, which he characterises by its differences with the Egyptian court and its similarities to contemporary America. Partygoers are gathered around a pool around which peacocks strut, their arrogance matching that of the humans watching them. The opulence on display here is more sophisticated and familiar to the filmgoer than the highly decorated and exotic patterns of the Egyptian court, with natural objects including flowers and plants, and white marble statuary all featuring. The exoticism that attaches to Cleopatra is given voice when an ingénue asks, 'Is she black?' to the great amusement of the others. Music follows a similar schema: the same theme as that heard in the Egyptian scenes, but played on a stringed instrument, producing a more gentle and refined sound. Less gentle and refined though are the partygoers themselves, who flirt and gossip about Caesar's betrayal of Calpurnia. In particular, we are shown that not all Roman wives are as faithful as Calpurnia. After a matron at the party notes that 'the wife is always the last one to know', a younger woman adds wittily, 'so is the husband, when it comes to that'.

Also introduced here are a number of key figures to the film's reading of Cleopatra, though she will only meet two of them. Brutus, Cassius and Casca are all characters that will be familiar to the audience from Shakespeare's *Julius Caesar*. Their function here is to explain the political problem Caesar poses in terms that the audience will understand. By pointing to Caesar's alleged plan to announce himself king, the film draws on America's notion of itself as a true democracy. In the 'Land of the Free', who will not empathise with Cassius' impassioned plea to his fellow conspirators: 'Was I not born as free as Caesar? And you?'

Calpurnia and Octavia offer two models for faithful wives; visually (both are blonde) and in their behaviour they present a contrast with the Egyptian queen. They will be discussed in more detail below. The final key figures, Antony and Octavian, also present a contrasting pair. Octavian is sullen, unsympathetic, and misogynistic – and, in his misogyny, delineated as the true villain of this female-focused narrative. Mark Antony is dashing, heroic, and impulsive. More interestingly though, he is presented as a modern celebrity, mobbed by partygoers, especially young women. His arrival at the party is framed as a mock triumph (echoing Caesar's own arrival in Rome in the next sequence). He is spectacularly dressed in crested helmet and gilded breastplate, heralded by fanfares and triumphal music and, in place of the reins of a triumphal chariot, he holds two giant mastiff dogs on a leash. In allegorical terms, if Rome is Hollywood, then Antony is precisely the kind of impulsive, sensation-seeking, magnificent movie star that the public loves, but the Decency League hates. As so often in this film and others, DeMille plays both sides: at the same time giving the public what they want, and critiquing it to placate cinema's morality guardians.

Seduced by spectacle

Cinema's popularity during the Depression Era of the 1930s has usually been explained by the desire for escapism. While this is clearly not the whole story (there were many successful films which showed a tougher social realism) it is certainly true that a large number of films from this period focus on luxury, fantasy, and spectacle. As a setting for film, the ancient world offered an apt canvas for such extravagant display. Its historical and cultural distance engendered an air of legend that legitimised the inclusion of fantastic opulence to entertain the Depression audience.

It is impossible to read the scene on Cleopatra's barge [see box: 'Cleopatra's barge'] as anything but a wholesale depiction of multiple seduction. Most obviously, Antony is seduced into an affair with Cleopatra. The sequence is littered with symbols of eroticism and troubling sexuality: the

29

Cleopatra's barge

Antony boards Cleopatra's barge with the intention of taking her back to the public square for their arranged meeting. Tying up his mastiff dogs at the entrance, he advances suspiciously into a palatial setting. Lyre music plays, and slave girls lay feather fans under his feet as he walks towards Cleopatra, who reclines in an undulating bower of more feathers, fanned by two male slaves, and covered in pearls. It is revealed that the men sent to fetch Cleopatra have already succumbed to this luxury, being 'awfully drunk'. Antony is resistant, and Cleopatra acknowledges her plan of seduction, announcing that she is 'dressed to lure you', and that she hoped he would be 'dazzled'. This gambit succeeds: Antony relaxes and is drawn in to the luxury that surrounds him with exotic foods, large goblets of wine, and spectacular entertainments. These include dancing girls, dressed in diaphanous gowns, who perform a sinuous dance around a garlanded bull. 'Clams from the sea' are dragged up in a net by black slaves: this opens to reveal more barely-clothed girls, draped in seaweed, the clamshells they hold filled with jewels. Cleopatra carelessly casts these out amongst the dancers and slaves, and invites Antony to do the same. Another dance has girls dressed in leopardskins staging a catfight. Antony's mastiffs can stand no more; they slip their collars and run off into the night. A trainer cracks his whip, and the cat-girls jump through flaming hoops. As the night goes on, the frantic pace begins to calm and Cleopatra's maid Charmian sings a hymn to Isis. As Cleopatra and Antony kiss, slaves draw a curtain across them and petals fall. The hortator sounds a steady rhythm and the oarsmen begin to row: in, out; in, out.

---

pearls that cover Cleopatra; the clamshells offered by the 'mermaids'; the feathered tunnel in which the Egyptian queen is found; the flaming rings through which the cat-girls leap. The arousal of Antony begins with scantily-clad and gyrating dancing girls, and is consummated with the pounding beat of the hortator. The cinema audience is also the subject of a seduction with cinematographic techniques used to draw the audience into DeMille's vision of opulence. Shots are centred so that our viewpoint mimics Antony's: we are with him as he enters the fantastic luxury of Cleopatra's barge, filled with feathers and pearls, precious stones and gold. (There was an extra-cinematic story around the film's release that DeMille had insisted on real gold for the goblets – despite the film being in black and white.) Feather fans intermittently obscure both Antony's and our viewpoint, teasing us with the spectacle that will embrace us. This spectacle proves to be one of extreme and careless excess to the point of wastefulness: a mass of roasted tiny 'reedbirds from the Nile', each one a single bite; a huge joint of meat, bitten into then discarded in favour of another; giant goblets of wine, emptied and refilled. Above all, this excess is represented by the clamshells filled with jewels that the mermaids present. When Cleopatra persuades Antony to join her in casually strewing them amongst the slaves and performers, it is perhaps a more

significant turning point than the sexual seduction that ends the sequence. Antony has relinquished the discipline of Rome: the Depression
audience joins him, immersing itself in the luxury of waste.

Games of gender

As a role model for women, Cleopatra, as an adultress, possible murderer
and eventual suicide victim, remains a dubious choice, even for a contemporary audience. However, at the time of the film's release, she was used
to sell all sorts of consumer goods, the advertisement of which invited their
purchasers to identify with the Egyptian queen. DeMille achieves this by
putting Cleopatra's dangerous aspects to the service of a glamorous reputation, while simultaneously domesticating her character development.
Thus Cleopatra can provide the female audience of the 1930s with an
alternative model to the 'New Woman' to aspire to – in both their real lives
and their fantasies.

The film traces the development of Cleopatra as a woman, in two ways:
literally, as she grows from a girl to a mature woman; and narratively as
she changes in the audience's estimation from 'the wickedest woman in
history' to a model who will stand by her man even unto death. Cleopatra
starts the film as a frivolous young girl, who heedlessly uses her sexual
allure on Caesar to her own advantage without thought of the political
consequences for him, or sisterly regard to the suffering of his saintly wife
Calpurnia. After Caesar's death, she is more serious – but her new
worldliness leads her cynically into a similar situation with Antony. When
it becomes politically necessary, she actively investigates ways to rid
herself of him, showing a distinct lack of proper feminine sentiment for her
man. It is only when he is provoked back into action that she reverts to
what is deemed to be the 'natural' (that is, subservient) role for a woman,
as shown in the scene described [see box: 'Antony becomes a man'].

This domestication of Cleopatra is doubly important because throughout the film we have seen what a disastrous effect she has on men.
Octavian is particularly misogynistic, but there is some truth when he
describes her as 'this poisonous snake that saps our men'. In fact, we have
seen what a bad influence she can be on upright Roman males early on
when Caesar is late after his first night with Cleopatra ('the first morning
he's been late since the day he was born'). Cleopatra saps men of their
self-discipline, and more – think of Antony's mastiffs, the embodiment of
his masculinity, running away from the overt femininity of the barge. The
film's dialogue also notes the loss of Antony's masculinity, with Cleopatra
condescendingly urging him to 'Be a good boy'. This is in particular
contrast to Antony's earlier description of women: 'They can't think – they
can't fight – they're playthings for us.' The words come back to haunt him
at his suicide, when he makes judgement upon himself before driving the
sword in: 'Antony – the plaything of a woman!'

Antony becomes a man

Tipped off by King Herod that the powerful factions in Rome would look more kindly on her if Antony were eliminated, Cleopatra determines to poison him. However, Herod also tips off Antony. As they sit down to dine, Cleopatra pours wine but Antony refuses to drink. To allay his suspicions, she drains a cup of the same, but then drops poisoned petals into his cup. As he is about to drink, a messenger arrives declaring, 'Rome have declared war! Mark Antony is a traitor.' Antony leaps into action, shouting orders, striking out physically, and dismissing Cleopatra contemptuously. Cleopatra is transfixed: she falls to her knees, declaring 'I've seen a god come to life! I'm no longer a queen – I'm a woman.' [Fig. 5]

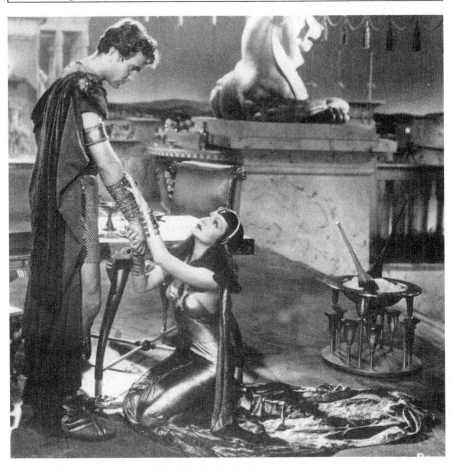

5. The 'New Woman' surrenders.
Cleopatra and Antony, *Cleopatra* (1934).

1. *Establishing the Conventions: Cleopatra* (1934)

If Cleopatra is dangerous to men, her relationship with other women is more complicated. As discussed previously, the film's moral stance with regard to Cleopatra as a woman is established at Calpurnia's party, where both Calpurnia and Octavia (representatives of Rome and the Western tradition) are implicitly compared with the Egyptian queen. If the film is to conform to the Production Code, viewers should be encouraged to take the side of these wronged (or about to be wronged) wives and against the adulterous Cleopatra. It is hard to see why we should root for the rather silly Octavia, but Calpurnia is a different matter. A model hostess, her admission at the end of the sequence that she knows about Caesar's adultery forces us to reassess thoughts that she is simply naïve and downtrodden. Her sad pragmatism regarding her husband's betrayal and selfless plea to him not to go to the Senate on the fateful day – 'not for me – but for you!' – should also turn the viewer against Cleopatra. However, at the moment when the film threatens to fall into a simple moral dichotomy of the virtuous Calpurnia and the wicked Cleopatra, DeMille inserts a complication. We soon discover that Cleopatra is herself the naïve one: truly in love with Caesar and failing to understand that his reasons for marriage are more political than romantic. When Apollodorus tells her that Caesar 'didn't love you', Cleopatra, as much as Calpurnia, is drawn as victim of romantic love. Cleopatra is not only 'the other woman', she is also 'everywoman', ultimately dependent on the love of a man.

Cleopatra, then, is quite a woman, but it is worth noting that there is one aspect of womanhood that is denied to DeMille's Cleopatra: 'the maternal'. The casting of Colbert meant a Cleopatra who was almost boyish in her figure, as was appropriate for the fashions of the day. She's fashionable, but not fertile. Unlike Elizabeth Taylor's Cleopatra almost thirty years later, the fecund roundness of a figure that had borne four children was not part of this version of the story, and nor were the children themselves. Cleopatra's reproductive powers are limited – to cultural reproductions of herself.

Suggested further viewing

Cabiria (dir. Pastrone, 1914)
This silent film, set in Carthage during the Second Punic War between Carthage and Rome, was innovative for its time, and included many of the features seen as characteristic in later films set in the ancient world. Cabiria is a young girl, sold into slavery in Carthage and subsequently presented as a sacrifice to the god Moloch, a fate from which she is rescued by a Roman nobleman, Fulvio Axilla and his slave Maciste. Maciste was played by a former dock worker (Bartolomeo Pagano) as a strongman figure, becoming the cinematic ancestor of the bodybuilder Hercules that defined the Italian peplum cinema of the 1950s and 60s. The depiction of the temple of Moloch, with its repugnant practice of child sacrifice, identi-

33

fied evil with the Oriental, a standard assumption for films to come. The film was one of the first to use tracking shots (known afterwards for some time as 'Cabiria shots'), in which the camera was moved on a 'dolly'. In contrast to the more usual static viewpoints, tracking shots produced more dynamism and a greater sense of audience involvement in the action. The film's scriptwriter, the poet and Italian nationalist Gabriele D'Annunzio, had great ambitions for *Cabiria* as a cultural product rather than mere entertainment. Released shortly after the Italo-Turkish war, it claimed ancient Rome as direct ancestor and legitimising authority for the current Italian political regime, presaging the use of Roman symbols by the Italian Fascists.

Sign of the Cross (dir. DeMille, 1932)

DeMille's first film set in ancient Rome was based on the stage play by Wilson Barrett, already well-known to popular audiences. It presented the conflict between Rome and early Christianity, personalised through the romance of the Christian girl Mercia (Elissa Landi), and the Roman prefect Marcus Superbus (Frederic March). Marcus is also desired by Poppaea (Claudette Colbert), wife of the Roman emperor Nero (Charles Laughton). His declared preference for Mercia makes her the target for Poppaea's vengeance. The film responded to the more loosely-enforced guidelines of the early Production Code with open eroticism and violence, authorised by the allegedly educative value of the ancient historical setting. This flouting of the guidelines included the lesbian 'Dance of the Naked Moon' and Poppaea's revealing asses' milk bath. There is also an extended arena sequence which establishes many of the staple features of such scenes in films to come, including multiple combats (one between Amazons and pygmies), Christians killed by wild animals (including crocodiles and lions), and implied death by bestiality. In 1944, the film was re-released for a Second World War audience with a number of cuts to remove any traces of pre-Code licentiousness, and a new prologue introduced by an army chaplain on a military flight over Rome.

The Last Days of Pompeii (dir. Schoedsack, 1935)

Edward Bulwer-Lytton's 1834 novel, *The Last Days of Pompeii* had been a great success with readers before being adapted for stage, opera and as a pyrodrama (spectacular stage show with added pyrotechnics). It was produced as a film by Italian filmmakers, twice in 1913 and again in 1926. However, the 1935 Hollywood film had little in common with the book other than the title. Rather it adapted the currently popular gangster film (e.g. *Little Caesar* (1931), *The Public Enemy* (1931)) to the ancient world. Marcus (Preston Foster) is a blacksmith who becomes a gladiator in an attempt to raise money to save his injured wife and son, but after their deaths continues in the cynical realisation that 'It's easy to get money – all you have to do is kill!' The film follows Marcus' various moneymaking careers as gladiator, slave trader, and eventually arena owner in Pompeii, taking in a journey to Judea where his adopted son Flavius is healed by Christ. In the final scenes, a grown-up Flavius has himself been condemned to death in his father's arena, but the fighting is halted by Vesuvius erupting. Flavius is saved, and Marcus is finally redeemed by saving others, though he perishes himself. The special effects were accomplished by Willis O'Brien who had recently done the same for *King Kong* (1933) and later became Ray Harryhausen's mentor.

The Roman Epics of Classical Hollywood:
Quo Vadis (1951)

Introduction

Prior to the success of *Gladiator* in 2000, mentioning classical antiquity on film was certain to invoke thoughts of the epic films produced in the post-Second World War period by Hollywood studios. Mostly set in Rome, these films often employed the same central plot device: an upstanding but pagan Roman soldier is converted to Christianity through love for a chaste Christian maiden, and is subsequently instrumental in the defeat of a decadent emperor (or his representative). Their stocklist of characters and events became core signifiers for cine-antiquity: evil emperors and vampish scheming empresses; brave gladiators and innocent virgins; crowd scenes and banquets; chariot races and arena combats. Persisting in popularity over time and appealing to broadly constituted audiences, the dominance of this style in re-presenting antiquity on film is such that viewers seem more likely to measure 'authenticity' by inclusion of the visual precedents they established than by any adherence to historical facts.

The Roman epics were large-scale productions, hugely expensive to produce with their vast crowds of extras, extravagant costume and set design, innovative use of technology, and prestige casts. In addition to *Quo Vadis* (the focus for analysis in this chapter), titles included *The Robe* (1953), *Ben-Hur* (1959), *Spartacus* (1960), *Cleopatra* (1963) and *The Fall of the Roman Empire* (1964). Their expense and extravagance makes them especially interesting as illustrations of the influence of commercial factors on representations of antiquity. In brief, the more that a film costs to produce, the more it will be expected to return that outlay in box-office takings. This agenda prompts more promotion and wider dissemination of the product, but also a more conservative approach to morality and representation. Such large-scale productions were also associated with the prestige and reputations of the studios, both because of their technical virtuosity and their economic scale. Their 'event' status made them ideal candidates for awards, which in turn encouraged their more widespread and longer-lasting dissemination. It was the dominance of the studio system in post-war Hollywood that made epic film production economically possible, and encouraged its hegemony over cine-antiquity: but it also threatened to halt the creative evolution of representations of its most popular topics.

2. The Roman Epics of Classical Hollywood: Quo Vadis (1951)

Filmmaking has always been commercially driven, and as cinema grew in technical sophistication, this became more explicitly foregrounded. The expense of equipment and increasingly large number of personnel needed to produce a film made small studios economically unviable. They folded or were swallowed up by their better-funded peers. By the late 1920s, Hollywood was dominated by five major studios, with another two minor studios. These studios owned not only the means to produce films, but also the cinema chains in which they were mostly exhibited and an extensive and efficient publicity machine to sell their films to the public. In addition, they held popular actors under contract to perform only in their films. The studios could dictate which films were shown and in what order they appeared in the programme. They could force independent cinemas to pay for films that they did not want in order to get a chance to screen high profile films like epics, which would have been pre-sold to the viewing public as events in themselves. Despite legislation in 1948 to break the studios' monopoly over exhibition, the major studios still wielded significant power until the mid-1960s when the advance of television and changes in audience demographics dictated a reassessment of commercial practices. Epic films had their part to play in this story of the rise and fall of the studio system. Famously, the enormously expensive 1963 epic *Cleopatra*, starring Elizabeth Taylor and Richard Burton, has often been said to have almost bankrupted Twentieth Century Fox.

For the studios, Roman epic films were not just attractive because they were popular with audiences. In their narratives of power and spectacle, they stood as a metaphor for the power of the studios themselves; in particular, their power to recreate and to control previously unseen worlds. For the audiences, the attraction was more straightforward. In a post-war world still in the grip of austerity measures, they offered the chance to escape into a world of luxury, decadence and spectacle: monumental, finely-decorated buildings; muscular men in gleaming breastplates; beautiful women decked in jewels and dressed in exquisite brightly-coloured fabrics; and, perhaps above all for a hungry audience, the feasts, with their tables spilling over with fresh fruit and roasted meats. The display of all this extravagance was well suited to show off the capacity of new film technologies such as Widescreen, Cinemascope, and Technicolor. And in turn, the possession and use of such new technologies once again showed off the power of the studios.

Pinning down a definition of an epic film is not as easy as one might imagine. In 2008, the American Film Institute listed their top ten epic films (of which two are set in ancient Rome and another one in Biblical times). Their definition of epic film is 'a genre of large-scale films set in a cinematic interpretation of the past'. This definition seems rather sweeping, but in fact discounts many films that viewers would consider epic: for instance, science-fiction and fantasy films like *2001: A Space Odyssey* (1968), *Star Wars* (1977), or the *Lord of the Rings* trilogy (2001-2003).

Genre definitions are always difficult. The film scholar Richard Maltby has noted that while 'audiences, producers and critics all discuss movies in generic terms ... they often mean something very different by them' (2003: 74). However, we can point to some key characteristics which, if lacking, make it difficult to describe a film as epic.

An epic film is certainly a production on a large scale, in terms of budget, resources, locations and often casts (prestige as well as numbers). This dictates a presentation in which spectacle and grandeur are fore-grounded, making the ancient world with its monumental architecture and extravagant emperors an ideal topic for epic film. However the success (as an epic) of a film like *Reds* (1981), ninth in the American Film Institute's top ten list, shows that grandeur does not have to derive from material wealth and show. The film recounted the life of John Reed, an American journalist who chronicled the Russian Revolution. Here, and in other epic films that do not include visual opulence, it is a grandeur of themes that makes the film 'epic'. The genre requires a narrative that connects its characters to great turning points or influential ideas in the history of mankind, though within the on-screen narrative the characters themselves may have only an inkling of the significance. The fact that epic films tend to be set against a backdrop of well-known historical events puts us as viewers into a particularly privileged position, assured in our ability to assess the outcome of events far better than the on-screen characters themselves. Thus epic films can serve a particular function for audiences by enabling us to review, assess and validate our histories, identities, and cultural communities.

All of the Roman epic films are broadly 'historical'. However, their narratives adapt historical fiction rather than historiography: a key point to remember, given the criticism often levied that they are historically inaccurate. Narratives were mostly drawn from highly successful popular novels like Henryk Sienkiewicz's *Quo Vadis?*, General Lew Wallace's *Ben Hur*, and Lloyd C. Douglas' *The Robe*. These novels integrated fictional characters with genuine historical figures and events, and had few qualms about reshaping the latter if it was necessary to fit the purposes of the narrative. Some had already been adapted to live performances for popu-lar audiences as 'toga dramas', or had previously been adapted for the cinema, so the films were able to build on popular awareness of the narratives and established conventions for live action re-presentations. The trend for film adaptations from literature also extended in the same period to smaller-scale films set in ancient Rome: *Caesar and Cleopatra* (1945), *Androcles and the Lion* (1952) and *Julius Caesar* (1953), for instance, were all adapted from well-known plays.

Seemingly paradoxically, film epic was never particularly interested in ancient epic. Even the best-known ancient epics – the *Iliad*, *Odyssey* and *Aeneid* – were mostly avoided by Hollywood, despite widespread popular knowledge of their stories. One reason for this may be found in the fact that the epic poems draw their narratives and characters from mythology. Classical Hollywood's primary drive for realism could not easily accommodate the gods, heroes and monsters of ancient myth. One borderline exception is *Ulysses* (1954), a joint US/Italian production starring Kirk Douglas, filmed in Italy with an Italian crew and mostly Italian cast, and scripted by Hollywood writers Hugh Gray (historical adviser on *Quo Vadis*), Ben Hecht, and Irwin Shaw. The film has been critically acclaimed as an intelligent and thoughtful adaptation of Homer's poem, capturing much of the fantastic quality of the *Odyssey* but (like the 1956 *Helen of Troy*, another US/Italian production) it does not have the narrative or visual feel of a Hollywood epic film. Another possible exception is *Troy* (2004) which combined events from the *Iliad* and *Odyssey* for its plot, but set them in a quasi-historical setting, eschewing the gods and rationalising the supernatural.

The dominance of Rome over Greece as a location for historical epic films has been much noted. Derek Elley (1984: 52) suggests a number of reasons why this may be the case, including the absence of an imperial age, and the lack of dramatic events, with the development of Greek civilisation being rather 'a tale of perpetual adaptation'. Nevertheless, there were two attempts to produce Greek historical epic films in the post-war period, neither very successful at the time of their release: *Alexander the Great* (1956) and *The 300 Spartans* (1962). Reasons for their relative failure (compared with the Roman epics) may be found in stylistic flaws: *Alexander the Great*, for instance, takes a highly earnest approach and forgets to entertain its viewers, while *The 300 Spartans* places a juvenile couple as prime movers of the narrative – in keeping with the dominance of teenagers in films of the times, but inappropriate for the conservative epic film audience (see Chapter 5 for further discussion). Interestingly, the resurgence of the ancient world epic film in the twenty-first century has seen the same historical narratives used by two new epic films: *Alexander* (2004) takes as its focus the career of the Macedonian conqueror, Alexander the Great, and *300* (2007) retells the defence of the pass at Thermopylae by a small force of Spartans.

This popularity in cinema of a small number of historical narratives and settings, and their reappearance at particular times, gives us a clue to the special utility of Rome as a setting for epic films in the post-war period. The stories of both Alexander and Thermopylae involve the victory of Greece (standing for the western world) over the Persians (standing here for Orientalism and the East). Recent epic films featuring these narratives appeared at a time of East-West conflict (oil-driven wars in the Middle East, the rise of radical Islam). Similarly, the post-war Roman epics were released into a world seeking validation for the sacrifices of the Second World War and the potential for further losses threatened by the Cold War between the western nations (especially the USA) and the Communist Eastern bloc. They used narratives of the sacrifices of early Christians to describe the (morally justified) triumph of freedom and democracy over tyranny. Visual and verbal parallels figured Roman emperors as Nazis, Fascists and Communists, and early Christian converts as god-fearing Americans. *Quo Vadis* is an especially good example of this trope.

The Roman epics of post-war Hollywood cinema have been so dominant in creating popular perceptions of the ancient world that it is surprising to discover how few there actually were: it is a struggle to list a dozen between *Quo Vadis* in 1951 and *The Fall of the Roman Empire* in 1964, even including such borderline examples as Mankiewicz's *Julius Caesar* (1953). Why is it that these films are so well embedded in the popular imagination? Partly this is to do with the commercial impulse: the large-scale promotions needed to attract greater audiences, the major awards, conservative family-friendly (for the main part) morality and apparent educational value have prompted repeat screenings on television, often at holiday times when they occupy long swathes of the programme schedule and large audiences can be guaranteed. Narratives of early Christianity like *Quo Vadis* and *Ben Hur* have become staples of network television at Easter, for instance. However, it is more than just repetition and prestige that has produced the popular audience's ongoing affection for Roman epics. With their spectacular sets, grandiose narrative ambitions, attractive casting and all-round exuberance they remain, above all, great entertainment.

Background to case study

The immediate source for the 1951 film was the historical novel *Quo Vadis?* by the Polish author Henryk Sienkiewicz (1846-1916), first published as a serial in Polish daily papers in 1895. The title was drawn from the Christian tradition of a revelation to the apostle Peter as he fled from Nero's persecutions. As he left Rome, a vision of Christ appeared to him. He asked the vision, 'Quo vadis, domine?' ('Where are you going, master?') Christ replied that, because Peter was abandoning his people, he was returning to Rome to be crucified a second time. Peter turns back to return to Rome in the understanding that this is where the church will be established, despite his own inevitable death on Nero's orders. *Quo Vadis?* was a huge international success, being translated into more than 50 different languages. However Sienkiewicz was better known in his home country for a series of historical novels set in Old Poland. In 1905, he received a Nobel Prize for Literature for his 'outstanding merits as an epic writer'.

The novel weaves the fictitious romance of the Roman Marcus Vinicius and the Christian Lygia into a backdrop of events and figures drawn from Roman and early Christian history. The far from straightforward course of this romance is used as a vehicle to showcase the decadence of Rome, led by its emperor Nero. In particular, the effects of that decadence and corruption on good intelligent men are drawn out in the central figure of Petronius, Vinicius' uncle and Nero's 'Arbiter of Elegance'. Love and lust are identified as competing principles for a good life, and respectively associated with Christian monotheism and Roman pantheism. Vinicius eventually embraces the love of Christ and receives the earthly rewards of love from Lygia and her rescue from a public and particularly brutal death. Though he shuns the new religion, Petronius is finally redeemed by love for his Greek slave Eunice, and a good death by his own hand. Nero remains a victim of his lustful desires and cowardice, and cannot reconcile himself to his inevitable death; instead he dies in violence and terror.

Translated into English, the full title of the novel was given as *Quo Vadis?: A Narrative of the Time of Nero*. In the context of nineteenth-century conflicts between the intellectual trend towards rationalism and popular adherence to a more literal and historically-based Christianity, Nero was a significant figure. Long identified in Christian narrative traditions as the 'anti-Christ', he offered a potent symbol of oppressive and anti-religious forces for a popular audience. In addition, given the topics of Sienkiewicz's other novels, the novel has been read as a patriotic allegory of Catholic Poland's struggle against imperialist oppressors Germany, Austria, and Russia. Thus the main narrative source for the film was already, as a literary text, subject to interpretation as a vehicle for the discussion of modern political and moral conflicts.

Sienkiewicz drew on several ancient sources for the historical events and characters of his novel, in particular Tacitus and Suetonius. Tacitus is the main source for the figure around which the narrative operates: Gaius Petronius. Petronius has been identified as the author of the *Satyricon* (discussed in more detail in Chapter 8) and is described by Tacitus as Nero's 'Arbiter of Elegance', his guide in matters of taste and culture (*Annals* 16.18). Nero's favour drew the enmity of Tigellinus, the Prefect of the Praetorian Guard and another of Nero's inner circle, who convinced the emperor that Petronius had been involved with conspirators against him. According to Tacitus (16.19) Petronius chose to pre-empt his inevitable demise by opening his own veins, and before dying composed a scurrilous letter to Nero listing the emperor's depravities and those who had been his partners in them. In the novel, this letter is given content not described in the historical sources: referring to Nero murdering his mother, brother and wife, but claiming that his greater crime is his despoilment of the arts: poetry, music and dance. The film repeats this revisionary strategy, citing, in a final flourish of ironic detachment, Nero's abysmal songs and poems as the reason for Petronius' suicide.

The influence of Tacitus can also be seen in the cinematic Nero's decision to deflect blame for the devastating Great Fire of Rome that destroyed more than half the city from himself to the (already unpopular) Christians (15.44). Suetonius also mentions the fire, stating openly that Nero was responsible (*Life of Nero* 38). He comments approvingly on the

41

oppression of the Christians (16), although unlike Tacitus, he does not link the two. However, it is Suetonius' descriptions of Nero's vices that have most influence on Sienkiewicz's emperor: prowling the streets of Rome at night provoking violent brawls; murdering his mother Agrippina and adopted brother Britannicus, among others. More minor historical figures mentioned in Suetonius also appear in the novel: for instance, Locusta the poisoner; Phaon, Sporus, and Epaphroditus, members of Nero's household. Phaon retains a notional place in the 1951 film as the name of the architect responsible for the new Rome that will rise in the place of the fire.

The popular success of *Quo Vadis?* as a novel made it an unsurprising choice for early cinematic adaptation. After a very early one-reeler made by Pathé in 1901 which presented a sequence of tableaux from the book, the first proper film version was made by the Italian Cines Company, directed by Enrico Guazzoni and released in 1913. A six-reel film playing at the unusual (for the time) length of two hours, the film has become recognised as a milestone in film history for its genuinely cinematic adaptation of a literary narrative, and use of a variety of points-of-view to develop unprecedented depth in its storytelling. A remake was released in 1924, also made in Italy by the German director Georg Jacoby and the Italian Gabriellino d'Annunzio (son of the Italian poet and nationalist, Gabriele d'Annunzio, who had his own role in the history of epic cine-antiquity through his involvement in the seminal 1914 epic *Cabiria*). Released into a Fascist Italy which had adopted ancient Rome as its patriotic model, its portrayal of a decadent Roman society and governing regime did not mesh with the spirit of the times and it was not well received by critics or viewers. After this failure, the next *Quo Vadis* was the 1951 film, the first American adaptation of Sienkiewicz's novel.

The 1951 film retains the narrative framework of the novel, but telescopes the timescale and reduces the extent to which a number of key characters feature. In particular, the apostles Peter and Paul, and their mirror image, the traitorous 'philosopher' Chilo Chilonides are diminished. These three characters are key to the novel's proselytising tone, so become mostly surplus given the film's lighter touch on the topic of religion. The character of Marcus is revised to better fit the expectations of a modern audience about how a hero should behave: for instance, incidents in the novel where he kills a slave in anger and viciously punishes others are not included. Poppaea is also revised in keeping with audience expectations, becoming a more stereotypical evil female, a vamp. She is without sympathy in the film, being totally motivated by adulterous lust for Vinicius. In contrast, the novel treats her in a more even-handed fashion providing a backstory about the death of her infant daughter and her superstitious belief that Lygia was to blame to explain her antipathy. Audience expectations and conventions also inform the religious scenes: Jesus is not shown speaking directly, and we do not see his face; except when Peter describes the Last Supper, when an onscreen enactment of Da

Vinci's familiar painting provides a legitimising cultural filter. There are changes in the film to the timing of events for the sake of narrative economy. For instance, the novel follows the historical sources in placing the death of Seneca before that of Petronius. In the film Petronius dies before Seneca, allowing the latter to convey the Arbiter's letter to Nero. Finally there are revisions which give the narrative a better fit with the timely themes by which the narrative is governed: Nero is played as a figure of ridicule, an echo of the propaganda strategies used to deflate the image of that more recent political bogeyman, Adolf Hitler. This also gives the film a humorous element, an important part of the most successful epic films, reducing some of the inevitable pomposity that accompanied the grand themes and moral lessons.

Two key themes inform the 1951 cinematic adaptation of Sienkiewicz's narrative, both concerning an ideological conflict: freedom versus tyranny, and Christianity versus paganism. They were especially timely given the date of the film's release, soon after the end of the Second World War and while the ideological conflict of the Cold War was at its height. Having such clear and purposeful themes served as an authorising strategy, almost a moral justification, for the cuts and revisions made to the characters and plot of the original text. Nothing should stand in the way of telling such an important and evangelising story.

As with all films, it is crucially important to situate *Quo Vadis* in the circumstances of its production. Rights to film the text were obtained by MGM Studios before the outbreak of the Second World War, and a variety of directors, writers, and leading actors were proposed and discarded before the production began shooting. In 1949, shooting was scheduled to begin with John Huston writing and directing, and the lead roles played by Gregory Peck and Elizabeth Taylor. However, Peck was hospitalised with an eye infection, and the prospect of holding up an expensive and complicated shooting schedule resulted in postponement. By the time shooting actually began in 1950, Huston's politically-driven script had been replaced by one that put more focus on the religious aspects of the story, though, as we shall see, it still retained a political message.

The cast had also changed. In the leading roles were the robustly American Robert Taylor as Marcus Vinicius, the English rose Deborah Kerr as Lygia, and the English-born (with polyglot European ancestry) Peter Ustinov as Nero. Previously proposed candidates to play Nero, the film's villain, had included Wallace Beery, Orson Welles, Charles Laughton (who had already played the character in DeMille's 1932 film, *Sign of the Cross*), and Robert Morley. Like Ustinov, Laughton and Morley were both British, recalling the aural casting conventions already noted in Chapter 1. There were good economic reasons for this: assets frozen in Europe as part of the post-war economic reconstruction could be released in the form of actors' fees paid in sterling. Such casting did nothing to discourage the audience's opinion that nothing said moral decadence and

43

imperial decline like a British accent. At least, such was the case in a male character; conversely, the same accent in a leading female character signified purity. To complete the paradigm, the male heroic lead would usually be played by an American actor. However, usage of these conventions was developing into something more nuanced than the original 'British, bad: American, good'. They had become a subtle way of reinforcing the cultural and (increasingly) political imperialism of the USA, with America shown as the new way that would both sweep away the corruption of power-wielders in the Old World, and simultaneously liberate its people (represented by the female lead).

The use of such conventions put the emphasis on individual characters as fundamental building blocks in the viewer's understanding of the narrative. This focus on the desires and characteristics of the individual as motivation for narrative action was key to a larger system of representational conventions which governed the way that the ancient world (and all other cinematic 'worlds') were presented in Hollywood cinema. The system has become known as the 'classical Hollywood style'. Films produced by Hollywood studios in the period from the end of the First World War to the beginning of the 1960s were subject to certain rules for narrative style. These emphasised regular and predictable causality, linearity of time and space, and psychological motivations as drivers for narrative action. In other words, they sought to produce cinematic representations which seemed to mimic real life: an 'invisible cinema' that situated the viewer as eavesdropper, an unseen watcher seated in the dark of the cinema. In turn, the need to artificially disguise the artifice of cinema dictated the way that shots were staged, lit, and edited. For example, key characters in a scene will be centred in the foreground, in focus and clearly lit. Dialogue between two characters is often edited into a shot/reverse shot sequence, with shots of each character alternated as they take their turn to speak, mimicking the way that we might look at each speaker in turn. The purpose of editing is to promote continuity: to make each action within a scene and each scene within the larger narrative seem to follow inevitably. This imperative for naturalism also promoted the use of more colloquial dialogue and accents, contributing, in the case of examples of cine-antiquity of the period, to the notion that the ancient world was just the same as the modern world, but in fancy dress. As a result, antiquity was as good a location for the discussion of modern moral and social concerns as any modern setting.

Principal photography on *Quo Vadis* was completed at the Cinecittà studios in Rome. The notion of 'authentic' location shooting was not the primary driver here: unlike *Jason and the Argonauts*, for example, *Quo Vadis* did not have a narrative reason to shoot amongst ancient architectural ruins (see discussion in Chapter 6). However, the same post-war economic reconstruction policies that made employing British actors advantageous also imposed limits on the amount of money that American businesses could take out of the local Italian economy. With audiences hungry for the escapism of the cinema and a ruined home film industry, Hollywood was making good returns in Italy which it could not export. Turning it into value-added exportable products like expensive epic films was a clever way to move the money back home. In news stories seeded by the studio's publicists, this commercial strategy was retold as a heroic tale of generous America coming to the rescue of broken Europe with stories of rebuilding the studios before filming could begin, feeding hungry children with leftover food from the banquet scenes, and providing work for thousands of locals as extras.

Another strand of pre-publicity aimed to give the film the authority of an educational text by emphasising academic connections and the extensive research that had gone into the script. The academic background of the researcher Hugh Gray is particularly highlighted in studio publicity. Gray had studied Classics at Oxford, and went on to be involved in the writing of other historical epic films, including *Ulysses* (1954) and *Helen of Troy* (1956). In the early stages of the film's production, Gray worked closely with John Huston to produce a script that was historically valid (though not necessarily historically accurate). The amount of research in ancient sources that he had undertaken was claimed to total four volumes of notes, which according to studio publicity, were to be handed over to the University of Rome on the film's completion. However, after Huston was removed from the project, Gray's contribution was downgraded to an advisory role. In the final film, he does not have a writing credit, but is named as 'historical adviser and lyrics composer'.

The huge costs involved in producing *Quo Vadis* called for an equally hyperbolic campaign to attract audiences on its release, including a vast number of commercial tie-ins. Publicity emphasised the great quantities involved in the film's production: an excess of extras, sets, costs, and research. However, the notion of excess was most accessible to the viewer in the sheer spectacle and luxury that the film presented to them onscreen. From the gleaming breastplates of the Roman soldiers through to the monumental architecture of ancient Rome, the extravagance of the feasts and the glamour of the dresses worn by the female leads – and all in glorious Technicolor. By March 1954, *The Hollywood Reporter* was able to report that the film had recouped its production costs, and it was not until April 1956 that the *Daily Variety* reported the final booking in a screening run that had been continuous since its first premieres in late 1951.

Of course, it was not possible to please everyone. The film had mixed reviews from the critics. Bosley Crowther in the *New York Times* called it 'a staggering combination of cinema brilliance and sheer banality, of visual excitement and verbal boredom'. It received eight nominations for Academy Awards, but failed to win any. Nevertheless, in more than half a century since it was made, *Quo Vadis* has maintained an attraction for new audiences for its extravagant and enticing vision of antiquity. In particular through its regular television screenings, it has continued to exert an influence on popular ideas about ancient Rome and its emperors.

Plot summary

Returning from a successful military campaign, the Roman commander Marcus Vinicius (Robert Taylor) meets Lygia (Deborah Kerr), daughter of a conquered foreign king and hostage of Rome, now adopted daughter of Aulus Plautius and his wife Pomponia. All three are secretly members of the new sect of Christianity. Entering Rome in triumph, Marcus confides his desire for Lygia to his cynical and world-weary uncle Petronius (Leo Genn), the 'Arbiter of Elegance' for the emperor Nero (Peter Ustinov). On Petronius' advice, Lygia is removed from her adopted family and taken to Nero's palace, where she is dressed for a feast by Acte (Rosalie Crutchley), Nero's former mistress. At the feast she is seated with Marcus, but catches the eye of Nero's empress Poppaea (Patricia Laffan), who desires Marcus for herself. Nero tells Lygia that she is his gift to Marcus and, despite her horror, orders that she be taken to his house. On the way there, the litter is ambushed by Ursus (Buddy Baer), Lygia's giant protector, and the girl disappears.

Meanwhile, Petronius realises that his slave Eunice (Marina Berti) is in love with him, and takes her with him to Antium where Nero has taken the court. On his uncle's advice, Marcus consults the soothsayer Chilo about Lygia's disappearance. He takes Marcus, with Croton the wrestler as bodyguard, to a secret meeting of Christians where the apostles Paul and Peter preach about the life of Christ. They follow Lygia and her companions home through the streets of Rome. But Ursus detects them, knocks Marcus out and kills Croton. Marcus awakes to find Lygia nursing him. She admits she loves him, and he proposes marriage, even agreeing to adopt Christianity. However, Lygia's declaration that she loves Christ equally to Marcus sparks another row. Marcus storms off to join Petronius and Eunice in Antium with Nero – and Poppaea.

However, their peace is broken by the message that Rome is on fire. Nero and his circle watch the flames from the roof of his palace, while the emperor sings of the burning of Troy. Meanwhile Marcus finds Lygia through the panicking mob, and leads many to the safety of the river. The mob accuse Nero of starting the fire and, on Poppaea's jealous advice, he blames it on the Christians and orders their arrest. Petronius decides to end his own life before Nero orders it, and Eunice chooses to join him in death.

Peter leaves Rome but, after seeing a vision of Christ, decides to return to an inevitable martyrdom. Lygia is arrested along with her adopted parents and other Christians. Marcus tries to free her, but is also thrown into prison. They witness the deaths of their Christian friends in the arena including Pomponia, who is killed by lions and Aulus Plautius who is burned at the stake. Lygia is tied to a stake to face a bull while Marcus is forced to watch from the emperor's box. However Ursus kills the bull, and the crowd demand their release, against Nero's wishes. Marcus announces the arrival of Galba to overthrow Nero, and the people respond by attacking the imperial palace. Nero kills Poppaea, but does not have the courage to kill himself, having to rely on Acte's help. As the film closes, Marcus and Lygia are leaving Rome to start their life together.

Key scenes and themes

Decadence and spectacle

While Sienkiewicz's novel was subtitled in some translations as 'A Tale of the Christ', LeRoy's film should perhaps have been labelled 'A Tale of the Anti-Christ'. Despite its ostensible moral focus on a virtuous Christianity, the real star of the film is the outrageous emperor Nero and his extravagantly immoral court. In the ambivalent, but undeniably entertaining, world of Hollywood cinema, audiences were cynically enabled to have their cake and eat it too. Spectacular Roman epic films encouraged them to congratulate themselves on their own virtuousness, while simultaneously enjoying the glamour of onscreen decadence. Rome's corrupt ethics and profligate luxury are made explicit in the sequence where Lygia is taken to an evening's entertainment at the imperial court [see box: 'Nero's feast']. The scene is narratively crucial in establishing Lygia's righteous Christian virtue, but the main attractions for viewers lie in the sex, violence, excess, and spectacle.

The corrupt decadence of the Roman court is illustrated in every aspect of this sequence: the crowd's enthusiasm for the death of the wrestler; the lewd public behaviour; Poppaea's approval and promotion of adultery (for herself and her husband); the excessive eating and drinking; and the idea that some humans are chattels to be exchanged as rewards for military service, regardless of their own wishes. Romans are also distinguished from Christians in their attitude to religion, with the emperor referred to as a living god.

Lygia is distanced from this world in a number of ways: physically by her refusal to take part in the drinking, carousing and violent spectatorship, and morally by her (to Marcus, incomprehensible) horror at Nero's assumption that her virtue is in his gift. Cinematically, she is also distanced by her placement in the shots: she is frequently placed at the bottom right of the frame and facing away from the camera, set apart from the Roman men and the events they are approvingly watching. Head and shoulder shots are in soft focus, presenting her as a softer and more fragile character than other hard-edged partygoers, especially Poppaea. She and Poppaea are also compared through their costumes. Both wear blue, but Poppaea's dress is a pale, silvery-blue, shining satin, giving the impression

Nero's feast

Lygia and Acte enter a room filled with music, dancing, laughter, and colour. Lygia is led to a couch, passing scantily-clad dancers and entwined couples. She is soon joined by Marcus and Petronius, who remarks on Lygia's beauty, saying 'Everything's there but the smile' before leaving them to join the emperor. Marcus sits close to Lygia and tries to kiss her, but she repels him. They are offered wine, but again Lygia refuses. All stand as the emperor and his empress enter and are seated. Marcus asks Lygia, 'Have you ever seen your emperor and your god this close before?' With a wry smile, Lygia answers, 'No, I have never seen Nero this close before.'

A single dancer begins to perform, and the camera now turns to Nero, who is watching the scene in a bored fashion through an emerald eyeglass. Spotting Lygia and Marcus, he is taken with the girl's beauty, encouraged by his wife Poppaea. However Petronius persuades him that she is not so beautiful ('Too narrow in the hips'). As the dance ends, a partygoer calls out for Nero to sing and, with apparent reluctance, he agrees. To his own accompaniment, he sings of the burning of Troy, to the backdrop of a flaming torch, and the audience's acclaim.

After Nero's performance there is wrestling, to the great excitement of male and female partygoers. Marcus boasts, to Lygia's obvious distaste, that the wrestler Croton has 'killed over 300 opponents!' The fight reaches a climax, and at Nero's thumbs-down signal, the victorious Croton breaks his opponent's neck. The wrestler salutes his emperor with a straight-armed salute, reminiscent to the audience of those so recently seen in Nazi and Fascist regimes. [Fig. 6]

Nero now comes down from his raised platform for a closer view of Lygia and informs her that he has made a gift of her to Marcus 'for his devotion to me and his service on the battlefield'. Lygia is horrified, and when Marcus tells her, 'Live with me – love as you were meant to love,' she angrily replies, 'What difference does it make if I love now that you own me?' Marcus sends her off with a Praetorian guard to be taken to the house of Petronius, while he obeys a summons from the empress.

of a metal shell: dress as armour. Lygia's is a deeper matte blue, covered in sparkling gems, evoking the more natural imagery of a starry sky or sun-dappled sea. This association with nature validates Lygia's moral viewpoint as one that is god-given rather than (hubristically) created by man.

Despite this clear moral agenda the cinema audience are encouraged to identify, not with the virtuous Christian maiden, but with the decadent court in their pleasurable consumption of the various spectacles. As Lygia and Acte enter the room, the camera pans round away from its focus on the two women, so that their view of the scene is also revealed to us in a single lingering shot of the whole room. We are invited to be amazed, impressed, and enticed by the mass of bright colours, the gilded decoration, the celebratory music, the exotically-dressed dancers, and the luxurious food. This latter luxury is represented on the one hand by the

6. Might is right. Wrestlers at Nero's banquet, *Quo Vadis* (1951).

excess of overflowing bowls of fruit, but on the other by the tiny roasted birds that Nero and Petronius toy with: illustrating the gourmandising luxury of the rich, not having to eat merely to satisfy hunger. The pleasures of watching are extended to giving us dedicated views of the erotic dance in progress as Lygia enters, and of the oiled and muscled bodies of the wrestlers, fighting to the death. We are even given the viewpoint of the

49

emperor and empress themselves, with green and red-toned scenes (spectacular in Technicolor) as we watch with Nero and Poppaea through their emerald and ruby eyeglasses. Thus, the power of Nero to create spectacle is tacitly identified with the power of the Hollywood studio.

Freedom and tyranny

Politics and morality are closely associated in *Quo Vadis*, with the political consequences of moral decadence drawn as tyranny. This theme is signalled in the spoken prologue that opens the film that declares, over images of massed soldiery and ragged, mistreated slaves, that in imperial Rome, 'The individual is at the mercy of the state ... Rulers of conquered nations surrender their helpless subjects to bondage', before noting the imminent victory over such practices by the 'humble cross'. The imagery, strikingly similar to newsreel images of the herding of Jews from the ghettoes during the Second World War, is repeated later in the film as the Christians are herded into the arena. [Fig. 7]

More than just a lesson from ancient history, the film presents Rome as a metaphor for more recent political 'tyrannies' like Nazism and Communism. The film's tyrant is Nero, named in the prologue as the 'anti-Christ', an epithet familiar to post-war audiences from its use in anti-Hitler propaganda. More verbal references to recent political events punctuate the script. The Holocaust is signalled with Nero saying that he will 'exterminate' the Christians, and noting that 'When I have finished with these Christians, history will not be sure that they ever existed.' Petronius warns Nero of 'the judgement of history'. In return, Nero's response to Petronius' suicide is to give the order, 'Burn his books!' The latter recalls directly the pre-war campaign by the Nazi regime to burn all books that appeared to contradict their ideology. In addition to the verbal references, there are also visual cues to the audience to identify the iconography of Roman imperial tyranny with that of more recent regimes: the wrestler's straight-armed salute mentioned above is one. These are especially prominent in the sequence of Marcus' triumph [see box: 'Marcus' triumph'].

Although television was gaining in popularity by the 1950s, newsreels screened as part of a cinema programme were the more common way for most viewers to access moving pictures of public events and figures. Before the war in particular, films of ritualised public celebrations in both Nazi Germany and Fascist Italy had been commonly distributed as expressions to the rest of the world of the growing power of those regimes. Through these films, and through the official and innovative cinematic records of Nazi gatherings made by Leni Riefenstahl, a visual vocabulary of totalitarian power was established and widely disseminated. This included the use of typically Roman symbols such as the eagle and the fasces, the trope of vast massed crowds to demonstrate support, and the juxtaposition of tiny human figures against monumental architecture, implying the inevi-

7. Christians herded by Roman guards in the arena, *Quo Vadis* (1951).

tability of history. Particularly relevant to this sequence are newsreel films showing Nazi and Fascist leaders attending march-pasts. For example, a 1938 Pathé item has Hitler on a visit to Rome, observing a vast military parade with Mussolini. The leaders stand on a balcony with their close advisers behind them, framed by monumental columns and guarded by soldiers in gleaming breastplates. Eagles are much in evidence, and some shots frame the march against a backdrop of ancient architectural remains. An insistent military drumbeat sounds throughout the clip, while marchers are shown processing diagonally across the screen. Members of the crowd give the straight-arm salute, and the two leaders salute the marchers as they pass. The familiarity of newsreel items such as this would have confirmed to the audience of *Quo Vadis* a strong visual identity between the Roman emperor and modern tyrants.

51

Marcus' triumph

The Forum is filled with a vast crowd awaiting the appearance of the emperor and the start of the triumphal procession. In front of the imperial palace, a chorus performs a celebratory hymn while dancers with pink and purple cloaks circle an altar. In the background is a huge banner with the imperial eagle outlined in gold. Vestal priestesses dressed in white appear, and their leader prays to the Olympian gods whose statues stand on either side of the altar space, including 'Zeus, father of the gods, and Nero his divine son!'

Meanwhile Marcus waits impatiently in his chariot. He is told that he cannot enter the Forum until the emperor appears on the balcony. But within the palace, Nero is reluctant to appear to his people, calling them 'that foul-smelling rabble' and complaining, 'This mob tortures me.' Finally, after Petronius appeals to his artistic vanity, he passes out onto the balcony to the sound of trumpets, accompanied by his empress Poppaea and her pet leopards, and other members of his inner circle. He gives the straight-armed salute to the crowd who cheer wildly. However, among them are those who dissent. The camera closes in on one woman who hisses 'Wife-killer! Mother-killer!' and pronounces that 'everyone knows he is a beast', before her husband silences her. The camera pans across the crowd to reveal the apostle Peter, who replies that, 'No man is a beast ... he is but sick ...'. But Nero hears only the cheers. 'How they love me!' he beams.

On his signal, the procession begins with flower-girls strewing the path. They are followed by massed drummers who fill both eyes and ears, with their insistent regular drumbeat, and visually dominate the screen in a regimented diagonal pattern of red, white and gold. These are followed by standard-bearers. Eventually we see Marcus, in gleaming golden breastplate, standing in a golden chariot pulled by four white horses. Behind him stands a slave, holding a gilded laurel wreath over his head and intoning the traditional formula, 'Remember thou art only a man.' But Marcus is fruitlessly scanning the crowd for a glimpse of Lygia. As he passes the imperial palace, he salutes Nero, who returns the gesture. While Marcus is facing away from the crowd, we see Lygia pulling her cloak around her head, and hurrying away.

The triumph is structurally paralleled later in the film in the sequence showing the burning of Rome – itself reminiscent of newsreels of the Blitz in London and other cities. Here again are the people of Rome in their masses, out on the street, but this time the noise is terror rather than excitement. Marcus is again at their level, but identified negatively as 'one of them – Nero's soldiers!' Lygia is in the crowd, but this time found by Marcus rather than unseen, and Nero and his court again watch the action from a raised viewing point, in this case the roof of the palace, while the emperor plays his lyre and sings of the Fall of Troy. In its parallels to the earlier celebration, this sequence reveals the dark truths that lie behind the tyrant's apparent love for his people, and, in Nero's choice of subject matter for his song (the destruction of Troy), the mytho-historical inevitability of his demise.

Petronius and the blacklist

Like all cultural texts that achieve more than a passing impact, *Quo Vadis* is receptive to a number of possible readings. Less explicitly than some other themes, *Quo Vadis* can be viewed as a film about performance and the arts, with the ancient authors Petronius, Seneca and Lucan all named, Nero's artistic attempts highlighted, and so many of the characters 'performing' an identity that disguises their real selves, to protect themselves against the governing power. In particular, the film can be read as a critique of artistic censorship and repression, with the paranoid and sycophantic imperial court presented as a metaphor for the Hollywood film industry itself. Its poster boy in the film is that anonymous author, Petronius.

During the post-war period, hundreds of writers, actors and other film industry personnel were actually or effectively blacklisted for alleged Communist sympathies. Although some degree of contact with Communist groups had been widespread among writers and artists in more idealistic pre-war years, by the post-war period disillusion had set in for many. In 1947, the House Un-American Activities Committee (HUAC) began an investigation into claims that Hollywood had been infiltrated by Communist sympathisers who were using popular movies to disseminate their political views and indoctrinate audiences. Called to testify at hearings that persisted into the 1950s, few of these acknowledged any direct connection or agreed to name or confirm the names of others said to have been involved. A refusal to answer direct questioning about Communist Party membership was considered an admission of guilt in itself, and in 1947 the studios signed a joint statement blacklisting ten writers who had done just this: the 'Hollywood Ten', as they became known, were subsequently also imprisoned for contempt. Others were damned by association, or by being named in various unsubstantiated lists. Some of the accused moved to Europe where anti-Communist feeling was not so strong, and some writers were able to continue working under pseudonyms. However, for many the consequences of the HUAC hearings were felt not only on careers, but also on personal lives: depression, marriage break-ups, and alcoholism were common.

Epic films set in the ancient world have had a peculiar part to play in this story. *Spartacus* (1960) was the first film to defy the blacklist openly by crediting one of the original ten blacklisted writers, Dalton Trumbo (for more on this, see Chapter 4). Another of the Ten, Albert Maltz, wrote the original script for *The Robe* before being blacklisted, and his name did not appear on the film's credits when it was released. A further example was *Alexander the Great* (1956), the first major film by the writer and director

Robert Rossen following his rehabilitation from blacklisting after he agreed to name other sympathisers: the film's focus on political disillusionment and personal betrayal chimes with Rossen's own story. The original script for *Quo Vadis* was written by John Huston, a prominent supporter of those accused by HUAC. Though he escaped blacklisting himself, many of his films were censored by the studios for their political aspects, and in 1951 he left Hollywood and moved to Ireland. In his autobiography, he writes of his ambitions for the film as a political allegory, and his removal from it by Louis B. Mayer, the head of studio, who wanted more focus on entertainment. Despite his replacement as a writer, it is clear that the spirit of Huston's original script remains in the film's resolute anti-totalitarianism. A more explicit reference to censorship and repression in the arts can be found in Petronius' letter to Nero, delivered after his suicide [see box: 'Farewell Petronius'].

Petronius' letter critiques the effects that occur when those in power are allowed to control the arts. In the context of the activities of HUAC and the studios, and the blacklisting of writers and performers, it notes the negative consequences on creativity of the forced conservatism and adversity to risk-taking that such activities produced. Nero's response mirrors the response of the studios, in destroying the careers of those blacklisted and even retrospectively removing their credits from films.

It is pertinent here to return to the sources for the film. As mentioned above, Petronius' letter listing Nero's crimes was attested by Tacitus, though he did not note any mention of Nero's artistic efforts. In both the historical sources and the novel, Seneca's forced suicide predates that of Petronius. However, revising these events makes it possible for the critique to be delivered to the emperor (standing in for the studios) by a writer, as the film itself does. In addition, Petronius' own historical status makes him the natural icon for such an endeavour. His authorship of the first-century novel the *Satyricon*, a bawdy and witty satire on Roman social mores is generally agreed, but has never been confirmed. Putting one's name to such a critique of the kind of behaviour led by the emperor himself would have been a dangerous act. Although in the film, the novel is not mentioned, it does make a passing appearance in the novel, when Petronius buys a copy of the manuscript for Marcus, explaining to him that he is unnamed as author in order to avoid the fate of less tactful writers. As an author who challenges the mores of the powerful, and has to keep his identity hidden, there is a clear parallel between Petronius and blacklisted Hollywood writers in the post-war period.

As well as the letter, there is an earlier critique of the power of the Hollywood studios by Petronius. In the party scene at the court, there is an out-of-character moment where he seems to offer a direct and serious criticism of Nero quite different to his usual witticisms. When the emperor talks of the need for first-hand experience of burning a city to inspire his poetry, Petronius says sharply, 'Burn a city in order to create an epic?

54

'Farewell Petronius'

A gentle fade reveals to the viewer another Roman party: but this time without the raucous vulgarity of Nero's feast. Refined music plays and guests (including Seneca), dressed mostly in white and muted shades, recline convivially around a shared table. There is generosity without excess, with slaves refilling drinks, but no overflowing displays of food or luxury. At the head of the table are Petronius and Eunice, reclining towards each other and forming, with the flowers and drapery in the background, a vision of calming symmetry that is largely maintained throughout the sequence. The hierarchy and relationships of voyeuristic power seen in Nero's party are absent here; rather there is a feeling of comradeship and equality. This is made explicit with Petronius' speech, in which he tells Eunice that she is no longer a slave, has been given ownership of his property, and should address him by his name, Gaius.

Revealing that he knows he has lost Nero's favour, Petronius declares that he will thwart the emperor's plans to make him suffer, noting that 'This evening is my ... signature' and explaining that 'it is not enough to live well. One must die well.' He calls in his physician who quickly opens his veins. Eunice seizes the blade and opens her own, determined to die with her lover. No blood is seen: rather it is symbolised by the red flowers placed between the two. Petronius now dictates a letter to be sent to Nero, in which he notes the emperor's responsibility for the deaths of his wife and mother, and for the burning of Rome, but declares that his greatest crimes are against the arts, citing 'your second-rate psalms – your mediocre performances'. He goes on, 'mutilate your subjects if you must, but ... do not mutilate the arts. Brutalise the people, but do not bore them, as you have bored to death your friend, the late Gaius Petronius.' As Petronius slumps lifeless against the equally lifeless Eunice, Seneca stands and delivers a brief eulogy, saying, 'Farewell Petronius. With you perishes the best of our Roman world.'

The letter is delivered to Nero, who is at first angry: 'Without permission? It's rebellion – blasphemy!' but then calls for his 'weeping vase' to mourn his 'dearest friend and truest critic'. On reading the letter, however, his countenance changes, and in a fury he screams in impotent vengeance, 'Destroy his house ... burn his books ... beat his memory into the ground!'

That's carrying the principle of art for art's sake too far!' The later sequence, which this conversation prefigures, showing the burning of Rome is undoubtedly one of the most 'epic' aspects of this film, both intra- and extra-diegetically: publicity stories noted that it took three months of planning and twenty-four nights to film. The sharp-eyed will also have noted though that the motto of M-G-M, the studio that made the film, is *Ars gratia artis* – which translates as 'Art for art's sake.' It would appear that it was not just Nero who was the butt of Petronius' wit.

If this critical reading was perhaps too carefully coded to reach ordinary filmgoers in the 1950s, it is more transparent to informed modern viewers, who have the benefit of historical hindsight, and easy access to background information that is not controlled by the studios' publicity machines. Petronius warns Nero about the 'judgement of history'. Perhaps such judgement may be made, not only on the Roman emperor, but also on the misused power of the post-war Hollywood film industry itself.

Suggested further viewing

The Robe (dir. Koster, 1953)

Adapted from the popular 1942 novel by Lloyd C. Douglas, *The Robe* relates the story of Marcellus Gallio (Richard Burton), a Roman tribune who is detailed to lead the soldiers attending Christ's crucifixion and wins Christ's robe in a game of dice. Before this, Marcellus has gained the enmity of the imperial heir Caligula by bidding successfully against him for a Greek slave, Demetrius (Victor Mature). Marcellus is sent to Jerusalem where Demetrius meets and begins to follow Christ. After the crucifixion, Marcellus dons the robe and is immediately struck with a maddening remorse. He returns to Rome, close to insanity. In an attempt to cure him, he is sent back to find and destroy the robe. In Cana he finds Demetrius, who hands him the robe. This time he feels a great peace, and converts to Christianity. He returns to Rome with Peter as a missionary, but is arrested on the orders of Caligula, now emperor. Refusing to renounce Christ, he is condemned to death and is joined in this by his childhood sweetheart Diana (Jean Simmons).

As the first film to use CinemaScope, *The Robe* was technologically innovative and seen as an important tool in the studios' plans to defend themselves against the growing popularity of television. It was followed by a sequel, *Demetrius and the Gladiators* (1954) which again starred Mature, and was filmed on the same sets just as filming for the first film finished.

Ben-Hur (dir. Wyler, 1959)

Ben-Hur was the third film to adapt the popular novel of the same name by General Lew Wallace, published in 1880. The director William Wyler had in fact worked as an assistant director on the chariot-race sequence in the very successful 1925 version. The narrative is highly equivocal, resonating with both the anti-tyranny agenda and the consequences of the Hollywood blacklist.

The film's hero is Judah Ben-Hur (Charlton Heston), a wealthy young Jew whose path crosses that of Christ at a number of key points. The narrative opens with Ben-Hur's childhood friend Messala (Stephen Boyd) arriving in Jerusalem as a Roman tribune detailed to seek out Jewish opponents to Roman rule. The two argue when Ben-Hur refuses to name dissidents, and later when the Roman governor is accidentally injured by a falling tile, Messala has his former friend and his mother Miriam and sister Tirzah arrested. Ben-Hur is sent as a slave to the galleys where he eventually attracts the interest of the Consul Quintus Arrius (Jack Hawkins). When the ships are attacked, Ben-Hur rescues Arrius, who takes him back to Rome, adopts him as his son and trains him as a charioteer. Returning to Jerusalem, Ben-Hur takes part in a chariot race with Messala. Ben-Hur wins and Messala is fatally injured, but reveals before he dies that Miriam and Tirzah are in a lepers' colony. Encouraged by Esther, a former slave, he takes them to Christ to be healed, but instead Ben-Hur finds Christ on the way to crucifixion. Fearing that any hope for curing their condition is about to be lost, Ben-Hur along with Miriam and Tirzah journey along to Calvary to see Christ put to death. As witnesses to the event, Miriam and Tirzah are healed by their faith, and Ben-Hur is released from his desire for vengeance.

The Fall of the Roman Empire (dir. Mann, 1964)
Unusual in the genre for claiming its inspiration from a work of historiography (by Edward Gibbon) rather than a novel, this serious and pessimistic film was the last of the post-war Roman epics. Released a year after Mankiewicz's *Cleopatra*, it was massively expensive to produce and did not achieve sufficient box-office returns to avoid the producer Samuel Bronston filing for bankruptcy. However it has since been critically acclaimed and was partly adapted for the plot of its successor, *Gladiator*, in 2000.

The plot opens on the Germanic frontiers of the Roman empire. The emperor, Marcus Aurelius (Alec Guinness) has summoned the provincial governors to announce his choice of successor. This is not to be his natural son Commodus (Christopher Plummer), but his adopted son Livius (Stephen Boyd), who is in love with the emperor's daughter Lucilla (Sophia Loren), herself promised in marriage to the Armenian king. However, the emperor is murdered before the announcement can be made public. Livius supports Commodus' accession, but Commodus' ideas about governing the empire by force and brutality are quite different to his father's, which sought to establish peace. Livius opposes Commodus and is sentenced to death along with Lucilla who has tried to assassinate her brother. Commodus challenges Livius to a gladiatorial-style combat in the Roman Forum in which he is killed by Livius who then rescues Lucilla. The film ends with the imperial throne up for auction to the highest bidder.

Peplum Traditions: *Hercules*
(1958, US release 1959)

Introduction

Peplum cinema, despite being one of the most prolific cinematic genres in which antiquity is represented, has never enjoyed the critical attention that it deserves. It always seems to be the poor relation to other genres. Within discussions of the ancient world on film, it has been forced to play second fiddle to big-budget Hollywood Roman epics. Within the study of Italian cinema, it is Italian neo-realist drama or the work of individual high-profile directors that dominates discussion. Even within the field of Italian genre films, it is the 'spaghetti western' that has attracted all the scholarly attention. The dismissive name says it all. The films are called peplum (pl. pepla) films in reference to the extremely short tunics worn by the actors. This name was coined by French critics when the first films were released. A similar nicknaming was applied to the large number of Italian westerns which were released shortly after the release of the peplum films and dubbed 'spaghetti westerns' by American reviewers. However, while the 'spaghetti western' has been renamed the 'European Western', and enjoys a reasonably active life on the art-house cinema circuit, peplum cinema is rarely re-screened at the cinema and seems destined to be stuck with its unfortunate sobriquet (the alternative 'sword and sandals' is not much better).

Conventionally peplum cinema refers to the large volume of films produced in Italy between the late 1950s and the mid-1960s that took as their subject matter a story involving a hero or adventurer from the ancient world. They have a number of distinctive elements. Muscular bodybuilders (often American) were cast as the heroic leads. Female love-interests were pretty, slim, and always in need of rescuing. The storyline traditionally involved the destruction of a brutal tyrannical regime, and there was normally a sexually voracious, vampy female who tried to seduce the hero away from his task of overthrowing tyranny and rescuing his 'true' love. Opponents tended to rely upon extra-natural resources (e.g. sorcery, mythical monsters, advanced technology) to advance their schemes, only to be thwarted by the natural strength and stout heart of the hero. Other regular features included the presence of elaborate dance sequences performed by scantily-clad women, set-piece demonstrations of heroic strength (e.g. bending bars, wrestling animals), and the very noticeable dubbing of voices, especially for the UK and US releases. This last feature was a common one in Italian films of this period which almost always post-synched sound as there was rarely any budget for live sound recording. Consequently the sound for these films has a slightly unnatural air, and in the English versions the effects can be truly comic.

The production of peplum films needs to be seen in the context of Italian genre filmmaking. Unlike high-art films, genre films tended to be cheap, quickly-made productions. They normally came in what has been termed 'hit and run' cycles in which a single and often much superior work inspired numerous imitations, generally of much lesser quality. Peplum, then, belongs in a sequence that includes the opera film, the film *giallo* (erotic, crime melodramas), the dialect comedy, the horror film, the 'sexy' film (pseudo-documentary films about life in nightclubs), and ultimately the spaghetti western. These films were produced for the mass-market cinemas regularly attended by all members of the Italian film-going public, especially its poorer, rural members. The *seconda* and *terza visione* cinemas charged substantially cheaper ticket prices than the so-called 'first-rank cinemas' (*prima visione*), which tended to show high-quality, first-run films. With over 11,000 venues, Italy enjoyed one of the highest cinema attendance rates in Europe in this period, and the bulk of atten- dees went to mass-market cinemas. Christopher Wagstaff describes the typical viewing environment for peplum cinema:

> Cinema-going in Italy was a habit; people went to the local cinema, in their own street or the next one. The film changed every day or two, and people did not bother to check what was on. They went after dinner, when they had finished eating, regardless of when the film began: this would generally be sometime before ten o'clock, which was when the last show began. They would watch the film round to the point where they came in; during the film show they would talk to friends, sometime paying only sporadic attention to the film. (Wagstaff 1995: 114)

Italian film directors have occasionally expressed nostalgia for this type of chaotic cinematic experience. Giuseppe Tornatore celebrated this lost world in *Cinema Paradiso* (1988) and it was recreated by Federico Fellini in one of the opening scenes of *Roma* (1972) where he depicts a trip to the cinema based on memories from his childhood in 1930s Rimini. In such an environment, features of peplum films such as their loose plots and preference for spectacular display rather than complex dialogue become understandable.

The origins of peplum films can be traced to the silent film classic *Cabiria* (1914) directed by Giovanni Pastrone. This lavish production, set in the time of the Second Punic War, introduced audiences to a number of features that would be replayed in peplum films. All the classic elements of peplum film are here – the classical setting, the muscles, the foreign villainy, and the barely repressed sexuality. The figure of Maciste would go on to be one of the most popular figures in Italian genre cinema. The character was clearly modelled on Hercules. His name is derived from the Doric word *makistos* (Attic Greek = *mekistos*) which means 'tallest', 'greatest', and 'largest' and which the writer for *Cabiria*, Gabriele d'Annunzio believed was an alternative title for Hercules. In this he seems to be slightly mistaken as the word in the context of Hercules only appears as a geographical epithet referring to a town by the name of Makistos, rather than one describing Hercules' attributes (i.e. Hercules *Makistios* = Hercules 'from Makistos', not Hercules 'the greatest', cf. Strabo, *Geography* 8.3.21). The success of this Herculean character meant that he reappeared in numerous outings in the 1910s and 1920s, and became a staple of peplum films in the 1950s and 1960s.

One of the factors that distinguish peplum cinema from other examples of genre films is the tremendous success that it achieved overseas. While comedy based on Italian dialects was destined never to travel well, peplum cinema managed to achieve very respectable box-office figures in the US, UK, and France. As we shall see, the break-through film for international box-office was *Hercules* (original 1958 Italian title: *Le fatiche di Ercole*). Produced for the chaotic viewing environment of the Italian mass-market cinema, peplum's preference for spectacle rather than narrative or dialogue made them well suited to the casual environment of the American drive-in cinema, the 'B' programme of UK cinema, or later the family living room as the films were replayed on television.

The other factor that assisted the widespread distribution of these films was the routine use of co-production arrangements in their creation. In a strategy to avoid being swamped by American films, a number of European countries in the post-war period passed protectionist measures to assist the survival of their local film industries. In Italy, these took the form of requiring that Italian films be shown for a certain number of days each month, tax relief for Italian films, and the prohibition of profits from foreign films being exported to their home countries. Both France and Spain enacted similar provisions. The idea of entering co-production arrangements between European countries was first mooted by the head of the Universalia studio, Salvo D'Angelo, who pointed out that there was much to be gained from branding films as the product of two countries. Not only did this make them eligible for tax relief in two jurisdictions, but it also made it easier to raise finance for film production. In time even tri-national co-productions were introduced. This form of production also proved attractive to American studios whose Italian profits were unable to leave Italy. To satisfy so many different national audiences, peplum films were not only re-dubbed into different languages, but also re-edited before distribution. Heroes were renamed. Maciste in the Italian version of the film might reappear as Samson in the French and German releases, Goliath in the Spanish version, and Hercules in the US and the UK. The cuts made to the film could be quite severe with some films losing up to twenty-seven minutes of screen time from their original length.

The production of peplum films peaked in the early 1960s. In total over 170 films were made. At its height, approximately 10% of the Italian film industry was involved in peplum filmmaking. In the early to mid-1960s, peplum films constituted the bulk of Italian film exports, with up to three times as many peplum films being exported as the more highly-regarded Italian neo-realist and art-house films. Initially, the plotlines of peplum films were deeply indebted to classical myth and history. However, over time, more and more increasingly outlandish plots were developed and the films moved away from their classical origins. Thus, we find Hercules fighting opponents as diverse as aliens (*Hercules against the Moon Men*, 1964), vampires (*Hercules in the Haunted World*, 1962), the Incas (*Hercules against the Sons of the Sun*, 1964) and a surprisingly large number of Mongol hordes (*Hercules against the Barbarians*, 1964; *Hercules against the Mongols*, 1963; *Hercules in the Valley of Woe*, 1961).

Like all Italian genre film cycles, peplum cinema inevitably came to an end as the Italian public's appetite for these films waned and new genres such as the western arrived to take their place. The lack of an Italian film production base meant that the genre died out in the US and UK as well where audiences were getting equally tired of these 'sword and sandal' affairs. The decline in peplum films was almost as rapid as their success. There were some attempts at revival. *Hercules in New York* (1970, released in the UK under the title *Hercules goes Bananas*) was one such attempt. The film is famous now for two things: it gave Arnold Schwarzenegger his first film role (in true peplum tradition Schwarzenegger's voice, owing to his strong Austrian accent, was dubbed in by another actor), and a fight sequence involving perhaps the least convincing bear costume ever worn by an actor in a motion picture. The genre was also the subject of an affectionate parody in *Hercules Returns* (1993) in which Australian comedians replaced the soundtrack of *Hercules, Samson, Maciste and Ursus* (1964, *Ercole, Sansone, Maciste e Ursus gli invincibili*) with their own comic voice-overs.

Background to case study

How does one measure a film's success? It is impossible to escape this question when discussing *Hercules* (1958). If one limits oneself to just the finances, then this film was an unquestionable triumph. The precise figures are hard to quantify. Newspapers report the final US box-office receipts at variously five, ten or eighteen million dollars. This discrepancy is largely due to the principal source of the figures being the film's often less than reliable or consistent promoter, Joseph E. Levine. Although *Hercules* did not enjoy quite the same magnitude of success in the UK owing to its limited distribution, its sequel *Hercules Unchained* (1960) earned substantial receipts and was named the 'most successful film in 1960' in a survey conducted by *Films and Filming*. Even accounting for the lavish costs expended in the promotion of the film (Levine stated that the publicity cost over one million dollars, another slightly doubtful figure), *Hercules* clearly made a handsome profit.

Yet by other criteria the film's status is more problematic. Certainly it has never received critical acclaim. The tone was set by the first reviews of the film. The *New York Times* reviewer, Richard Nason (1959), reviewed the film under the headline 'Weak Hercules' and he described the film as 'a slow-pace and stilted affair studded with routine spectacles'. The only enjoyment he derived was from the unintentionally bad dubbing ('[Reeves'] voice has the querulous pitch of a bank clerk's') and he concluded his review by saying that 'an added market for the film might be found among students of Greek, who would have occasion to reflect on what happens to classics legends when they fall into certain hands'. Nason's review is not untypical and its sentiments were reflected in a number of the newspapers. So, for example, even though *Hercules* had only limited distribution in the UK and critics were not invited to comment on it, the *Times* nevertheless could not resist having a dig at the film. It was particularly critical of Reeves ('a remarkable physique but no noticeable acting ability') and the musical soundtrack ('The music, which veers oddly in style from Puccini to Ravel and back via Respighi, is at least consistent in its loudness'). Indeed, the only aspect of the film which seems to have won plaudits from the critics was the cinematography, in particular the picture quality produced by a European variant of Cinemascope called Dyaliscope which proved very effective at retaining sharpness when condensing widescreen shots into a 35 mm format.

The universal critical reaction against the film is a little surprising as newspaper reports prior to the film's release seem sympathetic. Reports from correspondents in Italy describe its production and are intrigued by its 'unknown star', Steve Reeves. On hearing the storyline, the *Chicago Daily Tribune* even advised its readers that if they wanted to imagine what the Greek Olympics was really like then they should go to watch Reeves as he puts on displays of archery, javelin, and discus. Yet in reviewing the final product, they struggled to find anything good to say about it. This discrepancy probably has more to say about the dependency of newspapers on editorial sent by studios for a film's pre-publicity than any change of heart on the part of reporters.

One way to explain the success of *Hercules* is to see it as just the product of a slick advertising campaign. Certainly, it was his successful marketing of this film that propelled Joseph E. Levine into the ranks of one of America's leading producers. Levine was late in coming to prominence. He was 54 when *Hercules* was released. Prior to its release, he had been a small-time promoter based in the New England area. He had some previous commercial success with his importation and promotion of *Godzilla*

3. Peplum Traditions: Hercules (1958, US release 1959)

(1956) and *Attila* (1954). Previous Italian films imported and distributed by Levine had been largely high-quality Italian neo-realist dramas such as *Rome, Open City* (*Roma, città aperta*, 1945) and *Bicycle Thieves* (*Ladri di biciclette*, 1948). In 1958, Levine saw *Il fatiche di Ercole* and acquired the distribution rights for $120,000. Its appeal to Levine was simple. 'It had musclemen, broads and a shipwreck and a dragon for the kids,' he is reported to have said. The following year the film was re-titled *Hercules* and launched with a campaign that combined saturation advertising with block-booking of cinemas, opening it in 624 movie houses simultaneously. This latter feature was a new one in cinema practice. In promoting his film, Levine was assisted by the recent court-mandated fragmentation of the film industry. It was the break up of the Hollywood monopoly on production and distribution that allowed distributors like Levine to thrive and prosper.

The promotional campaign for *Hercules* and its sequel *Hercules Unchained* was pervasive. It featured extensive billboards, press advertising, lavish press parties, and a giant cut-out of Reeves which toured the country. There were numerous product and commercial tie-ins associated with the film. Sometimes the link between Hercules and the product advertised was not entirely obvious. For example, the campaign which likened the job of a Macy's price-checker to Hercules' labours ('armed with only pencils and pads, they low the spectre of high price') must have raised some questions in the minds of readers. Levine's marketing was not subtle. 'SEE heroic Hercules rip down the lavish palace of lustful pleasure! SEE him crush the savage ape-men who guard the Golden Fleece. SEE Amazons lure men to revels and violent death,' promised the standard press advertisement.

In dealing with Joseph Levine, it is easy to get swept up in the rhetoric. He was a figure who always played himself larger than life. It is no accident that his name features in a larger typeface than the names of any of the actors in press advertisements for *Hercules*. He never doubted his ability to sell a film. 'You can fool all the people if the advertising is right,' he famously quipped. Yet the success of Hercules can't be put down entirely to marketing. Despite Levine's claims, it would be a mistake to underestimate the shrewdness of the audience. The size of Levine's campaign may have been unprecedented, but its tactics weren't. As the reviewer for the *New York Times* pointed out in his review, 'At this point in the history of film promotion it seems hardly necessary to state that the picture bears out little of the breathless excitement of its advance building' (Nason 1959: 32). The audience were wise to Levine's tricks and still they came in droves. And not only for *Hercules*, but for the numerous sequels and spin-offs that dominated the Italian peplum output for the next six years. In fact, for all his posturing, Levine did not seem to understand the phenomenon that he claimed to have created. In an interview in October 1959, Levine claimed that, despite the enormous success of *Hercules* in the summer, the end of the popularity of peplum was close at hand and that he could see a market for only a couple more films. Levine, true to his principles, moved out of peplum quite quickly. What he did not foresee is that it would take another six years before audiences would get sick and tired of this muscle-bound hero.

The attraction for film companies of peplum cinema is easy to see – epic-style films produced at half the cost of Hollywood productions. The audience appeal needs some elucidation. *Hercules* pioneered a number of elements that together formed a distinctive cinematic vocabulary. It promoted a new version of the classical hero as well as creating a narrative in which that heroism could be displayed to best effect. This novel formulation had found its moment. To American middle-class audiences stuck in the rut of 9-to-5 jobs and the comfy domesticity of suburban existence, *Hercules* offered a world of danger, desire, and physical health. The sun always shone, and problems were simple and easily solved. Fathers could enjoy the erotic thrills provided by the Amazonian dance routine while children watched as the hero battled monsters. In the first century BC, Cicero remarked that he envied the simplicity of Hercules' life where choices were easy and right and wrong so simply defined. For the post-war audiences battling with the problems of industrialised, Cold War existence, it was easy to see Cicero's point.

Plot summary

The hero Hercules (Steve Reeves) has been called to the city of Iolco by its king Pelias in order to train his son, Iphitus. Unknown to Hercules, Pelias harbours a dreadful secret. Pelias acquired his throne by organising the assassination of his brother, King Aeson. This act was performed by the hired rogue, Eurystheus. Plagued by guilt and increasingly paranoid, Pelias hopes that after Hercules' training, Iphitus will prove man enough to take the burden of the kingship from him. On his way to Iolco, Hercules rescues Princess Iole (Sylva Koscina), the daughter of King Pelias. As they return to the palace, Iole recounts her still vivid childhood memories of the night of her uncle's assassination. She tells Hercules that the death of Aeson has been blamed on his former friend Chiron, the captain of Aeson's bodyguard. Chiron is also alleged to have kidnapped King Aeson's son, Jason, and stolen the Golden Fleece, the symbol of kingship in Iolco.

On arrival in Iolco, Hercules proves extremely popular with the youth of the city who wholeheartedly embrace the new athletic and health regime he brings to the town. Hercules proves less popular with Iphitus whose arrogance and sense of self-importance make him jealous of Hercules' ability and popularity. When Iolco is attacked by the Nemean Lion, Hercules rides out to protect the city. He is followed by Iphitus who is attacked by the lion and killed. Hercules defeats the lion, wrestling it with his bare hands. Pelias is distraught by the loss of his son, and curses

Hercules (whom he holds responsible for his son's death) demanding that he capture the Cretan Bull as penance for his actions. In the meantime, Hercules has become aware of his increasing affection for Iole. Knowing that it would be impossible for him to have a relationship with her whilst he is immortal and invincible, he asks the gods to remove his immortality. They do so. It is this new vulnerable, mortal Hercules who must face the Cretan Bull.

Hercules tracks down and kills the bull, but arrives too late to save its latest victim. This turns out to be Chiron who has raised Jason (Fabrizio Mioni) to manhood in a wilderness hideaway. He entrusts Jason into Hercules' care and asks him to restore Jason to the throne of Iolco. Before he dies, Chiron explains that the Golden Fleece was lost as they fled from the palace on the night of Aeson's murder and that the fleece is now located in the far-off land of the Colchis.

Predictably, Jason receives a chilly reception when he returns with Hercules to the court of Pelias. In order to rid himself of this rival, Pelias demands that Jason recover the Golden Fleece before Pelias will accept his right to the throne. Jason vows to undertake a voyage in the just-completed boat, the Argo, to retrieve it. Hercules promises to assist him in this endeavour and they are joined by a number of other famous figures from antiquity (Orpheus, Castor and Pollux, Asclepius, and Ulysses). In order to sabotage the voyage, Pelias ensures that the assassin, Eurystheus (Arturo Dominici) is amongst the crew of the Argo.

After adventures, which include escaping an island of Amazons, beating off a tribe of ape-men, and slaying a dragon, the crew returns with the Golden Fleece to Iolco. Unfortunately, just as they reach port, the fleece is stolen by Eurystheus and spirited away to Pelias. Hercules promises to retrieve the fleece, but is knocked unconscious and imprisoned. Jason and his men make their way up to the palace of Iolco, but without the fleece, Jason is unable to claim the kingship. Pelias attempts to arrest Jason. Fighting ensues. Meanwhile in the dungeon, Iole has discovered Hercules and revives him. He breaks out of his prison and arrives just in time to turn the tide of battle. Seeing that his side has lost, Pelias commits suicide by taking poison. Jason is proclaimed king and Hercules and Iole sail off into the sunset.

Key scenes and themes

Staging Greece

Film, especially populist film, has always favoured Rome over Greece. There are a number of reasons for this. The presence of convenient Roman historical narratives; the desire to pitch dissolute paganism against emergent Christianity; the metaphorical value of the Roman empire as a paradigm of modern imperialism; the cinematic opportunities provided by the displays of wealth and colour in Rome – all of these help explain cinema's predilection for Rome. The notable exception to this trend in popular cinema is peplum film. The majority of peplum films are set in Greece. For marketing purposes, US and UK releases of these films may have preferred the Romanised versions of characters' names - for example Hercules, rather than the Greek Heracles - but that was normally their only concession to the presence of Roman antiquity. Peplum cinema provides an almost unique opportunity to examine the way in which Greek visual motifs operate within popular consciousness. The vision of Greece that peplum cinema offers refracts a notion of Hellenism that had already been established outside cinema within the genres of history painting, drama, and popular fiction.

In attempting to create a vision of Greece, filmmakers needed to develop a new cinematic vocabulary. Costuming, music, and landscape were all deployed to create a vision of Greece that stood in contrast to Rome. We gain a sense of this new aesthetic from the opening scene of *Hercules* in which a variety of elements are utilised to locate the viewer within the world of mythical Greece.

Iole's chariot accident

The scene opens with a shot of a shepherd playing his pipes and tending his goats. He is perched high up on a promontory that falls away sharply to the sea. The landscape is dry and wild. Trees are sparse. This peaceful rural scene is violently interrupted by the arrival of an out-of-control chariot. The chariot runs perilously close to the cliff edge. Suddenly we see a tree being ripped out by its roots. The tree is lifted up by a bearded man who throws it in front of the horses to make them stop. Overcome by events, the female driver of the chariot faints into the arms of the bearded stranger. Hercules has met Iole [Fig. 8].

Hercules doesn't begin with lavish civic settings. There is none of the usual opulence, grandeur, or casts of thousands normally associated with the ancient world. Instead, it begins with two individuals in a rural landscape. We recognise that we are in the ancient world because of the chariot and the shepherd and his panpipes. Yet it is not quite the ancient world that we are used to seeing in Roman epic drama. This place is austere. In avoiding lavish display, the film signals that it is located in a place far removed from Rome. The only sign of civilisation is a small temple in the far background. The costumes also signify that we are in a different place. No rules of Roman morality are being observed here. The woman wears a tunic, totally unsuitable for a Roman matron. She shows a lot of thigh, but there is a classical purity about her. The hero wears no armour, but a tunic made of skins. Welcome to Greece.

This opening scene establishes a number of visual conventions that will be observed throughout the rest of the film. The first is a preference for simplicity in set design. Greek interiors tend to be comparatively sparse

8. A chance encounter in the wilds of Greece.
Hercules and Iole, *Hercules* (1958).

spaces. There is none of the massing of decorative objects or huge swathes
of rich fabric normally associated with Roman palaces. This Greece was a
wild and primitive place. The Roman appropriation of the classical aesthetic forced set-designers towards the archaic. The statuary, objects, and
architectural elements all take their cue from either archaic art or the
Greek Bronze Age. Instead of the lushness of the Roman imperial throne
room, the palace of Pelias is a dark, sinister, rough-hewn affair, suitable
to the temperament of its master. Costuming also participates in this
dynamic. The only time we see anything approaching such luxury occurs
when the crew are washed up on the island of the Amazons. Here the
exoticism and strangeness of the Amazons' island is confirmed by its lush
interiors. This change in decor is a sign of just how far the crew has
travelled from their Greek homeland. The simplicity of costuming also
adds to the impression of the comparative poverty of Greece. In Roman
epics, plain garments often identify a character as oppositional to the
dominant Roman power structure. It is the dress of the rebellious Christian or the unbowed gladiator. We know that these figures stand apart
from Rome because they refuse to participate in Roman aesthetics. Here
again simplicity is oppositional, only this time it marks out a space for
Greece, the only civilisation of the Mediterranean that can rival Rome in

terms of its legacy for western civilisation. *Hercules* also reverses the Roman practice of colourful clothes for women and white togas for men. In this film, colourful patterned clothes tend to be worn by the men of Pelias' court whilst the women wear white or subtle colours.

The potency of certain signifiers of Roman culture created a number of problems for establishing a distinct Greek look. Rome had already co-opted so much that was Greek that it left little room for a distinctive cinematic vocabulary of Greekness. For example, there is nothing inherently Roman about chariot races. Our earliest account of them occurs in Homer's *Iliad*. Yet after so many gladiatorial epics, the chariot race became synonymous with Rome in the popular mind. Greece could never have its chariot races without looking parasitic on Rome, and generally they are avoided in peplum cinema. Nevertheless, despite these disabilities, *Hercules* did succeed in creating a film with a distinctive Grecian ethos. The comparative scarcity of armour in peplum films is a good example. Peplum epics tend to eschew the use of armour. The combination of cloak and muscled cuirass, although a Greek invention, is so firmly associated with the Roman legionary that it proves impossible to reclaim or be rid of its Roman associations. For this reason, when armour does occur, it tends to be of simple design, often harking back to medieval designs rather than anything classical. In *Hercules* the soldiers wear scale-mail decorated with cross-hatches. The overextended crests on the helmets echo early Greek bronze figurines. The other obvious area of avoidance is the tendency to steer clear of using red fabric in either costume or decoration. Again the associations with Rome prove too strong even though there is a distinguished Greek tradition of wearing red: the cloaks of the Spartan warriors are the most obvious example. Instead, in peplum we see a preference for a light colour palette using light blues, whites, and gold.

In establishing a cinematic version of Hellas, *Hercules* exploited signifiers that were unquestionably Greek. Red- and black-figured pottery, Greece's most distinctive art form, provided the inspiration for the wall decoration of the palace of Pelias. While Greek letters, even if they were used on anachronistic tombstones or arranged into gibberish on Aeson's bloody note to Jason, gave viewers a sense that they were venturing into foreign territory. The sense that we are in a world before history is magnified when the Argo reaches its destination in Colchis. This really does turn out to be 'the place that time forgot'. The crew are attacked by a group of early hominids whilst Jason has to retrieve the Golden Fleece which is guarded by a Tyrannosaurus Rex. Greece is a strange place.

Another way in which on-screen Greece was established was through constant reference to mythological exemplars. Greece has long been viewed as a place of myth. Apart from a couple of notable examples (e.g. the *Giant of Marathon* and the *Colossus of Rhodes*), peplum has always favoured myth as the source for its plot line. So *Hercules* co-opts the story of Jason's quest for the Golden Fleece for its narrative structure. This story was one of the major mythic cycles in ancient Greece. References to the story are preserved in numerous vase-paintings, plays, and poems. The most famous version of the epic was written by the third-century BC poet Apollonius of Rhodes, who is jokily listed in the credits for the film. For the student of Greek mythology, there are many other references to enjoy: Orpheus playing the lyre to encourage the rowers; Asclepius' knowledge about the medicinal properties of poppies; the name of the assassin being the same as the name of the king who commanded Hercules to perform his labours; the young Ulysses (Greek Odysseus) being told that one day a knowledge of the bow will prove important to him.

This preference for staging Greece over Rome is partially a product of Italy's post-war desire to escape the legacy of the fascist filmmaking of the immediate past. Italian fascist ideology had made much of Rome's glorious history. From the very beginning of the Italian fascist movement links had been drawn between the name of the party and the *fasces,* the bundle of rods carried before a Roman magistrate to signify his office. Mussolini clearly projected himself as a new Augustus, leading his people to a reawakening of the Roman empire. Fascist aesthetics and ideology constantly invoked ancient Rome.

Fascist control of cinema began in September 1938 when the Italian fascist government banned the distribution of all foreign films. Into a market that had been dominated by American films, we now saw the release of Italian realist dramas, often reflecting fascist concerns about the family, religion, and the past. Films such as Alessandro Blasetti's *The Old Guard* (1934) which featured heroic fascists, or *The Iron Crown* (1941), a lavish, symbolic epic set in the medieval period about the search for a leader, exemplify this spirit. The most obvious example of the cinematic appropriation of the ancient Roman past was the film *Scipio Africanus* (1937). This was fascist Italy's most spectacular costume epic and celebrated ancient Rome's conquests in Africa during the Second Punic War. Produced during Italy's war against Abyssinia, and heavily backed by Mussolini's government, this was at the time the most expensive Italian film ever made. Drawing upon Rome's imperial past it justified Italy's expansionist present. One famous anecdote recounts that when Mussolini visited the film set during production, he received an ovation from thousands of extras dressed as Roman legionaries just as if he were a Roman emperor. The film won the Mussolini Cup for Italian cinema at the Venice Film Festival in 1937. This co-option of the classical past for such obvious political purposes meant that the Roman state, the fasces, the triumphal march, the torchlight parades – all these standard features of the epic film were now discredited. Ancient Rome had an ideological charge that was best avoided.

The body of the hero

Criticism of Steve Reeves' acting misses the point. Hercules is not produced through voice, gestures, or facial expressions. *Hercules* is as much about how a hero looks as how he acts. The use of bodybuilders for the role of the protagonist is one of the peplum's most distinctive features. Although this usage has a precedent in the rural strongman heroes of Italian peasantry, it was the spectacular success of Steve Reeves in *Hercules* (1958) that established the dominant paradigm of the bodybuilder hero for post-war pepla. Reeves offered a radically new form of the male hero, one in which the body was foregrounded far more significantly than ever before. Conventionally cinematic male beauty had resided in the face, now it resided in the chest, arms, and legs. Pepla displays more male flesh than any other genre. Normally, it is the female body that is held up for the cinema's gaze. Pepla puts the male body onto the agenda as well.

The film relishes Reeves' body. It continually engineers moments to show it off, and Reeves, the professional bodybuilder, knew how to pose himself for the camera. So, for example, as Hercules tears down the portico of the palace, the film lingers over his straining chest and arms, his lateral muscles perfectly spread in a classical bodybuilding position. It was an image that was replicated in numerous print advertisements for the film. The first time the audience gets to see an extended repertoire of Reeves' bodybuilding moves occurs in the sequence set in the training ground of Iolco [see box: 'Training the body'].

Here the film attempts to answer the question, 'What are these bodies for?'. The film explicitly links bodybuilding with sport, competition, exercise, and personal development. The first time we see Hercules, he is flanked by two companions in imitation of the victor's podium of the Olympic Games. Around him the youth of Iolco run, leap, and throw. All this activity is serving a higher goal – ethical and intellectual perfection. The old men of Iolco may complain that Hercules is causing the youth to neglect their studies, but as Hercules shows in the sequence involving the archery competition, he is offering a philosophy that harnesses body and mind together. Iphitus is used as the counter-example to show what happens when the body is developed at the expense of mind and character. His arrogance and laziness mean that he has no place in Hercules' gymnasium.

In so strongly grounding the image of Hercules in anatomy, *Hercules* is following a long established tradition. The paradigm was established for western culture by the discovery of the Farnese Hercules in the sixteenth century. This statue, over three metres high, was discovered in the Baths of Caracalla and was used by the Farnese family to decorate the front court of their palace. As a centrepiece of one of the most important collections of art by one of Rome's most prominent families, the Farnese Hercules was always destined to be in the spotlight. The statue is almost certainly a copy

70

Training the body

In a sudden jump from the darkness of Pelias' palace, we find ourselves in a brightly lit field. A line of bare-chested men throw javelins into the sky; the movement extending their upper bodies and showing off their muscles. A montage of training sequences then ensues. We see the same well-built frames running and jumping in unison. They wrestle on the ground, straining against each other to gain advantage. All this activity is too much for one young man who lies out on a stretcher. He begs the doctor to let him complete the marathon. 'They've all become fanatics since Hercules arrived. They seem to worship nothing but strength,' exclaims the doctor. Other figures join in, complaining about how the young have been swept up in an enthusiasm for exercise to the neglect of almost every other aspect of their lives.

The camera pans up to Hercules standing proud with his arms crossed on a rocky outcrop. He is stripped to the waist and wears only a short skirt. His muscles gleam in the sunshine. He is flanked by two equally impressive bodies that one of the doctor's companions informs us are Castor and Pollux. This trio gaze out over the training ground below. Suddenly a young man pole vaults up to the outcrop to join them. Hercules praises him, but also encourages him to improve his landing: 'If you want to become champion, you must work.' The young man agrees: 'I want to be like you Hercules ... My father said that you put strength ahead of everything, but I know that you want us to use our forces to serve our intelligence.'

Their conversation is interrupted by the arrival of Iphitus who arrogantly strides into the arena. The other men disperse. Hercules berates Iphitus for turning up so late for training. Iphitus shows little remorse. To teach him a lesson, Hercules challenges him to hit a target with an arrow from a great distance. Iphitus fails and feels humiliated in front of the crowd of onlookers. He claims that hitting such a target is impossible. Hercules then turns to the young man that he was previously conversing with and says that with the right intelligence even a boy like this could hit the target. Iphitus challenges Hercules to prove it. Just then Iole arrives in a chariot. Determined to impress her, Hercules instructs the young man in the art of archery. The young man shoots and is successful.

Outraged, Iphitus challenges Hercules to a discus competition. Iphitus throws a great distance, but Hercules throws his discus out of the arena. Alarmed and defeated, Iphitus flees from the hero.

of an original statue by the fourth-century BC sculptor, Lysippus. It was much copied in antiquity and over 80 examples survive from all parts of the Greco-Roman world. It depicts the hero at rest after completing his labours. Behind his back he hides the golden apples of the Hesperides, the collection of which was one of the last of his labours. Yet it is easy to lose the apples – indeed, this is part of the 'game' of this statue – in the great slabs of flesh that make up this Hercules. To describe the Farnese Hercules as 'hyper-muscled' is an understatement. The Farnese Hercules takes

71

us beyond naturalism. He bulges and ripples. We're just glad he's at rest. Imagine if he started to flex.

It is no accident that the Farnese Hercules has always been a favourite of the bodybuilding community. Eugen Sandow, the traditional father of bodybuilding, used to cover himself in chalk dust and strike a pose in imitation of the statue. The Farnese Hercules represents the ideal to which bodybuilders aspired. It is almost a cliché of bodybuilding biographies that their subjects were inspired to take up bodybuilding after seeing either a real Greek statue or a picture of one. When bodybuilders think of Greek statues, they are thinking of the Farnese Hercules.

In casting Steve Reeves (the bodybuilder par excellence) as Hercules we see the coming together of two different discourses – a popular conception of the Greek hero combining with the aesthetics of bodybuilding culture. This was not only new, it was risky. It is easy to forget this. At the start of the chapter, we asked a question about how we should measure the success of *Hercules*. Perhaps the best measure of the success of *Hercules* is that it made the showcasing of Reeves as Hercules seem so inevitable, so healthy, so natural. We couldn't be further from the truth.

First, it should be noted that films starring Hercules were not standard cinema fare. Ever since the rise of Romanticism, Hercules had been out of favour as man's favourite hero. For nineteenth- and early twentieth-century audiences, Hercules was in many ways too perfect. His triumph was too inevitable. There were no successful films of the labours because watching twelve episodes of a hero arriving only to triumph was too monotonous. Indeed, despite its Italian title translating as 'The labours of Hercules', the film didn't take the sequence of labours as its plot. Instead, it preferred to use the story of Jason and the Argonauts with a nod to the labours being given by Hercules' actions in wrestling a lion and bull. The film strips Hercules of his labours as it strips him of his invincibility. This is a hero who can bleed and die.

Secondly, we should note that Hercules lent his star-power to Reeves, and not the other way round. At the time of the release of *Hercules,* Reeves was not the aspirational figure he would later become following the film's success. Reeves may have been 'Mr Pacific Coast' (1946 & 1947), 'Mr America' (1947), 'Mr World' (1948) and 'Mr Universe' (1950), but hardly any member of the general public knew his name. Bodybuilding, despite enjoying great popularity at the turn of the century had fallen seriously out of favour in the period between the wars. There was something unnatural about spending so much time developing and contemplating these bodies that didn't do anything. It was tainted by suspicions of homoeroticism, and bodybuilding magazines had been seized as obscene publications. The sleazy nature of the sport had been seized upon by Mae West who had toured the country with her risqué reviews featuring numerous bodybuilders. The problematic status of bodybuilding was demonstrated in the musical film *Athena* (1954). This film, whose plotline

72

involved a sympathetically satirical look at bodybuilding and vegetarianism, was Reeves' only significant role before *Hercules*. It was a box-office disaster, and prompted Reeves to go to Europe to look for work in the film industry there. It was whilst he was searching for work overseas that Reeves was invited by Federico Teti to take the lead in *Hercules*.

Hercules rescued a hero who had been languishing in popularity and rehabilitated a sport in need of a makeover. Almost overnight, the sport of bodybuilding was brought into the mainstream. Advertisers created such a demand for bodybuilders that specialist agencies were created. There was suddenly a call for bodies. Over the next five years, there was practically a conveyor-belt running from the muscle beaches of California to the film studios of Rome and southern Italy. The list of actors who have played Hercules reads like a roll call of the most illustrious names in bodybuilding. Mark Forest (Mr Venice Beach, 1954), Reg Park (Mr Universe, 1951, 1958 & 1965), Peter Lupus (Mr International Health Physique, 1960), Reg Lewis (Mr Universe, 1957) and Mickey Hargitay (Mr Universe, 1955) have all lined up for the role.

The lure of women

Voyeurism in peplum comes from two directions. As we have seen above, it is a genre that is very much interested in staging the male body. However, the female body is also regularly put on display. Two different binaries operate in organising the display of female flesh. The first is that the female body is defined against the male. Whereas the male body is signified by its rugged, strong, outdoor appearance, female bodies tend to be smaller, weaker, and paler. They are bodies made for indoors. They are incapable of acts of strength. Hercules might be able to train a young boy to fire an arrow across an arena, but one is left with the strong impression that such activity would be beyond Iole, no matter how much instruction she received. The second binary occurs within the types of female bodies represented. One of the distinctive features of peplum is its strongly demarcated gender roles. Women tend to come in two types. Good, homely, virginal girls who are constantly in need of rescuing and sexy, depraved vamps who are often instigators of chaos and mayhem and who need a strong man to put them in their place. The former type of women is much more modest in appearance. Her short skirts might show off her thighs, but that is the most revealing that she becomes. In contrast, the vamp often leaves little to the imagination [see box: 'Dancing Amazons'].

'That's no job for a princess', Hercules remarks as Princess Iole attempts to fix her chariot wheel after her accident [Fig. 8]. The flip side of the concern with masculinity expressed in the *Hercules* films is an attempt to regulate and straitjacket female roles. Peplum cinema is remarkably conservative with the roles that it offers women. These roles are strongly colour-coded. Heroines wear whites and blues, whilst vamps wear red and

---

Dancing Amazons

Music floods our ears. The dance is already underway. With cymbals made from shells in their hands, the Amazons in perfect synchronicity rise, whirl, leap, and writhe. It is less a dance and more like a rhythmic gymnastics routine. Only the flowing diaphanous clothing makes us realise that we are not in the gymnasium. The scene cuts to the faces of Castor and Pollux. Goblets in hand, they are intoxicated, partly by the drugged wine, partly by the girls in front of them. We return to the Amazons. They spin around like tops. Side kicks show off their legs and buttocks. An Amazon watches on contentedly, admiring her sisters. Her smile seems to suggest some secret knowledge. We are shown scenes from the various couches surrounding the dancing display. Asclepius thinks his couch companion is too melancholy. 'We're not going to a funeral this morning,' he exclaims. A rueful smile crosses the face of the woman as she looks away. Drunk on wine, the men laugh hysterically, not noticing the sneers on the faces of their female companions. The dancing continues until the women collapse on the ground, seemingly spent.

---

black. Peplum cinema was never subtle, and its treatment of female roles was clumsy. Yet there is something paradoxical in this attempt to promulgate a Madonna/whore gender dichotomy. For in trying to repress female sexuality, peplum cinema has a tendency to make their evil female characters the most interesting and captivating of the women on the screen. These sexually voracious women often end up with more screen time and better dialogue. In contrast, good girls end up looking a little bland.

Hercules conforms to this pattern with Queen Penthesilea of the Amazons getting as prominent a role as Iole. Admittedly, Penthesilea is not as vampy as some of the 'bad girl' queens of peplum cinema. It is a law of the Amazons that all men who step foot on the island must die and she is trapped by fate and tradition into plotting against the life of the crew of the Argo and her great love, Jason. Wrestling with the dilemma about how to reconcile her love of Jason with her position as queen, Penthesilea struggles with a burden as great as Iole's when she finds out that her father is a murderer and a usurper. In cinema promotion the two women received equal billing. As one advertisement put it, 'The rest of the cast may be unfamiliar to you, but they fit their roles equally well, from the classic beauty of Sylva Koscina as Iole to the lethal loveliness of Gianna Maria Canale as the Queen of the Amazons.' Two sides of the same coin.

Of course, *Hercules* wasn't taking any risks in its portrayal of Amazons. Their sexual appeal goes all the way back to antiquity where they are regularly portrayed as scantily-clad and in provocative positions. For example, classical sculpture never follows the tradition of the one-breasted Amazons, preferring instead to always offer two perfectly-formed breasts for the viewer's contemplation. It is their lack of inhibitions that makes

Amazons so attractive. There has always been a fascination with fatal women.

Hercules manages to conflate two such dangerous groups in its 'Island of the Amazons' episode. For, while the imagery is Amazonian, the underlying story is based on the story of the Lemnian women. Jason encounters these women on the island of Lemnos in Book 1 of Apollonius' *Argonautica*. The women of Lemnos were famous in antiquity for slaughtering all the men on their island out of a jealous rage. The men's crime had been to prefer the company of the courtesans and slave girls that they had captured in war to their own wives and daughters. It is these women who were the prototypes for the Amazons in *Hercules*. Even the reference to the volcano that wiped out the men of the Amazonian island is a refraction of the history of Lemnos' own highly volcanic nature and its association with the foundry of the smith-god Hephaestus.

The western tradition of male voyeurism on Amazonian women continued into cinema. The silent film classic, *The Amazons* (1917) started the trend. The year before the release of *Hercules*, Anna Marie Nabuco had starred as Queen Conori in *Love Slaves of the Amazons* (1957) which likewise featured scenes of dancing, drugging, and seduction (promotional tag: 'This is the Lost Tribe of White Women Savages! Each a Beauty ... Each a Deadly Trap for the men they make their love slaves!'). A decade earlier, audiences had received similar fare when Amira Moustafa as Queen Zita had attempted to steal the husband of Patricia Morison in *Queen of the Amazons* (1947).

Promoters clearly knew their audience when they scheduled *Island of Lost Women* (1959) as the feature to accompany *Hercules* in US drive-in cinemas. This film was equally breathless in its promotion, promising 'Loads of Hidden Untouched Beauties' in a 'Hidden Paradise'. Yet, in case one needed reminding that these films were not all about sleaze, beneath these promises, patrons were also advised that children received a discounted ticket price and a free playground was provided for their enjoyment. As Levine realised so successfully, peplum cinema was multilayered. It offered action and adventure for the children along with plenty of female and male bodies for the enjoyment of adults.

Suggested further viewing

Hercules Unchained (Italian title: *Ercole e la regina di Lidia*, dir. Francisci, 1959)
Steve Reeves once again stars in this quickly produced sequel to *Hercules* (1958). Sylva Koscina plays Iole and Joseph Levine was heavily involved in its production. The film repeats the formula developed by director Pietro Francisci in *Hercules*. Once again an ancient narrative is coopted to provide the plot. In this case, the film is set against the story of Aeschylus' *Seven Against Thebes*. While travelling to Thebes to stop the war over the

throne between the brothers Eteocles and Polynices, Hercules stops to drink at a spring. The water is drugged and Hercules loses his memory. He is taken to serve in the pleasure gardens of Omphale, the Queen of Lydia. Fortunately, Hercules is followed by the boy Ulysses who helps the hero regain his memory. As Hercules' memory returns so does his strength, and he is able to escape from the Lydians and return to Thebes. He arrives too late to prevent the war between Eteocles and Polynices. However, he does manage to rescue Iole who has managed to get caught up in events in Thebes, and bring the fighting to an end. The film was heavily promoted for its battle scenes and the licentiousness of the court of Omphale. Critics, though not enamoured of the peplum genre, were kinder to this film than its predecessor.

Hercules and the Captive Women (Italian title: *Ercole alla conquista di Atlantide,* dir. Cottafavi, 1961)
British bodybuilder Reg Park plays Hercules in this film. Made in 1961, it is a much more representative example of standard peplum fare than either *Hercules* (1958) or *Hercules Unchained* (1959). The story works together mythic elements about the shape-changer Proteus, the castration of Uranus, and the civilisation of Atlantis to create a story about a mad queen and her quest for world domination. Typical peplum themes such as the liberation of subject peoples and the seductive power of women are explored. Running through the film is a strong Cold War anxiety about nuclear proliferation. It is through uranium (created by the blood of Uranus) that Antinea, Queen of Atlantis plans to enslave the world.

The Colossus of Rhodes (Italian title: *Il Colosso di Rodi,* dir. Leone, 1961)
Sergio Leone is most famous for his work as a director of 'spaghetti westerns', but prior to these films he found himself caught up in the Italian film industry's love affair with the ancient world. By the time he came to direct *The Colossus of Rhodes*, Leone had established credentials in the area of cine-antiquity. Previous work included involvement in the directorial units of *Fabiola* (1949), *Quo Vadis* (1951), *Helen of Troy* (1956), *Ben-Hur* (1959), and *The Last Days of Pompeii* (1959).

Unlike other examples of pepla, this film is based on historical events rather than mythological ones. As the title indicates, its subject is the Colossus of Rhodes and it tells the story of the creation and destruction of this ancient wonder, which in this film turns out to be a mechanical marvel, part statue, part weapon of war. Rory Calhoun stars as Dario, a visiting Athenian who finds himself caught up in political intrigue in Rhodes. The plot is complicated involving coup and counter-coup, but includes many of the standard peplum elements including vampy women (principally the over-sexed Diala played by Lea Massari), duplicitous foreigners (in this case the Phoenicians) and numerous scenes of choreographed combat.

Roman History on Screen: *Spartacus* (1960)

Introduction

Rome may be eternal, but the cinematic representation of its history is patchy. By tradition, Rome was founded in 753 BC and its last emperor in the West was Romulus Augustus who was deposed by the German chieftain Odoacer in AD 476. Yet of the 1200 years of Rome's existence, only a few decades are ever represented in film. Within the genres of films about ancient Rome, the depiction of historical narratives is curiously prescribed.

For example, early Rome is largely absent. This omission is striking because stories about the first kings of Rome and the founding of the Roman republic were a standard feature of eighteenth- and nineteenth-century cultural representations of Rome. Ever since the Renaissance, artists and dramatists had been drawn to figures such as Lucretia whose suicide after her rape by Tarquin provided the catalyst for the overthrow of Rome's monarchy. Such stories were a staple of the French history-painting tradition. Every artist who wanted to make a name for himself was obliged at some point to turn their attention to stories from Rome's foundation. Authors such as Livy provided compendia of anecdotes that could be translated into exciting, often morally uplifting, images.

Even relatively obscure incidents could be elevated into canonical scenes. The leading French history-painter, Jacques-Louis David's *Oath of the Horatii* (1784), for example, depicts a now little-discussed story from Livy concerning the dispute between Rome and the neighbouring town of Alba Longa. According to Livy, in each town there lived a set of triplets (in Rome, the Horatii, and in Alba Longa, the Curiatii) and it was decided that the dispute between the towns should be settled by combat between the two sets of brothers. In the course of combat, two of the Roman brothers are killed before the final Roman triplet can kill all of the Curiatii. Triumphant the last of the Horatii returns to his family. However, upon his return, he discovers his sister weeping for one of the Curiatii, a man to whom she had been betrothed. For such disloyal sentiments, he slays her on the spot. The harshness of the punishment was seemingly endorsed by the Roman people who acquit him for the murder.

This tale of self-sacrifice and duty that transcended familial bonds made the story a suitable subject for David who received a royal commission for the piece. The fame of the image only increased with the outbreak of revolution nearly five years later where its sentiments seemed even more pertinent. Yet the ideals that the story eulogises, and which make it so suitable for a newly-minted republic that is keen to suborn all competing bonds of affection beneath its revolutionary zeal, are precisely the sentiments which make the story so unsuitable for cinema. Cinema, especially popular cinema, occurs in a post-Romantic age where love justifies all. The idea that we might unquestioningly celebrate the death of two brothers in the service of the State or the murder of a woman for loving the wrong man are ideas that translate uncomfortably into modern cinema. Eulogising the act of putting country before family seems totally divorced from modern sensibilities. The image of the Roman consul Lucius Junius Brutus sentencing his sons to death in 509 BC for plotting to overthrow the republic in order to restore the monarchy may have played well in the eighteenth century (as numerous depictions record), but it is unlikely to provide suitable material for a conventional screenplay.

Other popular stories from the days of the early republic prove equally uncomfortable to translate. For example, the story of Romulus' murder of his twin brother Remus in a dispute over the founding of Rome is a difficult story with which to engage an audience. No matter how the story is set up, it is hard to sympathise with Romulus. Was the murder of Remus worth the establishment of Rome? For the Romans, the answer was certainly yes. Modern audiences have difficulty making the same leap. If nothing else, the echoes of the story of Cain and Abel are too strong. It is hard to empathise with a fratricide.

It is telling that one of the few attempts to film this story, *Duel of the Titans* (1961, UK title: *Romulus and Remus*) avoids the traditional myth-historical narrative and replaces it with a narrative more in line with standard peplum conventions. Remus (Gordon Scott) is transformed into a standard villain, proud, and impious. Here the founding of Rome plays second fiddle to a disputed love interest as Romulus (Steve Reeves) and Remus vie for the affections of Julia (Virna Lisi), daughter of the king of the Sabines. As always in peplum, the plot proves subordinate to spectacle and the display of muscles. Amongst other liberties taken with the traditional storyline was the inclusion of a scene involving a gratuitous but amazing volcanic eruption and the recasting of Rome's enemies, the Sabines as a depraved, degenerate society (trailer: 'Italy, a land possessed by the Sabines, a tribe addicted to strange, orgiastic fertility rites'). Publicity for the film stressed the way that the pseudo-mythical plot pitted the star of *Hercules* (Reeves) against the star of *Tarzan* (Scott). In many ways, it is this semi-mythical bout that the film is really interested in depicting, not an accurate version of the foundation story of Rome.

The inability of popular cinema to play stories from early Rome in any way straight is seemingly confirmed by another film produced in 1961, *Romulus and the Sabines* (also released under the title *Rape of the Sabines*). This sex-comedy starring Roger Moore as Romulus was billed as 'the bawdiest story in history' and retold the story of Romulus' abduction of Sabine women to provide wives for his followers and so ensure the continuation of his newly founded city. In this version of the tale, the uncomfortable sexual politics of the story are elided in favour of a romantic love story about the attraction between a vestal virgin (played by Mylène Demongeot) and the young dashing Romulus. In keeping with the humorous atmosphere of the film, all responsibility for the actions of the Romans is displaced by making the abduction the result of a competition between Mars and Venus. Moreover, the film goes out of its ways to play down the resistance of the women to their forced abduction. As the trailer for the film exclaimed: 'You couldn't exactly call it stealing. You see, while some young ladies resented it, there were others who delighted in THE RAPE OF THE SABINES.'

The middle and late republican periods fare only a little better. Again the patriotism of the narratives often makes them unsuitable fodder, especially for post-war cinema. The Italian dictator Mussolini's strong personal involvement in the production of the Italian epic, *Scipio Africanus*, ensured that such narratives would always be greeted with suspicion. In a post-colonial age, watching the empire of Rome expand seems positively indecent. Audiences had become too suspicious of empires to be disposed to greet them warmly on screen.

In addition, the complicated politics of the late republic make the period difficult to adapt for cinema. This was a period in which numerous alliances were made and broken, and figures regularly change sides. It is noticeable that the stories that have been most regularly translated to the screen are not new stories lifted from the history books, but stories which have been already assimilated into Western literature through various adaptations. Producers have traditionally seemed happier translating Shakepeare's *Julius Caesar* into cinema than commissioning entirely new scripts based on the life of the Roman dictator. The late republic lacks the moral clarity necessary for advancing plotlines. The problem with late republican politics is that everyone seems compromised. Policy all too regularly gives way to pragmatism and even the heroes (or more correctly, especially the heroes) end up with blood on their hands. Only when the action moves away from Rome does it seem possible to render some of this turbulent politics onto celluloid. The numerous films about the life of Cleopatra allow the filmmaker to tell the story of the politics of the late republic at one remove. By focusing on how that politics affects just one individual – the Ptolemaic queen – audiences can gain some idea about the shifting tides of Roman affairs.

It is perhaps telling that the most recent attempt to depict the politics of the period was not a film, but a multi-part television series, HBO's *Rome*. Here the extended format allowed the various intricate political machinations of Caesar, Antony, and Octavian to develop over time so that viewers did not drown in a sea of intrigue. Moreover, by telling the story of the fall of the republic through the eyes of two bit-players, Titus Pullo and Lucius Vorenus the series provides useful guides for viewers. The audience vicariously learns about republican politics as Titus and Lucius are drawn into affairs of state and matters are explained to them.

The other periods that are poorly served by cinema are the periods of the late empire and the continuation of the Roman empire in the East in Byzantium. A number of factors combine to make these periods less attractive for filmmakers. The unfamiliarity of the historical narratives of the period makes it less easy to win over audiences. In addition, these periods are more visually challenging for audiences familiar with the tropes of classical art. Byzantine emperors do not look at all like emperors of the popular imagination so many of the visual clues which audiences rely upon and enjoy are missing. Finally, the conversion of the Roman empire to Christianity deprives plots of one of their standard narrative features, namely the depiction of the plight of persecuted Christians under Rome. Feature films depicting the persecution of pagans by Christians are a rarity. The most notable exception is *Agora* (2009), which depicted the murder of the pagan female mathematician Hypatia by a group of fanatical Christians in fifth-century AD Alexandria.

Even within stories of Christian persecution, there is a preference for stories set during the reigns of the Julio-Claudian emperors. The large-scale (and better attested) persecutions of Christians under Decius (AD 201-51) and the so-called 'great persecution' under Diocletian and Galerius in AD 303 tend to be ignored. This seems to reflect a general Protestant sensibility on behalf of filmmakers and American audiences who prefer that their Christians have neither priests nor liturgy. Instead, cinematic Christians huddle together in prayer and witness without any of the accoutrements of the established church. The preference for the primitive first generation of Christians stresses the vulnerability of the Christian faith in its infancy. By placing these stories chronologically close to the time of the Resurrection, these narratives link the Roman films with the equally established cinematic genre of biblical epics. They start to occupy the place of sequel or 'spin-off'. Film advertising for Roman epic often stressed the films' similarity with biblical epic and both films appealed to the same market.

Roman historical narratives rarely escape the introduction of large-scale fictional elements into their plots. In many ways, cinema prefers to anchor its narratives around a few established historical facts and then embroider their stories to suit audience tastes and fashions. For example, numerous films are set around the explosion of Pompeii in AD 79, but few incorporate other historical details into their storyline. A number of these films either adapt or were inspired by Edward Bulwer-Lytton's novel *The Last Days of Pompeii*, but none are able to match this novel for its inclusion of historical and archaeological detail.

The need to supplement historical accounts is understandable. There are few accounts from the ancient world that are told with such completeness that they do not need to be supplemented. In particular, few stories contain the necessary romantic elements that make them ideal for popular adaptation. Except perhaps in the case of Cleopatra, romance always needs to be added.

We see this in the case of *Spartacus* (1960). The historical facts surrounding Spartacus' rebellion are reasonably well known and consistent. There are plenty of sources about the life of a gladiator from which it is possible to conjecture his training and life before the rebellion. We are also well informed about Roman politics of the period and the pressures and anxieties that Spartacus' rebellion caused in Rome. However, Spartacus' emotional state is unknown to us. We know that he had a wife, but beyond that almost nothing. In order to avoid the protagonist of the account appearing one-dimensional, an alternative life needs to be invented for him in which we can see his hopes and his dreams. Spartacus, the man, needs to open up to us.

Films that claimed to depict episodes of Roman history constantly needed to balance competing interests. Their storylines need to be compelling. Historical facts provide boundaries within which these stories need to be situated. Conjecture to fill gaps in our sources is inevitable. It seems entirely plausible that Spartacus felt love and hope. But with whom? When? Why? These are questions that remain opaque. It is up to the filmmaker to decide whether the answer to such questions is one that tells a Roman story or a modern one.

Background to case study

The *Spartacus* screenplay owes its origins to a chance encounter in the library of Mill Point prison. In 1950, the imprisoned novelist and playwright, Howard Fast came across a book about Germany after the First World War. Inside he found the story of Rosa Luxemburg, who had been one of the key leaders in the German socialist movement that flourished after the war ended. Luxemburg had named her group of agitators the Spartacists, and her group and its aims appealed to Fast. In particular, he was attracted by Luxemburg's commitment to freedom, a commitment that would ultimately cost Luxemburg her life. It was a sentiment to which Fast could relate.

Fast was a victim of the anti-communist hysteria that swept America at this time. He had been imprisoned for contempt of Congress for failing to answer questions from the House Committee on Un-American Activities (HUAC) about his involvement in, and the activities of, the Joint Anti-Fascist Refugee Committee, an organisation primarily involved in providing food, shelter, and medicine to refugees from the Spanish Civil War who had been driven out by the Fascist leader Franco.

Fast's first thoughts on reading about Luxemburg were to write a novel about her life and activities. However, he felt that it was still too close to the Holocaust to recount the story of a German Jew imprisoned and later killed for her beliefs. Instead, Fast took his inspiration from the same person who had inspired Luxemburg, the slave leader, Spartacus. This would not be Fast's first novel about slavery. His earlier novel *Freedom Road* (1944) had tackled the topic of slavery in the US.

Fast neither possessed Latin nor was he able to travel to Italy. The main source for his novel was Cyrenus Osborne Ward's *The Ancient Lowly* (1883). This work first appeared in 1883 and a number of subsequent editions were printed in 1888, 1889, and 1907 (the edition used by Fast). The work was a minor classic in Leftist circles. Fast had received his copy as a gift from his instructors after finishing his instruction at the Communist Party training school.

Ward was a passionate advocate of the working classes. His first work was *A Labor Catechism of Political Economy* (1877) and he regularly toured the country advocating, amongst other things, the establishment of a party for the working man and the nationalisation of assets such as the railroad, telegraph, and telephone systems. In *The Ancient Lowly*, Ward attempted the monumental task of describing the lives of the working classes from earliest times until the reign of Constantine. Reflecting contemporary racial theory, the work begins by discussing the differing attitudes towards labour adopted by Aryan and Semitic peoples. It then discusses the Indo-Europeans before charting the story of slavery and its opposition in the Greek and Roman worlds. In such an account, Spartacus plays an important role.

Ward's account of the revolt of Spartacus is distinctive for the way in which it treats gladiators as symptomatic of a much greater malaise in Roman culture, namely the brutal maltreatment of slaves and the working class. Throughout his account he constantly aligns the two groups. For him, the working classes were effectively enslaved through their poverty and so the victories of Spartacus are a victory for all opposed to 'haughty landlords' and 'non-laboring grandees'. 'Spartacus was, in all respects, a working man' (Ward 1889: 223) and his defeat deprived the world of the opportunity for the 'permanent recognition of the honor and merit of human labor' (317). In addition, Ward was keen to see Spartacus' revolt as part of a general trend in Roman politics towards freedom and economic justice for working people. He links therefore Spartacus' revolt with other political events such as the redistribution of land advocated by the Gracchi and the agitation for equality amongst the Italian allies. Ward was particularly interested in the Roman institution of *collegia* which he regarded as ancient trade unions and he argues that the attempted regulation of these guilds fuelled support amongst the working class for Spartacus' revolt. Ward's account saw Spartacus' struggle as intimately linked with popular politics at Rome and a reflection of the spiritual corruption that attends the institution of slavery. Both of these were themes picked up in Fast's novel and their echoes can be seen in the Spartacus screenplay. In particular, the dual focus in the film on events at Rome and Capua reflects the tenor of Fast's novel.

Fast's novel was published in 1951. Owing to an unofficial blacklist of leftist writers he had been unable to get it published commercially and so was forced to self-publish the novel. The director of the FBI, J. Edgar Hoover seems to have intervened personally to stymie the publication of Fast's novels. In the environment of fear that operated at the time, no publisher was prepared to risk incurring Hoover's wrath. However, Doubleday, while declining to publish, did let Fast know unofficially that should he publish the novel himself they would buy a large number of copies for their bookstores. This provided enough of an impetus for Fast to risk publishing the novel.

Despite a deliberate policy on the part of mainstream US reviewers to ignore the novel, *Spartacus* proved to be a great word-of-mouth success. Fast went through four printings in the first year of the book's release. Meanwhile in Britain and Ireland, the book was welcomed with a number of positive reviews and orders flooded in. Not everyone was delighted by the novel's success. The *New York Times* berated it for its obvious political bias:

> Once it was possible to distinguish the creative writer from the pamphleteer in the works of Howard Fast. Unfortunately for his success in the field of the novel, his steady shift to the left has cast an increasingly hectic fever-flush on each of his recent productions. 'Spartacus,' his twelfth novel, is printed by the author himself. It is a far cry from such notable books as 'The Unvanquished,' [one of Fast's earlier novels] a dreary proof that polemics and fiction cannot mix ... it is obvious from the first page that Mr. Fast has not set out to illumine a poignant episode in ancient history. 'Spartacus,' like so much of his later work, is a tract in the form of a novel. Occasionally (when he is describing the inferno of a slave bivouac in the desert, the torments of a crucified gladiator, the life-and-death struggle in the arena) Mr. Fast's pages take on a brilliance that recalls his earlier work. But the Q. E. D. he proposes simply does not square with the geometry of history. (Heath 1952: 22).

The events leading up to the publication of Fast's novel were turbulent and the same could be said for the events surrounding its screen adaptation. In 1957, the successful actor Kirk Douglas read Fast's novel and saw its potential as a great film and star vehicle for himself. Douglas had already established himself as one of Hollywood's most talented actors. He had been nominated for Oscars for his roles as the boxer 'Midge' Kelly in *Champion* (1949) and the amoral producer Jonathan Shields in *The Bad and the Beautiful* (1952). Douglas enjoyed a reputation for his versatility as an actor with roles ranging from gunslingers (*Along the Great Divide*, 1951; *Gunfight at the O.K. Corral*, 1957; *Last Train from Gun Hill*, 1959) to jazz musicians (*Young Man with a Horn*, 1950) to the tormented artist Van Gogh (*Lust for Life*, 1956). Nor was Spartacus his first venture into classical antiquity. Along with Silvia Mangano and Anthony Quinn, Douglas had starred in the 1954 adventure film *Ulysses* based on Homer's *Odyssey*.

What distinguishes *Spartacus* (1960) from these earlier films was Douglas' personal attachment to the project. Other roles had been about displaying his acting talent. In this film Douglas wanted to establish his name as a producer. Early in his career, Douglas had established his own production company, Bryna Productions, named after his mother. Douglas approached Universal to allow Bryna to make *Spartacus*. Universal were initially reluctant, but came around when Douglas was able to convince the well-known stage and film actors Peter Ustinov and Laurence Olivier to take part in the film. It was Douglas' personal investment in this project that saw him take the bold move of employing the talented Dalton Trumbo to adapt the novel for film. Fast had initially been commissioned to produce the script, but in a move that would become common in the production of this film, Douglas had not liked the product ('it was too inactive and talky' – Hanson 2001: 135) nor the speed at which Fast worked and so Fast had been relieved from the duty of producing the script. Fast later sought to have his work acknowledged by a co-writer credit for the screenplay, but his claim was ultimately rejected by the Writers Guild of America.

Like Fast, Trumbo was a victim of the anti-leftist purges that had swept the US. Trumbo was one of the so-called 'Hollywood Ten', a group of film industry professionals who had also refused in 1947 to cooperate with the House Committee on Un-American Activities. All had declined to answer questions about their own membership of the Communist Party and they refused to name others who had been members of the Party or who they suspected of having leftist sympathies. For this, they were blacklisted by Hollywood studios who refused to employ them. Trumbo was jailed for 11 months for contempt of Congress. Even while blacklisted Trumbo continued to write screenplays, although they were always submitted under either pseudonyms or front men. His scripts and treatments for *The Brave One* (1956) and *Roman Holiday* (1953) were given Academy Awards for 'Best Story'. *Spartacus* was the first film for which Trumbo and Fast were publically acknowledged after their respective blacklistings.

Just as there had been production problems over the script, so too were there problems with the direction. Douglas had originally employed Anthony Mann to direct the film. Mann had established his reputation in well-regarded, often psychologically complex, westerns starring James Stewart (e.g. *Winchester '73*, 1950; *The Naked Spur*, 1953; *The Man from Laramie*, 1955). Unfortunately for Mann, the productive relationship that he enjoyed with Stewart did not eventuate with Douglas. Douglas was unhappy with the first few scenes shot by Mann and asked for him to be replaced.

Mann was replaced by the young director, Stanley Kubrick. Kubrick and Douglas had previously worked together on Kubrick's anti-war film, *Paths of Glory* (1957) in which Douglas played a disillusioned commanding officer who sees his men executed for refusing to undertake an almost certainly suicidal mission. Kubrick would go on to become one of Hollywood's leading directors with films such as *Lolita* (1962), *Dr. Strangelove* (1964), *2001: A Space Odyssey* (1968), *The Shining* (1980). In a film system renowned for its collaborative nature, Kubrick was unusual in the degree to which he has controlled his projects. He was always heavily involved in matters of casting, script, and production. This preference for control seems to explain his ambivalent relationship with *Spartacus*. Although initially happy to claim credit for *Spartacus*, Kubrick later in his career disavowed his involvement in the film. Certainly, he exercised less control over its production than he did on a number of other projects. Not only did he inherit a film where Mann had already shot a number of scenes, but Douglas frequently intervened in the production of the film and Kubrick and Douglas clashed on a number of occasions.

Given such a turbulent production history and its origins in the work of a discredited novelist and scriptwriter, there seems to have been every reason to doubt that *Spartacus* was destined for success. Certainly Universal, who were backing the film, had reservations about the project. They were worried about cost overruns and also about public reaction to the film. For this reason, a number of scenes planned in the script were deleted. Many of these were large battle scenes which were dropped either for reasons for expense or because they contained images deemed too gruesome and potentially upsetting to audiences.

Universal had some justification for their concerns. On its release the film was picketed by a number of conservatives. Local branches of the American Legion, the US veterans' association, picketed screenings and its national convention condemned Hollywood's employment of blacklisted writers. Such protests, however, proved to be a minority activity. Amongst the most famous attendees were the Kennedy brothers who were happy to be publicly seen at screenings of the film, and so effectively gave the film an official endorsement. First Attorney-General Robert F. Kennedy publicly attended the film and then a week later his brother President John Kennedy, accompanied by the Under-Secretary of the Navy, also went to see it. Such attendance was particularly marked because normally the President saw films privately at the White House rather than a public theatre. As he left the cinema John Kennedy told reporters that *Spartacus* was a 'fine' film. Many agreed. *Spartacus* was a huge commercial success upon its release. The film made $60 million dollars worldwide and was nominated for six Academy Awards; winning awards for Best Supporting Actor, Best Art Direction, Best Cinematography, and Best Costume Design.

Importantly, this success led to the end of the Hollywood blacklist. Challenging the blacklist was already in the air. Otto Preminger had independently announced that he was giving Trumbo a credit for his work on *Exodus* (1960). However, had *Spartacus* failed because of its use of blacklisted figures, then it is hard not to believe that the destruction of the blacklisting system would have been set back considerably. Universal debated for a number of months before allowing Trumbo his screen credit. They were clearly concerned about the opposition that they might face and the effect this would have on audiences. In the end, and together with *Inherit the Wind* (1960) which was released in the same year and featured a script by the blacklisted writer, Nedrick Young, *Spartacus* started a trend that other films were happy to follow. In the few years that followed the release of *Spartacus,* a critical mass of films openly sported blacklist writers and this oppressive period of Hollywood policy was ended.

Plot summary

The film opens in the Roman mines of Libya. Here we encounter the Thracian slave Spartacus (Kirk Douglas) who has been sentenced to death for biting a Roman guardsman who struck him whilst he offered succour to a fellow collapsed slave. However, he is rescued from his fate by Lentulus Batiatus (Peter Ustinov), the owner of a gladiator school who, attracted by Spartacus' strength and spirit, buys him for his school in Capua.

On arriving in Capua, Spartacus is quickly introduced into the life of the gladiator. It is a life both more brutal and more privileged than the one that he had enjoyed until now. Freed from the drudgery of back-breaking work, Spartacus is trained to fight and kill. One of the treats offered to the gladiators are the sexual services of young slave women. It is in this context that Spartacus first meets Varinia (Jean Simmons), a young British slave girl working in the kitchens of the school. Sensing her fear and unwillingness, Spartacus refuses to take advantage of her, especially when he notices Batiatus and his brutal trainer, Marcellus (Charles McGraw) peeping through the grille hoping to catch sight of the two lovers in action.

Matters progress when the wealthy Roman politician and general Marcus Licinius Crassus (Laurence Olivier) and his retinue arrive in Capua. Always eager to please the powerful, Batiatus arranges a display of gladiatorial combat for Crassus and his friends. After prompting from the women in his party, Crassus insists that the fight be 'to the death'. Reluctantly, Batiatus agrees. Two pairs are chosen by the women. The first pair is Crixus (John Ireland) and Gallino and the second is Spartacus and Draba (Woody Strode). While waiting for the combat to begin, Crassus catches sight of Varinia and taking a fancy to her arranges to buy her from Batiatus and have her delivered to his house in Rome. The first fight goes relatively straightforwardly with Crixus dispatching Gallino. However, in the second fight, when Draba manages to pin Spartacus against the wall of the enclosure, Draba refuses to administer the final blow. Instead, he turns his trident against the watching Romans and charges the viewing box. Sadly, before he can inflict any damage, Draba is struck by a spear from one of the guardsmen and Crassus dispatches him with a slash to the neck.

Following the death of the two gladiators, a sombre mood comes over the gladiatorial school. Spartacus' unhappiness is only increased when he learns from Marcellus that Varinia has been sold. Unable to take the insults of Marcellus any longer, Spartacus drowns Marcellus in a vat of soup. The other gladiators join Spartacus in his rebellion and quickly they overpower the guards. Sensing danger, Batiatius takes Varinia and escapes. Seizing weapons, the gladiators destroy the school and head for the hills.

The scene changes to the Senate of Rome and we learn that Spartacus' rebellious band has been successful not only in evading capture, but also in pillaging the countryside and attracting other slaves to swell their numbers. The Senate resolves at the instigation of the wily politician, Gracchus (Charles Laughton) to send part of the Legion of Rome led by Crassus' protégé, Marcus Glabrus (John Dall) to deal with Spartacus' rebellion.

Unfortunately for the Romans, Spartacus has transformed his band from a drunken rabble into a disciplined fighting force. Energised by the thought of bribing some pirates and sailing away to freedom, Spartacus and his men ravage the countryside freeing slaves and gathering booty with which to pay the pirates. In the course of one of their raids, Spartacus discovers Varinia who had escaped from Batiatus as he fled from Capua. Reunited, their love continues to blossom and eventually Varinia finds out that she is pregnant by Spartacus. Another slave who joins Spartacus' band is the poet and singer, Antoninus (Tony Curtis). Antoninus had previously been a slave of Crassus, but fled his master when Crassus attempted to seduce him.

The first obstacle that Spartacus faces in his bid for freedom is the pursuing Legion of Rome. Underestimating their opponents, the Romans fail to set up adequate defences on their camp and Spartacus takes advantage of this weakness to inflict a humiliating defeat upon them. Almost all of the Romans are killed, the Roman camp is destroyed, and Glabrus is sent back to Rome in disgrace.

Glabrus' defeat allows Gracchus to score points against Crassus and, after a heated meeting of the Senate, Crassus retires from public office to private life. However, Gracchus' ascendency in political life proves to be short-lived. The ever-increasing success of Spartacus and Gracchus' in-ability to deal with him causes Rome to become increasingly desperate for a solution to the slave problem. Eventually, the city turns to Crassus and offers him supreme command if he will eliminate Spartacus and his army of slave gladiators.

Crassus' first act is to pay off the pirates so that they will not assist

Spartacus in his plan to flee Italy. As a result, Spartacus finds himself trapped in the heel of Italy. Marching with legions from Rome and joined by the armies of Pompey and Lucullus, Crassus has Spartacus outnumbered. With nowhere to go, Spartacus is forced to engage with the forces of Crassus. The result is an inevitable defeat for Spartacus and his men.

Hoping to make an example of him, Crassus searches for Spartacus amongst the captives. Despite Crassus promising to spare their lives, the slaves refuse to surrender their commander. Instead, each in turn declares 'I'm Spartacus'. As punishment, Crassus orders the crucifixion of all the surviving captives. Their bodies are set up lining the Appian Way, the main highway into Rome.

Whilst inspecting the bodies that litter the battleground, Crassus comes across Varinia still alive and clutching her newly born child. Crassus orders that she be taken to Rome to be a slave in his household. Leaving Varinia, Crassus rides along the row of captive slaves. Among the slaves he encounters he recognises Antoninus and Spartacus. He orders the commander to hold off crucifying these slaves until the very end.

While the slaves march towards Rome, Crassus' enemy Gracchus and Batiatus plot to humiliate Crassus by stealing Varinia from Crassus' house. Sadly, for Gracchus, it is the last plot that he will hatch against Crassus. Crassus, exercising his new powers as dictator, arrests Gracchus and has him brought to the senate chamber. Here he explains that he intends to use his powers to proscribe all his political enemies, starting with Gracchus. It is a vision of the future that Gracchus wishes to have no part in and on returning home he starts to puts his affairs in order in preparation for suicide.

As a final act of revenge against Spartacus, Crassus demands that Spartacus and Antoninus fight each other to the death, the winner to be crucified. Neither Antoninus nor Spartacus will allow the other to suffer an excruciating death on the cross and so they fight, each hoping to dispatch the other quickly. In the end, Spartacus manages to kill Antoninus who dies professing his love for Spartacus. Meanwhile, Batiatus rescues Varinia and Gracchus as a final act arranges to smuggle her out of Rome. As she leaves, she catches sight of Spartacus crucified by the gates of Rome. As he dies, she holds up the child so that Spartacus can see that his son has survived and will live the life of a free man.

Key scenes and themes

Between athlete and animal: making sense of gladiators

Few Roman institutions are simultaneously so foreign and so familiar as the gladiator. Almost from the moment cinema first engaged with the depiction of Rome, it was confronted with the issue of how to depict the gladiator. The gladiator is a distinctive and peculiar Roman product and as such he creates problems for his representation. Ideally, he is best understood in the context of a deep knowledge of Roman religious practice, the Roman law of the person, and the function of the abject (the fascinating 'other') within ideological structures. Without such knowledge, the gladiator is unreadable and one flails around for metaphors trying to capture something of his nature.

The training sequence

The trumpets blast and the screen is filled with a close-up of a giant mannequin armed with a swinging ball-and-chain and a small shield. As the mannequin swings from side to side, blurry figures dance about it, dodging the swing of its lethal-looking weapon. Spartacus manages to duck, but his companion is not so lucky and, after receiving a blow to the head, he crashes to the ground. The scene cuts to another 'training machine' where wooden (later metal) blades swing round a pole as gladiators duck and weave to avoid being sliced. An overview shot of the gladiator school reveals it to be a hive of activity as gladiators run, swing from bars, and engage each other in mock combat. Almost every inch of the training ground is used. The frenetic energy of the scene is picked up by the soundtrack where the woodwind and brass blast away in a breathy staccato imitation of the energetic combatants. Chained together by wooden rods, the gladiators have nowhere to run as they face each other with wooden swords and tiny metal shields.

One witness to all this activity is Varinia, who gazes out at the gladiators from the next-door kitchen. Her look turns to Spartacus who finds himself drawn away from the world of gladiators by the woman who had been offered up to him in the preceding scene.

The pace of the sequence slows as Spartacus finds himself transformed into a live anatomical model for explaining the effect of various blows on the human body. The trainer Marcellus, using brushes dipped in various paint colours, illustrates the range of wounds open to the gladiator. Dabbing Spartacus' throat and breast in red, he shows the spots that lead to an instant kill. Blue marks drawn on Spartacus' thighs and arms mark the places where a blow will cripple an opponent. Finally, the locations to strike for a 'slow kill' are marked in yellow. By the end of the lecture, Spartacus' physique has become a primary-coloured map of the gladiator's art.

The origins of the gladiator lie in the funeral rituals of the Etruscans. Gladiatorial combat was first offered as part of the games commemorating the deceased. The custom was adopted by Rome in the third century BC and quickly became a popular spectacle. We even have one account of a town that refused to allow the burial of a prominent citizen until his heirs promised to provide a gladiatorial show. The attractiveness of gladiatorial games was soon recognised by politicians who were happy to use the pretext of commemorating the death of a relative to stage large popular games to advance their political causes. The funeral games staged by Julius Caesar for his daughter Julia in 46 BC are usually regarded as a paradigmatic example of such political use of the games, not least because in honouring a woman (who had died eight years before), these games broke new territory and their staging was so obviously designed to increase Caesar's political capital.

Gladiatorial combat also featured as part of the celebration of a number of religious festivals. Initially privately sponsored, they were part of a number of public entertainments, which also included such things as beast hunts, theatrical events, athletic competitions, and public feasts.

As gladiatorial combat rose in popularity so too did the size of the industry that supported it. Gladiatorial schools called *ludi* (sing. *ludus*) emerged for the training of gladiators and there was an ever-increasing demand for men prepared to fight in the arena. Gladiators were drawn from the ranks of enemies defeated in battle and condemned criminals. A man could be condemned to death, for example by crucifixion or being thrown to wild beasts, but he could also be sentenced '*ad ludos*' (to a gladiatorial school). Contemporary moralists often paint gladiators as the worst sort of criminals such as arsonists or murderers. Although later on free men could volunteer to become gladiators, the profession retained its low social position and this was enforced with a number of particular legal sanctions. Under legislation passed by Augustus, for example, freed gladiators were forbidden from ever attaining Roman citizenship. In Roman law, the gladiator belonged to a group of individuals (along with actors and prostitutes) who suffered *infamia* (lit. 'without good reputation') and so were subject to a number of legal disabilities. They were legally classed as untrustworthy, they could neither act as witnesses for legal documents nor hold municipal office.

Yet despite this revulsion, the gladiator also exercised a high degree of fascination for the Roman public. Roman literature, perhaps more in fantasy than reality, regularly portrayed gladiators as the object of sexual desire for Roman women. Graffiti attests to the popularity of individual gladiators and accounts of particularly splendid fights were celebrated by Roman popular culture.

The gladiator represents a paradoxical figure, simultaneously revolting and alluring. He exists at the point where the discourse of Roman law meets Roman religion and popular culture. He is the most recognisable feature of Roman culture, yet the Romans were always keen to stress the foreign origins of the institution. He's elusive, but he leaves traces everywhere. Central, yet almost impossible to grasp.

It is understandable then that cinema has struggled to capture the nature of the Roman gladiator and so has found it useful to employ various contemporary metaphors to help translate this Roman institution into more modern vernacular. One of the more common strategies that has been employed is the drawing of parallels between the gladiator and the modern sports star. The appeal of such a strategy is obvious. Through recourse to modern notions of fame, the Roman enthusiasm for gladiatorial combat and the cult of personality that seems to have attended gladiators is explained. The similarity in architecture between the modern sporting arena and arenas such as the Flavian amphitheatre (the Coliseum) just seems to underscore the parallel. The fact that the vast majority of gladiatorial combats did not occur in such momentous arenas is quietly forgotten. Of course, such a metaphor can never convey either the religious dimension of gladiatorial combat nor the legal and social disabilities under which the gladiator operated.

The notion of 'the gladiator as athlete' underpins the scene discussed above [see box: 'The training sequence']. With its focus on training and exercise, the gladiatorial school resembles the modern gymnasium, especially considering the focus on specialist training equipment running throughout the scene. Spartacus was released at a time when there was a revolution happening in the nature of exercise. This was a period in which an increasing 'scientific' approach was being applied to physical development. From the turn of the twentieth century, there had been an increasing reliance on specially designed training equipment. Initially, the adoption of such equipment had been sporadic, faddish, and limited to only a few converts. However, by the middle of the century, such equipment had become seen as an essential part of the modern gymnasium. Just as specific weight machines were designed to isolate and target particular muscle groups so too does the fanciful equipment dreamt up for the school of Batiatus target specific gladiatorial actions (jumping, dodging, etc).

The treatment of gladiator as sportsman sits alongside the other dominant metaphor of the gladiator as 'trained beast'. The dehumanising effect of slavery is one of the key themes running through the film. When Spartacus declares that 'we are not animals', he encapsulates the principal criticism of slavery in the film and underscores why slave revolt was inevitable and the institution was doomed. The idea that the ultimate horror of slavery was not the inevitable cruelty that attended it, but the fact that it objectified humans to the point where they become nothing but lumps of meat is constantly reinforced throughout the film. When the slaves first arrive at the *ludus*, Batiatus tells them what regime awaits them: 'A gladiator is like a stallion, you'll be oiled, bathed, taught to use your heads'; a statement that merges the two dominant metaphors of athlete and animal. Like cattle, the gladiators are branded. Throughout the film they are constantly subjected to indignities that bring out their sub-human status. They are locked into cages and, like livestock in a prize competition, their bodies are inspected. Most famously, in the scene prior to the combat before Crassus, the gladiators are inspected by the Roman women. It is this same objectifying frame that allows Marcellus to use Spartacus' body as a living mannequin in his demonstration of the effects of various blows in combat. By reducing the gladiator to just an assemblage of muscles, Marcellus perpetuates the notion that gladiators are bodies without dignity.

At the same time, it is worth noting that, for all its professed distress at the horrors of objectification, this film finds such objectification remarkably useful. The inspection scene by the Roman matrons is heavily laced with sexual innuendo and allows the audience to vicariously enjoy the Roman matrons' voyeurism. An inspection by Crassus would not have had the same effect. Similarly, a strong streak of voyeurism flows through Marcellus' delineation of Spartacus' physique. It is an impressive body and the scene allows the audience to enjoy it. Moreover, by providing us with Spartacus' body, the film offers us one meaning of what it means to be a gladiator – namely, the gladiator is nothing but a well-trained arrangement of obedient muscles. Here is *Spartacus'* answer to the question, 'What is a gladiator?'

Spartacus and the quest for freedom

Spartacus is simultaneously gladiator and slave, and it is this dual identity that allows him to participate in two distinct cinematic discourses about Rome. The first, as we have seen above, is his role in the perpetuation of Rome as the centre of spectacle and entertainment. The second is the notion of Rome as the paradigm of the oppressive, totalitarian state. This curious tension between the Rome that we love to see and the Rome that we fear to live under plays out in a number of ways in the film.

The story of Spartacus is the story of one man's struggle to be free. In this sense, the film seeks to make a unique historical circumstance a universal one. Just as the legal and social framework that created the gladiator was unique to Rome so too was its institution of slavery. The capacities, lifestyle, and treatment of Roman slaves differed markedly, not only from the slaves of ancient Greece and Egypt, but also the slaves of the Caribbean and the American South. Yet, as the voice-over that begins the film makes clear, the slavery of Rome is just one chapter in the history of this 'disease'.

In expressing its disgust for the institution of Roman slavery, *Spartacus* was following in well-trodden territory. Anxiety about slavery was a common theme in epic films set in Rome. *Quo Vadis* (1951), *The Robe* (1953), *Demetrius and the Gladiators* (1954) all identify slavery as Rome's greatest flaw. Moreover, in making Spartacus the vehicle for the discussion of issues relating to slavery and its legacy, the film again ventures onto familiar ground. As early as the first half of the nineteenth century, parallels were drawn between Spartacus' struggle against Rome and the struggle for the emancipation of slaves in the United States. For example, Robert Montgomery Bird's play about Spartacus, *The Gladiator* (1831), although intended as a rousing piece to stir up patriotism in the newly-

---

The arrest of Gracchus

Caesar strides into the atrium of Gracchus' house. At his back are two fully armed guards. He begs the pardon of Gracchus for the intrusion. Gracchus initially warmly welcomes him, but his face changes when he sees the guards. The political pupil has come to teach his master a lesson in politics. Caesar comes with orders to bring Gracchus to the senate. 'What I do, I do not for myself, but for Rome', he apologises to the old man. 'Poor helpless Rome', Gracchus replies.

The scene shifts to the senate house. Previously, it has been a scene of light and debate. Now it is dark and covered in shadow. The face of Crassus fills the screen. He barks at Gracchus, berating him for his populist politics. 'Did you think 500 years of Rome could so easily be handed over to the mob?', he asks. He then recounts the cruel sentence of crucifixion that he has handed out to the rebellious slaves. The same fate, he warns Gracchus, awaits any who 'falter one instant in loyalty to the new order of affairs'. Crassus continues, 'The enemies of the State are known. Arrests are in progress, the prisons begin to fill. In every city and province, lists of the disloyal have been compiled. Tomorrow they will learn the cost of their terrible folly, their treason.'

Gracchus then learns that although his name appears first on the list of traitors he is to be spared punishment and will instead be sent to a luxurious exile in the country. In return, Crassus demands that Gracchus become a tool of the new order. He intends to use Gracchus' influence with his followers to ensure their compliance with Crassus' new regime. 'You will persuade them to accept destiny and order and to trust the Gods', he says before dismissing the senator who shuffles from the senate house traumatised by his interview.

---

minted American republic, was often interpreted as making a plea on behalf of the contemporary emancipation movement.

Spartacus is a man 'dreaming the death of slavery two thousand years before it would finally die'. The film makes the abolition of slavery in the US the final step in a process begun many years earlier in the fields of Capua. Yet, the film makes greater claims than this. By dating the death of slavery to 'two thousand years' after the time of Spartacus, the film ensures that the contemporary civil rights movements of the 1960s are included as part of the eradication process. Slavery didn't die when Lincoln ordered the Emancipation Proclamation in 1863 or the Thirteenth Amendment to the US constitution was passed. No, *Spartacus* sees slavery disappearing from the earth only with the end of segregation and the granting of full equality. *Spartacus* not only preached this political message, it also enacted it. In a still largely segregated and discriminatory Hollywood, one of the key supporting roles was given to the African American actor, Woody Strode.

Strode's performance as Draba, the African gladiator who refuses to take Spartacus' life in the arena, stands in contrast to the usual depiction of Africans and African Americans at the time. Instead of a depiction of a brutal savage or a comic happy-go-lucky slave in the American South, Strode invests his character with a reserve and dignity that deliberately contrasts with almost every character in the arena. His bravery shows up the cowardice of Batiatus, his silent modesty stands as an accusation against the garrulous depravity of the Roman women, and his death at the hands of Crassus introduces the audience to the Roman's cruelty. Such a depiction fitted well with the trajectory of Strode's career. A star athlete, he had continually been in the vanguard of breaking down barriers of segregation in athletics and football. His acting career had similarly been path-breaking. Initially cast to play stereotypical roles such as the Ethiopian king in *The Ten Commandments* (1956) and an African native in *Jungle Man-Eaters* (1954) and the TV-series *Jungle Jim* (1955), his career would take-off with more substantial roles after he played the title role in *Sergeant Rutledge* (1960), a film that broke new ground in telling the story of a black man falsely accused of the murder and rape of a white girl. Indeed, *Spartacus* was not the first time that Strode had acted in a Roman epic. One of his earliest roles had been as the lion in *Androcles and the Lion* (1952). In addition, he had an uncredited role as a gladiator in *Demetrius and the Gladiators* (1954). In making the transition from mute extra to the noble catalyst for Spartacus' rebellion, we see the political message of the film enacted. Here was a film that refused to put black identity in the corner, but instead chose to speak out to contemporary black concerns through the parable of Roman slavery.

Yet Spartacus' story is broader than just the story of emancipation, as this scene makes clear [see box: 'The arrest of Gracchus'], it is also a story about resistance to totalitarian force. Slavery comes in many forms. Sometimes it is dependent on race, sometimes on status at birth, and sometimes on political persuasion.

The extent to which *Spartacus* offers political critique is the subject of debate. Right-wing critics opposed to the film were not shy of attributing a distinct leftist agenda to it. They played up the political affiliations of both Fast and Trumbo and argued that the film was a work of propaganda, one that smuggled its communist message under the cover of Roman togas and stories of slave rebellions. It is tempting to dismiss such claims as the alarmist fantasies of a vocal pressure group. All the correspondence relating to the film by Douglas and Trumbo never indicate anything more subversive than a desire to make a commercially and critically successful film. The film's box-office success would seem to confirm that their desire for a film with mainstream appeal worked. A comparison of the film script with Fast's novel shows that what left-wing politics existed in the story largely failed to translate into the cinematic version.

Yet if *Spartacus* doesn't advocate a specific political position that doesn't mean that it completely avoids criticism of contemporary and recent political situations. We feel this most strongly in the interchange between Crassus and Gracchus. Conducted in Rome's senate house, it is hard not to hear the echoes of the HUAC examinations here. The scene demonstrates how all too easily the language of patriotism slips into a language of repression and vindictive reprisal. It provides a perfect counterpoint to the great cinematic moment of the film, the famous 'I am Spartacus' sequence. The slaves' refusal to name Spartacus, thus condemning themselves to death, resonated all too strongly with a Hollywood still bearing the scars of the infamous anti-Communist purges and blacklists of the 1950s.

Pushing the social limits

One of the criticisms made against Hollywood's Roman epics is that they tend to reinforce conservative social agendas. Certainly this is largely the case when it comes to gender roles, and it would be hard to argue that *Spartacus* does much to depart from this tradition in its representation of women. Yet, in other respects, *Spartacus* embraces a much more radical and progressive politics. In particular, and almost uniquely for epic film, it confronts issues relating to sexuality, most famously in its 'Oysters and snails' scene [see box].

This scene never appeared in the final general-release version of the film. Universal Pictures, the Catholic Church's Legion of Decency, and the censors demanded a number of substantial alterations to the film to reduce the graphic nature of its violence and immorality. The 'oysters and snails' scene was the victim of one such round of cuts. The scene was just a little too ahead of its time. It was not until the following year that the film Production Code was altered to allow depictions of homosexuality that treated the topic with 'care, discretion, and restraint'. Even then, the first films to treat the topic tended to be British imports and the homosexuality that they depicted was normally the cause of suicide and despair rather than pleasure or fulfilment. The 'oysters and snails' scene was only restored in 1990 when Universal Pictures announced that they were going to release an anniversary version of the film. By that stage, Olivier was dead. His voice was dubbed by Anthony Hopkins.

The absence of representations of homosexuality is one of the more noticeable omissions in films set in the ancient world. The omission is all the more striking because the supposed liberalism of ancient sexuality was one of the major draws for filmmakers. Scantily-clad dancing girls and predatory empresses reclining on couches are all standard features of the repertoire. An ancient world full of sexual promise and adventure has been regularly displayed for the voyeuristic enjoyment of cinema audiences. Film advertising regularly promoted the level of sexual excitement that viewers could expect in these displays of 'depraved, pagan Rome'. Yet it was only ever heterosexual sex that was on offer. Displays of imperial effeminacy on the part of decadent emperors may have gestured in the direction of the homoerotic, but the issue of male sexual desire for other

> **'Oysters and snails'**
> Through a sheer curtain, we see Crassus bathing in a small pool, the size of a large bathtub [Fig. 9]. 'Fetch a stool, Antoninus', he calls as Antoninus enters the room from the left. Antoninus then joins his master in the pool and begins to massage Crassus' shoulders with scented oil. The ethereal sounds of Eastern strings and cymbals gives the scene an exotic soundscape. 'Do you steal, Antoninus?', Crassus asks. 'No, master', Antonius replies. Crassus then asks him whether he has ever lied or dishonoured the gods. To both questions, Antoninus replies in the negatives. Crassus continues his Socratic questioning of the slave. Does he refrain from vice out of respect for the moral virtues? 'Yes', replies Antoninus.
> Crassus then seems to change tack and asks whether Antoninus ever eats oysters and snails. Antoninus expresses a preference for the former and a dislike for the latter. At this point, Crassus returns to the question of morality and asks whether such preferences are moral issues or issues of taste. When Antoninus expresses the opinion that dietary choices are not governed by codes of morality, Crassus then uses this admission to express the view that matters of taste are different from appetite and so different from moral issues. Uncertain (or perhaps all too certain) about where this line of reasoning is heading, Antonius is forced to admit that 'it could be argued so, master'. As Antoninus strokes Crassus' arms, the Roman looks up into the face of his attractive slave. He then calls for his robe and while Antoninus dresses him, he confides that he is a person whose 'taste includes both snails and oysters'.

men was never directly addressed. Charles Laughton as Nero in *Sign of the Cross* (1932), a pre-Code film, has a very attractive, scantily clad boy as his attendant, but the precise relationship between the emperor and his slave is left entirely unspoken.

It was not that ancient homosexuality was an unknown topic. From the fin-de-siècle onwards, Greek homosexuality was an 'open secret'. Numerous early homosexual activists at the beginning of the twentieth century had advocated homosexual rights based on the acceptance that Greece had tolerated male-to-male love. Even those opposed to homosexual emancipation were fully cognisant of its prevalence in the ancient world. Indeed, it was one of the sources of anxiety about the promotion of the ancient world in the modern era. Popular novelists such as Marguerite Yourcenar (1903-1987) in her international bestseller, *Mémoires d'Hadrien* (1951, translated as *Memoirs of Hadrian* for UK publication in 1955 and US release in 1957) and Mary Renault (1905-1983) in a large number of her works repeatedly discussed ancient Greek and Roman homosexuality. Indeed, these authors expected their representations of homosexuality to resonate as contemporary desires. For example, even though Renault sets her novel *The Charioteer* (1953, released in the US in 1959) in the period of the Second World War, the homosexuality of the central characters is repeatedly discussed through allusions to the Greeks, indeed the title of the work itself is a reference to the *Phaedrus*, Plato's dialogue devoted to the topic of male love. For these novelists, it was impossible to discuss the ancient world without making reference to homosexuality; an imperative not shared by filmmakers. The most explicit representation of ancient homosexuality in Renault's work came in her trilogy of novels about the life of Alexander the Great, *Fire from Heaven* (1969), *The Persian Boy* (1972), and *Funeral Games* (1981). This latter collection of novels subsequently proved very influential on Oliver Stone as he prepared his film, *Alexander* (2004). Alexander's relationship with his companion Hephaes-

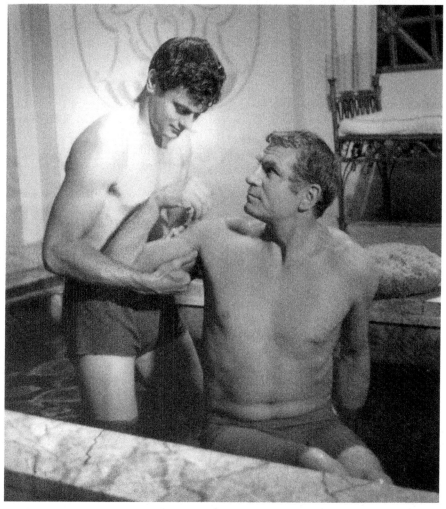

9. A scene too scandalous to show. Crassus and Antoninus, *Spartacus* (1960).

tion in the film was a direct result of Renault's popularising of Alexander's bisexuality.

Stone's depiction of Alexander's homosexuality created a scandal when the film was released. Yet in many ways, the scene from *Spartacus* is even more trailblazing. Not only was it produced (although not shown) so much earlier, but the scene treats the topic of ancient homosexuality with more subtlety and sophistication than Stone's depiction. In many ways, the scene in *Spartacus* presages contemporary thinking about male homosexuality. In the last decade, scholarship on classical homosexuality has moved away from associating male homosexual practice with any notions of fixed orientation. Rather than seeing the gender of one's sexual partner as a characteristic that defines one's identity, scholars have argued that ancient sexuality was far more attuned to aesthetic and status distinction. As a result issues such as the frequency of intercourse, the manner in which intercourse took place, the economic resources involved, the social status of the parties, and the sexual positions adopted were far more important than whether one's partner was a man or a woman. One might express a preference for one gender rather than the other, but this was only a matter of taste. In such a scenario, the parallel that Crassus draws with food seems particularly apposite and recent scholars have found themselves reaching for the same metaphor. David Halperin writes when dismissing the importance of gender in ancient sexuality:

> It would never occur to us to refer a person's dietary object-choice to some innate, characterological disposition or to see in his strongly expressed and unvarying preference for white meat of chicken the symptom of a profound psychological orientation, leading us to identify him or her in contexts quite removed from that of the eating of food ... In the same way, it never occurred to pre-modern cultures to ascribe a person's sexual tastes to some positive, structural or constitutive feature of his or her personality (Halperin 1990: 26-7).

In short, sex really was a matter of oysters or snails.

It would have been easy for *Spartacus* to fall into the trap of perpetuating a rigid dichotomy of sexuality. The woman-loving Gracchus would have been a suitable foil to the cold, homosexual Crassus. Yet *Spartacus* avoids such obvious arrangements. In making Crassus oscillate in his desires between Varinia and Antoninus, the film offers a level of complexity and sophistication that does justice to the more complex sexual protocols of the ancient world.

Suggested further viewing

Spartacus (Italian title: *Spartaco* or *Il gladiatore della Tracia*, dir. Vidali, 1913)
This early cinematic treatment of the Spartacus story is based on Raffaello

Giovagnoli's historical novel *Spartaco* (1874). Giovagnoli had fought with Giuseppe Garibaldi in the Italian Wars of Independence that led to the unification of Italy in the nineteenth century and his novel reflects his nationalist politics. The same politics was shared by the director of the film, Giovanni Enrico Vidali who used the film to send a powerful political message. Although the film in its initial stages follows the historical narrative of the Spartacus revolts, the final stages of the film depart radically from the historical facts. In this film, Spartacus defeats Crassus and is welcomed into Rome where after meeting some opposition he manages to unite all the disparate factions in Roman politics and establish a new reign of peace in the land. Shot in the Italian countryside, the film displays many of the standard features of Roman epics of the period including displays of muscle and arena combat against lions.

Julius Caesar (dir. Mankiewicz, 1953)
Produced by MGM Studios, *Julius Caesar* is one of the most famous cinematic adaptations of Shakespeare's play, which itself was heavily modelled on Plutarch's *Life of Julius Caesar*. Directed by Joseph Mankiewicz, who would later direct Elizabeth Taylor and Richard Burton in the infamous production of *Cleopatra* (1963), the film has an all-star cast, including a breakthrough role for Marlon Brando who played Antony. Suspicions about Brando's style of 'method' acting and his mumbling delivery were dismissed by his performance in this role for which he was nominated for an Academy Award. The cast was particularly noticeable for its associations with the stage and Mankiewicz's cinematic technique played to their strengths. The intense focus throughout the film on the play of emotions across characters' faces reflects his confidence in his actors' talents. Prominent actors included John Gielgud (Cassius), James Mason (Brutus) and Deborah Kerr (Portia). The film received great critical acclaim upon its release and was even cited by the Italian Ministry of Education in Rome as being of 'exceptional artistic values and of great cultural interest'. It was subsequently widely distributed within the Italian school system on account of its quality and historical subject matter.

Spartacus and the Ten Gladiators (Italian title: *Gli invincibili dieci gladiatori*, dir. Nostro, 1964)
Spartacus exists not just as an historical figure, but also as the embodiment of a set of virtues. Situated firmly within the peplum genre, this film demonstrates the way in which Spartacus, like Hercules, could be used as a branding device. Like *Spartacus* (1960), this film is also interested in using the figure of Spartacus to explore repression and the struggle for liberty. However, in this case, the historical circumstances are jettisoned in favour of a romp through the standard peplum clichés of endless fight scenes and saccharine love stories. The film tells a loose version of the Spartacus story from the perspective of Rocco (the bodybuilder Dan

99

Vadis), the leader of a band of ten gladiators who are sent out by Spartacus' former owner, Senator Varro, to recapture the escaped slave. They themselves are defeated and captured by Spartacus and in the process of fighting him are won over to his cause. Returning to Varro without Spartacus, the gladiators are imprisoned for their failure. Escaping through a combination of brute strength and the help of Varro's beautiful daughter Lydia, and joining up with Spartacus they lead a rebellion of slaves against Varro's repressive rule.

5

Greek History on Screen:
The 300 Spartans (1962)

Introduction

While the output of films depicting Greek historical events is considerably smaller than films about Rome, both Greek and Roman historical films share a number of features. Like the history of Rome, we only ever see small slivers of the history of Greece in cinema. Greek historical films tend to stick to a very limited series of events and narratives, largely the Persian Wars and Alexander the Great. Just as in the case of Roman historical films, Greek historical narratives are rarely complete enough to sustain an entire film without the addition of a number of fictional elements and subplots. Yet while historical films about Greece and Rome confront similar issues, there are also a number of features unique to Greek history and culture that pose particular problems for filmmakers. The small number of Greek historical films is not simply a by-product of a lack of interest in Greek history. Less than six months after the release of *The 300 Spartans*, Rex Warner's biography of the Athenian statesman Pericles would prove to be a bestseller. Rather, there is a genre-specific problem. For various reasons, Greek history is not an easy subject for the filmmaker. An examination of these particular issues is illuminating both about the nature of Greek culture and the pressures that operate on cinema.

Historical sources are always a problem for Greek history, particularly for its earliest periods. The line between history and myth is all too easily blurred. The ancient Greeks believed that they lived in a world where fantastic creatures still existed and that the marks of heroes of the previous age remained visible in the landscape. Indeed, in the fifth century BC, a general could plausibly claim to have discovered the bones of the Athenian hero Theseus and could take them in procession through the city for all to see. As a result, standard accounts of early Greek history all too often include supernatural elements that preclude them from being used as the basis for historical films. These accounts may have been 'history' to the Greeks, but are unrecognisable as such to us.

There were, of course, sceptical rationalising movements in Greece who attempted to remove or explain away such fantastic accounts about the past. Critics, such as the fourth-century BC intellectual Euhemerus, made their reputation by debunking myths and proposing alternative accounts

101

that explained the gods and heroes as just great men who over time had mistakenly had fantastic stories attributed to them (this technique of seeking a historical core behind mythic stories is known today as 'Euhemerism'). However, no complete alternative rationalist account of early Greek history survives. Instead, we have only fragments and passing comments. The rationalist historian Thucydides, for example, observes that Agamemnon's invasion of Troy probably had more to do with politics than the abduction of Helen (1.9.1), but he fails to expand on this idea to present an alternative account of the Trojan War. So while Thucydides provides precisely the type of rationalist frame that David Benioff was looking for when producing his script for *Troy* (2004), Benioff was left to his own devices to construct a version of the Trojan story that removed all references to the intervention of the gods or the supernatural.

Even when Greek historians write accounts of contemporary events that have minimal supernatural elements, there are still problems in transforming these narratives into film. Historical films are almost always a species of epic film and as such are limited by the same commercial pressures. They need to play to large audiences in order to be successful. This creates problems when there is a necessity to present difficult and unfamiliar material. We have already seen the problems that this causes for the cinematic depiction of the complicated intrigues of the late Roman republic. The problem is intensified for Greece.

Through a combination of topography, patterns of settlement, and historical circumstances, the geo-political landscape of Greece is exceedingly complex. Ancient Greece consisted of a patchwork of small, independent city-states each with their own laws, customs, and systems of government. Even in the period of the comparatively simple bi-polar politics of the mid-to-late fifth century BC when much of the Greek world divided in allegiance to either Sparta or Athens, there are still complicating factors. City-states swap sides in allegiance, each ally seems to have a different agenda and motivation. Telling simple stories about this period is difficult. Unfamiliar names and places all too easily pile up. Audiences may have heard of Corinth, but Phocis? When the city appears in *The 300 Spartans*, tellingly the speaker has to introduce his city as 'a small state, able to field only a thousand soldiers'. This could hardly have come as a surprise to the delegates at Corinth, and is purely for the cinema audience's benefit. Despite its size, Phocis is an important city historically. It is impossible to give an historical account of the background to the start of the Peloponnesian War or the rise of Philip of Macedon, the father of Alexander the Great, without mentioning Phocis. Yet Phocis is one of many such players and there are only so many times that films can stop and explain details.

Greek history is also complicated ethically as well as politically. The classical period of Greek history, the period most familiar to mainstream cinema audiences, is dominated by the Peloponnesian War, the war between Athens and Sparta. Yet this is a conflict that doesn't lend itself to easy ethical judgments. Neither side is completely in the right or the wrong. Arguably Athens, the city with which modern democratic societies sympathise as the first democracy, comes across in a worse light in the campaign. Her belligerence was one of the principal causes of the war. The empire that she was defending was a far from admirable institution. Athens treated her allies brutally. She behaved badly during the war, massacring, for example, the citizens on the neutral island of Melos. Counter-intuitively, it is militaristic Sparta that does most for the cause of Greek freedom in this campaign.

If Greek interstate politics is ethically complicated, so too are its interpersonal politics. As has been observed before, it is striking how important the opposition between Christian and pagan proves in orientating storylines and providing character motivations for films set in antiquity. Stories set in Greece are deprived of this organising dichotomy. What motivates 'good girls' to be 'good'? As Gideon Nisbet observes, films set in Greece can never have the frisson of repressed sexual desire that we find in Roman films: 'If *he* is pagan and likes girls, and if *she* is pagan and likes boys, why don't they spend the whole movie in bed?' (Nisbet 2006: 23). When Ellas tells Phylon in *The 300 Spartans* that they must resist their love and 'be strong', the audience is perfectly entitled to ask, as Phylon does, 'why?'. Her request to Phylon in reply that he remember that 'once the rain has fallen, nothing can put it back into the sky' seems extraordinarily coy and anachronistic. Furthermore, as Nisbet's statement implies, there are other considerations that apply particularly in Greece. Our pagan boy may also fancy other boys.

In the discussion of *Spartacus*, we raised the issue of homosexuality in Rome. The problem is only compounded in Greece whose reputation for homosexuality was such that even the Romans used the term 'Greek love' to refer to pederasty. Even if a film decides to ignore the issue, widespread knowledge about Greek homosexuality ensures that every sign of male intimacy and friendship is potentially miscoded. For example, *300* (2007) represses almost all references to the institutionalised homosexual relationships that existed between older and younger Spartans. However, that didn't stop many critics from seeing something deeply homoerotic in its endless displays of buff male Spartan bodies. As Todd McCarthy put it in his review of *300*, 'nowhere outside of gay porn have so many broad shoulders, bulging biceps and ripped torsos been seen onscreen as in *300*' (*Variety* 9/3/2007). This latent homosexuality was ruthlessly exploited by the *300* parody, *Meet the Spartans* (2008) where the closeted homosexuality of the Spartan king Leonidas operates as a running joke throughout the film.

Having seen the pitfalls, it is worth observing what films do with Greek history to tell their story. One obvious technique is to avoid too much historical detail or complexity. *The Giant of Marathon* (Italian title: *La battaglia di Maratona*, 1959) provides an extreme example. Arguably calling this film 'historical' is a travesty of the term. *The Giant of Marathon* presents a version of the story of the battle of Marathon as refracted through the lens of peplum cinema. Steve Reeves (*Hercules, Hercules Unchained, Dual of the Titans*, etc.) plays the Olympic athlete and leader of the Athenian Sacred Guard, Philippides, whilst opposite him playing his love interest, Andromeda, is Mylène Demongeot (*Romulus and the Sabines*). The historical errors in the film are legion. The Persian fleet were not equipped with ships with giant mechanical jaws, the Sacred Guard which Reeves supposedly commands is a fiction, Athens was never betrayed by a traitor called Theocritus. Such a list could be extended endlessly. Yet despite this, the key narrative arc of the battle of Marathon is retained. The film captures well the political situation of Athens at the time. Her nervousness about the possible overthrow of democracy by the Persians and the reinstatement of the deposed tyrant Hippias rings true. The famous runs between Sparta and Athens and between the Marathon plain and the Athenian city centre are included. The film cleverly exploits the little discussed Persian fleet's attempted attack on Athens following the Persian defeat at Marathon, turning this minor historical event into an underwater battle spectacular. Even the name Philippides is not without authority. Most accounts give the name of the Marathon runner as Pheidippides, but the film follows Herodotus in its naming of the hero.

Jettisoning inconvenient history and replacing it with cinematic clichés is one option. Quasi-historical films such as *Damon and Pythias* (1962) and even more *Colossus of Rhodes* (1961) belong to this tradition. Another technique is to avoid telling any grand political story and focus instead on the personal. In this, Greek history is fortunate to have a personality large enough to support an entire film, Alexander the Great. There have been two mainstream films based on the life of Alexander, Robert Rossen's *Alexander the Great* (1956) and Oliver Stone's *Alexander* (2004).

Both films have been praised for their historical accuracy. The pressbooks for Robert Rossen's *Alexander the Great* gush about the amount of research that Rossen put into his film, boasting that he 'painstakingly read through all those ancient writers who speak of Alexander'. We should expect such claims from pressbooks, but they have been followed by critics, with the film having been described as 'one of the most historically faithful of all movies about the ancient world' (Solomon 2001: 42). Similar claims were made about Stone's *Alexander* (2004); in this case perhaps with even more reason. Stone had the benefit of a number of historical advisors, most notably the leading Greek historian, Robin Lane Fox as well as academic advice from Fiona Greenland and Lloyd Llewellyn-Jones. Not only is the plot for the film grounded firmly in the ancient sources, but so are most of the props, costumes, and interior and exterior scenery. Huge amounts of time, money, and research were expended to ensure that every detail was as accurate as possible.

Intriguingly neither film is regarded as a great success. Both suffered at the box-office and critical praise for both films is thin on the ground. Rossen's *Alexander the Great* is regarded as one of his least successful films. Stone's film received almost universally negative reviews for being tedious. Shooting the life of Alexander the Great turns out to be harder than it looks. In many ways, the problems with Alexander are emblematic of filming Greek historical stories in general. The historical accounts fit awkwardly into the cinematic frame. These are stories made for biographies or multi-volume histories, not feature-length films. Stone cut out a number of battles from his *Alexander*, but that couldn't stop one critic from grumbling 'short life, long movie' (Clark cited in Cyrino 2010: 169). The tensions between grand abstract historical narratives and engaging personal stories keep threatening to overturn the project. Compounding the problem is the alienness of the environment. It appears to be more difficult to feel at home in Greece than it is in Rome.

Background to case study

Midway through the debate about how Greece should respond to the Persian invasion, the leader of the opposition to fighting against Persia gets up and shouts 'We have no time for history now, things are different today.' In one sense, the whole aim of *The 300 Spartans* is to show the audience that he is wrong. *The 300 Spartans* saw itself as an historical account with many things to say to contemporary circumstances.

The 300 Spartans is a Cold War film and needs to be viewed in this context. In the previous chapter, we saw how deeply Hollywood was involved with the policing of Cold War rhetoric. *Spartacus* may have signalled a breakthrough in the treatment of blacklisted artists, but it didn't alter the fundamental political dynamic. Fear of the threat posed by the Soviet Bloc continued to permeate US popular culture. Tensions between the United States and Russia had been building for most of the early 1960s. Only a month after the release of *The 300 Spartans* these tensions would boil over into the Cuban missile crisis and the world faced the very real possibility of nuclear war between the two superpowers.

During this period of fear and uncertainty many were looking for historical parallels to help elucidate the fraught and confused times. *The 300 Spartans* was not alone in seeing the clash between Greece and Persia as a precursor to the conflict between Communism and Democracy. In the year before *The 300 Spartans* was released, Stringfellow Barr published *The Will of Zeus* (1961), his magisterial account of Greek history from the Archaic period until the time of Alexander. While Barr's politics were liberal (some accused him of being leftist), his account of Greek history is suspicious of all forms of totalitarian power and he is fascinated by ways to oppose the loss of freedom. Like *The 300 Spartans*, Barr saw much value for contemporary politics in the study of Greek history. 'Mr. Barr, haunted by the present world crisis and our fumbling attempts to unite rival states in a peaceful community of nations, stresses the Greek failure to unite city states into a cooperative federation', reads one review (Prescott 1961: 41). The one exception to this general rule was the Greek coalition against Persia, and Barr gives it a prominent place in his account of Greek history.

Fuelling the interest in Greek history were a number of important recent discoveries arising from archaeological investigations. One of these relevant to the Persian Wars was the announcement in June 1960 of the discovery of the so-called 'Themistocles Decree', an inscription that detailed the plans Athens made in preparation for the Persian invasion. The discovery received wide publicity on both sides of the Atlantic with large spreads devoted to it. The *New York Times* featured the inscription on its front page; whilst on the inside it published a full translation with the technical Greek terms explained in parentheses. The inscription was seen as a foundational democratic document. 'The Athenian equivalent of the United States Declaration of Independence or the Gettysburg address', declared the inscription's finder, Michael Jameson (Knox 1960: 1). Moreover, the inscription was also seen as testament to the 'foresight and genius' of Themistocles who became recognised as the mastermind behind the Athenian preparations for the Persian War. All articles on the inscription single him out for praise for his brilliant command of strategy. Ralph Richardson's portrayal of Themistocles in *The 300 Spartans* as a brilliant strategist and wily politician fits neatly with this newly enhanced view of the Athenian statesman.

The Persian Wars effortlessly lent themselves to assimilation with Cold War rhetoric. It was all too easy to transform them into the story of noble, democratic free western states forced to fight against the aggression of a massive, despotic, totalitarian, Eastern power. Only a few years before *The 300 Spartans*, Nobel Prize-winning author William Golding made a pilgrimage to Thermopylae, a journey he had been planning for over twenty years. For Golding, visiting Thermopylae was a revelation; finally he understood why the battle mattered. Thermopylae's importance arose because of its place in the long history of the fight for freedom:

> I knew now that something real happened here. It is not just that the human spirit reacts directly and beyond all argument to a story of sacrifice and courage, as a wine glass must vibrate to the sound of the violin. It is also because ... that company stood in the right line of history. A little of Leonidas lies in the fact that I can go where I like and write what I like. He contributed to set us free. ('Hot Gates' reprinted in Golding 1965: 20)

Time and again, we see conflations between modern and ancient military agendas. It is this logic, for example, that sees the British decide to name one of their naval submarines *Thermopylae*, after the ancient battle. The links did not stop with the name. The motto of the submarine 'we shall fight in the shade' (appropriate for a submarine) is a punning appropria-tion of one of the most famous Spartan quotations from Herodotus' account of the battle of Thermopylae. In the same year as the release of *The 300 Spartans* the British naval submarine *Thermopylae* established official formal links with the modern town of Thermopylae. Everywhere people were only too happy to see themselves as the heirs of Leonidas and Themistocles.

The 300 Spartans ends with the line that, 'It was more than a victory for Greece, it was a stirring example to free people throughout the world of what a few brave men can accomplish once they refuse to submit to tyranny.' The invocation of 'free people throughout the world' makes the politics of the film quite clear. This is a story for western democrats. The ideological comparisons between East and West simmer throughout the film. It is hard not to read into Themistocles' speech at the Council of Corinth an implicit comparison between Communism and Democracy:

> These men are fierce, savage, bloodthirsty, merciless. But that is not the reason why we should fear them. That is not the source of their power. Their power lies in their unity. Unity, remember that one terrible word which will surely destroy Greece unless we counter it with a unity of our own. A unity of free men fighting together, resisting this united tide of tyranny.

This opposition between two types of 'unity', one free and one tyrannically imposed from above, is clearly informed by contemporary political discus-sions about the nature of the Soviet collective. Similarly, in (in)famously recasting the Spartan phalanx in the film publicity as the 'Incredible Flying Wedge' [Fig. 10], the film gives this military formation ('the clever-est strategy in the history of warfare') much more of the feel of the contemporary US/Soviet arms race where each side sought a decisive technological advantage over the other.

The ideology of the film may have been American, but its scenery was purely Greek. Filmed outside of the village of Perachora, the film benefited enormously from the assistance of the Greek government. Not only did it help in obtaining the location for filming, but the Greek army happily provided numerous extras to play the roles of Spartans and Persians. The use of location shots is most effectively shown in the montage of Spartans marching through Greece to Thermopylae. Over the course of a couple of minutes, the audience is treated to a variety of evocative Greek land-scapes. As Phylon and Ellas struggle to keep up with the army, we learn that Greece is a hard and unforgiving environment; at least that is one way of reading the rather comic inability of the Spartan pipers to keep their footing on the stony ground. Critics singled out the scenery for especial praise in their reviews. For many, it was the only thing worth-while about the film.

Certainly, the acting and script are rarely praised. The *Times*' critic was

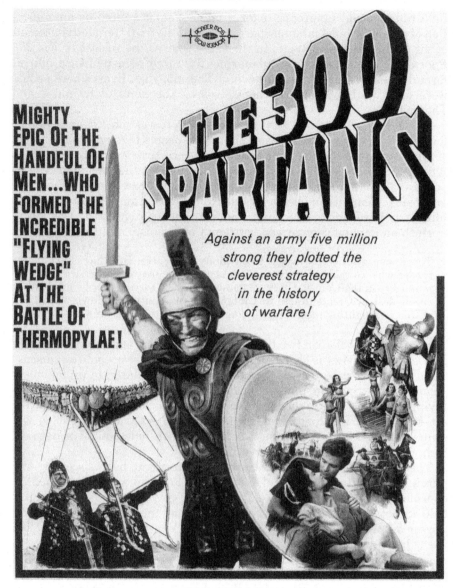

10. Beware 'the Flying Wedge'! Advertisement, *The 300 Spartans* (1962)

particularly virulent in his condemnation of the film. The film's dialogue was 'pathetic' and 'Richard Egan gives an acceptable account of an eager American soldier, whose name happens to be Leonidas'. 'It is shallow stuff, no more memorable than a weather report dated 480 BC', remarked the *New York Times*. Only Ralph Richardson (Themistocles) seems to have garnered any praise for his performance, but even here the praise is often back-handed. 'Actor's skill can't save "Spartans"' reads the headline for one review (*Chicago Daily Tribune* 12/9/1962: B6). Richardson's training as a classical stage actor made him suited to the role. He had first come to attention as Mark Antony in Shakespeare's *Julius Caesar* and he brought the same rhetorical stage presence to his performance as the Athenian orator.

After a short period in 'first run' cinemas, the film quickly moved to drive-ins where it was routinely paired in a double-feature with the Elvis Presley boxing film *Kid Galahad* (1962). The films make an interesting combination. Each in their own way eulogises the plain simple life and the necessity of fighting to achieve it. In *Kid Galahad*, Presley plays the role of a small-town mechanic who takes up boxing as a way of earning money and respect so that he can marry his sweetheart Dolly. Opposed by gangsters, he fights his way to achieving his dreams and his girl.

The 300 Spartans may have died in the cinema, but one feature that kept it alive in the public mind was its tie-in marketing. Two popular spin-offs of the film were a novelisation by John Burke entitled *The Lion of Sparta*, (which was the original title of the film script; in the US, the novel was also released under the film title *The 300 Spartans*), and a comic book version of the film produced by Dell Comics.

While the comic book follows the film quite closely, Burke's novel presents a much more complex story than the one presented in *The 300 Spartans*. Released in the run-up to the release of the film, *The Lion of Sparta* brings out the militarism and brutality of Spartan society. When Phylon (in the novel he is called Teucer) considers committing suicide, he encounters a couple about to cast their infant child over the cliff because the Spartan Council have judged it too sickly. This prompts him to rant against the nature of Spartan society and ultimately convince the parents to leave Sparta and seek a better life outside its territory. Such explicit criticism of the Spartan way is something we never see in the film. The novel is also more explicit about Spartan pederasty. Borrowing terminology from Plato about the heavenly love of men for men, the narrator of the novel, the seer Megistheus, describes the youth of Phylon: 'when he was a boy there had been many men who had loved him with the love which we held higher than the love of a man for a woman. I had been one of those who had admired from a distance – an ageing man myself, stricken by his youthful perfection, yet knowing even then that he was destined for the love of woman' (Burke 1961: 6). In bringing out these depths and complexities, Burke's novel doesn't so much whet the appetite for *The 300 Spartans*, rather it shows up the film's deficiencies.

Plot summary

As the introductory voice-over declaims, this film tells the story of 'a turning point in history, of a blazing day when three hundred Greek warriors fought here to hold, with their lives, their freedom and ours'.

The story begins with the massed forces of Xerxes entering Greece. Xerxes (David Farrar) is shown upon his throne reminiscing about his father's defeat at the battle of Marathon and swearing to avenge Persia for this loss. As Xerxes promises to fulfil Darius' dream of 'one world, one master', a Spartan spy, Agathon (John Crawford) is brought before the king. After initially sentencing the spy to death, Xerxes decides it is better to release him so that he can bring word of the size of Xerxes' army to the Greeks and so dissuade them from further resistance.

As he leaves the camp, Agathon encounters the Spartan Grellas (George Moutsios) who has accompanied the exiled Spartan king Demaratus to Greece in the company of Xerxes. Grellas asks Agathon to take a greeting to his son Phylon (Barry Coe) who still resides in Sparta. Agathon angrily rebukes Grellas for consorting with the enemy and strikes him with his whip.

Meanwhile in Corinth, the Greeks debate how best to meet the threat of Xerxes' invasion. Some states such as Corinth favour collaboration, whilst others such as Athens, led by their statesman Themistocles (Ralph Richardson), propose opposition to the invading army. The matter is decided when Sparta, represented by king Leonidas (Richard Egan), declares its support for Athens. Together a coalition of Greeks led by Sparta will oppose the Persian forces. Poring over a map of Greece, Leonidas and Themistocles plan to halt the Persian advance at Thermopylae.

Meanwhile in Sparta, the young Phylon has fallen in love with the young Ellas (Diane Baker). Together they meet on the hills above Sparta and discuss the upcoming war. Phylon proposes that he approach Leonidas to grant consent in his father's absence for him to marry Ellas. He is unaware that his father is currently seeking sanctuary in the camp of Xerxes.

Not all of Sparta agrees with Leonidas' plan to send Spartan soldiers beyond Corinth. Opposition comes from members of the Spartan Council led by a councillor called Xenaphon who lost his two sons in a battle with Athens. He is consequently blinded by hatred, and opposes an expedition to Thermopylae, which he argues only assists the safety of Athens not Sparta. Advice is sought from the Delphic Oracle, which reports that Sparta will be saved, but only at the loss of one of its two kings. This causes unease amongst the Spartan Council and they are reluctant to let the Spartan army march out against the Persians, especially as this expedition would violate the rules of the Carneia festival. Leonidas, knowing that if Sparta doesn't march it will be impossible to rouse the other Greeks against Persia, commands his personal bodyguard of three hundred men who are not bound by the rulings of the Council to assemble and to prepare to leave for Thermopylae. Leonidas storms out of the Council meeting warning the Spartans not to delay in sending more troops to support his expedition to Thermopylae.

Before Leonidas leaves for Thermopylae, Phylon asks Leonidas' permission to marry Ellas. Leonidas reveals that Agathon has informed him that Grellas is consorting with the enemy and refuses to grant consent to the marriage. In addition, he forbids Phylon from accompanying him and his men to Thermopylae.

Distraught at the news of his father's treachery as well as the loss of his chance to marry Ellas and his deprivation of a place in Leonidas' body-guard, Phylon climbs up the Taygetus mountains with the intention of committing suicide by throwing himself off a cliff. However, he is pre-vented from this act by Ellas who suggests instead that they follow the Spartan army to Thermopylae in the hope of persuading Leonidas to change his mind. Phylon is convinced and together he and Ellas travel to Thermopylae.

On arriving at Thermopylae, the Spartan forces fortify the pass and prepare to repel the Persians. The Persians are caught out by the Spartan military prowess. Xerxes' brother is killed in a skirmish and then, while Xerxes musters his forces for a counter-attack, the Spartans stage a daring night attack burning his tent to the ground.

While these battles occur, Phylon and Ellas have sought shelter with a nearby shepherd and his wife who have a hut by the pass. They live their life alone with only the brooding Ephialtes (Kieron Moore) for company. Phylon sneaks into the Spartan camp and joins the Spartans on their night attack against Xerxes' tent. In the course of events, he risks his life to save another Spartan. Leonidas is impressed by Phylon's bravery and welcomes him back into the Spartan army. The Spartan who Phylon saves turns out to be Ellas' father.

Xerxes reassembles his troops and charges towards Thermopylae. Time and again he is beaten back by superior Spartan strategy and bravery. Thousands of the best Persian soldiers are killed by Leonidas and his men.

In the hills, Ellas continues to live with the shepherd family. Ephialtes has fallen in love with Ellas and approaches her whilst she fetches water. However, he is rebuffed by Ellas and in his anger, he decides to punish her and her lover Phylon by revealing to Xerxes that there is a goat path that will allow the Persian forces to by-pass Thermopylae and encircle the Greek forces.

Word arrives from Sparta that no Spartan army is coming to relieve them. Grellas appears in the Spartan camp to inform them that Xerxes will soon have the Greeks surrounded. Leonidas prepares for a final confrontation with the Persians. He knows that he will in all likelihood be destroyed, but he also knows that if he can hold them off for long enough it will give the Greeks time to escape. Leonidas sends Phylon and Ellas to carry word to the other Greek forces. Phylon initially prefers to face death against the Persians, but Leonidas orders him and he reluctantly obeys. Leonidas is keen that word of his actions be carried to Sparta because he knows that his death will rouse the Spartans to fight for Greek freedom.

Surrounded by the Persians, the Spartans prepare for their final battle.

In the fighting Leonidas is killed. Xerxes stops the battle and declares that he shall spare the remaining Spartans if they will hand over the body of Leonidas. The Spartans refuse and Xerxes has them all slaughtered by his archers. The film ends with a shot hovering over the body of Leonidas while a voice-over praises the Spartan bravery and recounts how it was instrumental in inspiring the Greeks to their eventual victory over the Persians at Salamis and Plataea.

Key scenes and themes

The nature of Sparta

The society of ancient Sparta occupies a privileged place in western culture. Famous for its martial valour and praised for the simplicity of its lifestyle, many have found it inspirational, an ideal community whose form and values they would like to recreate in their own time. *The 300 Spartans* continues this tradition of imaginings about Sparta, both perpetuating received notions of Spartan life and challenging certain assumptions about how Sparta operated.

'With this or on this'

We see a group of young men in tunics marching in loose military formation through the street. Crowds of onlookers cheer them on, while martial flute music plays in the background. These youths are the next generation of Spartan soldiers and today they become men, taking their final oaths and receiving their precious shields and red cloaks. The scene cuts to Phylon standing before the men and women of Sparta.

In front of him stands Queen Gorgo who instructs him in the laws that govern the life of a Spartan warrior: 'You must treasure freedom above life, shun pleasure for the sake of virtue, endure pain and hardship in silence, obey orders implicitly, seek the enemies of Greece and fight them fearlessly until victory or death.' She then hands him his shield, reciting as she does so 'E tan e epi tas' [Fig. 11]. Ellas, who has been watching the ceremony, explains to one of the onlookers the meaning of the phrase: 'With this or on this. Either come home victorious with this shield or dead on it.' The ceremony completed, Ellas rushes forward to congratulate Phylon on becoming a full-fledged Spartan warrior.

If we are to believe the standard accounts, the life of a male Spartan citizen was a strange, complicated business. Separated from their families at the age of seven, Spartan boys lived in all-male bands until the age of thirty. For the first thirteen years of this period, they were regularly beaten and physically challenged. It was a system of education that was designed to induce qualities of hardness, obedience, and martial prowess. The only clothing Spartan boys received was a single red cloak a year. Their bedding consisted of reeds that they pulled out of the riverbank by

11. An education in Spartan duty. Gorgo and Phylon, *The 300 Spartans* (1962)

hand. At the age of twenty they applied for admission to communal messes. Admission to the messes was for life and this institution became the social centre of the Spartan citizen's existence. It was only at the age of thirty that Spartans could leave their barracks to marry and set up a household. Indeed, for the first weeks of marriage, a husband was not supposed to officially leave his mess, but would slip away in secret to be with his wife. Given such peculiarities, strategies of representation are difficult. How is it possible to capture such a life story? How can one indicate the character of such men? It is a problem that confronts not only filmmakers, but artists, writers, and historians as well. Telling the story in its entirety is difficult, particularly if you want to retain sympathy for the Spartan state as *The 300 Spartans* so crucially needs to do.

One popular method has been to reduce Spartan culture to a series of well-known stories or sayings. These hint at the brutality, but spare you the gritty details, giving you instead a memorable story or image. In this way, Sparta lives as a series of anecdotes. So, for example, children's books teach Spartan resilience through reciting the celebrated story of the boy who stole a fox and hid it under his cloak. Even though the fox started gnawing at his stomach, he endured the terrible pain rather than be caught stealing. Only when he dropped dead was the crime discovered. Such emblematic stories permit us to glimpse the key set of Spartan values that Gorgo rehearses above in her speech to Phylon – willingness to suffer in silence, obedience to the laws, indifference to luxury, and bravery in the face of insurmountable odds.

The film displays admirable commitment to such material. It repeats a number of the most familiar Spartan sayings known from classical literature. For example, when the Persians declare that their 'arrows will blot out the sun', Leonidas delivers the famous retort that in that case 'we fight in the shade'. The interchange repeats almost word-for-word the exchange given in Herodotus (7.226) between the Spartan Dienekes and a soldier from Trachis who warned him about the number of Persian archers that he faced. Similarly, the film ends with Simonides' famous epitaph for the Spartans killed at Thermopylae which was erected, according to Herodotus, on the spot where the last Spartans fell: 'O Stranger tell the Spartans that we lie here obedient to their word' (Herodotus, *Histories* 7.228). Remarkably these sayings are twice given in the original classical Greek (with modern Greek pronunciation). The first, 'With this or on this', is given in the scene described in the box above. The second is 'molon labe' ('come and take them') and constitutes Leonidas' reply to Xerxes' emissary's request that the Spartans surrender and hand over their weapons to the Persians (Plutarch, *Sayings of the Spartans* 51.11).

The decision to give the phrases in Greek has a curious effect. On the one hand, it disrupts the audience's ability to suspend disbelief and reminds us that we are watching drama, not events as they really happened. This is underscored when the woman asks for the Greek to be translated. The translation can't be for her benefit. After all, the conceit of the film is that as a Spartan woman she should be fluent in Greek. How can a Greek not understand Greek? When Ellas explains the phrase to her, she is really explaining it, not particularly subtly, to us, the audience. At the same time, for all the problems that the shift to Greek causes in continuity, it also serves to elevate the sentiments expressed. Wrapped in their original tongue, these Spartan sayings take on an added air of authenticity. They are like magical, semi-divine incantations, true nuggets of the Spartan ethos. We are drinking straight from the source of Spartan mythology.

However, there are limits to the way in which the film will blindly follow the standard script for eulogising Sparta. Gorgo may praise the Spartan constitution, but the film ultimately tells a different story and, in doing so, departs from a strong tradition running through western thought about the superiority of Spartan governance. Moreover, in questioning the nature of rule in Sparta, the film involves itself in wider questions about the Greeks and the rectitude of their commitment to free speech and debate.

From antiquity onwards, political theorists were fascinated by the strange form of government that Sparta enjoyed. Ruled by two kings, the constitution, like the Roman republican constitution, seemed to combine elements of monarchy, democracy, and oligarchy into a 'mixed constitution'. The most famous proponent in antiquity of the 'mixed constitution' was the second-century BC writer Polybius and ever since then there have been numerous advocates for the adoption of such a constitution. Wherever one goes, whether it is Renaissance Florence, Revolutionary France or America, unified Germany, or reformist England, it is always possible to find passionate believers in the Spartan form of government.

What is striking about the depiction of the Spartan government in *The 300 Spartans* is the way in which it departs from the generally positive depiction of the Spartan constitution. Representations of Sparta in the twentieth century, particularly cinematic representations, rejected the trend that one should look to Sparta to see how affairs should be ordered. Any confidence in Spartan governance falls apart in this film.

The problems with the system of dual kingship are exposed from the beginning of the film. Rather than providing an opportunity for one ruler to lead in battle and another to look after affairs at home, it is shown that the dual system promotes division and treachery. As Agathon leaves the Persian camp, he encounters Grellas and so we learn of the exiled Spartan king Demaratus and his retinue of exiled Spartans serving with Xerxes. We then cut to the inside of Xerxes' tent where Demaratus sits next to Xerxes sharing his food. Demaratus alludes to the story of his deposition from the kingship in Sparta when his rival king Cleomenes – alleging that Demaratus was not a legitimate son of a Spartan king – installed Demaratus' relative Leotychidas on the Spartan throne in his stead. Demaratus is light on the details of this sequence of events, but his passion and anger are clear. Being king of Sparta is clearly not a safe occupation. Moreover, this system which sent Demaratus into exile has, in doing so, given Xerxes a valuable tool in his conquest of Sparta. Demaratus will make a perfect puppet ruler for the Persian king.

Similarly, the Spartan Council are shown to be weak and foolish. They fail to see the big picture. Their excessive love of Sparta makes them unable to see their duty to wider Greece. They blindly follow tradition, superstitiously refusing to allow troops to move during a Spartan religious festival. The system of checks and balances, through which the dictatorial authority of the king was minimised, rather than producing the best outcome, instead leads to tragedy and the needless loss of life of the 300 Spartans. Instead of being the best form of government, the events surrounding the deployment of troops at Thermopylae show it to be the worst.

This motif of the Spartan government as a failed system proves to be an enduring one. It is picked up later in *300* (2007). Here the criticisms become even more extreme. In *The 300 Spartans* Leonidas criticises Xenaphon, his opponent in the Council, for growing so bitter with hatred over the death of his sons that he has become a danger to the State. His words are true, but Gorgo declares that Xenaphon's behaviour is understandable, possibly even forgivable. 'Dead children are not easy to forget, Leonidas', she reminds him. In *300*, there can be no forgiveness for the politicians of Sparta, in particular its chief magistrates, the ephors. They are shown as inbred degenerates driven by lust, greed, and envy. There is no good in them. They, and other leading politicians, sell out their king for a bag of Persian gold.

Oddly, in a film devoted to the concept of freedom, the plot seems to support the idea that the best form of government is benign kingship. If only Leonidas had been allowed to make all the decisions, then tragedy could have been averted and the Persians defeated all the more quickly. It was consultation and voting that proved his undoing. Indeed, the film is ambivalent about all democratic processes.

The Council of the Greeks at Corinth is shown to be far from perfect. 'People arguing while their house burns' is how Leonidas describes the Council. Xerxes tells Artemisia that his greatest chance of success lies with Greeks failing to unify. The scene then cuts to Corinth and we see a speaker offering precisely the type of advice that we know will lead to Persian success and the destruction of the Greeks. When the speaker makes his disastrous suggestion that each state should negotiate with Persia independently, his comments are not derided, but warmly received by the assembled delegates. Themistocles makes an impassioned speech in favour of unity, but he is almost undone by a rival speaker who asks him about an unfavourable oracle from Delphi. At the end of the meeting, the Council agrees to unite, but, as Themistocles remarks to Leonidas, it was a close run thing. 'I wouldn't care to go through an ordeal like that again', he sighs. So much for Greek democracy in action. It seems that it is only when kings and wily politicians combine to subvert the process that the correct decision is ensured.

This ambivalence about democracy sits alongside numerous examples of fine rhetoric devoted to the concept of freedom. The situation is all the more paradoxical given the amount of effort that the film expends in making Sparta a suitable vehicle for promoting a free and just society. In this film, Sparta is made over in the image of the modern liberal state. Indeed, at certain points, the film seems to be in denial that it is showing a story about Sparta at all. The first few minutes of the film as the title credits roll show us nothing of Sparta. It is only Athens, cradle of democracy, that we see as images of the Acropolis blend into an interior shot of the Parthenon. Thucydides once predicted that the impressive ruins of Athens would ensure that she always had precedence over Sparta in our collective memory, and the credits seem to show that he was right.

This re-making of Sparta can be seen in the depiction of how Leonidas conducts Spartan foreign policy. 'Sparta will fight whether others will follow or not', declares Leonidas. This brave piece of rhetoric which envisages a Sparta running the risk of facing the might of Persia alone flies completely in the face of the historical reality of the situation. Sparta did not need to convince other states to fight with words or acts of bravery. It could demand that its allies fight for her, and it was impossible for them to refuse her.

116

5. Greek History on Screen: The 300 Spartans (1962)

In *The 300 Spartans*, the Council of the Greeks is clearly modelled on the United Nations where sovereign nations meet to discuss and resolve important issues and pressing problems. Debate, not coercion is the order of the day. Each city-state is depicted as being free to make up its own mind about its relations with Persia. It is an attractive idea, but such freedom was certainly lacking in the fifth-century Peloponnese. While some states such as Argos were free to come to their own arrangements with Persia, it is the exception. The vast majority of states in the Peloponnese, including large states such as Corinth, were bound by treaties that obliged them to follow Sparta into battle, if she chose to enter the war.

Sparta dominated the Peloponnese as the leader of a large coalition of states, the so-called 'Peloponnesian League'. Its position was secured through a series of binding bilateral treaty obligations between Sparta and her allies, and one of the key clauses in these treaties was that Sparta and her allies 'have the same friends and enemies'. Effectively, this meant that should Sparta declare war then her allies were obliged to follow her. Sometimes they did so a little reluctantly, but in almost all cases once the call to arms was made then the member states of the Peloponnesian League provided contingents of men or ships to fight. Throughout *The 300 Spartans*, we hear constant references to Sparta providing inspiration to other states to oppose Persia, but the film is entirely silent on the fact that Sparta can command dozens of city states to fight the Persian invasion.

The reason why such political niceties are forgotten is obvious. Recognition of Spartan control of the Peloponnese threatens to blur the clear distinction between the free Greeks and the imperialist Persians. There is only room for one power that can threaten and pressgang subject states to war, and that is Persia.

If the omission of the Peloponnesian League is odd, the absence of the helots is even more striking. Ancient Spartan wealth and power was secured by its control over the huge conquered populations of nearby Messenia. Occupying a position between a slave and a serf, this oppressed population enjoyed few rights. Their lands were owned by Spartan masters and their produce was tithed to provide sustenance to the Spartan messes. The helots were treated as spoils of war. Each year the Spartans symbolically would declare war on the helots as a way of reaffirming their status as booty, chattels for their Spartan overlords. Literature about Sparta preserves numerous accounts of the brutal treatment meted out to helots. One story recounts how helots would be forced to get drunk by Spartans. The ensuing foolish drunken antics of the helot provided physical proof of their inferiority and a lesson reminding Spartans of the dangers of drink. Another tells how Spartan youths would be sent out to the fields to terrorise the helots, murdering any helot that they managed to capture outside at night.

Helots performed numerous household duties and even accompanied Spartans on campaign, performing the menial tasks that an army on the

117

march requires (feeding animals, carrying equipment, etc.). They should be ever present in our story, yet we never see a single one. All we see are what are euphemistically called 'servants'. The ugly face of Spartan power is hidden from the viewer. It is the equivalent of filming the *Gone with the Wind* story, but excising all reference to slaves. It's a fantasy, less troubling in many ways, but undeniably false.

Gorgo and the search for women

One of the problems that makers of Greek historical epics face is the absence of women from our sources. Even the under-represented women of Roman history seem plentiful compared to their Greek counterparts. This absence creates a problem because it potentially limits the range of stories that can be told within the narrative arc of the film. Filmmakers are faced with the choice of either perpetuating the gender bias of ancient accounts and limiting their accounts to just the deeds of men or violating their commitment to historical accuracy and inventing female characters. It has the potential to derail any opportunity for romance, as well as alienating a large section of the viewing audience. To this end, filmmakers have either invented female characters and plots (such as the love affair of Phylon and Ellas) or constructed rounded female characters from our fragmentary sources as they do with the figures of Artemisia and Gorgo.

Gorgo's code

The scene begins with a close-up shot of a boiling pool of water. It is one of the hot springs from which Thermopylae (lit. 'the hot gates') takes its name. From out of the pool emerges a wax tablet stuck on the end of a sword. The camera pans up to reveal Leonidas who proceeds to scrape the now soft wax from the tablet. Underneath the wax is revealed a message from Queen Gorgo. In order to prevent the message from being intercepted, she has cleverly hidden the message underneath the tablet's wax surface. To the casual enquirer, it would have looked like a blank wax tablet. 'My wife is a very clever woman', declares Leonidas.

In the figure of Gorgo, the wife of Leonidas, filmmakers were lucky to have one of the few female figures for whom we have a reasonable body of evidence. Sparta traditionally allowed its women more freedom than Athens. Indeed, the Spartan attitude towards women often scandalised the more repressive Athens. Yet despite this, we know little about individual women. The one exception is Gorgo. We first encounter her in our records as a young child of eight or nine in the court of her father, King Cleomenes of Sparta. Herodotus records that when Aristagoras was trying to persuade Cleomenes to assist him in his revolt against Persia – a revolt that would eventually precipitate the Persian Wars – he approached the king in Cleomenes' house as a suppliant (Herodotus, *Histories* 5.51).

Noticing that Gorgo was standing in the room, Aristagoras asked that she be excused so that he could outline his plan. Cleomenes refused to dismiss his daughter from such discussion and bade Aristagoras to continue with his entreaty. Aristagoras proceeded then to attempt to bribe the king. First by offering ten talents, and ever increasing the amount until he reached fifty talents. At this Gorgo could take it no more and cried out to her father: 'Father, this stranger will destroy you if you don't leave him'. Cleomenes, pleased with his daughter's response, took her advice and left. Thanks to Gorgo's intervention, Aristagoras left without Spartan help and Sparta avoided a costly and doomed military expedition.

The next time that we hear of her in Herodotus' account, she is married to Leonidas. Indeed, according to Herodotus, it was Leonidas' marriage to Gorgo that helped secure him the Spartan kingship. Leonidas had not been predicted to succeed to the Spartan throne. He had two older half-brothers, Cleomenes (the father of Gorgo) and Dorieus. Indeed, had Cleomenes been less ambitious and less prone to political intrigue then Leonidas would never have succeeded to the Spartan throne. However, when his plots against Demaratus were exposed, Cleomenes found himself impeached, an event which contributed to disturbing his mind and set off the sequence of events that led to his eventual suicide. Even then Leonidas would not have gained the throne had not his brother Dorieus been killed in Sicily. This left a spot open to either Leonidas or another relative Cleombrotus. According to Herodotus, the Spartans chose Leonidas because of his age and his marriage to Gorgo.

Herodotus' account makes Gorgo a key player in games of Spartan politics. She comes across as a shrewd advisor and a wise counselor, and this impression clearly forms part of the ancient tradition about her. For example, Plutarch attributes a number of smart and pithy statements to her in his *Sayings of Spartan Women* (*Moralia* 240 d-e). The scene involving the wax tablet is based on an anecdote preserved in Herodotus' account, which is designed to demonstrate the cleverness of the queen. According to Herodotus, Demaratus, although exiled in Persia, was not enamoured of the Persian plans to invade Greece and so sent word to Sparta to warn them of the king's plans. To avoid detection, he inscribed the message into the wood of a writing tablet and then covered the message in wax so that the tablet looked like a blank slate. This he entrusted to a messenger to take to Sparta, but while he entrusted the object to the messenger, he did not reveal the secret of the hidden message, lest the messenger be captured on his journey and the message discovered. Thus, the Spartans were initially confused by receiving a blank slate. It was only Gorgo who guessed the ingenious method that Demaratus had used and was able to reveal his warning to Sparta.

The film clearly knows about this tradition of a capable Gorgo, one able to meddle in the politics of the State. Yet apart from this moment involving the secret message to Leonidas, we almost never see it in the film. In this

119

respect, the passionate, eloquent, politically-engaged Gorgo of Zack Snyder's *300* (2007) is closer in spirit to the Gorgo of our ancient sources. The only time we see Gorgo taking charge in *The 300 Spartans* appears to be the scene discussed above where Phylon takes his Spartan oath of allegiance. Yet, at the very end of the scene, Gorgo's position is undercut. She is only inducting Phylon into the Spartan citizenry because his mother is dead. Normally, it would be his mother that would be performing the ceremony. Gorgo is acting as surrogate mother, not queen.

This idea of the domesticated, motherly Gorgo dominates in the film. Her character is trapped by the conventions of genre. Leonidas talks about politics, she talks about children. As we have seen many times before, films set in the ancient world operate with a reasonably rigid gender dichotomy. It is hard to be a 'good girl' and a player in the narrative. In order to be virtuous, one needs to sit on the sidelines. Her passivity is signalled in the prophecy that she receives from the Spartan seer Megistheus:

> He sacrificed a lamb and read the entrails. He said that there was wonderful good fortune for both of us. He said that you will be the Spartan King best remembered amongst men and he said that for centuries to come women will sing songs about my love for you.

The message of the prophecy is clear. Leonidas is the doer of deeds. Gorgo's role is to stand by adoring him.

It is the bad girls that get to play a part in the action. In *The 300 Spartans*, this role is fulfilled by Queen Artemisia of Halicarnassus. In Herodotus' account of the Persian War she enjoys a prominent role, possibly because Herodotus was also a native of Halicarnassus. Courageous and clever, she proved to be one of the best tactical naval commanders on the Persian side. She alone advised Xerxes not to engage the Greek fleet at the battle of Salamis. Xerxes ignores her advice and loses the war. During the battle of Salamis itself, she alone amongst the Persians distinguishes herself. This leaves Xerxes to famously declare that my 'men have become women, and my women, men'.

The first time we see her in *The 300 Spartans*, the film presents her as a force to be reckoned with. She strides confidently into Xerxes' tent boasting about the arrival of her ships. When Xerxes expresses surprise at seeing her, she exclaims, 'If my men fight, I want to be with them. That's the least that a queen can do for her subjects'. It is a sentiment that shows up Gorgo who seems content to send her man off to war while she keeps the home fires burning. Artemisia then proceeds to best Demaratus in a verbal joust. Only seconds before she arrived the Spartan king had been demonstrating his lethal fighting skills. Now he is unmanned by the queen's quick wit and scampers off to a corner of the tent to lick his wounds. 'A woman's tongue is far deadlier than the sword!' exclaims

Xerxes. The scene ends with Artemisia seductively arranging a date with Xerxes.

However, even with all this splendid initial character development, Artemisia is still very much sidelined in this film. Her personality is established, but we only really see her in one more scene where she lies still, being ravished by Xerxes while unbeknown to him the Spartans are sacking his camp. It is hard not to see her as a wasted opportunity. The film could have done much more with her. Yet, perhaps such criticism is misguided. The story of Thermopylae remains at its core a story about men, and *The 300 Spartans* knows this. On this level it succeeds. Critics have debated which is the 'manliest film' of all time. Intriguingly at least one critic is prepared to list *The 300 Spartans* as their most manly movie. Others disagree. For example, Todd and Brant von Hoffman (the authors of *The von Hoffmann Bros.' Big Damn Book of Sheer Manliness*) think that the most manly film is *Spartacus*. Such discussions are, of course, ridiculous. Yet they point to a truth worth commenting upon; namely that whatever we think of *The 300 Spartans*, its gender politics are deeply problematic.

Whose history counts?

Historical epics pose a number of unique problems for filmmakers. One of the many elements that they need to consider is the problem of conflicting historical sources. Even where there is a seemingly dominant tradition, our sources for events and people are almost never univocal. The filmmaker therefore faces a problem similar to the historian in the need to patch together and reconcile conflicting accounts to construct a narrative of events.

The account of a night raid on Xerxes' tent [see box: 'The night expedition'] is unknown from Herodotus' account. Yet one does make an appearance in our extant sources in Diodorus Siculus' account written in the final half of the first century BC. In his account, Diodorus takes Ephialtes' betrayal of the trail round Thermopylae as the catalyst for the night expedition. Soon to be surrounded by the Persians, the Spartans send the other Greeks away and make a daring attack on Xerxes' encampment as a last desperate attempt to forestall their destruction at Persian hands. Diodorus even goes so far as to declare that 'if the king had remained at the royal tent, he would have been easily slain by the Greeks and the whole war would have ended almost immediately' (11.10.3). Diodorus accounts for the king's absence by his decision to leave the tent to investigate the commotion that occurred when the Greeks first invaded.

There are few academic reasons to prefer Diodorus' account as a more accurate version of events at Thermopylae. Particularly as his discussion of the night expedition soon gives way to a rather confused account of the destruction of the Greek forces in which the night expedition and Herodotus' final battle collapse into each other.

121

The night expedition

As darkness falls, we see a line of Spartan soldiers standing up to their waists in water. The scene cuts to Phylon using the cover of darkness to sneak down into the Spartan camp. He grabs a Spartan shield, cloak, and spear and surreptitiously joins the Spartans as they wade out to the opposing shore where Xerxes' camp lies. Inside the camp, the Persians are distracted by the pleasures of drink and women. Women dance seductively by the light of the campfire. They do not notice the advancing Spartan forces creeping out of the sea. The Spartans run into the camp and head for Xerxes' tent. They spear the guards and burst inside. Dancing girls scatter in fear. Leonidas seizes one of them and interrogates her about the location of Xerxes. She reveals that he is not there, but in the tent of Queen Artemisia. Deprived of their prize, the Spartans retreat, setting fire to tents as they go. The flames quickly catch hold and pandemonium erupts in Xerxes' camp. Men and women scatter, horses run loose, and a number of Persian soldiers are killed in the ensuing melee. Amidst all this chaos, we see an oblivious Xerxes caught up in the arms of Queen Artemisia. They hear the noise of the commotion outside and Artemisia goes to the doorway to investigate. A slave arrives bearing news of the flames that have seized the camp. Alarmed, Xerxes orders his boat to be made ready in case he needs to make a quick exit. We see the Spartans retreating after their successful raid. Almost everyone escapes unscathed, except for Ellas' father who is struck by an arrow. The Persians race to seize him, but are beaten off by Phylon who returns to save him. Leonidas joins him and together they take the wounded soldier back to the Spartan camp.

Yet, it is clear that the tale of the night expedition was an important feature of the ancient tradition surrounding Thermopylae. Diodorus almost certainly gets his account from the fourth-century BC historian Ephorus whose account seems to have been particularly influential. Pompeius Trogus, writing shortly after Diodorus, also featured it in his account of the battle. More significantly, the biographer Plutarch (*c.* 50-*c.*120 AD) uses the absence of any mention of the night expedition in Herodotus as proof of the historian's perfidy and bias. In his essay *On the Malice of Herodotus*, Plutarch declares that Herodotus omitted reference to Leonidas' brave expedition because he wished to diminish the king's glory and because he wanted to discredit the role that the Thebans played in the final stages of Thermopylae when they and the Spartans and the Thespians stood alone against the Persian forces and undertook such bold manoeuvres (866b).

Again we may doubt the accuracy of Plutarch's claims; especially since his evidence for Herodotus' hatred of Thebes is a highly embroidered story about Herodotus being maltreated by the citizens of Thebes when he went there as a teacher. Nevertheless, Plutarch's criticism creates an interesting hypothetical. What would he have made of the film? On the basis of its inclusion of a night expedition, would he have preferred its account to the account of Herodotus? There are other elements in the film that he would also have enjoyed. One of the many criticisms that Plutarch makes about Herodotus as an historian is that he was a barbarian lover. Certainly, with its strong orientalism, the film – unlike Herodotus – could never be described as sympathetic to the Persian invader. We are left with a somewhat strange situation. Potentially a film that we would criticise for including unhistorical elements in its plot might actually have seemed more authentic to one of our ancient sources for precisely the reason that it included those unhistorical elements.

At stake here is a broader question about the nature of history and its relation to film. The night expedition serves a number of useful cinematic ends. It provides a useful device to reconcile Leonidas and Phylon. It breaks up the monotony of the sequence of land battles. It allows the film to develop the relationship between Xerxes and Artemisia. Artistically, it varies the colour palette of the film by adding an exciting action scene in the darkness of the Greek night. Given such cinematic advantages, the presence of the night expedition scene seems obvious. The film-makers were keen to include such an expedition even before they heard of Diodorus' account. Yet the question remains whether the decision to include it or any of the other anachronisms and historical errors should have given the director pause. The historical advisor to the film was against its inclusion. While ordinarily cinema should not be judged by the standards of the historian, does it make a difference if a film claims to be 'historical'? Is this claim of historicity just empty rhetoric, a piece of marketing hype to make the account seem more believable, more real? Or does it mean something more?

A parallel might be drawn with films that claim to be cinematic adaptations of literary works. Both the historical film and the adaptation profess to be limiting themselves. The director surrenders his freedom of play supposedly for a higher cause; namely, conveying a truth about a work or a set of events. The director enters into a contract with their audience that the original subject matter will not be significantly misrepresented. It is not the case that 'anything goes'. Endings cannot be altered. The spirit of the work should be preserved. The skill of the director depends on working within this reduced frame. Like the artist who paints with only a few colours or chooses to work in miniature, the genius lies in working within a set of self-imposed rules. Seen in this light, the failure to live up to the ancient sources is not an historical failure, but an artistic one. It looks like cheating.

Suggested further viewing

The Giant of Marathon (Italian title: *La Battaglia di Maratona*, dir. Tourneur and Bava, 1959)
Another film about a classic battle from the Persian Wars. This time the

battle is not Thermopylae, but the earlier battle, Marathon (490 BC). The film is best described as 'historical peplum'. Following his victory at the Olympic Games, Philippides (Steve Reeves) is appointed commander of the Sacred Guard, an elite Athenian unit designed to protect Athens from both internal and external enemies. Athens at the time is a dangerous place. The newly emergent democracy is under threat. The expelled tyrant Hippias and his supporters seek to overthrow the democracy and restore the tyrant to the city. Chief among Hippias' supporters is the politician Theocritus (Sergio Fantoni). In order to further his cause, Theocritus attempts to seduce Philippides using the wiles of his attractive servant Charis (Daniella Rocca). However, his plot fails as the virtuous Andromeda (Mylène Demongeot) has already stolen Philippides' heart. While Theocritus plots inside the city, Persian forces advance on Greece.

The film provides a useful contrast to *The 300 Spartans*, which looks rigorously historical in comparison and highlights the injustice of critics who were happy to dismiss *The 300 Spartans* as just another peplum offering. While the film fails as history, it nevertheless succeeds as another episode in the extraordinary myth-making that has sought to constantly repackage the battle of Marathon ever since the time of the Athenian empire. The Athenians claimed that gods and heroes fought alongside the Greek forces at Marathon. This film continues this process of imaginative reconstruction.

Alexander the Great (dir. Rossen, 1956)

Robert Rossen was another victim of the House Un-American Activities Committee (HUAC). Called to testify about the prevalence of communism in the film industry, he initially refused and was blacklisted. Two years later he recanted and gave the committee 57 names of figures with communist sympathies or affiliations. *Alexander* is the first film that Rossen produced after his blacklisting ended and it is tempting to read his experience of brutal bullying by HUAC into the film, most notably in the way that power seems to corrupt the personality of Alexander. Starring Richard Burton as the blond Alexander, the film tells the story of Alexander's life from his birth until his death at the age of thirty-two. The film plays strongly with the notion of tragedy, hinting at Alexander's complicity in the death of his father Philip (Fredric March) and showing Alexander's disillusionment as his dreams of conquering the world turn sour.

6

Myth and the Fantastic: *Jason and the Argonauts* (1963)

Introduction

Greek mythology has proved itself both highly suitable and somewhat problematic for cinema. Mythology offers stories and characters that have been very widely retold. Embedded in the traditions of western literature, they have often accrued the capacity for multiple signification. Mythic narratives and characters can be appreciated on a variety of interpretive levels. The name Achilles, for example, invokes (at the very least) warriors, weaknesses, and wounded heels. Those with more knowledge of classical literature may think of his rage in Homer's *Iliad* and his brutal treatment of the Trojan prince Hector; some will note his cultural status as a gay icon for the (much-debated) nature of his relationship with his friend Patroclus. Such ready-made narrative scaffolding made it possible for filmmakers to cut down on background explanation: especially useful for early films like *The Fall of Troy* (1911), which were at the same time very brief, and had to mostly rely on visual storytelling.

Myth's inclusion of supernatural beings like gods and monsters can be more problematic. On paper, or in the imagination, fantastic creatures enable us to tell stories that go beyond the limits of everyday experience. Even in static visual arts like sculpture or painting, they retain their capacity for inspiring awe. However, as moving, speaking figures on stage or on the cinema screen, fantastic creatures can seem absurd rather than awe-inspiring, silly rather than sublime. This was especially the case in pre-CGI films. Traditional cinema consumption, informed by the hegemonic classical Hollywood style, assumed belief in the reality of on-screen worlds, and peopling those worlds with fantastic creatures puts this belief in jeopardy. Consequently, it is in the genre of fantasy films, where the questioning of reality is a central theme, that myth finds a more natural cinematic home.

Defining fantasy films as a genre is not an easy task. In the cinema, fantasy has been popularly linked with horror and science-fiction. Well-known examples might include *Sleepy Hollow* (1999), *The Fifth Element* (1997), *Twelve Monkeys* (1995) and *Army of Darkness* (1993) – plus, of course, epic series like the *Star Wars* films (1977-2005), and the *Lord of the Rings* trilogy (2001-2003). Horror and sci-fi genres showcase fantasy as a matter of course, with their supernatural events and extra-terrestrial locations. However, they do not exhaust the range of genres which can include fantastic elements. Classic fantasies include romantic fantasies such as *A Matter of Life and Death* (1946) and *It's a Wonderful Life* (1946); revisionist fairytales like *Edward Scissorhands* (1990) and *The Company of Wolves* (1984); martial arts films in the tradition of *Crouching Tiger, Hidden Dragon* (2003) and *House of the Flying Daggers* (2004); and other less easily classifiable films like *Being John Malkovich* (1999) and *Big Fish* (2003). Films with fantasy elements that are inspired by Greek myth include *Orpheus* (original French title *Orphée* 1950), *Jason and the Argonauts* (the case study for this chapter), *Medea* (1969), *Hercules in New York* (1970), *Clash of the Titans* (1981), and *Mighty Aphrodite* (1995). These films present their narratives in very different styles, from arthouse opacity through slapstick comedy and family adventure film to post-modern morality tale. Combined with the variety of genres listed above, this diversity suggests that fantasy functions broadly and serves a variety of purposes.

At its core, fantasy depicts a departure from the real whether it is a violation of the laws of physics, the inclusion of animals unknown in nature, or the creation of impossible connections between cause and effect. However, the important issue is not so much the content of the fantastic, but its effect on the viewer. This has been most effectively studied by the structuralist critic Tzvetan Todorov, who provides a more formal definition of fantasy based on the idea of 'hesitation'. According to Todorov, one can recognise fantasy because it produces 'hesitation' in the interpreter (i.e. the reader or viewer). This hesitation occurs when an inexplicable occurrence produces the need for a decision, either on the part of the reader, or a character within the narrative: was it imagined or real – and if the latter, are the rules that govern reality different from those that were previously assumed? Todorov argued that it is in the hesitation that occurs between these two positions (between a commitment to the real and a desire to pursue the irrational) that the fantastic resided. The question that fantasy provokes is 'do I believe what I just saw?'.

Although Todorov's analysis was predicated on a small number of literary texts, and has been much criticised and debated, it offers a useful jumping-off point for thinking about the way we process what we see on screen when we view fantasy films. Consider, for instance, the moment in *Orphée* (1950) when the eponymous poet discovers that he can access the underworld through the mirror in his room using a mysterious pair of gloves. Viewers are cued to the supernatural status of the gloves by the curious manner in which Orphée puts them on – appearing to be made of rubber, they fly onto his hands, miraculously turning themselves inside-out in the process. As Orphée breaches, then enters the mirror-glass, his gloved hands pass through the mirror as if it were water. Both cinematic events, the behaviour of the gloves and the ability to pass through a solid mirror, are created through the manipulation of film technology to produce a 'special effect' (sometimes referred to as FX). In the first, the actor has been filmed taking the gloves off, and then the film has been reversed. In the second, a shot of Orphée's gloved hands passing through water is intercut with shots of him looking in a real mirror, and walking through an empty frame. Despite – perhaps even because of – the naïvety of these effects, a moment of fantasy viewing is produced as the viewer tries to simultaneously process the extra-cinematic question of how the refutation of reality is achieved by the filmmaker, and the intra-cinematic question of whether the character is dreaming.

The tension between realism and fantasy has been a source of inspiration for filmmakers ever since the earliest days of cinema. Filmmakers were quick to note the medium's dual potential for extraordinary reproductions of reality, and for making the extraordinary seem real. The Lumière brothers exploited the former, astounding audiences in 1895 by transporting them from a Parisian salon to become invisible eavesdroppers on scenes in other lives; allowing them to see, for example, workers exiting a factory at the end of their shift or trains leaving a station. Georges Méliès, working at the same time, took the other path, realising film's capacity for fantasy. A Parisian magician and showman, Méliès was filming in a Parisian street when his camera jammed and had to be restarted. When the film was played back, the pause in continuity had turned men into women, carriages into hearses: the first examples in live action cinema of the stop-motion effects described earlier in *Orphée*. As a successful conjurer, Méliès recognised the value of such a trick, and used it to present on screen the kind of stories that provoked wonder: tales of space travel, fairy tales, and often accounts of ancient myth. Fantastic sequences held Méliès' audiences in thrall, a visual representation of what ancient mythographers presented in words.

Travelling forward over a hundred years, the enthusiasm of recent cinema audiences for the kind of films listed above has shown that fantasy can still enthral an audience. However, for one of the most recent examples of mythology in cinema, *Troy* (2004), fantasy was eschewed. Instead a pseudo-historical approach was taken, removing the Olympian gods from the narrative and offering rational explanations for other mythical elements such as the weakness of Achilles' heel. *Troy*'s attempts to historicise myth may have been at least partly responsible for the film's rather tepid reception at the box-office. Filmmakers should have noted audience resistance to their historicising process when a pre-release attempt to change the film's title to *The Trojan War* was withdrawn following highly negative feedback from film fans. Reviewers' responses to the decision of director Wolfgang Petersen to excise the gods from this retelling of the Trojan War narrative were more mixed. Although some critics castigated the film for its departure from Homer's *Iliad* (the canonic retelling of the myth and the film's acknowledged inspiration), others applauded it, with one critic dismissively pointing to the unmissed absence of 'snowy-haired Brit actors, wandering round up to their ankles in dry ice carrying thunderbolts'. The criticisms bring into focus the problems and choices that are associated with putting the immortals on screen. What *does* a god or goddess look like, for instance, and how are their divine commands enacted? Or, perhaps more pertinently, what will audiences accept in these matters?

Gods, heroes and monsters are the features that divide ancient myth from other narratives as far as adaptation to cinema is concerned. The least problematic of these figures for cinema are heroes and heroines. As we shall see in the discussion of Disney's *Hercules* (Chapter 9), modern and ancient notions of heroism are fundamentally incompatible. However, on a superficial level, the two discourses share enough features to allow audiences to accept the reality of heroes. All one needs is an attractive young man or woman with a good figure. They don't have to be extremely muscular (Hercules is the most notable exception), but they do have to have a touch of 'star quality' about them (even if they aren't already stars). The mythic hero isn't a role for the everyman. Extra-cinematic factors help blend notions of ancient and modern heroism. For example, pre-release publicity may draw the reader's attention to heroic aspects of the actors' lives outside the world of this particular film; to previous roles, or even post-film employment. Todd Armstrong who played Jason in *Jason and the Argonauts* (1963) went into US army training after completing the film; editorials in the UK pressbook compared this with his onscreen role, describing him as 'a practising warrior'. The casting of Diane Kruger as Helen in *Troy* was preceded by a lengthy press campaign on the search for someone to play 'the most beautiful woman in history (sic)', repeating the same tactic used when casting Rossana Podestà as Helen in the 1956 film *Helen of Troy*. Often the task of portraying iconic heroes is given to relative unknowns, the cultural accretions of myth seemingly easier to carry by actors who have not accumulated too much baggage of their own. The sometime champion bodybuilder Arnold Schwarzenegger, for instance, had his first film role in *Hercules in New York* (1970), where his name appears in the credits as 'Arnold Strong'.

If heroes can be created through good looks and some studio publicity, monsters demand more technical responses in their creation. Conveying the otherness of monsters can involve the application of a variety of techniques, from low-tech solutions like costume and make-up, to stop-motion filming, and the superimposition of a number of images using mattes. In *Ulysses* (1954), for instance, the giant Cyclops, Polyphemus, was played by the actor (and former Olympic wrestler) Umberto Silvestri, with effects created by the use of extensive make-up to indicate his single eye and low angle camerawork to create the illusion of height. These images were then combined in post-production with film of Ulysses and his companions shot from a high angle. In *Jason* and *Clash of the Titans* (1981), an alternative strategy was used, with fantastic creatures (including the Harpies, the Hydra, and Medusa) portrayed through the use of animated 3D models, filmed separately then integrated in post-production with live action sequences. Their animator, Ray Harryhausen, has argued that it is the technique of animation that 'liberates the fantasy in the story' (Wells 2002: 95). Certainly animation's capacity to create worlds where natural laws are completely absent encourages an anarchic spirit of freedom, and can enable the discussion of more sensitive topics: adoption in *Hercules* (1997), homosexuality in Barry Purves' *Achilles* (1995), agnosticism in *Jason* (see Chapter 9 for more on animated films). However, the notion of a fully animated fantasy produces problems for Todorov's definition. With animation unreal by definition (whether drawn or 3D), there is no moment of hesitation. Fantasy's capacity to make us pause and question what we have previously accepted as reality is therefore not present: the liminal qualities of the fantastic world tip into outright escapism. In *Jason*, this problem is avoided by blending animated sequences with live-action, re-igniting the hesitation of the fantastic, and foregrounding debates about the role of both fantasy and the gods in human culture.

Background to case study

Jason and the Argonauts has become widely known for its special effects and animated sequences, used to put gods and fantastic creatures on-screen, and created by Ray Harryhausen (1920-). Harryhausen's Dynamation system used mattes to integrate live-action footage with 3D models. These were animated through tiny changes of position, shot one frame at a time: the laborious stop-motion technique. Produced many years before the introduction of computer-aided techniques, all animation and other special effect sequences in the film were designed and enacted by Harryhausen himself. Such extremely labour-intensive production meant that only short sequences could be produced. As a result, the gods and fantastic creatures in *Jason* are mostly not a continuous presence in the narrative, but are used to punctuate the action with spectacular setpiece sequences.

Harryhausen himself is now one of the most discussed and respected figures in animation, lionised by critics, fans and the industry, and the recipient of an Academy Award for lifetime achievement in 1991. But in advertising at the time of the film's original release in 1963, he was scarcely mentioned. Potential viewers would have looked elsewhere for the film's attractions: to the cast, the characters, the story, and the spectacle. They would not have known from the credit hidden at the foot of the posters for 'Associate Producer Ray Harryhausen' the extraordinary extent of Harryhausen's involvement in the origination and formation of this cinematic Argonautica.

Harryhausen's interest in animation and fantasy began when he saw *King Kong* as a teenager in 1933. Animating the eponymous primate was the work of Willis O'Brien, and in 1949, Harryhausen's (largely self-taught) skills of animation were rewarded with the position of assistant animator to O'Brien on another gorilla movie, *Mighty Joe Young*. The film won an Academy Award for its special effects which, although credited to O'Brien, are now widely acknowledged to have been mostly the work of Harryhausen. Moving on to work on a series of monster and science fiction films with titles like *The Beast From 20,000 Fathoms* (1953) and *Earth vs the Flying Saucers* (1956), Harryhausen developed his special contribution to animation techniques which he named Dynamation. This technique filmed animated models as the filling in a sandwich of two separate pieces of live-action film, one used as a background and one as a foreground. Through this technique Harryhausen achieved his aim of realistically integrating models and live actors and so maximised the viewer's suspension of disbelief in his fantasy worlds.

In his early career, Harryhausen's role was as enabler of other people's fantasies through his masterful and imaginative use of special-effects techniques. However, in 1955 he began a collaboration with producer Charles H. Schneer in which his animated creations and effects took a greater role in driving and defining the narratives of films. Their first film was *It Came From Beneath the Sea* (1955), which depicted a giant octopus terrorising San Francisco; later films like *Earth vs the Flying Saucers* and *20 Million Miles to Earth* (1957) translated the 'monster' theme to a sci-fi setting. In 1958, Schneer and Harryhausen turned their attention to another fantastic milieu, the world of fairy tales and legend. These presented advantages over the earlier monster movies. They possessed widely known stories and had greater appeal for a larger, and potentially more profitable, mainstream family audience. At the same time, they still allowed Harryhausen to showcase his ability to blend realism and fantasy. The first film in the series was the first Sinbad film, *The Seventh Voyage of Sinbad*. It was released in 1958 (two more were released in 1974 and 1977) and it was followed by *The Three Worlds of Gulliver* in 1960. For Harryhausen, who found Greek myth 'a vivid world of adventure with wonderful heroes, villains, and most importantly, lots of fantastic creatures' (Harryhausen and Dalton 2003: 151), it was a short step from these legendary tales to the narratives of ancient mythology. The mode of film production which had now been established by Harryhausen and Schneer entailed that the form of their mythological retellings should be driven by the animations and effects that the narrative facilitated.

Evidence for Harryhausen's use of ancient mythology as inspiration for his fantastic creations can be found in many of his films. Besides *Jason* and *Clash of the Titans* (1981), Harryhausen claims to have a number of other uncompleted mythological projects including a film on Atlantis, another retelling the story of Daphnis and Chloe, and an adaptation of the Roman poet Virgil's epic work, the *Aeneid* (which was to have been produced after *Clash of the Titans*). Myth-inspired creatures also appeared, including a giant Cyclops in the first Sinbad film and a Siren in *The Golden Voyage of Sinbad* (1974). According to Harryhausen, he and

6. Myth and the Fantastic: Jason and the Argonauts (1963)

Schneer saw Greek myths as 'the type of stories ... where you had to use every trick that you could possibly conceive in order to render the mythological concept on the screen' (Wells 2002: 97). For their first fully-realised adaptation of Greek myths, Harryhausen and Schneer considered narratives about Perseus (which they later filmed in *Clash of the Titans*) before settling on Jason and his quest for the Golden Fleece because it seemed the most flexible myth for adaptation.

Jason is one of the oldest Greek mythological heroes and (inevitably) each of the retellings we have revises his story. The film collates elements from various versions, adding its own interpretations to suit Harryhausen's effects and the target family audience, which he had been cultivating ever since his fairytale films. Perhaps the best-known version of the myth for modern audiences is the *Argonautica,* an epic poem by Apollonius of Rhodes, written in Alexandria in the third century BC. Apollonius' version includes many of the incidents, characters and monsters found in the film (albeit in different forms), including Talos the Man of Bronze, the Harpies, and Aeëtes' earth-born warriors. The film also drew inspiration from another source, Pindar's *Fourth Pythian Ode* in having Pelias usurp the throne from Jason's father Aeson. Another incident in the same sequence adapts a story from other myth collections (most notably the so-called *Library of Apollodorus* and Diodorus Siculus), in which Pelias murders Jason's family. The film presents this episode early in the film, with Jason's young sisters as the victims. This alteration establishes the moral schema for the film, with Pelias an uncontentious villain from the start for a modern family audience, as the murderer of a young girl and baby.

Although his poem remains the major source for the film, Apollonius' portrayal of heroism is far from the classical Hollywood norm. His Jason is a famously 'helpless' hero, who relies on the other Argonauts and (strikingly) the magic of the Colchian princess Medea. She helps him achieve the tasks her father Aeëtes sets him, and overcome the serpent that guards the fleece. In the film, Jason and Medea adopt more conventional attributes for adventure film hero and heroine. Jason is resourceful and brave, and a natural leader of the Argonauts. Medea is highly decorative (a key sequence has her performing an erotically-charged temple dance, covered in gold paint), has to be rescued from the sea by Jason, and gets herself shot trying to save her man. More interesting is the film's portrayal of Hercules, played by the theatrical actor Nigel Green. Harryhausen has stated that he wished to distance his retelling of Greek myth from those produced in the peplum films. For this reason, the film eschews the typical bodybuilder Hercules. Green's Hercules is quite different from these. He is bulky rather than muscled, greying, and clearly older than the peplum hero. He enters the narrative arrogant and reckless, and leaves it (after provoking a sequence of events which prove personally catastrophic) thoughtful and grave. This is a Hercules clearly more complex than the

131

often one-dimensional peplum heroes and, in his flaws, closer to the Heracles of ancient Greek myth.

A brief survey of other films that include Jason illustrates how antici-pated audiences can dictate what is included and omitted from the mythological variants. *Jason and the Argonauts'* commitment to family values is brought into relief through comparison with these other versions. The 1958 *Hercules* (discussed in Chapter 3) showed parts of Jason's quest in its narrative, explicitly crediting Apollonius as a scriptwriter. To cater for its slightly more mature audience, it included an extended scene involving the Argonauts' seduction by the Amazonian women, a scene entirely omitted in *Jason and the Argonauts*. Similarly, another film retelling, Pasolini's *Medea* (1969), played to an adult arthouse audience, so was able to present even more explicit sexual and violent scenes. These included the episode where Medea murders her own brother to delay her father's pursuit. The 2000 television film *Jason and the Argonauts* added contemporary references for its multi-cultural, post-feminist audience with a black Orpheus (perhaps referencing the 1959 film *Orfeu Negro*), Atalanta as a female Argonaut, and an implied incestuous relationship between Medea and her brother Apsyrtos.

As we can see, there is a fair degree of flexibility in the Jason myth and this flexibility enabled the narrative in the 1963 film to be restructured around Harryhausen's special effects sequences. These sequences allowed Harryhausen to promote his vision of ancient Greece as a realistic world inhabited by magical creatures. However, they also had the effect of prioritising a reading of *Jason* in film criticism and fan writings as a vehicle for showcasing animation and special effects. The disadvantage here is that reading the film simply as a spectacular visual and technical achievement diverts attention from its highly sophisticated narrative. This narrative was first sketched out, in conjunction with Harryhausen and Schneer, by Jan Read (whose previous scriptwriting credits included an adaptation of Tennessee Williams' play, *The Roman Spring of Mrs Stone*), and developed by Beverley Cross (a successful dramatist who had won awards for his adaptation of H.G. Wells' *Kipps* as the musical *Half A Sixpence*). It is a mistake to underplay the narrative in this film as it offers, amongst other elements, an intelligent and complex discussion of the relationship between men and the gods – a genuine cine-mythography.

We first encounter the film's desire to explore the relationship between the mortal and divine early in the film when Jason declares to Hermes that he does not believe in the gods. Hermes then transports Jason to Olympus 'so that you will believe', but as Jason's encounter with Zeus and Hera unfolds, it is the gods' intentions towards humanity that appear more in question and Jason seems right in his doubts. Jason's wavering 'belief' is not about the existence of gods, but whether they are benevolent protec-tors of mankind, or callous chess-players with men as their pawns, fit only for sacrifice. Intriguingly, this theological question is one to which Harry-

6. *Myth and the Fantastic:* Jason and the Argonauts *(1963)*

hausen could especially relate. In the documentary film *The Harryhausen Chronicles,* Harryhausen compared the role of the animator with the ancient gods:

> [the animator is] putting on screen images that appear to be alive, and you're controlling exactly what they do, and that's why this concept in Greek mythology appealed to me so much – that the gods were manipulating humanity.

Thus Harryhausen makes the identification between the intra-cinematic relationship between the gods and men, and the extra-cinematic relationship between the animator and his models. If myth is, as has been argued, always ultimately about the relationship between man and the gods, who better to understand that relationship than the animator, who regularly invents, directs, and enacts the 'life' of his models?

The other factor that drove this project was Harryhausen's self-declared missionary zeal to restore the place of fantasy in a cinema he saw as becoming obsessed with anti-heroes and the mundane. In finding a place for fantasy, he was particularly keen to distinguish his cinematic Greece from peplum films which he noted 'seldom visualised mythology from the purely fantasy point of view' (Harryhausen 1972: 85.) In 1963, these were beginning to run out of creative steam with increasingly absurd hybrids like *Hercules Against the Mongols.* However, there were other reasons Harryhausen may have wished to distance Jason from the Italian genre. The pepla's association with B-movie values, both in their low budget production quality and their focus on eroticism and (often sadistic) violence was similar to the monster movies Harryhausen had worked on in the 1950s. This was not likely to attract the more mainstream family audience which had made *Sinbad* an international success. Besides profit though, there was also the matter of principle. The fantastic elements of the pepla were firmly situated in their heroes' implausible, but still undeniably human, muscled bodies while the gods, creatures and monsters of myth were largely ignored. For Harryhausen, fantastic cinema was about escapism rather than aspiration: 90 minutes of suspending disbelief in the idea that giant gorillas could threaten New York, or that gods and winged creatures existed on the earth.

Harryhausen may have wanted to distinguish his film from peplum cinema, but studio publicists had other ideas. Both spectacle and eroticism – the standard clichés of pepla – were prominent in publicity for the film, and this undeniably had an effect on how critics reacted to it. *Jason and the Argonauts* was marketed to potential viewers primarily as an action adventure film rather than a fantasy. We see this most clearly in the pressbooks for the UK release. These pressbooks were published by United Artists and offered ready-made articles for inclusion in film fan magazines and local newspapers. Written editorial pieces here stressed the film's

133

adventure aspects and its exotic locations. Cinema managers were advised that '*Jason and the Argonauts* is based on one of the world's great tales of adventure, and a major part of your promotion of the picture should be based on this angle'. And, as has already been mentioned, articles noted the involvement of the actors in previous adventure films, and drew an extra-cinematic parallel between Todd Armstrong's US military training and his role as ancient Greek warrior. Additionally, the standard 'authenticity' ploy in promoting cine-antiquity was not overlooked. So Schneer's travels around Europe to seek out authentic locations ('places believed to have been described by the soothsayers of ancient Greece') are duly noted and much is made of the fact that the Harpies sequence is actually filmed in the remains of a Greek temple in Paestum in Sicily.

While the fantastic creatures were overlooked in written editorials, they do find their place in the visual publicity for the film. But again we notice that the publicity can't make up its mind whether this film is a type of peplum film or something else. Talos, the man of Bronze, one of Harryhausen's most distinctive fantastic creations might appear in the background of the film poster, but the insert pictures all show action shots more reminiscent of peplum films, such as Jason rescuing the helpless Medea and leading the Argonauts into battle. We notice a similar ambivalence in the lobby cards for the film. All the famous Harryhausen creations are there (Talos, the Harpies, the Hydra, Triton holding back the Clashing Rocks, and the skeleton warriors), but they are joined by images such as a gold-painted Medea from the dance sequence – a scene straight out of classic peplum cinema. Even the theatrical trailer refuses to escape from peplum conventions so while it includes most of Harryhausen's animated sequences, it also can't resist a reference to Medea as 'the temple dancer – mysterious, exciting – and exotic'. Most interesting is the inclusion in the trailer of the end of the battle with the skeleton warriors, showing Jason escaping by jumping off a cliff into the sea. As a strategy for promoting a narrative this is akin to printing the last page of a novel; it's a literal cliffhanger. It also confirms the primacy of spectacle over narrative, at least in the eyes of studio publicists.

On its original release, the film failed to achieve the success enjoyed by *Sinbad,* performing well in the UK (in the top ten box-office successes of the year), but less well in the US. Press reviews were varied. *Variety* (5/6/1963) picked up on the family viewing angle, noting its 'moppet appeal', and calling it 'a sure delight for the kiddies and a diverting spectacle for adults with a taste for fantasy and adventure'. The British *Monthly Film Bulletin* (Sept. 1963) described it as 'fun', though 'enjoyable more for its special effects than any directorial flair,' and located it in the tradition of 'Méliès and Flash Gordon'. However *The New York Times* (8/8/1963) was less complimentary, grudgingly concluding that 'this absurd unwieldy adventure ... is no worse, but certainly no better, than most of its kind', suggesting the feared comparison with the pepla may have

134

indeed had a negative effect. Despite this unenthusiastic reception on release, the film has since gained iconic status as well as the great affection of many. It was given a theatrical re-release in 1978, and it is a constant presence on television schedules, often being shown on satellite television on the Sci-Fi Channel (fantasy providing the link here between mythology and science-fiction). Through such widespread and continuous exhibition, *Jason and the Argonauts* has become one of the best-known and most popular films inspired by the ancient world. In 1991 when Ray Harryhausen received his Oscar for Lifetime Achievement, the actor Tom Hanks told the audience, 'Everybody thinks that *Citizen Kane* was the greatest movie ever made. But if you were young in 1963, you know the real answer is *Jason and the Argonauts*.'

Plot summary

The film opens with Pelias' (Douglas Wilmer) attack on Thessaly, in which he murders Jason's father Aristo and incurs the wrath of Hera by killing Aristo's daughter Briseis in the goddess's temple where she has sought sanctuary. Hera (Honor Blackman) decides to help the then-infant Jason to regain the throne.

Returning as a grown man, Jason (Todd Armstrong) declares his intention to travel to far-off Colchis to find the Golden Fleece, and prove to the people of Thessaly that 'the gods have not deserted them'. However, Jason has his own doubts about the gods and their intentions towards humans, as he tells the seer in the ruined temple of Hermes. The seer (Michael Gwynn) is revealed to be Hermes himself, and transports Jason to Olympus where Hera tells him that she will help him in his quest, despite the opposition of Zeus (Niall McGinnis). In order to retrieve the fleece, Jason challenges the shipbuilders of Greece to construct the finest boat ever made. To crew it, he holds an athletic competition to select the finest and strongest sailors. Those successful in the competition for a berth on the Argo (the boat is named after its maker Argos) include Hercules (Nigel Green) and Pelias' son Acastus (Gary Raymond), sent by his father to sabotage the mission.

Hera guides them to the Isle of Bronze where Hercules angers Talos, the island's Man of Bronze, who destroys the ship before Jason defeats him. But Hercules' protégé Hylas (John Cairney) is lost in the struggle and Hercules decides to stay on the island. The Argonauts, provoked by Acastus, threaten to revolt but are placated by the appearance of Hera who tells them to sail to Phrygia. Here they find the blind seer Phineas (Patrick Troughton) being tormented by the Harpies. The Argonauts capture and imprison the Harpies, and in return Phineas directs them to Colchis, giving Jason a talisman of the god Triton as a token of gratitude.

At the Clashing Rocks, they are threatened with shipwreck, but when Argos tells him to pray, Jason declares his lack of belief in the gods and casts the talisman into the sea. The god Triton emerges and holds the Rocks apart for the ship to pass through. Safely reaching the other side, they rescue a survivor of a previous wreck, the priestess Medea (Nancy Kovack), who sails with them to Colchis. Before they arrive, Jason and Acastus fight and Acastus disappears overboard. Reaching land at Colchis, Jason goes alone to visit its king Aeëtes, who invites the Argonauts to a feast, but then imprisons them. It emerges that Acastus has reached Aeëtes first and persuaded him that Jason is planning to attack. Medea helps them to escape and takes Jason to the Fleece where he kills the Hydra guarding it. However Aeëtes collects the Hydra's teeth, and sows them in a field where they emerge from the earth as skeleton warriors. In the battle that ensues, two of the Argonauts are killed but Jason escapes and is reunited on the Argo with Medea who joins them for the journey home.

Key scenes and themes

Myth into fantasy

The model animator Barry Purves explained the difference between Computer Generated (CG) animation and model animation: 'CG is good for making the fantastic seem real, whereas puppets are more suited for making the fantastic seem credible, which is not the same at all' (Purves 1998). In *Jason and the Argonauts*, Harryhausen uses model animations to persuade his audiences to believe in ancient Greece as a natural location for fantasy. Our introduction to this fantastic 'reality' is found in the Argonauts' first halt at the Isle of Bronze, where they encounter Talos, the Man of Bronze. There are two further creatures borrowed from myth to fuel the fantasy agenda in *Jason and the Argonauts*, the Harpies and the Hydra. In all three cases, Harryhausen adapts and revises the mythological versions to suit his animating techniques and the demands of the narrative.

For example, just as in myth, the Harpies appear in the film as Phineas' tormentors. However, the scaly blue skin and webbed bat-like wings of the cinematic Harpies contrast dramatically with the bird-like feathered wings seen in ancient vase paintings of these mythical creatures. Harryhausen's Harpies appear more like aliens than mythical creatures. They seem to have come straight out of science-fiction. In fact a test reel made by Harryhausen for an earlier unrealised film project called *The Elementals* in which 'giant humanoid bat-creatures' invade Paris shows strikingly similar figures, suggesting that an earlier model may have been 'recycled' for this retelling. In contrast, the film's representation of the Hydra as a many-headed snake-like guardian is true to classical depiction, but not true to standard mythic accounts, where it occurs, not in the Jason cycle of myths, but as the object of one of Hercules' Labours.

136

6. *Myth and the Fantastic: Jason and the Argonauts* (1963)

In the case of Talos, Harryhausen takes the mythological character and adds popular signifiers for ancient Greece and elements from science fiction to create the Man of Bronze. In Apollonius' version of the myth, Talos is the watchman of Crete, who tries to prevent the Argonauts from landing on the island. In the film, he is one of a group of giant statues forged by the gods, who comes to life to seek vengeance for a blasphemous theft by Hercules.

Talos, Man of Bronze

Hunting for food, Hercules and his protégé Hylas arrive at a valley of bronze statues on plinths and, inside one plinth, discover the treasure house of the gods. Despite Jason's warning that the Argonauts should take nothing from the island but food and water, Hercules helps himself to a giant brooch pin to use as a spear. He and Hylas start to leave, but run when they hear an eerie metallic creaking as the bronze statue begins to move. Seeking vengeance for the blasphemous crime, the statue first chases the pair, then attacks the rest of the Argonauts who flee to the ship and try to leave the island. Their way is blocked by Talos standing astride the harbour. The ship is wrecked, and Jason calls on Hera for help. She tells him about Talos' weak spot – the plug at his heel. The Argonauts manoeuvre Talos into position, and Jason unscrews the plug, venting Talos' lifeblood of molten metal into the sand. As Talos falls, he takes one final victim – Hercules' protégé Hylas, crushed beneath his huge body.

Talos is one of the best remembered features of *Jason and the Argonauts* [Fig. 12]. His imagery is an interesting confection of Greek and science-fiction iconography. On posters for the film, he is shown in poses that utilise two key cultural signifiers for ancient Greece. The first is his distinctive helmet. The crested helmet is one of the most commonly deployed props in films set in Greece. The silhouette of Talos' crested helm recalls publicity for other films set in Greece including *Alexander the Great* (1955) and *The 300 Spartans* (1962). The other signifier is even more potent. As the Argonauts attempt to flee the island, Talos is shown striding the harbour entrance in a reprise of popular ideas about the Colossus of Rhodes, a figure specifically mentioned by Harryhausen as an inspiration for the scene. The Colossus also influences the size of Talos, over 100 feet high onscreen. In case the significance of the pose was not clear, the identification was reiterated in the tagline that often accompanied promotional shots of Talos: 'The Epic Story That Was Destined To Stand As A Colossus Of Adventure'. Finally, as a piece of statuary, Talos represents the remnants of antiquity most familiar to popular audiences from museums, ruins and public architecture.

There is a second set of signifiers attached to Talos, this time more modern, and situating the film in a secondary discourse of cinematic science fiction and fantasy. Talos' metal construction recalls that modern marvel (and threat), the robot: the identification supported by the creak-

12. Talos the Colossus. On the Isle of Bronze, *Jason and the Argonauts* (1963).

ing sound effects and its jerky stop-motion movement – described by Harryhausen as 'deliberately stiff and mechanical' (Harryhausen 1972: 90). Its mask-like face and sightless eyes are a standard conceit in the science-fiction of the time, denoting inhumanity. Anxieties about robots arise from the idea that we might lose control over the technology we create; that the machines might turn out to be superior. This contemporary fear is enacted in Talos' attack on the Argonauts – but at the same time it also draws us back to antiquity. The statue's literal 'animation' gives notice to the viewer that they are now in a magical land where the remnants of the ancient world may come to life. Unpicking the significations of Talos we can see the richness of Harryhausen's creation and also appreciate that these fantasy figures do not come from a vacuum, but are the product of a number of conscious decisions by the animator to produce a multi-layered result.

Fantasy into myth

The last of Harryhausen's animated creatures are perhaps also his best-known: the skeleton warriors. Appearing at the climax of the film for a battle with Jason and two of the Argonauts, the skeleton warriors are a fantastic import, replacing the Earth-born men of the myth. The sequence

> **Battling the skeleton warriors**
>
> Having killed its guardian the Hydra, Jason, Medea and the Argonauts are escaping with the fleece when they are cornered by Aeëtes and his men. Aeëtes sows the teeth of the dead Hydra, and skeleton warriors sprout from the ground, attacking Jason and his crew. Sending Medea, Argos and most of the Argonauts back to the ship, Jason and two companions battle the skeleton warriors amid temple ruins [Fig. 13]. While his companions fall to their opponents, Jason escapes by leaping from a cliff into the water, followed, lemming-like, by the skeletons.

13. Battling the skeleton warriors. Jason in Colchis,
Jason and the Argonauts (1963).

has become so well-known that it has spawned its own 'mythology' about the time taken to produce the animation, while the iconography of the skeleton warrior has been successfully reproduced in a variety of popular cultural texts.

Much has been made of the labour and time taken to produce the sequence: four and a half months for four and a half minutes of film, with Harryhausen single-handedly animating seven individual models and integrating them in fight scenes with live actors. However, the skeleton warriors are (like the Harpies) actually an example of Harryhausen's economical practice of importing creatures from other narratives: the original skeleton warrior was created for *Sinbad*. One great advantage a skeleton has for stop-motion animation is its paucity of expression. Animating expressions on seven individual models would have been an additional burden on Harryhausen's animating skills. Even so, the animation is so persuasive it is impossible not to see them seeming to wear the most ghoulish of grins.

If the Harpies introduced a science fiction element into mythology, the skeleton warriors are rather creatures of horror films. For the viewer, an animated skeleton produces all sorts of anxieties about human mortality. Like the homicidal bronze statue Talos, it is an apparently lifeless object turning against us, the living. In this instance though, it is not the artefacts man has produced, but man's own body that turns against him. Skeletons symbolise our own mortality: they are what is left when the worms have eaten our flesh. There is an added horror in their empty eye sockets. As with Talos, if eyes are the window to the soul, there is no soul at home here. The skeleton warriors were the subject of the censor's displeasure; he declared that a scene where a decapitated skeleton feels around for its lost head would have to go if the film was to receive the desired 'U' certificate. The very notion of this scene shows that this was more black humour than horror. What effect can decapitating a skeleton or, indeed, stabbing an empty ribcage have? Bernard Herrmann's musical score plays a vital role here in defusing the horror and promoting the black humour of this scene, with staccato strings, brass and percussion echoing the *danse macabre* enacted on screen.

The iconography of the skeleton warrior has retained its popularity in popular culture, featuring in various texts since Harryhausen's sequence first appeared. In Sam Raimi's *Army of Darkness* (1992), the black humour and apt musical score of *Jason* is taken one stage further, with the skeleton army marching into battle playing composer Danny Elfman's *March of the Dead* on drums made of skulls and flutes made of leg bones. In *Terminator* (1984), the horror of Arnold Schwarzenegger's cyborg character is revealed as he strides out of an apparently fatal blaze, flesh burnt away: a skeleton warrior indeed. There was even a children's cartoon series for television, *The Skeleton Warriors*, which screened in the USA from 1993-94. Like many other elements of films inspired by the ancient world, the skeleton warriors have more recently also made the crossover into gaming, appearing in the *Dungeons and Dragons* role-playing games, and in video games including *The Legend of Zelda* (Nintendo). For many consumers of popular culture, one of the least authentic features of Harryhausen's retelling of the Jason myths is also the best-known.

Man and the gods

Although critical and audience attention has largely focused on Harryhausen's model creatures, the film also includes other special effects, sometimes using live actors. Many of these are used to show man's interactions with the Olympians. Putting the gods onscreen means wrestling with some key iconographic issues. What should the gods look like? How do they communicate with mortal men? In the film, Harryhausen offers a number of solutions. On the occasions when gods openly appear to men, they are shown as men made huge. For instance, when Hermes first appears to Jason, and again when he meets Zeus and Hera in Olympus, or when Triton appears to hold apart the Clashing Rocks, scale indicates divinity. At other times when they appear in the mortal world, gods are in religion-related disguise: Hera appears to Pelias as a temple priestess, while Hermes opens the film's narrative as Pelias' seer, reading the omens before his attack on Thessaly. The third, and perhaps most interesting solution proposes a scheme of symbolic exchange between the Olympians and men. In the mortal world, the gods are represented by inanimate cult objects: the temple statue of Hera, the bronzes on the Isle of Bronze, Hera as ship's figurehead [Fig. 14], Phineas' talisman of Triton. In Olympus though, the situation is reversed – gods appear like mortals, men are clay figurines.

Jason visits Olympus

Having declared to Pelias his intention to seek the fleece to restore the people's belief in the gods, Jason meets the king's seer in the ruins of a temple, in which he recognises one of the fallen statues as Hermes. He tells the seer that he does not believe in the gods, upon which the seer grows in size and reveals his true identity as the messenger god Hermes. Hermes transports Jason to Olympus, where Zeus and Hera are moving pieces on a game board. Zeus mocks Jason to the other Olympians and challenges his self-reliance, saying that 'no man calls upon the gods unless he wants something.' However, Jason refuses his assistance, though he accepts Hera's offer of help, limited to five times.

There is an obvious contrast here between the ruined temple – the home of the gods in the mortal world – and the perfection of Olympus. The fallen statues stand as a metaphor for man's loss of belief, while Olympus is conservatively portrayed as a pillared marble temple set in the clouds, all in white and gold. In this scene, as in many others in the film, associations are created by appropriate use of sound design: the home of the Greek gods connotes notions of a Christian heaven by the use of harp music and triumphal organ chords during Jason's transit with Hermes. The game of strategy played by Zeus and Hera, in which heroes, monsters, and a model Argo are moved around a board like chess pieces, provides a powerful metaphor for the gods' power over the lives of men. The metaphor has an important cinematic afterlife in fantasy films with the imagery reused in *Clash of the Titans* (1981 and 2010), and Disney's *Hercules* (1997).

The importance of the gods to the narrative is confirmed by their structural position in the film. Gods form a frame for the film's narrative: the opening shot is of Hermes disguised as the seer, reading the portents

14. Man shapes the gods. The shipyard at Thebes,
Jason and the Argonauts (1963).

for Pelias' invasion; the film closes on Zeus' ominous declaration: 'I have not finished with Jason.' Theology is central to this film. The language of belief suffuses the dialogue. The film constantly seeks to calibrate the relationship between god and man. It is a complex relationship. On the one hand, the absolute power of the gods is shown through the chessboard. On the other hand, the belief of man seems crucial to the gods' existence. Zeus, for all his omnipotence, seems curiously concerned about what mortals think of him. Hera explains his concern when she remarks to Zeus that he is 'the god of many men. Yet when those men no longer believe in you, then you will return to nothing.' In offering this novel, and distinctly un-classical, formulation, the film ventures into new territory. By giving a degree of agency and power to man, it solves the problem of how men can be held responsible for their actions. At the same time, it provides a motive for the intrusion of the supernatural into the mortal realm; the gods need to appear because they need men to continue to believe. It is only with such a theological superstructure that a film like *Jason and the Argonauts* can work. Few films theorise the fantastic as explicitly as *Jason and the Argonauts* and the film is all the stronger for it.

142

There is a second point to this discussion of the lives and motivations of the gods. As we have seen, the gods also work meta-cinematically as a metaphor for the animator. As the controlling influence on the film, Harryhausen might be read as playing out the role of Hermes who, as the first onscreen character, is structurally identified as our primary point of contact with the divine. The messenger god Hermes is the conduit between mortal and immortal worlds, just as Harryhausen negotiates the bridge between reality and fantasy, live action and animation. As the animator transports his audience to a land of magical fantasy, his apotheosis Hermes delivers Jason to the home of the gods. Most tellingly, Hermes describes himself in the film as a 'bringer of dreams', a phrase that alludes to Harryhausen's own description of animation as something that 'creates the illusion of a dream' (Wells 2002: 96). Thus, as Hermes transports Jason to Olympus so that he will believe, Harryhausen asks the cinema audience to abandon their taste for reality and the mundane, and believe for a while in fantasy: in gods, heroes and monsters. When Hera warns Zeus that he will be finished if people stop believing in him, it is not hard to see the anxiety that must attend every animator or producer of special effects.

Suggested further viewing

Hercules in New York (dir. Seidelman, 1970)
The film opens in an Olympus oddly conceived as a formal (and quite suburban) English rose garden with clipped box hedging, utterly different from Harryhausen's grandiose vision in *Jason and the Argonauts* or *Clash of the Titans*. Hercules (Arnold Schwarzenegger) is bored in Olympus, and following a father-teenage son argument about this, Zeus accidentally casts him down to Earth. Here he is befriended by a New York pretzel seller (Arnold Stang), becomes a celebrity through his prowess at wrestling, courts a professor's daughter and gets involved with the mob, before returning to Olympus.

Schwarzenegger's movie debut saw him following in the footsteps of his own bodybuilder heroes, Steve Reeves and Reg Park, in playing Hercules. The contemporary New York setting took the anachronisms of the later peplum films (see Chapter 3 for a brief survey) to their logical extreme. The film is now viewed mainly for the novelty value of Schwarzenegger's first film performance. Already a champion bodybuilder, Arnie had no previous acting experience, and retained a dense Austrian accent, revealed in the recent original voicetrack DVD releases of the film (in the theatrical release, his voice was dubbed throughout). In fact the film was produced as a vehicle for Stang, a bespectacled New York Jewish comedian. Schwarzenegger was cast as his physical opposite, and punningly renamed 'Arnold Strong' in the credits. Despite its low-budget aesthetics, it often does a good job of subverting the conventions of Hercules films. For instance, in many of the films, Hercules is first found by water; in this subverted version he is *in* the water, dredged up by a fishing boat out of New York harbour. Other subverted conventions include javelin-throwing, a wonderfully staged chariot race (Arnie drives a hot dog stand), and a 'Labour' in which Hercules defeats a wild beast in combat – a man in a bear suit in Central Park.

Clash of the Titans (dir. Davis, 1981)
Perseus (Harry Hamlyn) falls in love with the beautiful princess Andromeda (Judi Bowker), and succeeds in winning her hand. However, she has been promised to the monstrous Calibos, son of the goddess Thetis. In revenge, Thetis declares that Andromeda must be sacrificed to the Kraken. On the advice of the Stygian witches, Perseus seeks out and kills the Gorgon Medusa, and uses her fatal gaze to destroy the sea-monster.

Another of Harryhausen and Schneer's productions, *Clash of the Titans* appeared almost twenty years after *Jason and the Argonauts*. Its style owes more to the fairytale narratives of the two Sinbad films that immediately preceded it, with fantasy the driving force and anachronistic (for ancient myth) themes of forgiveness, pity and mercy. Elements of the myth cycle are thoroughly reorganised to serve the romantic quest narrative, and (as with *Jason*) to showcase the special effects. For instance, rather than using the winged sandals of myth, Perseus travels on the winged horse Pegasus in his quest to slay Medusa, although in myth Pegasus appears only after Medusa's death, when he is born from her corpse. Other special effects include a helmet of invisibility, a mechanical owl (Bubo), a two-headed dog (Dioskilos), and the sea-monster Kraken (imported from Scandinavian myths). Most impressive is Medusa, with her serpentine body and animated snake-hair. Rather than the discrete sequences of *Jason*, some of the animated elements and effects appear for extended periods. The complexity of this animation meant that Harryhausen could not accomplish it alone. Instead, a team worked on the special effects. The film is aimed at a more adult audience than *Jason*, with partial nudity, failed suitors burnt alive, and a cruel and merciless Zeus played by the renowned British theatrical actor, Laurence Olivier. Other distinguished casting for the gods included Claire Bloom as Hera, Ursula Andress as Aphrodite and Maggie Smith (wife of the scriptwriter Beverley Cross) as Thetis.

Percy Jackson and the Lightning Thief (dir. Colombus, 2010)
Percy Jackson (Logan Lerman), a 17-year-old living in modern-day America, discovers that he is in fact the son of the Olympian god Poseidon (Kevin McKidd), and finds himself accused of stealing Zeus' lightning bolt. With his best friend Grover (Brandon T. Jackson) who turns out to be a satyr, he is taken to Camp Half-Blood, a training camp for demi-gods, and meets Annabeth (Alexandra Daddario) daughter of Athena and Luke (Jake Abel) son of Hermes. With Annabeth and Grover, Percy embarks on

6. Myth and the Fantastic: Jason and the Argonauts (1963)

a quest to rescue his mother Sally from the Underworld. However when they meet with Hades (Steve Coogan), he reveals that Luke is the lightning thief, and a battle between Luke and Percy ensues. Percy triumphs and returns the lightning bolt to Zeus (Sean Bean) before returning to the camp.

The film was adapted from Rick Riordan's novel for young adults, *The Lightning Thief*. Riordan wrote the story for his own son who had been diagnosed with dyslexia and Attention Deficit (Hyperactivity) Disorder. The book's hero, Percy, is also dyslexic, the suggestion being that there is a supernatural and heroic reason why he perceives the world differently. Percy stands for Perseus, and aspects of the relevant myths are incorporated, including the beheading of Medusa. The film was widely read by reviewers as an alternative Harry Potter (especially as the director Chris Columbus had also directed the first Potter films), and some of the interrelationships between generations certainly play out similarly, with the gods often as disparaging of mortals as Voldemort's followers were of Muggles. Unlike the gods in *Jason* though, these Olympians generally stay away from manipulating events in the mortal realm. Gods and mortals alike are portrayed as flawed, with the suggestion that the future lies in the hands of the young demi-gods, who may (or may not) combine the best of both worlds.

7

Art Cinema: *Fellini-Satyricon* (1969)

Introduction

So far the discussion of the representation of antiquity in cinema has focussed on popular, commercial films. However, there is another genre of film practice that is equally interested in antiquity. This is the genre of 'art films'. As we shall see, the self-consciously distinctive nature of these films makes it difficult to define what constitutes an 'art film'. Part of the problem with definition is that it is easier to recognise what these films are not (i.e. widely-distributed, industry-driven products with a broad appeal) than identify the constituent elements that unify them. People tend to know one when they see it, but drawing up a list of criteria to define what constitutes an 'art film' is practically impossible. Some films have large budgets involving multiple personnel, others are made on the most meagre of resources using only a few staff. Some prove widely popular with audiences, others are only beloved by a select group of critics. Even the terminology proves difficult. Some dislike using the term 'art film' in a broad sense preferring to restrict its use to only high-culture films from the early part of the twentieth century, the films for which the term 'art film' was coined. Some prefer to use a designation that stresses place of production ('European cinema'), others stress the place of reception or the mode of distribution ('arthouse' or 'indie' films), still others prefer to characterise them by the intellectual movements to which the films seem affiliated ('modernist' or 'avant-garde' cinema).

One of the few common elements in the 'art film' is the strong presence of an 'auteur' (French: 'author') whose vision dominates the final product. Underpinning the notion of auteurist cinema is the idea of film as the projection of a particular and unique personality, a personality who is free to act without (e.g. commercial, moral) restraints. Although, even this is not always straightforward. On the one hand, in theory, every film has an 'auteur' in the form of its director. On the other hand, almost no film is just the product of one man. Even the most dictatorial directors find that the ideas and decisions of set-designers, composers, costumiers, casting agents, cameramen, lighting-directors and producers become inevitably incorporated into their films. The long list of credits that come at the end of the film are not an empty ritual, but are a highly-regulated testament that precisely quantifies the wide range of contributions made by members to a finished cinematic product.

146

7. Art Cinema: Fellini-Satyricon (1969)

The origins of the intellectual analysis of the role of the auteur and auteurist cinema can be traced to François Truffaut's famous essay 'On a certain tendency of the French cinema' in *Cahiers du cinema* in 1954. One of Truffaut's aims was to reclaim the title of 'art' for film. The term 'art film' had been around since the earliest days of cinema, and many artists were attracted by the potential of cinema when film first began. However, the rise of large professional studios and the increasing use of generic formulae in popular cinema had debased the notion of cinema as art. In reasserting cinema's claim to art, Truffaut stressed the contribution of the director's personal style as being crucial for the appreciation of the film. The rest of the personnel, most notably the scriptwriter, thus became completely secondary. Criticism should centre around the director's distinctive style. In such a scenario, film becomes a particularly personal expression and the cultivation of personal style is the implicit aim of the director's art.

Such analysis prompts two questions. First, how does one create a sense of personal style? The answer to this lies in the various cinematic techniques available to the director to make the film distinctive from other cinematic products. For example, this could include such elements as a predilection for a certain type of shot such as extended tracking shots or extreme close-ups. Alternatively, it can be through the use of recurrent thematic motifs or a preference for certain types of narratives, especially non-linear narratives. Even certain types of production techniques (e.g. the use of improvisation) can contribute to making the film distinctive. Whatever technique is used, the aim of the director, if they want their film to be regarded as art, is to distinguish it using such techniques from mainstream fodder.

The second question concerns how such a style should be assessed and is much more difficult. It requires analysis not only of how a film distances itself from other similar treatments, but also how the film fits within a particular director's oeuvre. In the case of the representation of the ancient world, this means that films should not only be analysed against other depictions of Greece and Rome, but also located within a body of work in which the depiction of the classical world may rarely feature.

Superficially, the economic position of art cinema looks bleak. By their very nature, unique and idiosyncratic films tend to be less popular than industry-made commercial fare. They inevitably take more risks and with risk comes a greater chance of failure. Yet, the cultivation of a distinctive style does have certain commercial advantages. Once a certain style is developed it can be used to market a film. Audiences know, on one level, what to expect even if that expectation is to expect the unexpected. Most art cinema directors would shudder at the notion that they represent a brand. Yet, as we shall see in the case of *Fellini-Satyricon,* the director's name was an important part of the marketing of the film and ensuring its production and distribution.

147

The term 'art cinema' was first coined to describe films of stage production and adaptations of literary works. Although the genre has expanded to include a much wider range of films, work that adapts or derives inspiration from literary texts still constitutes a significant strand in 'art films'. This has important consequences for the representation of antiquity because the intellectual sophistication and consequent high prestige attached to classical texts has ensured that they have regularly been the subject of cinematic reworking.

We can see this process most clearly in relation to Greek tragedy. Over fifty films take one of the Greek tragedies as their starting point. Sometimes these films employ a relatively straightforward theatrical aesthetic in their cinematic versions of the tragedy. A good example of such a film is Jean Prat's *Les Perses* (1961), a film adaption of Aeschylus' play, *The Persians*, produced for the French national television broadcaster. The film is characterised by the 'staginess' of the production. The set is modelled on a Persian palace, but the broad balconies and ramps mimic a stage-set. Even the traditional three doors of the classical stage are preserved in the set. Adding to the sense of theatre, the characters wore masks and the camera shots largely imitated natural viewing patterns. The production stuck reasonably faithfully to the original script and was well received by critics. Particularly popular were the chorus of Persian noblemen whose masks were derived from Achaemenid art. The soundtrack by Jean Prodromidès went on to become one of the best sellers of the year.

In contrast, other directors prefer to take a more interventionist approach to their versions of Greek tragedy, ensuring that they firmly leave their stamp on the work. One of the most intense engagements with Greek tragedy can be found in the work of Pier Paolo Pasolini (1922-1975). Novelist, poet, and filmmaker, Pasolini exerted tremendous influence over Italian avant-garde culture from the 1950s until the time of his murder seemingly at the hands of a hustler in 1975. One of the central themes in his cinematic works was a desire to engage with the central texts of western culture. He directed films based on Boccaccio's *Decameron*, Chaucer's *Canterbury Tales*, *A Thousand and One Nights*, the *Gospel of Matthew*, and the Marquis de Sade's *120 Days of Sodom*. It was natural that Greek tragedy should also come within his view. Pasolini produced two works based on tragedy, *Oedipus Rex* (Italian title: *Edipo Re*, 1967) and *Medea* (1969) along with a documentary about preparations for a cinematic version of the Oresteia set in Africa, *Notes for an African Orestes* (*Appunti per un' Orestiade africana*, 1970). Both of Pasolini's tragedies are distinguished by the incorporation of a large amount of extra-textual material (particularly scenes from the mythic history of the characters prior to the events depicted in the tragedy) as well as a free approach to the text. *Oedipus Rex* (1967) includes material from both of Sophocles' Oedipus plays – *Oedipus Tyrannus* and *Oedipus at Colonus*. In both

148

Oedipus Rex and *Medea*, the sources of Pasolini's inspiration range widely. The sets evoke North Africa as much as Greece. The costumes are influenced by African, Papua New Guinean, and Georgian tribal designs. The soundtrack includes elements of Romanian, Georgian, and Japanese music.

A mid-position between these two extremes is presented by directors who remain faithful to the original play, but blend new elements and cinematic techniques so that they produce unique cinematic versions of the original tragedy. The Greek director Michael Cacoyannis' (1922-2011) three films based on Euripidean tragedies (*Electra*, 1962; *Trojan Women*, 1971; and *Iphigenia*, 1977) capture this approach. Assisted by the Greek government as a method of boosting tourism, these films were tremendously popular. In producing the film, the crew enjoyed unique access to important sites. *Electra*, for example, is shot in the ruins of the Bronze Age citadel of Mycenae. They had distinguished casts. *Trojan Women* stars Irene Papas, Katharine Hepburn, and Vanessa Redgrave. They also enjoyed critical success. Both *Electra* and *Iphigenia* were nominated for Oscars for 'Best Foreign Language' film as well as winning numerous international film awards.

The adaption of classical texts is not the only way the ancient world has impacted on 'art cinema'. Other aspects of classical culture, most notably mythic narratives have also been very influential. The archetypal status of Greek myths has seen many directors drawn to them for inspiration. For example, the important French avant-garde director, Jean Cocteau (1889-1963) produced a trilogy of black-and-white films based around the Orpheus myth.

The first film in the sequence is *The Blood of a Poet* (French title: *Le Sang d'un poète*, 1930) which takes the form of loosely-connected surreal sequences. The film opens with a bewigged artist drawing a face on a canvas only to see the mouth start to move. Alarmed, he rubs out the mouth only to discover that the mouth transfers itself to his hand. In desperation, he wipes his hand on a statue which transfers the mouth to the statue and allows it to speak. The statue, an imitation of the Venus de Milo, instructs the artist to leap through a mirror in the wall, which transports the artist to a long corridor full of locked doors. Looking through the keyholes, the artist sees a series of bizarre scenes including a slow-motion execution of a Mexican, the flagellation of a child covered in brass bells, and a striptease performed by a disembodied hermaphrodite reclining on a chaise-lounge. Suddenly a hand appears and gives the artist a revolver and commands that he shoot himself. This he does, but the bullet does not kill him, its just transforms him into a blood-splattered classical poet. The artist then turns around and returns through the mirror to confront the speaking statue. Grabbing a hammer, he smashes it to pieces causing a cloud of fine plaster dust to rise up. The dust transforms into a snow-filled scene and we find ourselves observing a snowball fight between children. As the fighting continues, it becomes

149

increasingly more violent. One boy's leg is broken. Another is strangled by a scarf. Finally, one boy throws a snowball of such solidity that it knocks one of the boys unconscious. Terrified, the children scatter, leaving the boy to bleed to death in the snow. The last scene of the film involves a card game being played over the corpse of the boy while an audience applauds from opera boxes above. Finally one of the card-players pulls out a gun and shoots himself dead. His female companion walks away from the table leaving his body in a pool of blood.

As one can see from this synopsis, this film is no straightforward retelling of the Orpheus tale. Instead, it chooses to adopt motifs drawn from the mythic story of Orpheus to tell its tale of a poet and his relationship with his work. For example, the journey through the mirror represents a descent into the Underworld. This particular motif proved popular with critics and Cocteau reprised it in his second Orpheus film, *Orphée* (1950). This second film, while set in contemporary Paris and including a number of experimental elements was designed to be more recognisably based on the myth of Orpheus and his attempt to rescue his wife Eurydice from Hades. *Orphée* told the story of a poet whose beloved is killed by the chauffeur of a princess (representing Death) and who journeys into a dreamscape to retrieve her. In the final film in the sequence, *Testament of Orpheus* (1959), Cocteau returns to the more avant-garde aspects of *Blood of a Poet* to give an account of poetic inspiration. Featuring a cast of well-known figures such as Pablo Picasso and Yul Brynner, this film shows a poet travelling through a series of landscapes in pursuit of poetic truth.

Cocteau's trilogy demonstrates that even when a single director confronts the same sets of issues in a series of films, his versions will often vary dramatically in terms of form, style, and content. It is easy to spot the differences in approach in Cocteau's three films. Despite their common origins in the myth of Orpheus, scenes from one film do not easily transpose themselves into another. They share a common sensibility and approach to filmmaking, but are independent products. For such reasons, it is difficult to generalise about art film as a genre. Each film needs to be taken on its own merits and be seen as a unique product.

Background to case study

On 10 August 1968, the *New York Times* published an announcement about the next project by the celebrated Italian director, Federico Fellini (1920-1993). The film would be an adaptation of Petronius' *Satyricon* and feature 'a vast fresco of comedians old and young portraying the bawdy days of Petronius Arbiter in ancient Rome'.

It is hard to determine precisely what expectations this announcement created for the cinema-going public. Petronius was hardly a household name. In the popular imagination, the figure of Petronius, the emperor

Nero's confidante and so-called 'arbiter of taste', was most closely associated with his appearance in *Quo Vadis* (1951). Leo Genn won plaudits for
his portrayal of this disillusioned courtier who finally tires of the corruption of Rome and commits suicide after penning a letter denouncing Nero's
depravity and lack of talent. Indeed, Henryk Sienkiewicz's depiction of
Petronius in his novel *Quo Vadis* determined the popular understanding
of the figure for the twentieth century. In the commendation for the award
of Sienkiewicz's Nobel Prize for literature in 1905, the awarding committee singled out his depiction of Petronius for particular praise:
'Sienkiewicz has constructed a psychological picture that gives a strong
appearance of truthfulness and is extremely penetrating ... The entire
description is perfect in its genre.' Similar praise was handed out by Harry
Thurston Peck, Professor of Latin at Columbia, in his influential essay
'*Quo Vadis* as History' (1898): 'As to the delineation of historical characters, high praise must also be given here. Petronius ... is a picture filled
out with plausibility and skill from the slight sketch preserved in Tacitus.'

If most readers of the *Times* would have had only a vague idea about
Petronius, they would have been even less familiar with the content of the
Satyricon, the Latin novel which since the sixteenth century had been
attributed to Petronius. The novel exists in a fragmentary state. Both the
beginning and the ending are missing. Sometimes we only have a single
sentence out of a chapter. The amount that survives represents a small
proportion of the complete work (parts of three books out of possibly
twenty-four). The over-arching narrative of the work concerns the, often
erotic, adventures of the principal narrator Encolpius, in particular his
obsession with the boy Giton and his attempt to secure his love against his
rival Ascyltos. Along the way, numerous vignettes are sketched out. The
most famous among them is the detailed description of the banquet held
by the boorish, wealthy freedman, Trimalchio (the so-called *Cena Trimal-
chionis* 'Dinner of Trimalchio').

Adaptations of the text for American audiences were few. However,
Fellini's promise of a humorous offering follows an established trend.
Previous popular representations of the text had a propensity to stress the
work's eroticised content and its humorous nature. One of the earliest of
the twentieth century's comic *Satyricons* was Randolph Carter's *Arms for
Venus* (1937), which ran on Broadway and was described by *Variety* as 'an
orgy of laughs'. Seven months before the US release of Fellini's *Satyricon*,
the *New York Times* in its review of William Arrowsmith's translation of
Petronius' text introduced the work to American audiences by describing
it as 'a Roman Vaudeville'. Two years after Fellini's film opened, the
composer Bruno Maderna's musical version of the *Satyricon* proved a
comic hit with audiences.

The cast list that Fellini proposed for his adaptation of the *Satyricon*
seemed to confirm this strongly comic vein. Mae West was said to have
been signed up to play a part along with Groucho Marx, Jimmy Durante,

and Danny Kaye. *The Beatles* were supposed to have agreed to provide some of the music and also act in a few scenes. A couple of months later Fellini confirmed this cast list and even added a few extra names such as Terence Stamp and Mickey Mouse. These stars would be combined with 'many Italian comedians' to produce a unique version of Petronius' text. Given such casting discussions, it was perhaps understandable that many thought that Fellini's *Satyricon* was destined to be a light-hearted romp. Indeed, this perception lasted right up until the release of the film in the US. The film had its opening in the US at the Little Carnegie Theater on 11 March 1970. In the promotional material for the launch, the film was described as an 'Italian-made comedy-drama'.

In fact, what Fellini produced was a film that was much darker and more challenging than many expected. The change in casting provides a means through which it is possible to trace the changing conception of this project from its initial planning to final delivery. None of the names floated by Fellini in his early interviews about the *Satyricon* ever made it into the film. The accessible popular ballads of the Beatles gave way to the more avant-garde and experimental electronic work of Nino Rota and Andrew Rudin. Sometimes these casting changes were for entirely practical reasons involving the availability of the actors. According to her biography, Mae West (who Fellini had also tried to hire for his *Juliet of the Spirits*) cooled on the idea of involvement in the project when she discovered that the 'erotic witch' (Oenothea/Enotea) that she was being asked to play was a mother. Terence Stamp proved too expensive. However, these changes in personnel also reflect a change in the nature of the project.

At the start of the planning of the film serious consideration was given to making the film a musical. Fellini had earlier toyed with the idea of producing a musical based on the *Satyricon* while still a law student at university in Rome in 1939. The musical was supposed to offer a satire on the rise of fascism in Italy in the 1930s. However, the problem of censorship and fitting the political content of the satire with the text had dissuaded Fellini from proceeding with the musical proposal at the time. He revisited the idea in the initial stages of brainstorming for the film. The idea of a musical also suited one of the sources of the inspiration for the film – Fellini's childhood experiences with sword-and-sandal epics.

Cinematic depictions of the ancient world had exerted an important influence on Fellini. On a number of occasions, Fellini told about the impact of going to see movies featuring ancient Rome with his father. His very first movie was a gladiator epic, which he saw at the age of six at the impressive neo-classical cinema, the Fulgor, in the main street of his hometown in Rimini. The experience stuck in the mind of the young Fellini, eventually reappearing a couple of years after his *Satyricon* as a reworked scene in *Roma* (1972), Fellini's largely autobiographical film about moving as a child from Rimini to Rome. In the scene, the young child is captivated by a black-and-white gladiator film about scandalous events during the reign of Claudius. The film exerts such an influence on the imagination of the child that when he later hears gossip that the wife of the pharmacist is 'worse than Messalina', he can only imagine her in terms of the wicked empress of the cinematic orgies that he has seen on screen. Another image that had impressed itself upon the director came from his experience of going as a young reporter in the early 1940s to the great Italian film studio of Cinecittà and seeing the extras from one of the numerous historical epics produced in the period. What struck him was the humorous juxtaposition of actors dressed as gladiators and soldiers in togas, helmets, and breastplates sitting around the studio bar drinking fizzy lemonade. The cinematic potential of this blend of mundane modernity and the exoticism of antiquity appealed greatly to the director.

Such biographical information is important because one of Fellini's distinctive characteristics as a filmmaker is the way in which he imports and translates personal experience into cinema. Fellini has always resisted the label that his films are strictly autobiographical. However, it is undeniable that he repeatedly draws on personal memories to create his scenes.

The most clearly autobiographical film by Fellini is *Amarcord* (1973), a film set in the Rimini of Fellini's youth and featuring a coming-of-age story that draws heavily on his own childhood. The title, which means 'I remember' in the local dialect, indicates that this is a very personal reminiscence. Yet this autobiographical sensibility can be seen flowing through Fellini's career from his earliest works. Fellini's first commercial and critical success was his film *I Vitelloni* (1953). The title of the film ('little calves') is slang from Fellini's hometown of Rimini and refers to 'lazy, spoilt, feckless youths'. The movie traces the meanderings of a group of overindulged friends as they waste their time in an Italian provincial town. Fellini, who was once berated for being a 'vitellone' by an elderly citizen upset at his behaviour, drew heavily on his childhood in Rimini and his experience of the youths of his hometown in constructing the story. Similarly his experience as a filmmaker and journalist have been imported into a number of films, most notably *8½* (1962) and *La Dolce Vita* (1960). The former is a film about a director suffering from 'director's block' as he makes a post-apocalyptic science-fiction film and the latter is the story of a journalist's adventures in Rome's demi-monde.

Given its origins in childhood pastimes and comic juxtapositions, it is understandable that the initial tone of the *Satyricon* should have been light. Of course, Fellini's *Satyricon* was never going to be standard comic fare, but what turned it into a more serious, abstract, and imaginative film was another desire that had been pressing upon the director. This was the idea of creating an alternate world, a complete vision that could mimic the director's dreams. Just as he was about to start production of *Juliet of the Spirits* (*Giulietta degli Spiriti*, 1965), Fellini expressed this desire to make a new kind of film:

Up until now, I've always done stories where the requirements of the plot, or the setting, or the fact that the action is meant to be taking place in the present day, have prevented me from transfiguring everything in the way that I'd like – the furnishing of a room, the face of an actor, the general atmosphere of a scene. That's why, from time to time, I dream of making a film with historical costumes and in color to tell a fable relating solely to the imagination, which would not have any clearly defined intellectual, ethical structure: reality within the imagination (Canby 1984: 15).

This idea of a version of reality that claimed to be historical, but in fact escaped normal conventions and operated outside the bounds of traditional narrative found its fulfilment in the *Satyricon*.

Part of the reason that the *Satyricon* should prove the vehicle for the director's desire to create an entirely fantastic world was Fellini's discovery about the great potential for his imagination that setting a film in ancient Rome would provide. Fellini read widely on the topic and had the advantage of advice from the classicists Luca Canali and Ettore Paratore, the latter one of the leading authorities on Petronius. Yet, what struck him after his enquiries was the incompleteness of our knowledge about the ancient past and the licence that this gave him:

Suddenly, I realize that we don't know one damn thing for sure about Rome thousands of years ago. It is one big *nebuloso*, full of myth, fairy tale, Cecil B. DeMille information. Now I am excited, because I know that the picture will be a trip in the dark, a descent by submarine, a science-fiction, a psychedelic picture! I know that I want no help from books, from archaeology, and I feel better. A voyage into total obscurity! An unknown planet for me to populate! (Burke 1970: 99).

This idea of Fellini's *Satyricon* as a 'science fiction' set not in the future but the past has proved popular with critics. It captures the sense of alienation one feels in watching this film. Whatever past Fellini is showing, it is not one shared by the audience.

This reorientation of Fellini's cinematic project towards 'a trip in the dark' is reflected in the move away from well-known actors in the film's casting. Fellini wanted to start with a blank slate. 'I want people to look at the picture without the help of a star to guide them ... I realize that if I put in some well-known actor, the audience identifies with him and his past roles ... For *Satyricon* I do not even look for actors with strong charisma; just interesting faces', he said in the same interview. In this instance, nothing was to detract from the director's vision.

If the faces weren't to have charisma, that didn't mean that they shouldn't be pretty. A desire for beautiful boys to play the male leads can be traced to early in the film's production. At one of the interviews where Fellini was still talking about casting Mae West, the interviewer noted that a casting call had been made for 'beautiful boys' for the film. A good number turned up, many of them inexperienced at acting with only a sense of their own good looks making them think that they were suitable for the film. A few were deluding themselves. 'Some of them are so ugly ... Almost as ugly as those who were here when he was casting the freaky ones', whispered one of Fellini's assistants to the reporter who had stumbled into the casting (Shivas 1968: D21).

In the end, no Italian boy proved beautiful enough for the male leads, although a number did make it into roles as extras. Fellini had always tried to mix amateurs and professionals in his films. 'I like actors, but amateurs make things more credible', he declared. For the cast of the *Satyricon,* Fellini recruited local meatworkers, peasants, gypsies, greengrocers, and market gardeners. This preference for amateurs and the unknown continued into the casting of the lead roles. The roles of Encolpio (Encolpius), Ascilto (Ascyltos) and Gitone (Giton) were given to Martin Potter, Hiram Keller and Max Born respectively. Potter was a British actor who, prior to the *Satyricon,* had enjoyed only minor roles in major stage productions and television series. Similarly, neither the American-born Keller nor the British Born had any substantial film experience before the filming of the *Satyricon.* All actors shared a similar love of alternative theatre. Prior to filming the *Satyricon,* Keller had starred in the Broadway production of the counter-cultural musical *Hair.* Max Born arrived on set with shoulder-length hair, a love of Eastern mediation, and a desire to 'chuck all the old ideas away and start understanding things' (Zanelli 1970: 5). For Fellini, their lack of experience and even their lack of Italian was an advantage. It was all about the look. 'Their faces are right. So they don't speak a word of Italian, it makes no difference' (Burke 1970: 99). This sense of the lack of force of personality was only intensified by the casual dubbing of the actors that gives their presence a dreamlike and insubstantial quality, an effect further exacerbated by the slight distortion produced by the use of anamorphic camera lens which produce a much flatter, shallower depth of field so that characters seem to be moving in more distinct, slightly unreal planes.

The filming of *Satyricon* took place almost entirely in the studios of Cinecittà. The few outside scenes were shot nearby; Focene on the coast near Rome's Fiumicino airport served as the location for the beach scenes. Cinecittà was a studio with which Fellini had a particularly close association. Large sections of *La Dolce Vita* had either been filmed or produced there. Cinecittà also had a strong association with films set in the ancient world. The studio had been founded at the instruction of Mussolini in 1937, and had become the home of large-scale Italian cinema ever since that time. In the 1950s, the lots had been used for the filming of ancient epics such as *Quo Vadis* (1951), *Helen of Troy* (1956), *Ben-Hur* (1959) and *Cleopatra* (1963). More recently, the studio's association with the ancient world has been strengthened with use of the studio for the filming of the HBO TV-series, *Rome.* It was a studio that was used to handling large sets. For *Satyricon,* a number of very big sets were constructed under the direction of the architect Luigi Scaccianoce and the designer Danilo Donati. Fellini only had a limited budget for the film and constantly felt its restrictions. Financiers, principally the United Artists studio, had raised around 2 billion lire (US$ 3.3 million). Fellini worried that such money would barely fund the credits for what he intended. At one point in production, Fellini joked about a solution to his money problems, '[We will have] very beautiful credits. The rest of the time the screen will be blank. We lock the doors and the audience must imagine its own film. It is very creative for them' (Shivas 1968: D21). Yet, despite these financial constraints the production values of the film did not suffer. This was largely due to the ingenuity of Donati who was often able to find cheap substitutes for expensive-looking props and finishes. For example, the large mosaic of Trimalchio is composed entirely of candy. Donati, who had just a year previously won acclaim (and ultimately an Oscar) for his work on the costumes for Franco Zeffirelli would become one of Fellini's favourite designers. They would collaborate a number of times, including Fellini's *Casanova* (1976) for which Donati would win his second Oscar.

The marketing of the film placed great prominence on Fellini's name. 'Rome. Before Christ. After Fellini.', declared one of the most prominent film posters. (In fact inaccurately: the *Satyricon* is set in a world that although indeterminate is after the birth of Christ.) The film was actually released under the title of *Fellini-Satyricon*. However, this had less to do with the marketing cachet of the director's name than the fact that the release of Fellini's *Satyricon* coincided with another rival *Satyricon* project by Gian Luigi Polidoro (director) and Alfredo Bini (producer). At the time, there was some suggestion that these two filmmakers had produced their film in an attempt to cash in on Fellini's project. Such accusations were unfair. The pair secured the rights to the name *Satyricon* before Fellini (hence the need to devise a new title for Fellini's film) and far from being a cheap rip-off, the film actually had a budget of $1.6 million.

While Polidoro and Bini had been successful in securing the rights to the name *Satyricon*, this seems to be the only real success that they enjoyed with this rival *Satyricon* project. The film opened before Fellini's, but its run was short – only four days. Authorities objected to the obscene content of the film, and shut down the film, arresting Polidoro and Bini on the charges of making an obscene film and corrupting the morals of a minor (one of the actors). This second charge was dismissed by the court and, while the court did rule that the film was obscene and ordered the removal of about 100 feet of film, both Bini and Polidoro were handed suspended sentences. The film was then released to Italian audiences, after the necessary cuts had been made. However, despite the fact that punishment of the producers and the confiscation of the film made it briefly a cause célèbre for Italian liberals, the film sank without a trace. It was largely ignored by Italian newspapers. The film was never seen outside Italy. In the end, in order to safeguard the Fellini film, United

7. Art Cinema: Fellini-Satyricon (1969)

Artists bought the world rights for Polidoro and Bini's film and refused to release it, ensuring that the only *Satyricon* available to international audiences was Fellini's.

Despite the director's deliberate attempt to present an alternative and idiosyncratic version of ancient Rome, there was much that was deeply conventional about the marketing of the film. In particular, the strong associations between Rome and sexuality were stressed. Trailers for the film presented audiences with scenes of writhing bodies and promised scenes of depravity and excess; all the standard tropes of the popular conception of the Roman empire. As we have seen earlier, the genre-defying nature of the film made it difficult to describe to audiences and the marketers of the film can perhaps be forgiven for turning to hoary old clichés to promote the product.

Fellini did not expect his film to do well at the box-office. On set he joked about this, describing the film as 'one long suicide' (Zanelli 1970: 10). The reaction to the film was mixed. Critics were divided in their responses. The film won the Critics Prize at the Venice Film Festival and a number of critics praised the film and listed it amongst the best films of 1970, although one did note that while he included it on his list, 'this has not been an especially brilliant year for movies' (Canby, V. in *New York Times* 27/12/1970: 61). Others were not as kind. John Simon in a review entitled 'A spanking for *Fellini Satyricon*' was extremely critical. Describing the film as 'a gimcrack, shopworn nightmare', he criticised the liberties that Fellini had taken with his original text:

> There is no excuse for the chaotic magpie's nest that Fellini has made of the work, depriving it of any meaningful structure, tossing into it garbled bits of literature, history, art history, languages from ancient Greek to modern German, obviously self-serving allusions to his own earlier films – every-thing out of whack, topsy-turvey and gratuitous – unless astounding the bourgeoisie can be called a valid motive. (Simon 1970: 99)

Four years later, he returned to this theme. In a retrospective piece on the director, he singled out *Satyricon* as the start of the 'tragic deterioration of Fellini's genius'. Others were happy to endorse Simon's verdict. Willard Van Dyke, Director of the Department of Film at the Museum of Modern Art wrote that 'this Fellini film lacks the sense of style that was so apparent in *8½*, but it also lacks the dramatic values. Instead, it substitutes the stylishness of interior decorators and acting below the level of a high school pageant' (Van Dyke 1970: 80).

The film has similarly divided classicists. Gilbert Highet, popular critic, professor at Columbia, and well-regarded writer on the classical tradition, liked the film with some qualifications. Highet relished the fact that it avoided the standard errors of most motion pictures in making 'everyone too straightforward and too modern'. In his review entitled 'Whose *Satyricon* – Petronius' or Fellini's?' he drew attention to the wide variety of

157

classical texts which influenced the film. Other critics have been only too happy to join him in pointing out this variety of texts that *Fellini-Satyricon* draws upon. These include not only Petronius' text, but also Apuleius' *Golden Ass*, Horace's *Odes*, Suetonius' *Lives of the Twelve Caesars,* and Tacitus' *Histories*. Indeed, this lack of exclusive fidelity to Petronius' text has become a divisive issue for critics. In one of the first reviews of the film in the *New York Times,* John Simon drew attention to the fact that the wife of the suiciding couple cites Hadrian's epigram on his departing soul even though the line was composed a century too late to be included in Petronius' text. For him, this typified Fellini's sloppy pretentiousness. In contrast, Thalia Pandiri and Robert Baxter from the Department of Classics at Smith College wrote to the *New York Times* defending Fellini's techniques, praising this practice of quotation, and arguing that it had excellent classical precedent in the work of many Roman writers such as Virgil who had been happy to quote other authors. For them, Fellini's use of multiple allusions to other texts only added to the film's richness.

Plot summary

Fellini-Satyricon eschews a traditional plot in favour of a series of loosely connected episodes. The film begins with Encolpio (Martin Potter) raging that his fellow student with whom he shares an apartment, Ascilto (Hiram Keller) has stolen his slave lover Gitone (Max Born) from him. Encolpio confronts Ascilto at a bathhouse. A fight ensues and Ascilto confesses that he has sold Gitone to the actor, Vernacchio (Fanfulla). Encolpio then visits Vernacchio's theatre and witnesses a macabre theatrical performance in which one of the actors has his hand cut off. Vernacchio is initially reluctant to return Gitone to Encolpio, but is forced to do so when a magistrate in the audience threatens him with punishment.

Gitone and Encolpio then walk through the streets of Rome on their way to Encolpio's apartment. Along the way, they encounter many fantastic scenes of Roman life. A detour takes them through one of Rome's brothels. Eventually, Encolpio and Gitone arrive home and make love to celebrate their reunion.

Their peaceful co-existence does not last long. Ascilto bursts into the apartment and wakes up the sleeping lovers. Both Encolpio and Ascilto agree that they can no longer bear each other's company and agree to go their separate ways. They divide their possessions, but when it comes to the ownership of Gitone, they let the slave decide. Unexpectedly, Gitone chooses Ascilto and he and Ascilto depart leaving Encolpio distraught.

Suddenly, an earthquake erupts and Encolpio's apartment block is destroyed. The scene jumps abruptly to a light-filled art gallery in which Encolpio encounters the poet Eumolpo (Salvo Randone). Encolpio accompanies Eumolpo as he makes his way to the villa of his patron, Trimalcione (Il Moro, Mario Romagnoli).

While at the villa, Encolpio and Eumolpo enjoy a sumptuous feast and a variety of entertainments. Unfortunately, Eumolpo is unable to endure a life of flattering his patron and his poetry any longer. Drunk, he accuses Trimalcione of plagiarising his verses from Lucretius. Enraged, Trimalcione orders his slaves to throw Eumolpo into the furnace in the kitchen. Eumolpo is dragged off to meet this ghastly fate.

The scene shifts to outdoors as Trimalcione's party makes its way to view the tomb that Trimalcione is constructing for himself and his wife. Trimalcione then acts out his funeral and demands that his guests mourn for him. While at the tomb, one of the guests tells the story of the 'Matron of Ephesus'. The film retells this darkly humorous story about a woman who is forced to desecrate the corpse of her husband to save the life of her new lover.

We then see Encolpio and Eumolpo wandering through a field. Eumolpo is still alive, but has been severely beaten by the servants in the kitchen. Exhausted, Encolpio collapses and falls asleep. No sooner has he closed his eyes, than he is roughly woken. The scene has shifted to a beach and Encolpio, Ascilto, and Gitone (now reunited) have been captured by the slaver Lica (Alain Cuny) who searches the world for people and objects that he thinks will please the emperor. The three companions are loaded onto Lica's ship. During the voyage, Lica takes a fancy to the beautiful Encolpio and arranges to marry him on the deck of the ship. Unfortunately for Lica, a palace coup forces the emperor to commit suicide before the slaver can deliver his valuable cargo. The new emperor's forces seize Lica's ship, Lica is killed, and Gitone is taken.

The scene shifts to a villa where a wealthy couple make preparations as a result of the changed political circumstances. The slaves are freed and the children are sent off to safety. Once these arrangements have been made the couple commit suicide. A little later Ascilto and Encolpio stumble onto the scene. They discover the corpses of the couple and explore the now deserted villa, encountering a slave girl whose sexual favours they enjoy.

There is another abrupt transition and we find Ascilto and Encolpio in a desert landscape. In a nomadic caravan lies a woman with an insatiable desire for sex. Ascilto joins the long list of men who try to bring her relief. Meanwhile, Encolpio learns that the companions of the woman are taking her to a hermaphrodite who has miraculous powers.

Ascilto and Encolpio hatch a plan to steal the hermaphrodite and sell him for a fortune. Killing his attendants, they escape with the hermaphrodite. However, the hermaphrodite proves too sickly to travel and dies as they transport him away from his shrine.

We next see Encolpio fighting a man in a minotaur costume. Hunted through a labyrinth, Encolpio collapses at the minotaur's feet begging for mercy. At this point, it is revealed that the combat is all an elaborate ruse, part of a rite to the god of laughter. Encolpio is rewarded with a woman, but discovers that he has been cursed with impotency. Onto the scene

159

comes Eumolpo who has recovered from his beating and risen to be master of a nearby city. He promises to arrange a cure for Encolpio's condition. This is eventually achieved when Encolpio sleeps with the witch Enotea (Donyale Luna).

While Encolpio is seeing Enotea, Ascilto gets into a fight and is mortally wounded. Encolpio wanders on alone and arrives at the seashore in time for the funeral of Eumolpo. At the funeral, Eumolpo's will is read in which he promises a share of his fortune to any who is prepared to consume his corpse. Greedy mourners begin to devour the flesh. Disgusted, Encolpio leaves the scene in a trading ship that Eumolpo had chartered for a trip to Africa. A voice-over begins to recount Encolpio's voyage. The film ends mid-sentence.

Key scenes and themes

The joy of the fragmentary

The lack of linear narrative and the desire to embrace the fragmentary are often seen as two of the most distinctive features of Fellini's film. This reaches its climax at the end when, as the screenplay declares, 'everything cracks and crumbles ... It is all transformed into an antique fresco; a discolored fresco in Pompeiian colors' (Zanelli 1970: 273). In the final act of the film, Encolpio is literally transformed into a fragment of wall-painting and, as the camera pulls back, we can see other scenes and characters of the film have been rendered into frescoes. The fresco of Encolpio joins with a depiction of Gitone, Ascilto and Vernacchio. Another fragment contains a depiction of Trimalcione, his wife Fortunata, and Eumolpo. Enotea and the wizard who cursed her make up another fragment. In front of them stands yet another fragment of fresco depicting the suicidal couple. As the camera pans back still further, we see that these frescoes form part of a now dilapidated structure perched on a cliff above the sea. The organising principle of the film is displayed. We have been witnesses to a ruin. The disconnected scenes are just fragments from a large whole. Fellini intended this final scene to be revelatory. Yet, in many ways this last dénouement is just the final instance of a motif that has been building up throughout the film.

The scene in the gallery is introduced by an abrupt transition [see box: 'The scene in the gallery']. Indeed, none of the other transitions between scenes in the film can rival this one in violence. One moment we see Encolpio's apartment block being torn asunder by an earthquake. Men and women are screaming. Walls are crumbling. Frenzied horses run wild. And the next moment – silence. The darkness of Encolpio's quarters in the Suburra gives way to a brightly-lit gallery [Fig. 15]. Only gradually does sound return to the scene and when it does, it is gentle and melodic. We find Encolpio on the left of the screen. The camera moves – having briefly lost him – to reinsert him into the centre of the action.

160

The scene in the gallery

Encolpio wanders around a brightly lit gallery. On the walls are paintings from all different periods of classical art. Still smarting from losing his beloved Gitone, Encolpio scoffs at the scenes of love that are depicted. His obvious derision of the scenes catches the attention of the poet, Eumolpo. These fine works of art cause the poet to lament the current state of the arts. Such work would be impossible to produce today. People are too obsessed with money. No one is prepared to suffer poverty as artists did previously to achieve greatness. Our love of food, drink, and sex has made contemporary audiences forget the arts. Romans would prefer a bag of gold to the works of Apelles and Phidias, laments Eumolpo.

15. Learning to love the fragmentary. Gallery scene,
Fellini-Satyricon (1969).

All around Encolpio are famous works of art. They are supposed to be recognisable to the viewer. Fellini intended that the audience should have a sense here that they had seen them before. Knowledgeable viewers will spot reproductions of well-known frescoes from Pompeii and Herculaneum, depictions of maenads and couples from Attic vases, a slab of enlarged cuneiform script, a medallion portrait showing Septimius

Severus and his family, and frescoes from Knossos, to name just a few of the images. In a film which has been characterised by an aesthetic that rendered the ancient world as foreign and alien, the images are a welcome sight, a reassuring vision of the ancient world as we know it and see it in museums and galleries.

In spite of the diversity of their origins, one element unites these images. All are fragments. Some are more damaged than others, but none is complete. In these fragments of art, Fellini found a metaphor for his mutilated text. Fellini found inspiration for his *Satyricon* in the work of the archaeologist. In numerous interviews he compared his role as a director to that of an archaeologist. His film would reconstruct Rome 'as the archaeologist does, when he assembles a few potsherds or piece of masonry and reconstructs not an amphora or a temple, but an artifact in which the object is implied, and this artifact suggests more of the original reality ... Are not the ruins of a temple more interesting than the temple itself?' (Zanelli, 1970: 4).

In a meta-theatrical moment, Fellini even includes such an archaeologist working on a fragment in this gallery scene. In the centre of the room, we see a restorer attempting to repair a broken image on the canvas. The image is taken from a black-figure vase by the Amasis painter in the Cabinet des Médailles in Paris. It depicts two maenads. One has thrown her arms around the other in an ecstatic embrace. The other maenad stands holding out a hare, a traditional lover's gift. In the original vase, the hare is being offered as a gift to Dionysus.

Contemplating these canvases is designed to teach us how to watch this film. The experience of the film is like viewing the frescoes of Pompeii: moments of perfect clarity in which every detail is crystal clear are interspersed with unbridgeable gaps. The mind tries to make sense of the absences. It tries to bridge these gaps to make a complete picture. Sometimes it succeeds, more often it fails. There are limits to the power of the restorer. In the same way, the viewer can see that the various scenes of *Satyricon* are connected and it is possible to construct a rough over-arching narrative, but some doubts remain. Some scenes stubbornly refuse to fit. It is impossible to say with certainty where every scene belongs. There are questions that can never be answered.

Numerous critics have praised Fellini for his desire to embrace the fragment. Where others had only seen the text of Petronius as flawed by its corruption, Fellini seized the opportunities that such a mangled text provided. It is worth noting that Fellini was not the only artist to see the potential of the fragment expressed in the *Satyricon*. At precisely the same time as Fellini was producing his *Satyricon*, Stanley Silvermann and Peter Raby were producing a musical-opera version of the *Satyricon* for the Stratford Opera festival. It is striking that this production also eschewed narrative in favour of the fragment. The fragmentary nature of the piece was highlighted by the decision to have each different scene composed in a contrasting style from electronic to pop to grand opera. Fellini's film coincides with a time in which many in the arts were finding beauty in the damaged and discarded. To the attuned sensibility, the *Satyricon* reminds you of the pleasures of the partial and incomplete. Absence stimulates the audience, goading them on. Fellini wanted his audience to struggle with the film: 'They must fight preconceptions about movies having to tell them a story with a start, a development, an end; preconceptions about myself personally, because they know before that Fellini always tells them some story. This is not an historical picture, a Cecil B. DeMille picture' (Burke 1970: 99).

These fragments are not just celebrated here for their form. Their content also matters. The images resonate with the content of the film. Maenads capture the wildness of the women. The numerous intertwined couples echo the film's erotics. In one canvas in the corner, we see a reproduction of a famous comic play, the *Amphitryo*, which celebrated Zeus' seduction of Alcmene through the ruse of assuming the guise of her husband. The story of adulterous gods using their powers to create confusion and mischief among mortals reminds us just how far this world is separated from the world of Christianity. A number of these images have strong homoerotic connotations. In addition to the coded lesbianism of the maenads in the central canvas, figures from Greek myth who were beloved by homosexuals sit alongside scenes of homosexual love such as the reclining male couple positioned under the window taken from the Etruscan Tomb of the Diver. Encolpio recites the names of these figures. First is Ganymede, the Trojan youth abducted by Zeus to Mount Olympus where he spent the rest of his days serving his lover as a cup-bearer. Next is Narcissus, the man who died after falling in love with his own reflection, a figure who thanks to psychoanalysis has become the paradigm of homosexual desire. Finally, he identifies Hyacinth, the boy beloved by Apollo who died as the result of a contest between Apollo and Zephyr, the West Wind, over the boy. As he died, Apollo turned him into a flower. These themes of homosexual love as dark, passionate, and often tragic flow through the film. The walls of this gallery contain all the stories that this film wishes to tell us.

What is Rome?

Arguably Fellini's favourite subject is Rome. Although born in Rimini, Fellini lived almost all of his adult life in the Italian capital and a number of his films depict the city. The most obvious film dedicated to Rome is – as the title suggests – *Roma*, but other films are also keen to explore the city, its sights, and its regions. Both *La Dolce Vita* and *8½* feature sequences that either take the viewer through the city or help capture its unique aspects. It is within this context of explorations of Rome – the city as opposed to the civilisation – that we should locate the *Satyricon*. Fellini is interested in giving a sense of place as well as time and values.

A trip through the Suburra

The camera follows Encolpio and Gitone as they walk through the streets of the Suburra quarter in Rome. Around one corner, we see a colossal head of an emperor being transported by horses. Fires burn in the streets. Encolpio and Gitone joke with an old prostitute seated outside a brothel. Catching sight of the magistrate who has been pursuing them since the theatre of Vernacchio, they duck through a door heading towards the nearby brothel.

As they wander through the door, they first catch sight of a man sacrificing an animal to discover if his wife is fertile. A pimp soon ushers Encolpio and Gitone into the depths of the brothel. Nearby aristocrats arrive by rafts through the sewers, all eager to obtain a night's pleasure. The brothel is composed of a series of rooms in which every sort of sexual desire is satisfied. Scantily-clad young children dance around an old man. Satisfied customers walk out of the rooms leaving indifferent prostitutes behind them. Rows of men stand around muttering inarticulately. Hawkers offer strange wares to passers-by.

Leaving the brothel, Encolpio and Gitone arrive at their apartment block. The block is built around an *impluvium*, a wide low basin which is designed to catch rainwater. A woman washes her clothes in the water. In order to reach their apartment, Encolpio and Gitone are forced to climb a steep staircase. As they climb the stairs and make their way through the galleries, we catch glimpses of the lives of the other inhabitants of the region. In one apartment a woman lies naked alone. Another is crowded with people and a fight between men spills outside. Suspicious neighbours stare out at us as we pass by. In one room a fire threatens to break out. A bandaged man calls out to his wife from another apartment. A man is seen defecating in the corner of his apartment while outside a man plays a soulful tune on a lyre. The shot changes and the camera pulls back from Encolpio and Gitone to give a complete view of the apartment block. We can see it bustling with activity as the camera pans to the sky.

Fellini had no time for the conventional Rome of epic cinema. Instead of epic's gleaming white marble, he offered a darker more gritty view of the city. The soundscape of the Suburra scene [see box] also defies convention. There are no fanfares of trumpets here. Instead, there is a discordant mix of sounds. Electronic notes cascade. Primitive drums beat an urgent tempo. Cymbals clash and gongs sound. Horses gallop furiously, but produce no noise.

In choosing to show life in the Suburra quarter, Fellini avoided more typical locations such as the Forum or the palaces of Palatine or the temples of the Capitoline. In antiquity, the Suburra was regarded as a notorious area for its prostitution and cheap accommodation. Epic film had, of course, ventured out of the imperial palaces before. Trips to the Christian catacombs were a regular feature of the genre. However, these trips beyond the Palatine were more about formalising a sense of pagan/Christian opposition than creating a sense of the reality of life in the ancient city. In the same way as the dull, homespun fabrics of Christian costume contrasted with the rich colours and elaborate embroidery of imperial garb so too did dark, simple Christian dwellings contrast with the impressive bright gleaming marble palaces and temples of Rome's pagan rulers.

In this sequence, Fellini picks up the cosmopolitan nature of life in Rome. The cityscape is designed to evoke North Africa as much as classical Italy. Fellini took seriously the notion of Rome as 'world capital'. The Suburra sequence is designed to show what such a lofty description might look like on the ground and in the alleyways of the city. Filmed in the largest of the studios of the Cinecittà complex, the magnitude of the ancient city is made apparent. The size of the city and the idea of journeying through it are emphasised by the use of a tracking shot that follows the actors through the quarter. This is one of the few tracking shots that Fellini allowed himself in the film. Even here, the shot is not a conventional tracking shot. It fails to keep track of Encolpio and Gitone. Losing them in the crowd, the camera becomes distracted by some incidental detail. Initial plans for the film specified no tracking shots. In keeping with the contemplatory nature of the film, Fellini wanted his film to be composed exclusively of static shots with no camera movement. Although this stricture was soon broken, no other sequence gives as great a sense of movement as this one.

The Suburra is not only large, it is also rich in diversity. Every age, body-type, and ethnicity is found here. The *Satyricon* is polyglot. Numerous languages occur throughout the course of the film. Characters speak Italian, Greek, Turkish, German, Latin of varying degrees of proficiency, along with invented and nonsensical tongues. Even the inscriptions and graffiti reflect this linguistic diversity. The Latin is deliberately ungrammatical to give the impression that it is written by someone for whom Latin is not their first language.

The sequence begins with Encolpio and Gitone watching a colossal head of an emperor being drawn through the city. The image replays an earlier sequence of Fellini's from *La Dolce Vita* (1960) in which he has a giant statue of Jesus fly through Rome carried by a helicopter. Here appropriately Christ has been replaced by the emperor. In *La Dolce Vita* the transportation of the statue of Jesus is all about the installation of a new monument. Here we are not so sure. Is this head being taken to complete a statue or has the statue been torn down? Similarities have been noted between the scene and the dragging of the body of the emperor Vitellius through the streets of Rome after he was deposed.

Roman politics begins the shot, but Roman pleasure dominates the scene. The majority of the scene involves wandering through a crowded, labyrinthine brothel. Roman erotic art provided the inspiration for a number of the images within the brothel. One of the works that stimulated Fellini's imagination was the collection of erotica assembled in Jean

165

16. Rome without its grandeur. Brothel scene, *Fellini-Satyricon* (1969).

Marcadé's *Roma Amor* (1961). One of the features of this work is the attention that it pays to Pompeian frescoes of couples performing intercourse. Such frescoes which feature isolated figures in sparse undecorated rooms clearly influenced the design of the film [Fig. 16]. Indeed, flicking through the pages of *Roma Amor* produces an effect not dissimilar to wandering through Fellini's brothel as scene of intercourse gives way to yet another scene of intercourse. The inscriptions that adorn the brothel are also borrowed from Pompeian archaeology. Outside one of the booths, we see the inscription 'Bacchis II XXXVII', an abbreviated message inspired by actual examples meaning 'the second prostitute called Bacchis, her price is 37 pieces of silver'.

When discussing Fellini's depiction of sex, one critic observed 'There's always something prudish about sex in Fellini's films, it's almost anti-erotic, possibly because sex so often has its roots in adolescent fantasies that have nothing to do with love' (Canby 1993: C15). It is an acute observation. Even in the Roman brothel scene, a lot of the imagery came not from Roman material, but from Fellini's puberty. Whilst he was a young man in Rimini, conversation among Fellini's friends would often turn to sexual fantasies. A number of the various scenarios imagined by Fellini and his companions were included in the scene. This juxtaposition of modern sexual fantasy and ancient sexual aesthetic creates a unique amalgam, a recipe for Rome that stands outside of time. It is another way of making Rome an 'eternal city'.

A world before Christ

The advertising for the *Satyricon* proclaimed that this was a film 'Before Christ. After Fellini.' The director seems to have risen to the implicit challenges in both statements. Not only is this film a distinctly personal vision, but it is a vision which is serious about capturing a world before Christianity. For Fellini, it was through the pagan mindset that it would be possible to re-capture Rome and it was this idea that drove him through the project: 'It is always difficult to identify the reason why you do something ... what stimulates me is to try to create characters of the same psychology before Christ, before the invention of conscience, of guilt ... That's the real reason to do the picture. To see what people were like 2,000 years before Catholicism' (Shivas 1968: D21). For Fellini, this was not an idle exercise in ancient history, but a project with contemporary urgency. It was from the pagan pre-Christian past that we might learn to live in a modern godless post-Christian world.

The hermaphrodite

A pool shimmers, reflecting the domed mosaic ceiling above. We see a crowd of worshippers, kneeling or sitting on the floor. A veiled woman makes a prayer on behalf of her sick son. In front of her, two attendants stand over a wicker manger set against a grotto wall. The shot shifts to show the crowd of suppliants. A mad man dressed only in a loincloth and bonnet spins around erratically. A man on crutches limps towards the pool while an old man leaves a tray of offerings on the pool edge. We catch a view of the valley outside. A fat man staggers forward whilst a member of his party leaves gold chaplets for the hermaphrodite.

Singing fills the cavern as we again survey the crowd. A man with a bandaged head and a palsied hand stands at the back awaiting his audience with the blessed child. The attendants raise the child out of his manger. He is an albino and seems terribly weak, unable to stand without support. As he is shown to the crowd, the suppliants raise their hands in adoration or bow their heads.

Even within the context of a film replete with freakish bodies, the albino hermaphrodite is one of Fellini's most startling creations. The role was played by a genuine albino from Naples, Pasquali Baldassare. The scene involving the hermaphrodite was one of the first scenes shot by Fellini. It was also one of the most difficult. Fellini had problems getting precisely the right degree of languidness in the performance from the boy that he desired. Language also proved a problem, with Fellini having to use the boy's father to translate into the Neapolitan dialect that the boy understood.

In his treatment for the film, Fellini makes clear that the inspiration for this scene was the site of Lourdes in the French Pyrenees. Its famous grotto became a site of pilgrimage for Catholics following appearances of the Virgin Mary there in 1858. The place is especially well-regarded by the sick, a number of whom claim to have received miraculous cures after visiting the site. Each year, thousands of pilgrims make the trip to Lourdes in the hope of being healed of illnesses and diseases which medicine is unable to cure. For pilgrims, the waters of the grotto have particular importance as it was this water that the Virgin Mary herself commended pilgrims to drink. Pilgrims bathe in the water as a sign of devotion and take flasks home as relics.

Initially, in both the treatment and the screenplay, this scene was intended to occur in a dilapidated temple of Ceres. There are still some elements of this original conception, most notably in the circular roof of the chamber. However, the associations with Lourdes have been strengthened by collapsing the temple into a grotto and making a feature of the large pool of water that separates the hermaphrodite from the worshippers.

Other Catholic imagery informs this scene. The moment where the attendants hold up the pale boy to the crowd references both the practice of the exposure of relics (Fellini was very keen that the genitals be exposed at this point) and the iconography of the *Pietà*, Michelangelo's celebrated depiction of Mary cradling the corpse of Jesus in the Vatican. The women cover their heads and kneel and pray in a manner reminiscent of Catholic liturgy. Even the votive offerings in the shape of the object of supplication, whilst based on ancient precedent, can also find their echo in contemporary religious practice in rural Italy.

This juxtaposition of Catholic rite and pagan context sets up a number of competing ideas. On the one hand, it is deliberately blasphemous. The mimicry of Jesus by replacing him with an intersex albino clearly mocks Christian faith. On the other hand, the scene is strangely comforting. Here is a world that despite its apparent strangeness is recognisable. Roman religion is not alien, but rather seems to operate according to known rules and adhere to an identifiable aesthetic.

Critics such as Erich Segal (1971) have criticised Fellini for his inability to escape his Christian sensibilities ('Fellini left the church, but the church never left him'). He was not alone in making such claims. In an interview with Fellini, Alberto Moravia suggested to the director that his version of antiquity bore a remarkable resemblance to the pagan world as imagined by the early Christians and that it failed to think outside the Christian paradigm (Zannelli: 29). Such scenes as this one seem to lend support to this claim. Yet this perhaps misreads this scene. The scene with the hermaphrodite is designed to feel disturbingly and scandalously familiar.

We are supposed to feel the presence of Christianity here. Elsewhere, rituals are staged to express the foreignness of Roman religion. When a fortune-teller interprets Trimalcione's future from the sound of his belching, the scene is comic, but also designed to allude to the ancient art of cledonomancy, in which certain significant sounds or names can be interpreted to portend important events. This is a moment when the Romans seem definitely not like us.

The film is punctuated by such rituals, many informed by actual ancient religious practice. When Encolpio and Gitone make their way to the brothel at the start of the film, they encounter a couple who have asked a priest to interpret the blood of a sacrificial victim to determine whether the woman is fertile. The scene is based on the Roman (and Near-Eastern) practice of haruspicy in which the organs and entrails of victims were inspected to determine divine will. Although the ritual was limited to organs rather than blood, the film is accurate in its depiction of the motives of the couple. Questions about fertility and legitimacy of children represent a substantial proportion of the inquiries received by oracles in antiquity.

Later we see Trimalcione asking blessings from his household gods, three miniature gold effigies presented to him on a plate. Again Fellini focuses on a particular Roman religious custom. The gods that Trimalcione anoints are the *Penates*, Roman spirits associated with the inner parts of the house. Along with the *Lares*, they made up a group of familiar spirits or 'household gods'. Such gods were central to the religious life of the family. Famously, when Aeneas, the founder of Rome, flees burning Troy, one of few things that he takes with him are his *Penates*.

This desire to capture something of the religious life of the Romans can also be seen in the marriage between Encolpio and Lica. The scene is a dense set of allusions to ancient literary texts and practices. The idea of the marriage ceremony seems to have been inspired by the story of the marriage between the Roman emperor Nero and the slave-boy Sporus. The story is recounted in one of Fellini's favourite texts about ancient Rome, Suetonius' *Lives of the Twelve Caesars*. In his biography of Nero, Suetonius recounts how Nero fell in love with a young Greek slave boy Sporus and dressed him as a woman and even staged a sham marriage ceremony with him, a rite Nero repeated later with another beautiful slave, Doryphorus. The outline of the marriage ceremony, Fellini borrows from Jerome Carcopino's *Daily Life in Ancient Rome*, one of his regular source texts. This gave details of Lica's costume, the saffron robe and the veil fixed with a wreath, as well the sacrifices, the showering of nuts, and the cries of 'Felicitas'. Onto this was grafted other texts. For example, the suggestion that the husband put aside his boys now that he has a wife is taken from Catullus 61, one of the poet's marriage songs.

Even the fantastic 'mirth ritual' in which Encolpio is chased by a gladiator dressed as a minotaur has some basis in Roman literature and ritual. The literary antecedent is Apuleius' *Golden Ass* in which the hero, Lucius suffers a number of shocking indignities as part of a celebration of the 'god of mirth'. While the *Golden Ass* supplies the ritual frame for the scene, we need to look elsewhere for the specific content. While there were no such religious rituals like the one depicted in antiquity, we do know that Romans often staged elaborate mythological pageants in which criminals were executed. Women might be tied to the horns of bulls to be stampeded to death in imitation of the death of Dirce, the woman punished for maltreating Zeus' beloved Antiope. Alternatively, a man might be dressed as Icarus and fired from a catapult. In such a world, the scenario of creating a replica labyrinth and staging the fight of Theseus and the Minotaur is not completely absurd.

Fellini's rituals are fantasies. Some are complete inventions. Some are borrowed from anthropological observations of distant tribal cultures. Others are a pastiche of ancient sources cobbled together to make a strange unity. Yet despite their divergent origins and widely differing form, they are united by a common purpose, namely to use sacred moments to make us rethink the categories of pagan and Christian so that the former become more familiar and the latter more distant.

Suggested further viewing

Orphée (dir. Cocteau, 1950)
This is the second in the trilogy of films that Cocteau made concerning the Orpheus myth. The film is set in 1950s Paris and tells the story of the encounter between the popular poet Orpheus (Jean Marais) and a mysterious woman known as the Princess (Maria Casares). Over the course of the film, it becomes clear that the Princess is the embodiment of Death who is assisted in her task of ending life by her henchmen, sinister leather-clad motorcyclists. Despite sensing danger Orpheus falls in love with the Princess and gradually his feelings for his wife Euridice (Maria Dea) start to flag. However, his passions are re-awakened when Euridice is killed by the Princess' henchmen and he makes a journey into the Underworld to retrieve her. The film is famous for a number of features, most notably its sequence where Orpheus travels into the Underworld through a mirror. Its combination of special effects and dream imagery helped make the film an important subject for artists and writers interested in the power of the subconscious and the archetypal status of myth.

Medea (dir. Pasolini, 1969)
Filmed in the wild, sparse landscape of Cappadocia in Turkey, this film loosely follows the plot of Euripides' tragedy about the foreign princess Medea who is abandoned by her lover Jason for another woman and who consequently murders her rival and her children by Jason. In Pasolini's version of the story, particular attention is given to fleshing out the

170

back-story of events prior to Medea's arrival in Greece. Indeed, many of the most notable scenes in the film occur in the first part of the film where the story of Jason's theft of the Golden Fleece from Colchis is told. Costuming, dance, and language all combine to construct ancient Colchis as a wild, tribal place. Crops are watered with the blood of sacrificial human victims. Pasolini's vision is clearly influenced by contemporary writings on anthropology and ritual. The film stars the opera singer Maria Callas as Medea and Giuseppe Gentile as Jason.

Mighty Aphrodite (dir. Allen, 1995)
Billed as a modern comic-tragedy, this film stars its director Woody Allen as sportswriter Lenny Weinrib who becomes obsessed with finding the mother of his adopted child. It is a decision he soon begins to regret as his pursuit of the mother leads to a series of personal disasters for himself, his wife (Helena Bonham Carter), and the prostitute mother of their child (Mira Sorvino). Inspired by the story of Oedipus, with occasional nods to the myth of Pygmalion, this film plays with the conventions of Greek tragedy. So, for example, despite being set in modern New York, it features a masked Greek chorus who comment on events and pass judgments on characters' actions. The film also makes use of classical plot devices such as the technique of *deus ex machina* whereby seemingly insolvable problems are resolved by sudden, unexpected, and unbelievably fortuitous events.

Satirising Cine-Antiquity:
Monty Python's Life of Brian (1979)

Introduction

The ancient world and its cultural artefacts tend to be associated with high culture and elitist pursuits. In contrast cinema, whether mainstream or, to a lesser extent, arthouse, has been considered part of a more popular cultural tradition. Fitting the two together is bound to be tricky. More successful examples of cine-antiquity, including all of the films discussed so far, have incorporated some element of humour to defuse this tension and avoid appearing too high-minded and didactic. Peter Ustinov's camp performances as Nero in *Quo Vadis* and Batiatus in *Spartacus* are good examples. However, there are also films that have taken a more consistently comic approach to antiquity.

There are various ways that cinema can derive comedy from the ancient world. Some films have adapted ancient comedies to the big screen. Given the context-specific nature of most comic drama, whatever the historical period, some degree of adaptation is usually necessary if the intention is anything more than presenting a record of a performance. However, the slapstick and farce found in some ancient comedies can still prove surprisingly familiar to modern audiences. *A Funny Thing Happened on the Way to the Forum* (1966) is an adaptation of a musical written by Stephen Sondheim, which itself adapted various elements of comedies by the Roman author Plautus including *Miles Gloriosus* ('The Swaggering Soldier'), *Pseudolus*, and *Mostellaria* ('The Little Ghost'). While some of the humour in the film does depend on the use of anachronisms, it succeeds overall in capturing the spirit of Plautine comedy with its multiple plot threads and its social satire. The action is driven by a gaggle of characters from the lower strata of Roman society: the clever slave, Pseudolus (Zero Mostel), the pimp Lycus (Phil Silvers) and the ineffectual younger son of the household, the ironically named Hero (Michael Crawford). Meanwhile the representatives of the more respectable orders of society – the two paterfamilias, the matron and the triumphant soldier – are mocked as lechers, fools, nags and braggarts.

Other films derive their comedy from juxtaposing ancient and modern worlds. In Woody Allen's *Mighty Aphrodite* (1995), the film opens with a costumed Greek chorus performing in the ruins of the Teatro Greco in Taormina, Sicily. They declaim in high style on the whims of the gods and the tragic fates of Achilles, Oedipus and Medea before concluding, with jarring inappropriateness, 'Take for instance the case of Lenny Weinrib. A case as Greek and timeless as fate itself.' The scene cuts to the modern day, where the New York sportswriter Lenny (Allen) and his wife Amanda (Helena Bonham-Carter) are at dinner with friends, discussing the possibility of adoption. Returning to the Greek theatre, Laius and Jocasta are introduced and muse, with the chorus, on the ungratefulness of children who murder their fathers, sleep with their mothers, and move out 'to ridiculous places – like Cincinnati'. This introduction establishes the chorus as commentators on the subsequent adoption. As the narrative continues, Lenny begins a hubristic search for the child's true parents, and ancient and modern worlds begin to overlap. Figures from the chorus along with others from Greek tragedy begin to appear in Lenny's everyday life: sometimes still dressed in costume but speaking lines from New York Jewish humour; sometimes in modern dress, like the blind beggar, Tiresias. After splitting up, Lenny and Amanda are eventually reconciled in the Greek theatre with the actors looking on. The film finishes with the chorus singing and dancing to the far-from-tragic song made famous by Louis Armstrong, 'When You're Smiling'.

In addition to these categories of humour, there is a growing group of films that derive their comedy from satirising previous examples of cine-antiquity. The *Oxford English Dictionary* defines satire as a poetic or prose composition in which 'prevailing vices or follies are held up to ridicule'. To succeed, satire relies on two things: first that the characteristics of its target will be sufficiently well-known that the audience will recognise them as belonging to the target; secondly that the audience is prepared to accept the target as an object fit for ridicule. By the mid-1960s, these conditions had been met for films set in the ancient world. They were both extremely well-established and widely disseminated as texts, and increasingly out of fashion with filmmakers and audiences.

There were general and more specific reasons for this decline in the representation of antiquity in film. Overall, box-office takings were down, partly due to the now rapid take-up of television. In its broad programming, this offered something for every member of the household. In response, mainstream film releases became more specifically targeted to particular age groups – adults, teenagers, children – rather than aiming at broader and more encompassing audiences. The post-war desire for escapism was also diminishing (discussed in Chapter 6). It was replaced with a contemporary wish for greater realism, actualised in the UK, for instance, in the popularity of 'kitchen-sink dramas' like *Saturday Night and Sunday Morning* (1960) and *The L-Shaped Room* (1963) – perhaps as a cultural route to validating the rapid social changes that were taking place, especially the invention of the teenager and the breaking down of class and other social boundaries.

Of the two most common cinematic styles in cine-antiquity, the peplum films had already fallen victim to their own inherent speeded-up evolution. The constant need to surpass previous titles in their fantastic combinations and sadomasochistic elements had resulted in films that were essentially parodies of the original films in the genre. Titles included *Hercules Against the Moon Men* (1964) which imported a sci-fi element into an ancient world setting, and *Hercules, Samson, Maciste and Ursus* (1964) which combined a late antique moral fable about 'the Choice of Hercules' with strongman figures from the Bible, nineteenth-century fiction and twentieth-century cinema. (The latter was used in 1993 as the basis for a satirical film, *Hercules Returns*. More details of this film at the end of this chapter.) The pepla continued to be screened and to exert an influence on ideas about the ancient world for large audiences, but this was mostly achieved through their adaptation for television in the popular series, *Sons of Hercules*. In the meantime, features of the genre like the eclectic juxtapositions of ancient and modern, the bodybuilder Hercules and dancing girls were already a topic for satire with the release in 1962 of *The Three Stooges Meet Hercules*. Transporting the three members of the popular comic act back to ancient Greece through the medium of a time machine, the film also manages to take in Roman galleys and a gladiatorial combat.

The epic films were the most prominent casualties of changing tastes. For audiences for whom Christian belief was no longer an imperative and anti-totalitarian conflicts a fading memory, the moral and political messages that provided narrative focus for the Roman epics held waning interest. In addition, the special utility that ancient world epics had had, as an alibi for screening eroticism and violence in the name of education, was no longer necessary in a society where such images were much more directly and easily available. As a consequence, ancient world epic films were no longer economically attractive for filmmakers. The gamble always inherent in epic filmmaking of betting on box-office income outstripping the enormous outlay was now seen as too risky.

This was especially the case after the financial disaster of *Cleopatra* (1963). The film began shooting in the UK in 1960, but the production was closed down after Elizabeth Taylor, who played Cleopatra, became seriously ill. After her recovery shooting recommenced, but had to be relocated to Rome for the sake of Taylor's health because of the English weather. As a consequence the budget soared, with early footage having to be reshot because some of the actors were no longer available, and the already vastly expensive sets and props being rebuilt from scratch in Rome. During filming the married Taylor started a scandalous affair with her equally married co-star Richard Burton (who played Antony), which provoked huge amounts of often hostile publicity. The director Joseph Mankiewicz's first cut of the film came in at six hours; he cut this to four hours after studio criticism, and then saw it cut again to just over three hours for theatrical release. The reduced length (and consequently sometimes incoherent narrative) has been blamed for the poor critical reception the film received. Nevertheless, it did gain four Academy Awards (for art direction, cinematography, costume design and visual effects) and was the highest grossing film of 1963. Despite this success at the box-office, the enormous costs incurred in making the film meant that it still made a huge loss, driving Twentieth Century Fox studios to the brink of bankruptcy.

With its over-blown budget, the over-dramatic private lives of its stars and over-long running time, not to mention the great self-regard of its pompous narrative and dialogue, *Cleopatra* was a natural target for satire, especially given the waning popular interest in ancient world epic films. Less than 18 months after its release, *Carry On Cleo* (1964) appeared in UK and US cinemas. The film was the tenth in a popular series of low-budget British comedy 'Carry On' films which featured a repertory cast indulging in puns, slapstick, and general bawdiness. The previous film in the series, *Carry On Spying* (1964), satirised the currently popular Bond films; *Carry on Cleo* followed the lead of its predecessor, taking elements of a specific film (in this case Mankiewicz's *Cleopatra*), but also aiming its satire at the whole genre. Posters for the film showed Amanda Barrie as a winking Cleo, reclining on a couch, a clear homage to Taylor's pose on posters for the original film. Credits poked fun at the epic genre's attitude to historical accuracy, stating that the narrative was 'from an original idea by William Shakespeare' and, in a classic Carry On *double entendre*, that 'certain liberties have been taken with Cleopatra'. There are many ironies about one film succeeding by virtue of another failing. As critics have pointed out, this is compounded in the case of *Carry on Cleo* where the film actually uses the discarded sets from *Cleopatra*'s early UK filming. However, perhaps the real final irony is that *Carry On Cleo* probably has at least as secure a place in cultural history as the film it satirised; in the UK, perhaps more so. It is frequently named as the best of the Carry On series, and its posters have appeared on postage stamps in the UK.

More recently, satire has given a new life to some of the peplum films through their inclusion in the long-running US television series, *Mystery Science Theatre 3000* (MST3K). Screened from 1988 to 1999, this series was based on the idea of a mad scientist who imprisons a man and forces him to watch bad movies in order to see how long he can endure before going insane. To survive, the man and his robot friends provide their own commentary to the films, referred to as 'riffing'. The films were shown in their entirety with the television characters appearing in silhouette at the bottom of the screen. The outrageous camp of many peplum films suited this absurd format and titles shown included *Hercules* (1958) and *Hercules and the Captive Women* (1961) as well as the previously mentioned *Hercules Against the Moon Men*.

The best satire treads a fine line between realism and farce, and it is in that liminal arena that it makes its most effective attacks. It can be devastating as a tool to ridicule folly, but it also runs the risk of being too crude, or too subtle, or misjudging its audience. And as the following case study will show, there is always the possibility that some consumers may miss the joke altogether.

Background to case study

Monty Python's Life of Brian describes the birth and adult life of a young man, born to a single mother in a stable in Bethlehem, acclaimed as a messiah for his wise teachings in the marketplace, scapegoated by the Roman authorities, and finally crucified. As the film's title and opening scenes make clear, its subject is not Christ. Rather it is Brian Cohen, whose loosely-virtuous mother has found herself pregnant by a Roman centurion seducer; whose impromptu 'teachings' on peace and co-operation only happen because he is trying to evade arrest as a member of a revolutionary group; and whose crucifixion is marked by the mass singing of a song which incongruously exhorts its listeners to 'Always Look on the Bright Side of Life'. Brian's life is a tragicomedy of errors and mistaken identity: from his birth, when the three kings who visit realise they are in the wrong stable and snatch back the gifts they've brought, to his death when his reprieve is given to another man who has jokingly claimed to be him. It makes for a satirical, absurd and occasionally surreal comic film with targets that include people's need to abdicate moral responsibility, the effects of organisation and authority on religious belief, and cinema's role in creating popular perceptions about antiquity and early Christianity.

Life of Brian was the third feature film from the Python team, and their second (after *Monty Python and the Holy Grail*) with a narrative structure, albeit one still owing plenty to the sketch format of the television show that developed the Python style. *Monty Python's Flying Circus* was a comedy sketch show produced for the public service British Broadcasting Corporation (BBC) and first screened between 1969 and 1974. It was written and mostly performed by a team of six: Graham Chapman, John Cleese, Terry Gilliam, Eric Idle, Terry Jones, and Michael Palin. It quickly gained a cult following for its absurdist treatment of a range of often banal subjects and its innovative responses to the formal structures of television comedy. In Python-world, sketches no longer had to end with a punchline; instead, a pipe-smoking colonel could stride onto the set, waving his arms at the camera to stop filming and declaring that it had all become 'too silly'. Sketches were linked with surreal animations (by Gilliam), often featuring, for no apparent reason, classical statues, giant hands and feet descending from the heavens, or barely decent Edwardian pin-up girls. Any sense of realism was resolutely rebuffed with female roles largely taken by men dressed in pantomime dame-style drag and speaking in falsetto voices. Although only four series were produced, the cult popularity of particular sketches (such as the Dead Parrot sketch, the Lumberjack

Song, the Spanish Inquisition sketch, and the Ministry of Silly Walks sketch) extended the influence of the show's unique style as fans began to memorise and repeat them for their own audiences. In 1974, the series also began screening in the US, massively extending the audience for its very British style of comedy. Since then its considerable influence on comedians in the UK and US has been widely acknowledged, from revue shows like *Saturday Night Live* to individual stand-ups like Eddie Izzard.

However *Monty Python* did not suddenly appear on the comedy scene fully-formed and without warning, like one of Terry Gilliam's animated giant feet. The six members of the Python team had previously built a substantial body of collective experience as writers, artists, and performers on television comedy programmes, with five out of the six first performing in nationally-toured comedy revues while at university (Palin and Jones at Oxford; Cleese, Chapman, and Idle at Cambridge). Among the programmes they were involved in prior to *Monty Python* were the anarchic children's show, *Do Not Adjust Your Set* (Jones, Palin, Idle and Gilliam), the comedy sketch show, *At Last the 1948 Show* (Chapman, Cleese and Idle) and the satirical topical sketch show, *The Frost Report* (all but Gilliam). This extensive previous experience (coupled with the fact that the show was screened very late at night when only a minority audience was expected) meant that the team were allowed considerably more autonomy than was usually the case in BBC productions. They had also gained a keen awareness of what worked and what didn't in the format of the comedy sketch show. For example, the understanding that a perfectly good sketch could be ruined by an inadequate punchline prompted the cast to find alternative ways of closing a sketch that weren't so dependent on a 'killer ending'. Other elements from these earlier shows also made important contributions to the development of *Monty Python*'s comedy cocktail. There is an easy transition from the political satire of *The Frost Report* to *Monty Python*'s more general satirical approach to the British class system and the social conventions that it dictated. This class consciousness was explicit in sketches like 'Upper-Class Twit of the Year' and 'The Gumbies', but it also informed virtually all the writing, providing an underlying thread of continuity and making the absurdism coherent. Other more anarchic innovative comedy of the time, like Spike Milligan's TV series *Q5*, shunned convention simply for the sake of absurdity and difference, but *Monty Python*'s unconventionality had a serious satirical point, however silly its content: it ridiculed the follies of a British society still paralysed by social class and conventions.

The first cinematic venture for the Pythons was *And Now For Something Completely Different* (1971), a compilation of existing sketches, designed to bring the material to a wider audience, particularly in the US. The second film, *Monty Python and the Holy Grail* (1975), offered new material and a (still fairly loose) narrative framework to hang it on. Combining the sketch format of the television show with the episodic

177

format of the Arthurian cycle, the film followed king Arthur (played by Chapman), his squire Patsy (Gilliam) and his knights (the rest of the Python team) on their quest for the Grail. Collectively and individually they encounter a variety of obstacles and characters (often also played by Pythons doubling up), including peasants who expound on the failures of various theories of government; knights who demand a shrubbery as tribute before they are allowed to pass; the Black Knight, whose extreme pugnacity leaves him demanding a fight even after all his limbs have been severed; and the rescue of a damsel in distress who is actually an extremely fey prince. Each of the sequences mocks an aspect of popular knowledge about the Middle Ages and the transmission of its history through popular culture. For example, Lancelot's rescue of Prince Herbert owes much to Errol Flynn in *The Adventures of Robin Hood*. The satire is most effective because of the genuine erudition that underpins it. Jones, who co-directed the film, has since become well-known as an author and television presenter of popular histories about the medieval period. Characteristic aspects of the television show are repeated in the film, including swipes at the class system; incongruous juxtapositions of historical with contemporary elements and the exotic with the banal; and the refusal to provide a conventional narrative closure. The co-direction of the film by Jones and Gilliam created some difficulties in production due to their contrasting directorial styles. However, it was a financial success, returning a gross of over £80 million for its £229,000 production budget, and has remained a favourite with audiences, being the most popular Python film in the US and voted fifth best comedy film of all time in a viewers' poll by *Total Film* magazine in 2000 among other acclamations in the UK.

There is general agreement among the Pythons that the seed of the idea for the next film came from Idle, who jokingly suggested that a good title would be *Jesus Christ: Lust for Glory*. This typical Python absurdist juxtaposition of peacemaker and gung-ho militarism drew on the title of a recent film about the abrasive Second World War US General, *Patton: Lust For Glory* (1970). Once the team had agreed that there were possibilities in the idea of a film about Christ, various ideas were proposed and discarded. The first focused on the idea of Christ as a carpenter criticising the shoddy construction of the cross. However, after further discussion and some quite serious scholarly research, it was agreed that it was difficult to find anything in Christ's life or teachings that would provide a sustainable source of humour. The focus shifted to the idea of a thirteenth disciple, who was always late and missed the important events. This plotline was favoured by John Cleese (who went on to star in *Clockwise* (1986), as a fanatically punctual headteacher forced into disastrous unpunctuality by events). Eventually the team settled on the idea of a parallel life, with its opportunities for misunderstandings and mistaken identities.

By the time serious writing development began at the end of 1976, members of the team were already working on other successful projects,

178

including the television series *Fawlty Towers* (Cleese) and *Ripping Yarns* (Palin and Jones), and the film *Jabberwocky* (Gilliam). However, a script draft was completed by early 1978, and production planning began. It was planned to shoot the film on location in Tunisia, taking advantage of the sets recently built for Franco Zeffirelli's television mini-series, *Jesus of Nazareth*. Days before the production crew were due to depart for Tunisia, the team learned that their financial backers, EMI Films, had pulled out. This was on the orders of their chief executive, Lord Bernard Delfont, who had shown the script to a friend on the board who was a prominent Roman Catholic, and had pronounced it to be blasphemy. (To mark this, the last spoken line of the film is: 'I said to him, "Bernie, they'll never make their money back on this one."')

As a considerable amount of money had already been spent on development and pre-production, the Pythons sued EMI Films, who eventually settled out of court. Idle and the producer John Goldstone then set off for America to try again to raise the financial backing. While there was reluctance among conventional backers to support the film, it was Monty Python's status as an icon of pop culture that eventually saved the film, with the newly-rich pop aristocracy keen to be involved. The Who's drummer Keith Moon offered to try to raise the funds, in return for which it was planned that he should play a cameo role as a 'blood-and-thunder prophet' (in the event, Moon died just before filming started). However, Idle had also mentioned the finance problems to his friend George Harrison, formerly of the Beatles, who raised the necessary £4 million (partly by mortgaging his own house) and set up the production company Handmade Films, with Denis O'Brien. Asked why he would do something so exceptional, Harrison replied that he wanted to see the film, prompting the later description by Idle of Harrison's belief in the project as 'the most expensive cinema ticket ever'. Shooting began in September 1978 and took just 41 days, with Cleese noting that the process was 'extraordinarily efficient' and the director Jones (directing solo this time after the conflicts with Gilliam on *Holy Grail*) 'very well prepared' (Sellars 2003: 11). Harrison appears very briefly in the film as 'Mr Papadopoulos, the owner of the Mount'. Another brief cameo is by the former Goon, Spike Milligan, himself a considerable influence on Python humour, who was in Tunisia on holiday at the time and found himself roped in, not entirely happily.

The main target of the film itself is in fact Python's regular *bête noir*, the British Establishment and the status quo. They particularly aim at four of its key features: the church, the class system, the law, and education. As mentioned above, Christ was not a target, and there is care to make this clear from the start of the film. The fact that there are two separate births is shown when the wise men abandon Brian and his mother Mandy for the real Messiah. Christ also appears in person (played by Kenneth Colley) delivering the Sermon on the Mount, with Brian in the audience. Following this there is also a scene where an extremely spritely ex-leper tries to extract money from Brian, claiming that his career as a beggar has been ruined since Christ cured him. The playing out of each of these scenes reflects the feeling of the team following their research that the humour they could extract from the life of Christ rested in the people and events that surrounded him.

A particular target however was the way that religious belief and ideas are systematised and controlled by religious laws and authorities. Christianity is not the only religion called to account here, with a general intolerance displayed in the crucifixion sequence – 'A Samaritan? This is supposed to be a Jewish section'... 'Pharisees separate from Sadducees' – and Judaic laws mocked more specifically in the early stoning scene. Laws pertaining to gender mean that women are barred from the stoning, but they attend anyway in their masses, all wearing false beards. As the priest in charge, Cleese combines elements of the bureaucrat, devoted to enforcing petty rules, and the schoolmaster (which he had in fact been) sending miscreants to the back of the crowd. The crime of the man to be stoned is, ironically in view of the film's later problems, blasphemy. The scenes following Brian's acclamation as a messiah also illustrate the way that belief is rapidly subject to organisation, with Brian finding his former colleagues from the People's Front of Judea (PFJ) putting together a speaking tour for him, and (comically) managing the supplicants: 'Those possessed by devils, try and keep them under control a bit, can't you? Incurables, you'll just have to wait for a few minutes. Women taken in sin, line up against that wall, will you?' Although not (ostensibly) a religious organisation, the revolutionary PFJ provide a useful (perhaps less precarious) metaphor for the Church, whilst also broadening out the target of satirical attack from just religious fanaticism to include political extremism, in this case the PFJ's political (and historically literal) zealotry about the Roman oppression of Judea.

It is the desperate desire for an object of belief that is most clearly a target for satire in this film. Part of the research undertaken by the Pythons in the early writing stages had revealed that there had been a kind of 'Messiah fever' in Judea at the time, with false messiahs often being identified by a colonised population eager for a local hero. The idea is actualised in the film when Brian is mobbed by followers after his impromptu speech in the marketplace; they scrabble around for signs and symbols to worship, fixing first on a gourd, then on a sandal. Brian's protestations that he is not the Messiah are met with the gnostic pronouncement that only the true Messiah denies his divinity, and by one follower telling him, 'I say you are, Lord, and I should know – I've followed a few.'

If religion is the most immediate target, it is not the only one. As with the television series, social class informs much of the humour, with Cleese's centurion and priest both illustrations of a bureaucratic middle class that stands between the Roman governing class of Pontius Pilate (played by Palin) and his unfortunately named friend, Biggus Dickus (Chapman), and the working-class trade unionism of the PFJ's committee meetings. In addition though, the film satirises the ancient world of epic films, which had had similar settings and subject matter and had formed so much of the cinema audience's ideas about what antiquity looked and sounded like. Jones in particular spent time watching epics including *Ben-Hur* (1951) and *Barabbas* (1961). Their influence can be clearly seen in many scenes in the film, including the opening pre-credits scene of the wise men visiting the infant Brian, and the monumental stone-cut credits themselves, both of which are borrowed from *Ben-Hur*.

Like the life of its eponymous hero, the film's reception was also marked by misunderstandings about identity, actions, and purpose. These ultimately led to accusations of blasphemy, still a common-law offence in the UK until 2008. The notion of blasphemy, or at least of offending Christian religious beliefs, had been a serious concern for earlier Roman epics, and it was still unusual to show Christ explicitly in mainstream cinema. Various tactics had been used to avoid this, for instance showing a part of the body but avoiding the face (a hand offering water in *Ben-Hur*), or staging a pastiche of an artistic representation (De Vinci's *The Last Supper* in *Quo Vadis*). However, Christ's actual appearance in the film was treated entirely respectfully; it was the people around him that were ridiculed, either directly (the ex-leper, Pontius Pilate) or by comparison (those who seek out prophets and those who seek to impose rules for religious belief). Jones in particular argued strongly that the film was heretical rather than blasphemous, because its challenge was aimed at the Church.

Moral crusaders like the Nationwide Festival of Light and other Christian groups strongly objected to the film, organising a campaign of pickets and leafleting outside cinemas in the UK. There were also protests outside cinemas in the US and a ban on screening by a number of local councils in the UK, and the whole of the Republic of Ireland and Norway. Most memorably two of the Monty Python troupe that made the film, John Cleese and Michael Palin, took part in a heated live television debate on the BBC's *Friday Night, Saturday Morning* in November 1979 with Mervyn Stockwood, the Bishop of Southwark and the journalist Malcolm Muggeridge, in which the two Establishment figures are widely agreed to have come off the worst. Stockwood and Muggeridge had attended a screening of the film, but missed the opening scenes which established it as a parallel life and not a life of Christ. As a result, their arguments that the film mocks Christ's life were aimed at a target that did not exist. Attacks against the film became personal and qualitative, with Stockwood dismissing it as 'undergraduate' and Muggeridge calling it 'tenth-rate'. Meanwhile Cleese and Palin were measured, thoughtful, and courteous. At the end, Bishop Stockwood signed off with the cheap sneer, 'You will

181

get your thirty pieces of silver.' The debate has itself become a landmark event in popular culture in the UK, marking the moment the Establishment very publicly lost their ownership of the moral high ground. In a rapid display of intertextuality it was itself satirised eleven days later in the BBC television sketch show, *Not the Nine O'Clock News*, with Rowan Atkinson playing a bishop defending his film, *The Life of Christ,* against accusations that it lampoons Monty Python, and in particular 'Our Lord John Cleese – even the initials are the same!'

In the end, the bans may have been more beneficial than harmful to the film, creating a buzz of public interest that extended far wider than the usual, rather cultish, Python fanbase. It may also have prompted a longer life for the film, in the sense that it is now discussed not only as a cinematic comedy, but also as something that marks a key moment in the histories of cultural censorship and moral and religious change in society. It was a financial success, costing about $4,000,000 to produce and grossing over $20,000,000 in its first year of release in the US, making it the highest-grossing British film in the US of that year; in the UK it was the fourth highest-grossing film overall. In contrast to Muggeridge's not entirely well-informed value judgement, it has also been voted best comedy film of all time in a number of UK polls, including those by the broadcaster Channel 4 in 2006 and the broadsheet newspaper *The Observer* in 2007.

Plot summary

Following a bright star, three wise men travel to Bethlehem, where they find a mother in a stable with her baby in a manger. They fall to their knees to worship the infant, and offer up their gifts. However, it soon becomes clear that Brian Cohen is not the child they were seeking and, snatching their gifts back, they move on to the next stable from which a radiant light shines ...

Time passes and Brian (Graham Chapman) is now a young man, still living with his mother, Mandy (Terry Jones). They witness Jesus giving his Sermon on the Mount, before moving on to take part in the stoning of a blasphemer, with Mandy wearing a false beard as women are banned. Returning to their hovel, Mandy reveals to Brian that his father is not Mr Cohen, but a Roman centurion. Brian dashes out, declaring that he is not a Roman: 'I'm Kosher, Mum! I'm a Red Sea Pedestrian, and proud of it!'

We next see him in the arena where he works selling exotic snacks to the spectators. Among the few viewing the games are a small group of revolutionaries, Reg (John Cleese), Francis (Michael Palin), Stan (who wishes to be called Loretta) (Eric Idle) and Judith (Sue Jones-Davies): the People's Front of Judea. Brian asks if he can join the group, and their leader Reg gives him a task: to paint the slogan 'Romans Go Home' on the citadel. Brian is caught by a centurion who corrects his Latin and makes him paint it correctly one hundred times. With the citadel now covered in anti-Roman graffiti, Brian is accepted by the PFJ, and joins them on their raid to kidnap Pontius Pilate's wife. Once inside the palace though, they meet members of the Campaign for a Free Galilee who are on the same mission. A fight breaks out and Brian is arrested. However, he escapes when Pilate's guards are seized with uncontrollable laughter at the prefect's lisp.

After a surreal interlude on board an alien spaceship, Brian returns to the PFJ's headquarters, but Roman soldiers soon arrive to search for him and, attempting to hide on the balcony, he falls to the marketplace below where an assortment of prophets are preaching to small crowds. To evade the pursuing soldiers, Brian begins to deliver some vaguely spiritual platitudes, but breaks off unfinished when the soldiers pass. His audience pursue him, demanding to know what he was about to say. He escapes out of the city and into the wilderness, chased by the crowd who are now hailing him as the messiah. Leaping into a hole to hide, he disturbs a hermit who breaks his vow of silence. In the chaos that ensues, the crowd clears, revealing Judith.

The next morning, Brian wakes up next to Judith. Opening his window, he is aghast to find a huge crowd outside. He tells them they should stop looking for people to follow and work things out for themselves. His pleas fall on deaf ears. 'You're all individuals,' he shouts. They reply, in chorus, 'Yes, we're all individuals.' Meanwhile, the PFJ are busy managing the crowd inside the house, all seeking the healing services of the newly identified messiah. Brian struggles outside, and is promptly rearrested.

Sent for crucifixion, Brian has an opportunity for reprieve as part of Pilate's annual Passover speech. However when the centurion asks for Brian of Nazareth, another prisoner claims to be Brian and is released in his place. One by one, people who could have rescued him – the PFJ, the Judean People's Front, Judith, his mother – all arrive and explain why they are not going to do so. Finally, Brian has no options left. But his neighbour on the cross tells him to cheer up, and the crucifixees end the film singing, 'Always Look on the Bright Side of Life'.

Key themes and scenes

Satirising epic films

In their television series, the Pythons were adept at subverting both programme and comedy conventions. A special target for their ridicule was the starched and outdated politeness that the BBC itself had come to stand for, with their dinner-jacketed continuity announcer (played by Cleese) turning up in a variety of incongruous settings and situations. In *The Life of Brian*, they did a similar job of demolition-from-the-inside on the outdated cinematic clichés and monochrome morality of the Roman epic film.

As discussed in previous chapters, the underlying moral agenda of the epics clearly associated the governing classes of imperial and pre-imperial Rome with tyrannical political regimes of the mid-twentieth century (Nazism, Fascism, Stalinism), while their opponents (slaves, Christians) were aligned with the 'free' people of the western world (primarily America). In this schema, Rome is irredeemable, needing a new order to sweep away corruption and immorality. However, *Life of Brian* includes a counter to this view in the sequence where the PFJ meet to plan their kidnap of Pilate's wife. Reg delivers a diatribe against the Romans, ending in the rhetorical flourish, 'And what have they ever given us in return?' To his annoyance, the group's members offer a list, including 'the sanitation, the medicine, education, wine, public order, irrigation, roads, a fresh water system, and public health' and ending in 'brought peace'. In this typically intelligent riposte to the cinematic orthodoxy, the audience is reminded that the Hollywood version of ancient history is not the only one. Rome is not always the bad guy.

Other conventional aspects of the Roman epics are also undermined. A very widely-known image from epic film is the publicity poster for *Ben Hur* (1959), which spells out the film's title in monumental carved stone letters. It is an image, while not used in the film's onscreen credits, (which instead superimposed text over a slow pan into Michelangelo's *Creation of Adam*), that draws on notions of timelessness and authority to validate its narrative; a vision of antiquity literally set in stone. The titles for *The Life of Brian* borrow this notion and subvert it, opening their animated title sequence with the title spelt out in monumental carved stone letters which prove anything but timeless as one of the letters breaks off, causing the infant Brian to fall off his cloud and crash onto more stone letters below. Further stone letters spell out the names of the stars of the film, before they too collapse and plunge Brian into a chasm, past a jumble of (aptly) Fellini-esque signifiers for antiquity, including the Primaporta Augustus, the colossal sculpted head of Constantine, trumpets, banners, and more prosaic images including tenements and washing lines. The collapsing letters are a timely reminder that we are constantly rebuilding our ideas of antiquity from fragments, and that no version is the definitive one (see Chapter 7). The titles collate some of the most often used visual clichés of cine-antiquity, but no Roman epic film would be truly epic without an arena sequence. *Life of Brian* does not avoid this cliché, but it does, happily, rewrite every conventional element.

The goriness and boredom in the arena scene [see box: 'In the arena'] show up the true absurdity of the sanitised and heroic Hollywood version of the gladiatorial combat. The messy reality of arena combats, or any other violence, is generally hidden in epic film; a good example is found in the red flowers that signify Petronius and Eunice's opened veins in *Quo Vadis*. Other aspects are equally subverted, with the small and apathetic audience contrasting with the usual packed and enthusiastic crowds in the films, and the distinctly unequal, unheroic combat itself. An early shot

184

In the arena

The sequence opens with trumpets sounding. A caption announces the scene as 'The Colosseum, Jerusalem'. The camera pans across a gory scene in the arena, which is being cleared after the previous bout. Bloody limbs are strewn around the floor. Another caption tells us that it is the 'Children's Matinee'. A cleaner tries to remove a ring from a hand, without success – so he takes the whole arm.

Establishing shots reveal that the arena is topped with arches, each containing a statue. There is a canopied dais decorated with a golden eagle for the wealthier spectators and stepped stone seating for ordinary viewers, but there are few occupants. Today's combatants are announced as 'Frank Goliath, the Macedonian baby-crusher and Boris Mineburg'. Boris turns out to be a weedy-looking man in a loincloth, armed with a trident and net, who tries to run back out of the arena, but is prevented by the closing of the gate. His opponent is a huge gladiator clad in heavy arm and leg plates and carrying a short sword. Boris drops his weapons and runs off around the arena, pursued by Goliath.

In the meantime, Brian wanders among the spectators, selling exotic snacks including, 'Larks' tongues. Wrens' livers. Chaffinch brains. Jaguars' earlobes. Wolf-nipple chips.... Dromedary pretzels, only half a denar. Tuscany-fried bats.' He approaches a small group who are deep in earnest conversation, asking them, 'Are you the Judean People's Front?' They recoil indignantly from any association with these 'splitters', and identify themselves as the 'People's Front of Judea'. Brian asks to join and avows his hatred of the Romans.

The chase continues on the floor of the arena to a desultory chorus of boos from the sparse audience. Eventually the gladiator, panting in his heavy armour, comes to a stop and drops dead of a heart attack. Boris celebrates his victory, and Brian is told by Reg that there is a task he can do for them.

---

from the floor of the arena looking up to the statues in their arched recesses seems inspired by Jean-Léon Gérôme's 1872 painting, *Pollice Verso*: the same painting which inspired Enrico Guazzoni's arena in *Quo Vadis* (1912), and Ridley Scott's in *Gladiator*. This act of homage situates the Python film more thoughtfully in the visual tradition of cine-antiquity.

Brian's job as a snack-seller enables two points to be made. The absurd nature of the snacks he has for sale (described by Judith as 'rich imperialist titbits') are not a world away from some of the luxury items proposed in previous films to illustrate the decadence of Rome. In DeMille's *Cleopatra* (1934), for instance, Antony is offered tiny reed birds. Cambridge Professor of Classics Mary Beard once proposed a 'dormouse test' for judging the quality of modern recreations of Rome, arguing that one should pay attention to the length of time 'before the characters adopt an uncomfortably horizontal position in front of tables, usually festooned with grapes, and one says to another: "Can I pass you a dormouse?" The longer

185

you have to wait before this tasty little morsel appears on the recreated banquet, the more subtle the reconstruction is likely to be' (Beard 2005). The humour underlines a serious point. No doubt there were luxury food items in ancient Rome for the wealthy few, just as there are people who will happily pay vast sums now for coffee that has passed through the gut of an Indonesian civet, and our historical sources give undue prominence to such gastronomy. The diet of most ordinary Romans would have been quite different, but it is the extreme and the ostentatious, so obviously parodied here, that we know and associate with antiquity, and that has happened because of the wide dissemination of these notions through film.

The other point made in this scene is the parallel between cinema itself and the arena. Brian carries his exotic wares in a tray strung around his neck like a snack-seller at a baseball game in the US. However, for a UK audience in the 1970s, it would have been equally reminiscent of an old-fashioned cinema usher, selling ice creams and soft drinks. Python had already used this figure in their television series in a sketch where a cinema usher sells albatross rather than ice creams. The sketch had become a cult favourite, and was repeated in the first Python film, *And Now For Something Completely Different*, which had been successful in the US, so it is reasonable to speculate that this reading (rather than a baseball game snack-seller) was the preferred one. Cinema is also referenced in the caption, 'Children's matinee', which notes the UK cinema practice of showing children's films on a Saturday morning, often filling the theatre at a time when it would usually be empty, and inducting children into the habit of cinemagoing. Through these cues, the arena is re-drawn as the ancient cinema, a conceit also found in more serious films like *Spartacus* or *Gladiator*, which again places this satirical epic back in the tradition of the films it seeks to subvert.

In class

One of the most persistent themes pursued by the Pythons in both television and film is the absurdities of the British social class system. This is also prominent in the film, with debates about class recurring at key structural points at the beginning and end of the narrative proper. In the first post-titles sequence, among the spectators at the Sermon on the Mount we see the full spectrum of society, each behaving according to stereotype. Mr and Mrs Gregory represent the upper classes, with their black slave holding a parasol to protect them from the sun; Mr and Mrs Big Nose are the aspirational middle classes, concerned with manners, proper language and prestige; and Mr Cheeky is the confrontational working class. The same characters appear again in the crucifixion scene at the end of the film, still arguing about what they perceive to be the proper conventions by which they should be treated, even in the face of death. In many ways these groups reprise the *Frost Report*'s famous 'I'm

186

upper class' sketch in which representatives of the upper, middle, and lower classes each play out the characteristics of their respective classes. The upper classes in this 1996 sketch had been represented by John Cleese.

Other characters also map modern conventions of class onto ancient characters: the aristocratic feyness of Pontius Pilate and Biggus Dickus with their natural assumptions of privilege and entitlement; the middle-class professions represented in bureaucrats like the priest at the stoning, or the liberal conscience-ridden centurion sending prisoners to crucifixion; the working-class family values and irrepressible good humour of Mr Cheeky, expecting his brother to rescue him from crucifixion, 'if he can keep off the tail for more than twenty minutes'.

Class behaviour and values were largely taught through education, so it is appropriate that one of the central scenes for this theme aims its satire here, and specifically at Latin teaching [see box: 'Romans go home'].

'Romans go home'

It is dusk. Moonlight reflects off the white marble of a giant naked statue of Pilate, as Brian stealthily approaches the walls of the palace. Foreboding music warns the audience of the jeopardy he is in as he takes out a brush and begins to paint red letters on the walls. The word 'Roman' is evident as the shot changes to reveal dark figures nearing, while Brian is too occupied with his painting to notice. The music rises to a crescendo as the centurion reaches Brian and claps him on the shoulder, asking 'What's this then?' The full graffito is revealed as ROMANES EUNT DOMUS which Brian translates as 'Romans go home'. Instead of immediately arresting and dragging off the terrified Brian, the centurion proceeds to point out the mistakes in his Latin composition, holding him by the ear and making him conjugate verbs and decline cases. The correct Latin phrase being reached, he tells Brian to write it out a hundred times before sunrise. Brian gets busy with the paintbrush, and by sunrise the walls of the palace are completely covered with the red-painted slogan, ROMANI ITE DOMUM. 'Finished,' he tells the soldiers watching him. 'Right,' replies one of the soldiers, 'now don't do it again!'

In the UK at the time of the film's release, education was very much an active arena for class conflicts and distinctions to be played out. From the late 1960s, the UK education system had been subject to reforms that removed the earlier two-tier system of grammar and secondary modern schools, replacing them with the 'comprehensive' school. At the same time, the curriculum was modernised, removing some of the more purely academic subjects such as ancient languages and introducing more vocational subjects. Middle-class parents who had previously been happy to send their children to grammar school now scraped together the funds for private schooling. By the 1970s, secondary education had become a passionately-argued class issue with a clear divide perceived between those educated privately and those educated in state schools. One marker of that

17. 'Romans go home'. The citadel in Jerusalem,
Monty Python's Life of Brian (1979).

divide was the continuing study of Latin, widely derided by progressive educational reformers as a 'dead language', but valued as a symbol of difference by those supporters of private education.

All of the five British Pythons had followed typical British middle-class routes through education, progressing from single-sex grammar or private schools to university at either Oxford or Cambridge. An essential part of this type of secondary education had been the study of Latin, until 1960 a compulsory requirement for admission to Oxbridge. The graffiti sequence reflects this experience of Latin teaching by rote in British schools; the centurion threatening to cut Brian's throat is an extreme manifestation of the bullying inherent in the system, and the instruction to write it out a hundred times a common punishment for minor misdemeanours. The Pythons had been criticised in their television output for intellectual elitism, particularly for their sketches that referenced philosophy. A joke based on an error in Latin translation and the pedagogical practices of schoolmasters in fee-paying schools might attract similar accusations. However the sequence is made accessible to a wider audience by the absurdity of the situation. The final reveal where the ancient palace is seen covered in red-painted graffiti is made more effective because the previous scenes had taken place in twilight: the shocking truth of Brian's crime against the jealously-guarded treasure of the middle-classes is revealed by the full light of day [Fig. 17].

In search of belief

There is no escaping the fact that *The Life of Brian* satirises aspects of religion. However, much of the criticism was mistakenly predicated on the notion that the target of the film was Christ. The Pythons were all clear that there was a good reason why this was not the case – they simply couldn't find anything to be funny about in the topic. Instead, the religious satire was aimed at the kind of figures and events who might have surrounded Christ, and who certainly cluster to modern-day prophets and evangelical figures.

The Pythons claimed that much of the religious satire was driven by ideas they discovered while doing historical research for the script. For instance, the mass crucifixion sequence at the end of *Life of Brian* was perhaps the most notorious and highly criticised part of the film, because of its light-hearted approach to such a central narrative of Christianity. Christ's death by crucifixion prompted the adoption of the cross as symbol of the Christian religion. But script research showed that crucifixion was actually a very common form of punishment at the time, not something exceptional to Christ. Christianity's claim to exclusive ownership of the cross as religious symbol is one of the features of organised religion that is satirised in the film. Also targeted are religious laws that seem dislocated from belief: for example, in the stoning scene, those laws that forbid half the population from taking part in justice simply on account of biological chance.

Another object of satire is the desperate need for people to have a focus for belief, and the unsound assumptions that can grow from this need. Again, the 'messiah mania' current at the time when the film is set, and discovered during script research, was the spur for this. There is a natural tendency for populations under the control of foreign powers to wish for a nationalist hero or leader to emerge from the people, so this narrative retains a modern resonance beyond that of religious belief. In fact, it is this that forms the thread that holds the story together, making *Life of Brian* the most narratively cohesive of all the Python films.

In the scene described [see box: 'I'm not the Messiah'] we see an extended critique of the operation of faith. The scene points out that the secret to religious success is not certain dogma, but structural ambiguity. It is only when Brian breaks off mid-sentence that the crowd become interested in the mystery of what has not been said. Like the opaque pronouncements of the other prophets in the marketplace, the statements most apt to provoke faith are those which are open enough to allow believers to map on their own desires and needs. Once this process has been kick-started, anything is open to interpretation: a dropped sandal, a

189

> **'I'm not the Messiah!'**
>
> Having fallen from the balcony of Matthias' house while hiding from soldiers, Brian finds himself among the prophets in the marketplace. In order to blend in and avoid discovery, he pretends to preach to a small group of sceptical onlookers who challenge everything he says. A brisk marching sound signals the arrival of the centurion and soldiers, which gives Brian's attempts at preaching a new urgency. However, once they have passed he stops abruptly mid-sentence, sparking a sudden interest in his previously apathetic audience. They begin to follow him, insisting that he finish and, working themselves up to a pitch of hysteria when he refuses, they start claiming his every action as significant. Brian is now desperate to escape his new pursuers, and races out of the city, dropping his sandal as he goes. Some of the followers see the dropped sandal as a sign, but cannot agree on its meaning. Others claim Brian's gourd as a rival symbol and the followers start to argue amongst themselves.
>
> In the meantime, Brian tries to hide in a hole occupied by a hermit, Simon, who accidentally breaks his eighteen-year vow of silence, alerting the followers. They hail Brian as their 'Master' and interpret everything he says as portentous, claiming 'a blessing!' when he tells them to go away, and 'a miracle!' when he points out the fruiting juniper bushes nearby. One man asks to be healed of 'a bald patch', while another claims to have been healed of blindness before falling into the hole. Only Simon holds out against the idea that Brian is the messiah, whereupon the followers declare him an 'unbeliever'. Shouting 'kill the heretic', they carry him off.

casual suggestion. And those who oppose the majority view are denounced and punished.

There is perhaps some irony that two of the key scenes concerning religion in the film are about the definitions of blasphemy (the stoning scene) and heresy (the scene described above), given that these were the very misdemeanours the Pythons were accused of committing themselves. In a telling exchange early in the film, Brian says, 'There's no pleasing some people.' And the ex-leper replies, 'That's just what Jesus said, sir.' [Fig. 18]

Suggested further viewing

Carry on Cleo (dir. Thomas, 1964)
Julius Caesar (Kenneth Williams) and the Roman legions are in Britain, in search of slaves. They find a primitive society, with the people still dressed in animal skins and living in caves, but return to Rome with a number of slaves including the ineffectual Hengist Pod (Kenneth Connor), his friend Horsa (Jim Dale), a fearless fighter, and Horsa's beloved, Gloria (Julie Stevens). An attempt on Caesar's life is thwarted by Horsa, but Hengist gets the credit and is made Caesar's bodyguard. Meanwhile Mark Antony (Sid James) is sent to Egypt, where he is seduced by Cleopatra

18. A man in drag and an ex-leper. Life in the market in Jerusalem,
Monty Python's Life of Brian (1979).

(Amanda Barrie) and plots with her against Caesar. Caesar travels to
Egypt, but Horsa is among the slaves rowing his ship, and again thwarts
an attempt at Caesar's assassination. On arrival in Egypt, a fearful Caesar
persuades Hengist to adopt his identity. Cleopatra gives Hengist an
aphrodisiac potion which has the effect of bolstering his manliness. He
kills Cleopatra's bodyguard, and escapes back to Britain with Horsa and
Gloria, where he puts Cleopatra's potion to good use with his wife Senna.
We leave Mark Antony and Cleopatra in the bath, and Caesar finally
assassinated by Brutus.

The film follows the well-established formula for the Carry On series of
puns, *double entendres* and contemporary British cultural references.
Cleopatra plays a surprisingly small role, with much of the plot concerning
the differences between the sophisticated Romans and primitive Britons,

191

a variation on the usual Carry On anti-authority agenda. Costumes and sets were re-used from those built for the aborted British filming of the 1963 *Cleopatra*, as were motifs like Cleopatra's make-up and milk baths. The 'voice of history' narration (also borrowed from previous epic films) was done by E.V.H. Emmett, whose authoritative tones would have been familiar to British cinema viewers from the Gaumont British newsreels. Cod-Latin is liberally scattered through the script, including Antony's exclamation when he sees Cleo for the first time: 'Puer ... oh puer ... oh puer', translated by the narrator as 'Boy ... oh boy ... oh boy'; and Caesar's alleged motto, 'Nihil Expectore in Omnibus', translated as 'don't spit on public transport'. The film has been critically acclaimed as the best of the Carry On series, but so many of the jokes are UK-specific that the humour can be unintelligible to a non-UK audience.

Hercules Returns (dir. Parker, 1993)
Brad McBain (David Argue) works for the vast Kent Cinema Corporation which exploits its monopoly on film exhibition with showings of cheap mass-produced serial films like *Rocky Meets Rambo, Rambo Meets Bambi* and *Rambo Eats Bambi*. Brad decides to resign and open his own independent cinema, the Picture Palace. Employing a short-tempered projectionist (Sprocket, played by Bruce Spence) and a publicist (Lisa, played by Mary Coustas) who has a habit of punching anyone who insults women, Brad plans to re-open the cinema by screening the last film exhibited there before it closed: *Hercules* (1958). However, on the night of the gala re-opening they discover that the film order has been sabotaged by Sir Michael Kent, the head of the Kent Corporation. The film they receive is not *Hercules*, but a little-known title called *Ercole, Sansone, Maciste e Ursus gli invincibile* (1964), and it is still in the original Italian. Brad, Lisa and Sprocket decide to re-dub the film on the spot, which is a huge success with the audience. After starting a fight with Brad, Kent is knocked out by Lisa, and the film ends in a celebratory party.

In this Australian film, the real star of the film is the comically over-dubbed version of *Ercole, Sansone, Maciste e Ursus gli invincibile* with the plot outlined above merely an excuse to showcase the over-dubbed film. This technique of comic over-dubbing had previously been used to great effect in the stage show, *Double Take Meets Hercules*, performed by Des Mangan and Sally Patience, and while this couple do not appear onscreen, it is their voices that give life to the peplum characters. The over-dubbed script is full of ribald 'Ocker' humour, and brings to the surface the underlying eroticism of the pepla with the two juvenile leads renamed 'Labia' and 'Testiculi'. It also taps into the association of the peplum films (with barely-there plots and even more barely-dressed bodybuilder heroes) with kitsch and gay culture, with Hercules ordered by Zeus to 'openly reveal to the world your homosexual tendencies'. However the framing narrative offers a more serious protest about the role of big corporations in encouraging formulaic cultural products.

Meet the Spartans (dir. Friedberg & Seltzer, 2008)
We are first introduced to the Spartan Leonidas as a baby with an implausible set of abdominal muscles and a beard. He grows up to marry Margo (Carmen Electra) and become king of Sparta. One day a messenger arrives bearing a demand from the Persian king Xerxes (Ken Davitian) for Sparta's surrender to him. Leonidas (Sean Maguire) kicks the messenger into a pit, followed by several other incongruously modern celebrities that he dislikes. The next day, he assembles his warriors to face the Persian masses. Unfortunately only thirteen have been recruited because of the strict specifications that they should be 'hunky, with deep Mediterranean tans, hot bods and well-endowed'. They travel to Thermopylae where their confrontations with the Persians include a dance-off and a series of mother insult jokes. The Spartans win, but are betrayed by Paris Hilton, a deformed Spartan who has been banned from joining the warriors. In the battle that follows, Xerxes is bonded with a convertible to become a Transformer robot, Xerxestron, but he strays too far from his power socket and crashes down on the remaining Spartans. Leonidas is crushed to death, but one blinded warrior, Dilio (Jareb Dauplaise), has returned to Sparta. A year later, he leads a new force of Spartans against the Persians, but goes the wrong way and ends up in Malibu, where he knocks down the (real-life) Hollywood actress Lindsay Lohan, leaving rehab.

Following briskly on the heels of *300* (2007), the object of the film's satire is mainly the extra-cinematic narratives around the original. Following reports that cast members for *300* had their musculature enhanced by make-up, for instance, one less-fit warrior in the later film has a 'six-pack' spray-painted onto his stomach. The well-publicised technique of filming the whole of *300* against a blue screen, with the backgrounds added in post-production, is also marked when Xerxes' army is revealed to be a blue screen. However there are also nods to older films, like this exchange between Xerxes and Leonidas which references Nero's verdict on the Christians in *Quo Vadis:* Xerxes threatens, 'When I'm through with you, you'll be written out of the history books!' to which Leonidas replies, 'That's fine, because I can't read.'

9

The Disney Version: *Hercules* (1997)

Introduction

Recent critical attention has not been kind to Walt Disney (1901-1966). In his review of *Hercules*, the cultural critic Stefan Kanfer summarised much contemporary feeling about Disney:

> The impresario couldn't draw with much panache, couldn't write dialogue or compose music or lyrics. He was a naïf and right-winger, biased against blacks, Jews and homosexuals. His taste could be vulgar, and his self-importance was notorious (Kanfer 1997: 17).

A recurrent feature of such criticism is the innate social conservatism implicit in the Disney Corporation's products, both those produced under Walt Disney's direction and those subsequent to his death. Some progressive family therapists have even advised against allowing children to watch Disney films or, if this proves impossible, then adults should intervene to mediate their child's viewing either by hi-jacking the stories to provide alternate endings or pointing out errors or misconceptions that the film is promoting.

Such criticism stands in contrast to the critical acclaim that attended the work of Walt Disney in the 1930s and 1940s. At this time, members of the avant-garde embraced his animations and his work received adulatory reviews in Paris and Berlin. The leading French director René Clair praised Disney's polymath abilities and described his artistry as 'sublime'. Amongst the most vocal of Disney's champions was the Russian director Sergei Eisenstein (1898-1948). Eisenstein has a claim to being one of the most influential directors of the twentieth century. The impact of his films, such as *Battleship Potemkin* (1925), *Alexander Nevsky* (1938) and *Ivan the Terrible, part I* (1944) and *part II* (1958), can be seen in the work of numerous directors right up to the twenty-first century. In addition, Eisenstein was an important early theorist of cinema. Famous for his championing of montage, Eisenstein was fascinated by the origins of the appeal of cinema and its relationship to earlier art forms. In any account of cinema, Eisenstein felt that Disney must have a prominent place. Indeed, he regarded him as one of the three most important figures in the industry and his work one of the greatest contributions that America made to art:

9. The Disney Version: Hercules (1997)

> I'm sometimes frightened when I watch his films. Frightened because of some absolute perfection in what he does. This man seems to know not only the magic of all technical means, but also the most secret strands of human thought, images, ideas, feelings. Such was probably the effect of Saint Francis of Assisi's sermons. Fra Angelico's paintings bewitch in this way. He creates somewhere in the realm of the very purest and most primal depths … He creates on the conceptual level of man not yet shackled by logic, reason, or experience (Eisenstein 1988: 2).

It is impossible to reconcile such views with those of Kanfer above. Kanfer's Disney is a man distinguished by the smallness of his talent and of his breadth of vision; Disney is a figure who ruined popular film. For Eisenstein, Disney is part saint, part genius. Yet, whatever opinion we decide to follow, it is clear that it is impossible to give a full account of cinema that doesn't include Disney.

The change in critical attitude towards Disney animation is the result of a number of factors. Certainly, changing attitudes and increased sensitivity towards issues of gender, race, and class have not served Disney films well. In addition, Disney films have come under increased scrutiny because of the dominance of Disney in the media market. The Walt Disney Company is the world's largest media and entertainment company enjoying a market capitalisation of approximately $70 billion, an annual turnover in the region of $38 billion, and an operating income of close to $6 billion. In addition to its animation studios, its film business includes the large studios of Touchstone Pictures and Miramax films. These film businesses are complemented by an extensive network of home distribution companies for the selling and rental of DVDs as well as commercial vehicles for the translation of films into live entertainment formats such as musicals or dramatic shows. Further opportunities for cross-promotional activities are provided by the parks and resorts division which includes five Disney theme parks (Anaheim, Florida, Tokyo, Paris, Hong Kong) as well as a private cruise line. The merchandising division of the corporation is the largest in the world and its publishing division (Disney Publishing Worldwide) is the world's largest publisher of children's books and magazines with a market penetration of 100 million readers each month in 75 countries. Finally, Disney is a large owner of media networks. These include one television network (ABC) as well as a number of cable channels, radio stations, and Internet businesses.

Far more than any other cinematic product, Disney films need to be seen in the context of an extensive network of complementary commercial pressures. Its films not only need to be saleable in a variety of international markets, but they also need to be translatable into small screen formats for home entertainment systems and television distribution as well as supporting a range of themed merchandise, resort entertainments, and book versions. Given such a range of diverse pressures that each film needs to satisfy, the tendency to rely on established formulae is understandable.

195

Hercules belongs to the so-called 'Eisner era' of Disney film productions. Traditionally, the animated cinematic output of Disney is divided into 'Silent and Early era' (1924-1937), 'Golden era' (1937-1967), 'Silver (post-Walt) era' (1967-1984), 'Eisner era' (1984-2005), and 'post-Eisner era' (2005-) films. However, these divisions are not impermeable. For example, while the beginning of the 'Golden era' is normally associated with the production of *Snow White* (1937), the first full-length, sound-synchronised, Technicolor, animated film, *Snow White* only makes sense when seen as a continuation of Disney's early experiments in colour and sound (e.g. *Silly Symphonies*) rather than a radical break from them.

The influence of the 'Golden era' productions on the style and formula of Disney films is unmistakable. Films such as *Snow White and the Seven Dwarfs* (1937), *Pinocchio* (1940), *Bambi* (1942), *Cinderella* (1950), and *Peter Pan* (1953), established a preference for young protagonists, a mixture of comedy and drama, and a strong musical element. The Disney Corporation has continually returned to these films for inspiration and the development of new revenue streams. Merchandise associated with these films continues to sell well and they occupy a central place in the formulation of the Disney brand.

The 'Eisner era' of production is one associated with renewal in the animated division of the corporation. After the death of Walt Disney, animated film revenues experienced a decline. Although features such as *Robin Hood* (1973), *The Rescuers* (1977), and *The Fox and the Hound* (1981) were commercial successes, it was felt that the animated output of Disney looked increasingly dated and was being left behind by other studios and cinematic formats. The tremendous success of live-action films such as *Star Wars* (1977) threatened animation's monopoly on the depiction of the fantastic and unreal. The low point for the animated division was the production of *The Black Cauldron* (1985), an expensive flop universally derided for its overly complex storyline and difficult to like characters. In 1984, in order to reverse declining revenues and protect the company from hostile takeovers, the board of Disney appointed Michael Eisner as its new chairman. Eisner had been previously president of Paramount Pictures. Instrumental in getting Eisner elected to this position was Roy E. Disney (Walt Disney's nephew and son of Roy Disney, the co-founder of Disney).

In return for his corporate support, Roy E. Disney was appointed in charge of the animated division of the company. This period is characterised by a back-to-basics approach in terms of animation. According to Peter Schneider (Senior Vice President), there were three cardinal rules to observe: 'Tell a great story; tell it with great characters; and always push the technological barriers.' The first film to demonstrate this new sensibility was *The Little Mermaid* (1989). Its character-driven storyline combined with a strong soundtrack and technically impressive underwater animation proved a tremendous hit at the box-office and started a chain of successes that included *Beauty and the Beast* (1991), *Aladdin*

(1992), and *The Lion King* (1994). In each film, we see a similar combination of elements: a young hero is forced to confront danger accompanied by physically-comic sidekicks. All the while, a popular musical soundtrack provides commentary on the film's developments. As we shall see, it is a formula that with minimal tweaking Disney applied to the story of Hercules.

Background to case study

In 1992, the animation department at Disney turned to Greece in its quest for new subject matter for development into an animated feature. Amongst a number of proposals, two were singled out for further development, a feature based on the story of the *Odyssey* and a feature based on the hero, Hercules. Ultimately, the decision was taken to proceed with the Hercules project. The reason for the decision to green-light Hercules over the *Odyssey* illustrates both Disney's production priorities and the form that the movie took. 'Hercules appealed to us because it didn't seem as sacred a thing as something like the *Odyssey*. We had to feel that whatever we chose, we would be able to take quite a few liberties', said Ron Clements, one of the film's directors.

The other director for the film was John Musker. Clements and Musker had been a directing team in three previous films (*The Great Mouse Detective, Little Mermaid*, and *Aladdin*). As directors, they originally had come to prominence when Roy E. Disney had been put in charge of the animation department. Both figures were poster-boys for the new Eisner-era Disney. *The Great Mouse Detective* (1986), their first co-production, is normally regarded as one of the first films to express the new reinvigorated spirit of the animation department. Following the disastrous flop of *The Black Cauldron*, Disney animation moved in a different direction. Budgets were tightened. The marketing of the films was more targeted towards a children's market. The production schedule was increased. *The Black Cauldron* had occupied all of Disney's animation resources for a three-year period. Now two to three projects would be prepared simultaneously. Thus, while *Hercules* was undergoing development, *Pocahontas* (1995) and *The Hunchback of Notre Dame* (1996) were being finalised. The lessons learnt from one film could now be quickly and easily imported into another.

A number of the successful features of *Little Mermaid* (1989) and *Aladdin* (1992) were replicated in *Hercules*. A popular catchy soundtrack was commissioned. Sidekick characters are used to provide much of the humour. The ratio of comedy to drama follows the traditional Disney recipe of 3:1. Just as the genie in *Aladdin* was a thinly disguised Robin Williams, so again, the look and style of prominent actors, in this case Danny DeVito and James Woods, influenced the depiction of the characters of Philoctetes and Hades.

Yet, although there is much that is similar with these previous productions by Musker and Clements, *Hercules* also represents some significant departures. The most obvious one is the graphic style employed in the animation. Rather than use in-house animators for the artistic lead in this film, Disney turned to the British cartoonist Gerald Scarfe to take on the role of production design. Musker had long been a fan of Scarfe's work and was instrumental in getting him on board for the project.

Gerald Scarfe made his reputation as a satirical cartoonist for magazines such as *Punch* and *Private Eye* in the 1960s. Later he became more famous as a political cartoonist for the *Sunday Times* for which his depictions of Margaret Thatcher were renowned for their savagery. Although primarily a cartoonist, Scarfe was not without experience in animation. Prior to his involvement in *Hercules*, Scarfe had been the animator and principal director of the celebrated animated short, *The Wall*, for the band Pink Floyd. He had also extensive experience designing for the theatrical stage.

As a cartoonist practising for the adult market, Scarfe was well positioned to be the aesthetic muse for this film which pitched itself at a slightly older, savvier, hipper market than previous Disney films. Unlike other films which aimed to please audiences from age six and upwards, *Hercules* was very much slanted towards the over-eleven market. His sharper lines and edgier graphics suited the more mature subject matter of this film. Translating Scarfe's vision to the team of animators were Andy Gaskill (Art Direction) and Sue Nichols (Production Styling). Both were experienced Disney professionals, having worked on a number of previous films. While Scarfe sketched out the broad-concept and aesthetic look, Gaskill and Nichols were charged with organising the animators to bring it to fruition. They were responsible for working out the nature of the lighting, props, costuming, and background. Most of the more quirky elements in the scenes were the product of their work.

In looking for their inspiration, members of the artistic team travelled to Greece and Turkey. Their itinerary in Greece included Mount Olympus, the Acropolis in Athens, Delphi, and Thebes. While in Turkey, in addition to major classical sites such as Ephesus, their travels also included a tour of the coast to see the rock-cut tombs of Lycia. The distinctive architecture of the tombs, which were carved into high cliffs, makes a frequent appearance in the film; such tombs providing Hades with his preferred place from which to watch the unfolding drama. In addition, a large amount of time was spent combing through standard works on Greek art. This initial research was distilled into the reference guides issued to all animators. The impact of this research is seen most effectively in the opening scene of the film, which features a run-through of the greatest works of classical art.

The other important creative input into the film was the song-writing team of Alan Menken and David Zippel. Menken was a well-established figure at Disney having won Academy Awards for his soundtracks for *The*

Little Mermaid (1989), *Beauty and the Beast* (1991), *Aladdin* (1992), and *Pocahontas* (1995). However, he had not previously worked on a Disney feature with Zippel. In many ways, it was a pairing that suited the production values and the narrative structure of the story. Zippel, a former lawyer, was a talented lyricist who enjoyed complex puns and wordplay. Menken's experience meant that he could easily adapt to a musical pastiche style that fitted well with the movie's post-modern sensibilities. Moreover, the most distinctive musical motif in the film, the gospel and blues-singing chorus of Muses, replicated a musical conceit that Menken had used earlier in his career. One of Menken's earliest successes had been with the musical *Little Shop of Horrors*, a musical that parodied early B-grade horror films. One of the features of the musical was a troupe of gospel-singers who provided meta-textual commentary and fill-in narrative in much the same way as the Muses do in *Hercules*.

In promoting *Hercules*, Disney followed its standard combination of print and digital media promotion. One feature that makes Disney promotion strategies distinctive from other film companies is the opportunity to cross-promote its films through its Disney stores, theme parks, and television channels. Stores started to receive Disney merchandise in advance of the film in order to whet the audience's appetite. Another cross-promotion strategy was use of a strategic tie-in arrangement with McDonald's restaurants. In January 1997 McDonalds and the Disney corporation signed a ten-year agreement to facilitate large-scale cross-promotion and *Hercules* was the first film to benefit from this arrangement. Hercules merchandise such as figurines, soft-drink cups, and tray inserts all appeared throughout the campaign to help launch the film. In Europe, Disney entered into an arrangement with the confectioner Nestlé to promote Hercules through the incorporation of Hercules figurines in their range of chocolates.

Another distinctive aspect of Disney's marketing of its films is the use of spin-off television shows to rejuvenate the franchise. In 1998, Disney produced *Hercules: The animated series* to capitalise on the popularity of the *Hercules* movie. The series premiered on the Disney Saturday morning show on the national ABC network where it proved tremendously popular. It continued to show on the ABC network until 2001 when it moved to the cable television channel Toon Disney. Episodes were made until 2008. The series was created as a prequel to the film and followed Hercules' adventures as a teenager at the Prometheus Academy, where together with his friends, Icarus and Cassandra, he battled both the snobbery of classmates such as Prince Adonis and the plots of Hades. Like the film, the series was characterised by a comic approach to myth. Icarus, for example, is shown as constantly frazzled owing to his close encounter with the sun and the inability of anybody to take Cassandra's prophecies seriously is a running joke.

One other post-release spin-off that was designed to capitalise on and maintain interest in the film was the 'Hercules on Ice' skating spectacular.

This was the first of the 'Disney on Ice' productions. The show, which toured the US, received almost universal critical praise and was often compared to the film in much more favourable terms. In particular, critics praised the depiction of Megara as a more lovable figure than the cynical and damaged character in the movie, and the character of Philoctetes who swapped a lot of his verbal humour for physical slapstick in the ice-capades version of the story.

Perhaps the most controversial aspect of Disney's promotional campaign for *Hercules* was the Disney parade in New York. In 1995, Disney purchased the lease on the derelict art-nouveau playhouse, the New Amsterdam Theatre on 42nd Street in Times Square, and began renovations. Disney's intention was to create a central venue that it could use for promotional screenings of its movies and a location for its theatrical spin-offs. Indeed, the latter is perhaps the most prominent use of the space; the New Amsterdam having been the location for the opening of the stage version of the *Lion King* in 1997. This renovation was heavily supported by city officials who were keen to see the New Amsterdam rehabilitated as part of their plan to clean up Times Square. To celebrate the re-opening of the New Amsterdam, Disney was able to secure an agreement from Town Hall to allow a parade from West 42nd Street to East 66th Street. The occasion of the parade was the première of Disney's new summer blockbuster, *Hercules*.

The logistics and cost of the parade were enormous. The city repaved one block of 42nd Street and filled all the potholes for the length of the parade route. Teams of electricians turned off all the streetlights along the parade route. Disney asked over 5,000 businesses to turn off their lights for the duration of the parade. Traffic around 42nd Street was closed from midnight on Friday to noon on Sunday. Most of Midtown was closed to traffic for the duration of the parade. Over eight miles of police barricades and 2,000 police officers were deployed. The clean-up operations involved 118 sanitation workers charged with clearing 350 specially-deployed rubbish bins.

The excessive cost of the event (only a proportion of which was covered by Disney) combined with the inconvenience and the perception that Disney was in receipt of special favours attracted criticism. The *New York Post* was particularly scathing in its editorial on the event. Letters-to-the-editor of the major New York newspapers took a similar line. These critics were joined by a number of New York chapters of industrial unions who were involved in strike action at the time against ABC, a Disney affiliate, and who objected to New York city officials condoning a celebration of the Disney corporation. Yet, despite this opposition, the event was also popular in many quarters. Approximately two million people came out to watch the parade, which featured, in addition to a giant Hercules striking poses as he stood atop Pegasus, thirty imported floats from the night-time parade at the Disneyworld in Florida. The audience for the event was further expanded through the televising of the parade on E! The Entertainment Channel, a cable channel owned by Disney.

The critical reception of the film was mixed. Some critics panned the film for being too commercial and too obviously aimed towards the merchandising market. Kanfer complained that far from being the offspring of Zeus and the wife of Amphitryon, this title character 'springs from the twin sources of Myth and Avarice'. Others found it too formulaic, a repetition of techniques previously seen in films such as *Aladdin*. Critics often compared Menken's score for *Hercules* unfavourably with his previous efforts. It is perhaps telling that although *Hercules* was nominated for an Academy Award, it failed to win, ending Menken's run of success.

The initial box-office was equally disappointing. In the first two weeks of general release, the film took only $58 million at the box-office. This compares with *Pocahontas* and the *Lion King*, which took $80 million and $119 million respectively in the same time period. The film eventually garnered $252 million in worldwide box-office, a respectable return, but not outstanding. Part of the reason for the comparative underperformance at the box-office was a misjudgement of the audience. The traditional secret for Disney success had been to produce films that appealed to the entire family. Such a formula became increasingly difficult as the audience fragmented at the turn of the twentieth century. Moreover, the target audience of the film, namely slightly older, but pre-teen boys, failed to be attracted in the requisite numbers, preferring to go to even more adult-oriented films such as *Men in Black* (1997) or *The Lost World* (1997), the sequel to box-office hit *Jurassic Park* (1993). At the same time, the film alienated younger viewers who found the darker vision of the film distressing. The lack of success of *Hercules* is noticeable given the lack of competition in the summer of 1997 for the child market. There were no other films, apart from *George of the Jungle* (1997), pitched at children that year. Analysts noticed the gap and predicted *Hercules* would do well. Such predictions only served to reinforce the sense of *Hercules'* failure. The final contributing factor was the run away success of *Titanic* (1997), which succeeded in smashing all previous box-office records. The film so dominated the takings that year that *Hercules* got lost. Ultimately, it was not the Titans that destroyed Hercules, but a ship named after them that sank the film.

Plot summary

The film begins with a prologue in which a singing chorus of Muses describe how Zeus (voiced by Rip Torn) created order out of chaos by imprisoning the destructive elemental Titans that formerly stalked the earth (song: 'That's the gospel truth'). The scene shifts to Mount Olympus where the pantheon of gods is assembled to celebrate the birth of Hercules, the son of Zeus and Hera (Samantha Eggar). All of the gods are enchanted by the young infant and shower him with gifts, his parents providing him with a small winged foal, Pegasus. Hades (James Wood) alone proves immune to the child's charms, and his hatred only intensifies when he returns to the Underworld and learns from the three Fates that his plans for domination will be undone should the adult Hercules ever take the field of battle against him. Hades hatches a plan to dispose of Hercules by first stripping him of his immortality and then killing the helpless infant. He entrusts the plan to his two bumbling sidekicks, Pain (Bobcat Goldthwait) and Panic (Matt Frewer). Unfortunately for Hades, these two demons fail to administer the full dose of the potion that will render Hercules mortal and defenceless. Instead, Hercules is left mortal, but retains his godlike strength. When Pain and Panic, in the form of serpents, try to kill the child he quickly dispatches them. Defeated, the two demons decide to return to the Underworld and pretend to Hades that they were successful in their mission to kill Hercules.

Unable to return to Olympus owing to his mortal condition, the infant Hercules is raised by Alcmene and Amphitryon, a peasant couple who find the child after it has been abandoned on earth by Pain and Panic. Ignorant of his origins, Hercules (Tate Donovan) grows up into an awkward adolescent, his exceptional strength proving more of a burden than a gift (song: 'I can go the distance'). Recognising the unhappiness of their adopted child, Alcmene and Amphitryon recount to him the strange events surrounding their discovery of him on a mountainside. Hercules realises that the gods must know the story of his origins and he sets off to the temple of Zeus to find out the truth.

On his arrival at the temple, Zeus manifests himself and reveals that Hercules is his son. Moreover, he tells Hercules that he will be able to return to his biological family on Mount Olympus, if he transcends his mortality and proves himself a 'true hero' on earth. In order to help him to achieve this end, Zeus reunites Hercules with Pegasus and sends him to undergo training with the satyr and hero-trainer, Philoctetes ('Phil'; Danny DeVito). After an extended montage of training-scenes (song: 'It's up to you'), Hercules feels ready to embark on his quest to become a hero. Phil advises him to head for Thebes. As they journey to Thebes, Hercules encounters a young woman (Megara, 'Meg'; Susan Egan) being menaced by a centaur river-spirit. Hercules rescues this 'damsel in distress' and the young hero is smitten by this gorgeous auburn-haired beauty. Unfortunately for him, Megara has already sold her soul to Hades and is acting as his agent on earth.

Hercules' actions in rescuing Megara bring to Hades' attention the fact of Hercules' continued existence. Afraid that Hercules may yet upset his plans, Hades immediately undertakes to destroy Hercules by arranging for the hero to go into battle against the giant Hydra. The pair is evenly matched, but Hercules eventually triumphs over his foe, burying the many-headed serpent under a pile of boulders. The Hydra is the first of a sequence of monstrous opponents sent by Hades to kill Hercules. Through an extended musical number (song: 'Zero to Hero'), we see Hercules triumphing over all of them, increasing his fame and fortune.

Unable to succeed by force, Hades resorts to guile and arranges for Megara to seduce the hero. Hercules falls deeply in love with Megara, refusing to heed the warnings given by Philoctetes, who accidentally uncovers Hades' plan about the danger she poses. Megara meanwhile has been bowled over by Hercules' honesty and integrity and refuses to assist Hades in his plans. When Hades sees how passionately in love these two figures are, he realises that he has the perfect leverage to enact his scheme.

Appearing before Hercules at the gymnasium, Hades offers Hercules a deal. After demonstrating that he has Megara in his clutches, Hades promises that if Hercules will give up his godlike strength for twenty-four hours then he will not do any violence to Megara. Hercules, reluctant because he knows that Hades will use this period to wreak havoc, agrees provided that no harm should come to Megara during the twenty-four hours. Hades and Hercules shake on the deal and Hercules discovers that his powers have gone.

Hades then bounds off to unleash the Titans and lead them in an attack against Olympus. The release of the Titans causes calamities on earth and Hercules stands by powerless to help. While he launches his attack on Olympus, Hades sends a giant Cyclops to kill Hercules. As Hercules and the Cyclops battle, Megara is accidentally injured by a falling column. This violates the agreement that Hercules made with Hades and Hercules finds his strength returned.

Hercules then ventures to Olympus where he manages to defeat Hades and the Titans. Unfortunately while he is away saving Olympus, Megara dies. Risking his own life, Hercules journeys to the Underworld to retrieve Megara's soul from the River of Death. It is this act of self-sacrifice which finally proves that Hercules is a 'true hero' and allows him to have his immortality restored. Finally able to return to Olympus, Hercules chooses instead to stay on earth with Megara. He has finally found a place where he belongs (song: 'A Star is Born').

Key scenes and themes

The nature of heroism

Hercules is the paradigm of the Greek hero. He's the archetype and the template for all subsequent versions of heroism. As Ron Clements, the director of *Hercules*, remarked, he's the 'first superhero'. Given his status, Hercules is the ideal vehicle for analysing the nature of western heroics. One of the constant questions running throughout *Hercules* is a question about the nature of heroism. The issue is central to the plot of the film. It

203

is Hercules' discovery of what makes 'a true hero' that allows him both to defeat Hades and reconcile himself to his family on Olympus. Allied to this theme are a number of other important themes in this film. For example, Hercules' quest for true heroism maps onto an ancillary concern about how one makes the transition from childhood to adulthood. Hercules' gangly, uncontrollable body at the start of the film exemplifies many of the problems that young men face as they approach puberty. Hercules' escape from his awkward adolescence represents the first step towards becoming a hero. Similarly, the concern with substance over style that underpins much of the criticism of consumer culture that one finds in this film is part of this broader quest for a definition of heroism. When Zeus advises Hercules to 'look inside your heart', he implicitly rejects all external trappings of fame in favour of an interior life predicated on a moral framework of self-sacrifice. This is the formulation that Disney offers as a notion of heroism.

The ancient mind would have had trouble grasping the notion of heroism offered in Disney's *Hercules*. The idea that there was such a man as a 'true hero' was one unknown in the ancient world. People were simply either heroes or they were not. Essentially, heroes were figures (usually from the past) who were offered some form of worship or commemoration such as ritual offerings on their graves or sacrifices performed in their honour. By defining heroism in terms of ritual function (i.e. anyone who receives cult is a hero), a large number of figures were recognised as heroes that we would not normally consider as such. We possess, for example, a few child heroes whose only claim to fame are distinguished parents. We even have one case of a dog worshipped as hero. Later in the Hellenistic period, wealthy benefactors would use their patrimony to establish cults to themselves and ensure that they were worshipped as heroes by their communities and descendants.

There was no moral requirement for being a hero. Heroes could perform the most horrendous, immoral acts. Achilles mutilated the body of his opponent Hector to such an extent that even the gods were outraged. Other Homeric heroes were no better. Agamemnon is shown to be a vain and ill-tempered ruler in the *Iliad*. Odysseus is wily and deceitful. Indeed, Hercules was no paradigm of good behaviour. He was as famous as a drunk or a glutton as he was a defender against evil. Ancient artists seem to have had as much fun depicting a fat, drunken, urinating Hercules (the so-called 'mingens-type') as they do showing him in more elevated poses.

Moreover, the implicit criticism of wealth and fame in the film contradicts much of the ancient ethos surrounding the hero. One of the defining features of the hero in the ancient world was his fame. A hero without fame was a contradiction in terms. Further, there was a direct correlation between fame and material rewards. Heroes expected to be rewarded as a natural consequence of their status. Sometimes they could be exceptionally mercenary. Hercules, for example, refused to rescue the daughter of

Zero to hero

The sequence begins with the Theban crowd staring at the pile of rocks under which the Hydra is buried. Hercules' destruction of the Hydra seems to have cost him his life. Suddenly, the clenched fist of the Hydra twitches and Hercules emerges, exhausted, but alive. Carried aloft by the adoring crowd, Hercules turns to Phil and says, 'You've got to admit – *that* was pretty heroic.' The scene cuts to the chorus of Muses and a jazzy musical number begins. Through a montage of scenes, the Muses recount the deeds of Hercules and show his increasing fame. Hercules' activities largely consist of defeating monsters sent by Hades. Only the extinguishing of an erupting volcano by placing a boulder on its mouth breaks up the otherwise endless repetition of monster-bashing. All the monsters of Greek myth are here. Even monsters outside the traditional Herculean mythic cycle are included. So while the montage begins by showing him skewering with an arrow the Erymanthian boar, traditionally the third of Hercules' labours, it soon shows him defeating the Gorgons and the Minotaur, monsters more often associated with Perseus and Theseus respectively. In a visual conceit first established in *Jason and the Argonauts*, Hades is shown controlling the monsters via chess pieces on a large game board. Interspersed among the scenes of monster fighting are scenes where Hercules is shown receiving the rewards of fame [Fig. 19]. Increasingly the hero is turned into a brand and used to market goods as diverse as action figures, soft drink, and sandals.

The visual imagery is underscored by the lyrics of the accompanying musical number, 'Zero to Hero'. These stress both the martial nature of Hercules' activities ('Who puts the glad in gladiator? Hercules! / Whose daring deeds make great theatre? Hercules!') and the monetary rewards that he received from them ('From appearance fees and royalties, our Herc had cash to burn / Now nouveau riche and famous, he can tell you what the Grecians earn'). The song and attendant sequence of images finishes with the line, 'Now he's a hero. Yes, indeed!'.

Well actually, no he isn't as it turns out. Almost immediately, the colour and volume disappear and the scene transforms to a darker and more sober scene set inside the temple of Zeus where Hercules re-enacts some of the previous adventures we have just seen for his divine father. Confident that he has now earned a place amongst the Gods, Hercules awaits his invitation to Mount Olympus. Sadly for him, his confidence turns out to be misplaced. Zeus informs him that he is yet to prove himself 'a true hero'. It takes more than fame or a capacity for violence to make a hero in the Disney universe.

the king of Troy from a sea-monster until he promised Hercules a set of fine horses. When the king reneged on the gift after Hercules' rescue of the princess, Hercules vowed to destroy the city. It is a story that is the very antithesis of chivalry.

This consideration of ancient notions of heroism brings into relief just how contrived is the version offered by Disney. The notion of heroism that Disney presents here is the product of a complex series of post-antique

19. Is there a difference between fame and heroism?
Disney *Hercules* (1997).

intellectual developments. The modern hero is a confection of a number of different ideas. It takes the Christian focus on the internal self, melds it with Romantic notions about the importance of the individual, and tops it off with a coating of twentieth-century self-help rhetoric. Looking for the origins of the version of heroism in Disney's Hercules one is better advised to read the letters of Paul or the Charles Atlas guide to physical development than any work of Greek mythology.

There is a further problem with the notion of heroism that Disney offers in this film. As a number of critics have noted, despite its rhetoric, the film seems to offer mixed messages about the relationship between fame and heroism. The film may claim that heroism is not a quest for glory, but its visuals and music revel in precisely the rewards that fame brings. This is especially shown in the 'Zero to Hero' sequence where the up-beat tempo of the music and the fast-paced editing specifically invite us to enjoy the spectacle. Further strengthening the viewer's association with this sequence are the specific images employed. This story of success is a version with which viewers are all too familiar. From the celebrity endorsements of sports shoes and soft drinks, to the autographs, to the rewarding of poor parents with glistening mansions, Hercules walks a path already trod by numerous basketball and football stars [Fig. 19]. His version of heroism is one that needs little extra validation. Rather than under-cutting traditional narratives about success, this sequence reinforces and amplifies them. Given that the sequence is designed – like so many other Disney sequences – to be replayed as a stand-alone segment (it is its own chapter on the *Hercules* DVD), its contradictory message obliterates many of the values that are supposedly the mainstay of the storyline of this film.

Indeed, in pushing too hard the eschewing of worldly possessions as a desirable aim, Disney threatens its own interests. Annalee Ward identifies the contradiction that lies at the heart of *Hercules* thus:

> This is the problem. Disney keeps waffling on the message it sends. Disney says that it wants to teach the lesson that a true hero is defined by the strength of his heart, but it also wants to teach the audience to value materialism: more stuff is good. After all, Disney needs to sell more to keep its profit margin acceptable for stockholders. (Ward 2002: 88).

This tension plays out in the plethora of tie-in merchandise that was produced for the film. The film may specifically ridicule the notion of Hercules merchandise such as action figures, soft-drink bottles, and sneakers. Yet it was precisely these items that the corporation and its affiliates produced to sell in its Disney-branded stores or to accompany the Hercules-themed fast-food meals at McDonald's. Disney's *Hercules* proves to be an exercise in doublethink where viewers are simultaneously encouraged to reject and desire consumer products.

These rival versions of heroism can be seen in the rival narrative arcs of Hercules and his trainer, Philoctetes. If the story of Hercules is a story about the discovery of a deeper, internal form of heroism, the story of Philoctetes is one where its showier, more superficial rival is shown to be triumphant. From the beginning, Philoctetes is only interested in surface. For him the way to heroism is through the development of muscles not ethics. When Phil talks about 'heart' he means endurance not morals. Heroism is all about 'going the distance'. His only interest is fame, creating a hero whose name will endure forever; a real 'star'. For all of Zeus' moralising about the true nature of heroism, the film ends with the Muses singing that 'a star (significantly not a hero) is born'. It seems that ultimately this film is all about making Phil's wishes, not Zeus', come true.

Rejecting the epic film

As we have regularly seen, representing antiquity on film inevitably involves working with a tradition. Not only is one competing with the plethora of classical motifs that permeate western culture, but one is also heir to a substantial cinematic inheritance. It is a heavy weight to bear and each director and genre reacts differently. The ironic, meta-theatrical response to this tradition offered in *Hercules* typifies many of the cultural products of the last two decades of the twentieth century. This was a period in which the in-joke and the parody reached their heights as an art form. This was particularly noticeable within the field of popular US animation where TV shows such as the *Simpsons* and *South Park* pioneered this approach and trained their audience to expect such meta-textual humour. In this period, it increasingly became seen that one of the functions of entertainment was to run a commentary on popular culture. No trend, fad, or fashion was immune. In many ways, it was a perfect fit of form and content. Just as animation offered an overly stylised version of reality that referenced, while never completely replicating, the original, so plotlines, dialogue and motifs from other cinematic, mythological, and popular narratives were referenced in a playful, parodic fashion.

The opening prologue sets the tone visually, musically, and comedically for the rest of the film. The film is all too aware of its cinematic predecessors and works hard in the prologue to signal that *Hercules* represents a departure from what has gone before. This rejection of older genres of epic

---

Prologue

The scene opens in what looks like the inside of an abandoned temple or perhaps the vault of a museum. The building reflects elements of classical architecture such as the domed ceiling of the Pantheon. The camera pans around a cluttered space composed of masterpieces of classical sculpture. In the foreground is a statue of Athena of the Phidian type modelled on the bronze example found in the Piraeus. In the midground reclines a statue of Dionysus taken from the east pediment of the Parthenon. In the background, classical and archaic statuary fills a wall of niches. All are modelled on recognisable types. The camera pans round and yet more statues come into view. Some are direct copies of famous statues. For example, we see the Zeus from Cape Artemision with a restored thunderbolt, the statue of Heracles from the east pediment of the temple of Aphaia at Aegina, and the bronze Terme boxer. Others, while not direct copies, take their inspiration from classical and neo-classical sculpture such as the work of the Danish sculptor Bertel Thorvaldsen. As the camera travels through this assemblage, we see in the distance a black-figure vessel highlighted by a shaft of light coming through the oculus of the dome. A gravelly voice-over (Charlton Heston) accompanies the scene, telling us about an age of gods and heroes. At the moment that a close-up of the vase fills the screen, the voice is suddenly interrupted by one of the figures on the vase coming to life. She berates the narrator for making the story sound like 'some Greek tragedy'. Suddenly, all the figures on the vase come to life and we are introduced to the Muses who tell the narrator to 'lighten up' and promise that they will take over the storytelling from this point onwards. In a musical number ('That's the Gospel Truth'), the Muses give the back-story to the film and recount how Zeus imprisoned the Titans and made life 'neat and smooth and sweet'. To illustrate their lecture and support their claim that they are speaking the 'gospel truth', the Muses refer to images on Greek vases. Having finished their story, the Muses step aside as the camera zooms in on a drawing of Mount Olympus on a plate. As the camera gets closer and closer, the drawing gradually morphs into the real mountain and the credits begin to roll.

---

film is dramatised by the replacement of Charlton Heston in the role of narrator by the Muses. As the star of *Ben-Hur*, Heston is a figure especially associated with epic cinema. His replacement by a troupe of sassy lounge singers tells us everything that we need to know about the shift in attitude embodied in this film.

This shift is further signalled by perhaps the most distinctive stylistic device in the film; the extensive use of Greek pottery as a decorative motif. Whereas the voice of Heston is associated with a gloomy room (part-museum, part-mausoleum) full of dusty, refined statuary, the world of the Muses is a bright, colourful landscape of gutsy, primitive, and ceramic-inspired images. According to the styling reference guides issued to all animators, the guiding shape palette for all forms in the film was the Greek vase. The bulging trunks of trees, the fall of shadows on undulating hills, the curve of Meg's hips as they meet her waist, even the splashes made by drops of water all imitate Greek vase shapes. The style of drawing imitates that found on Greek vases. Tendrils of vegetation normally found in the backgrounds of vase-paintings find their way into the undergrowth of *Hercules*. The subsidiary decoration on Greek vases such as key meanders and palmettes are regularly deployed throughout this film. The appeal of pottery to Disney's animators is easy to understand. Artists interested in the movement and expressiveness of line have always been interested in Greek vases. Yet this dominance of pottery represents more than just an illustrator's fancy. The rejection of the primacy of statuary and the turn to pottery repeats again the rejection of epic cinema. Statuary has regularly been regarded as the highest form of art, and it was routinely deployed as a classical signifier in epic films. No court of a Roman emperor ever seems complete without a few plaster casts of Greek athletes. Its only rival as a piece of classical *mise-en-scène* is the fluted column. No epic film ever embraced pottery in the way that *Hercules* does. In doing so, the film signals its break from the epic tradition. Rather than having any pretensions towards high art, this film is going to be populist and accessible. Moreover, it is going to break rules.

The figures that break most of the rules are the Muses. From their first appearance, they are upstarts. They don't operate in the same plane as the rest of the action. They slide across walls, imitate friezes, and animate pottery decoration. As Mike Show, who was in charge of animating these characters, remarked:

> They exist like drawings on a flat wall or as statues. They don't exist in the world with the other characters. You can put them on a wall, make a statue out of them, a bust, or on a plate ... They live in their own realm, their own two-dimensional graphic world (quoted in Thomas 1997: 219).

This liminal nature permits them to serve a particular narrative function. Disney takes the traditional role of a Greek chorus as commentators on passing action and combines it with an ironic sensibility. These extra-dimensional characters function meta-textually. They play-up the fictive nature of the action. They never let us forget that we are watching a story, not live action. As a stereotypical Motown act metamorphosed into a bevy of goddesses, they license the interjection of other anachronistic elements. From the moment Zeus is described as 'too type A to just relax', we know that this film intends to speak to contemporary mores. When Pain jokes that 'Hercules' may be a popular name like 'Britney', we permit the jokey reference to the popularity of Britney Spears because we've already swallowed so much of this contemporary referencing already. The Muses teach us to expect such moves.

The number of intertextual allusions in this film is too voluminous to catalogue. Gods resemble TV stars. Thebes owes more to an out-of-towner's view of New York than it does to any archaeological site. Music and lyrics often comprise a series of endless quotations from vaudeville through to pop. *Hercules* doesn't short-change you when it comes to ideas. The basic storyline of a hero saving the world and in the process discovering his humanity is one that has been used before. If nothing else, it is essentially the same premise as *Hercules* (1958). What distinguishes the Disney version is all the added embellishment. It is the postmodern bells and whistles that make this film unique. It is a rich recipe, and one not welcomed by all critics; some of whom found the tone of the film a little too flip. In her review in the *Washington Post* ('Disney's *Hercules*: Myth for the masses', 27/6/1997), Rita Kempley expressed her frustration: 'Chock-full of celeb cameos, puns, and contemporary camp, the movie is annoyingly hip. It wants to belong even more desperately than its title character.'

Sanitising myth

Time magazine film critic Richard Corliss voiced the criticism of a number of reviewers when he remarked, 'don't look for this plot in Bulfinch'. As they watched the film, viewers became all too aware of the fact that what they were watching owed more to Disney conventions than Greek myth. As we saw earlier, Disney has long enjoyed a reputation for the promotion of conservative social values. Critics have regularly derided the film corporation for its representation of race, gender, and sexual orientation, which they have seen as excessively normative and reactionary. Good women are always passive subjects waiting to be rescued. Men are heroic and find validation through action rather than emotions. Effeminacy in males is derided, but compassion in women is praised. Villains often perpetuate ethnic stereotypes. This situation seemed to be changing with the more recent Disney films (e.g. *Pocahontas, Mulan*) broadening the range of both gender and ethnic representations; this change reflecting a broadening of representation that occurred in US media in the 1980s and 1990s. Yet even here the corporation was not above tweaking the storyline

9. *The Disney Version: Hercules* (1997)

> **Rescuing a damsel in distress**
>
> As Hercules, Phil and Pegasus look on, a young woman, Megara, comes into view; she is being chased by a giant blue centaur through a river. Water flows everywhere. In the background, we can see a waterfall. The young woman and the centaur struggle in the water that pools around their feet. The centaur grabs the woman and lifts her up so that she and he are face-to-face. 'I like them fiery,' he exclaims. Unable to control himself, Hercules wanders into the river to confront the centaur and his captive. However, he finds his offer of assistance dismissed by the young woman who tells him to 'Keep moving, junior.' Hercules refuses to take the advice and begins his attempt to subdue the centaur. Released from the centaur's grip, Megara dries herself on a branch on the riverbank and watches the combat. Despite being initially unimpressed by Hercules' rather amateurish and bungling attempts at monster-fighting, Megara warms to the hero as the fight progresses. Finally, she is forced to ask Phil, 'Is wonder boy for real?' Having dispatched the centaur, Hercules returns to Megara and finds himself completely tongue-tied by her beauty. After introductions are completed, Hercules asks how Megara found herself mixed up with the centaur. 'Well you know how men are,' Megara replies, 'They think "no" means "yes" and "get lost" means "take me, I'm yours".' It is a conversation that the all-too-innocent Hercules is unable to follow. After spurning the offer of a ride to Thebes, Megara heads off into the sunset, leaving Hercules with the line, 'I'll be alright. I'm a big, tough girl. I tie my own sandals and everything.'

to fit their agenda. Thus, Disney felt at liberty to change the age, looks, and accomplishments of the historical Pocahontas as well as the ultimate outcome of her meeting with John Smith in order to make a more 'Disney' storyline. The problem faced in *Hercules* is that much of Greek myth operates in an ethical world far removed from Disney's conventional morals.

The scene in which Hercules meets Megara [see box: 'Rescuing a damsel in distress'] represents a confection of a number of Herculean myths. Its principal source is the adventures of Hercules and his love affair with Deianeira. Just as in the scene described above, the first time that Hercules and Deianeira meet, Hercules needs to wrestle with the river god Achelous for her. Although in this case, the river god took the form of a horned bull. The presence of the centaur Nessus refers to another later adventure. In that episode, Hercules and Deianeira come to the river Evenus and Hercules is tricked by Nessus into putting Deianeira on his back in order to allow him to carry her across the river. However, rather than ferrying her across to the opposite bank, Nessus attempts to abduct and violate Deianeira. Fortunately, before Nessus can succeed in his plans, Hercules cuts him down with a volley of arrows.

In the Disney version of these myths, Megara (Hercules' first wife) is

211

substituted for Deianeira and the incidents involving Achelous and Nessus are conflated. Nessus remains a sexual predator, but this time he was approached not for his assistance as a ferryman, but, as we learn later, as a potential ally in Hades' plan to overthrow the rule of Zeus. The directors of the film were quite open about their free attitude towards mythic traditions. As co-director John Musker remarked in an interview, 'We, Ron Clements and I, knew we would only make one Greek movie. We borrowed elements and made it a sort of stew of mythology' (Tucker 1997: 38).

It is foolish, for a number of reasons, to criticise a film for not following a particular mythic tradition. First, because the idea that there is such a thing as an authoritative mythic tradition is a myth itself. In antiquity, countless different versions of myths circulated, often with irreconcilable details. Names and deeds were frequently interchangeable. Secondly, it is foolish because it ignores the fact that writers in the Greco-Roman world regularly adapted myths to suit their own story-telling purposes. The point when dealing with treatments of myth is not to criticise the creation of a 'stew', rather the role of the critic is to comment on its flavouring. It is worth observing that the choices in adapting myth made throughout *Hercules* reflect a particular moral view. They represent a desire to repress notions of domestic violence, irrational anger, and sexual transgression in favour of a world-view that celebrates monogamous companionate relationships and the nuclear family.

Take, for example, the depiction of Hercules' relationships with women. In antiquity, these relationships are always flawed and often end in bloody circumstances. A prime illustration is provided by Hercules' relationship with Deianeira, discussed above. According to the standard mythic tradition, as Nessus lay dying from the wounds inflicted by Hercules' arrows, he whispered into Deianeira's ear that his blood was a powerful aphrodisiac and that she should capture some of his blood so that if Hercules ever strayed she could reinvigorate his love for her. Deianeira duly did so, only to discover that Nessus had tricked her. For when she applied the blood to Hercules' cloak, she discovered that it was a burning poison that caused such intense continuous pain that ultimately the hero was forced to end it by committing suicide on a burning pyre; his immortal soul then travelled up to the heavens where he was welcomed on Olympus as a god. So while both the Disney movie and traditional mythic account start the story of Hercules' ascent to godhead with the rescue of a damsel from a river guardian, one is a story of vengeance, adultery, poison and betrayal and the other is a cheery musical number.

Hercules is depicted as a bumbling sexual innocent. He doesn't understand Megara's implied rape reference. He is constantly wrong-footed by her beauty. It is Megara who calls the shots. She's a type of modern feisty woman, the 'tough gal' that Disney increasingly chose to feature in its late 1990s films. Her sisters are Esmeralda from *The Hunchback of Notre Dame* (1996), Audrey from *Atlantis* (2001), and Captain Amelia from

Treasure Planet (2002). Hercules' lack of worldliness makes him an easy dupe for her subsequent deception. It is hard to imagine a stronger contrast with the traditional mythic depiction of Hercules, which made him a womaniser of the first order. This is the man who famously deflowers the fifty daughters of king Thespius in one night. Later, he seduces Auge, the virginal priestess of Athena, and causes her to lose her position and be exiled from her family. Hercules leaves sexual turmoil in his wake. The story of his encounter with Megara is one of bloodshed, not coy kisses. Megara was famous in antiquity for being the wife whom Hercules slew during a bout of madness. The twelve labours were his penance for his crime. When Hercules declares to Megara 'I will never hurt you', the viewer who knows their mythology is left to laugh at the ironic humour of the statement and the boldness of Disney's sanitisation of myth.

If the depiction of Hercules' relationship with women seeks to normalise these relationships and remove any edginess, the same can be said for his relationship with parents. Unlike traditional accounts that make Hercules the product of an adulterous union between Zeus and the mortal Alcmene, in the Disney version of the story, Hercules is the legitimate son of Zeus and Hera. Alcmene and her husband Amphitryon are relegated to the roles of foster parents. Hera is a doting loving mother, not the hateful goddess who, raging at the betrayal of her husband, plagues Hercules for most of his life. 'We felt that illegitimacy would be difficult subject matter for a Disney movie ... We moved more towards making Hades the villain instead of Hera', Ron Clements said in an interview. This divine nuclear family lives – literally – in a gated community on Mount Olympus with the other gods. By representing Zeus and Hera as a normal nuclear family, the film manages to avoid the problem of the incestuousness of divine relationships. In myth, Zeus may be Hera's brother as well as husband, but in the Disney version only the latter relationship gets any air.

This constant privileging of the normative and domestic over the strange and transgressive turns Greek myth into a comprehensive rather than confronting narrative. Hercules loses any of the cultural accretions that make him distinctive. He becomes just another costumed superhero. Indeed, that is how Ron Clements saw him, 'a kind of superhero – the first superhero'. This may have been how Hercules first appeared to Clements, but it is remarkable to observe the amount of effort that was required to achieve this depiction. Greek myth turns out to be a far from convenient source for comic-book heroes.

Suggested further viewing

Fantasia (1940)
This bold, experimental film produced by the Walt Disney Company consists of seven animated sequences set to eight pieces of classical music. It was the first feature film shown in stereophonic surround sound and

was designed to offer a new genre of entertainment; one that combined the concert experience with the animated short. In keeping with its artistic pretensions, rather than being shown as a general release, the film was shown only in a limited number of high-end theatres and only for a limited run. Although a few critical responses were received from classical music critics, the general response to the film was extremely positive and the film is now regarded as one of Disney's finest products.

The film also represents Disney's most sustained engagement with antiquity prior to *Hercules*. In an extended sequence set to the music of Beethoven's *Pastoral Symphony*, the viewer is treated to an animated romp through the landscape of Greek myth. The sequence opens onto an Arcadian idyll dotted with neoclassical temples where creatures from Greek mythology romp. Pegasus and his brood of flying horses soar through the sky. Female centaurs bathe by pools whilst flying cupids plait their manes. Onto this scene arrives the god Bacchus who inaugurates a wild revel of dancing and drinking. Suddenly the fun is interrupted by an ominous storm cloud. Rain pours down and the wind blows. The god Zeus, clearly the prototype for the depiction of Zeus in *Hercules*, has arrived. Assisted by Hephaestus, Zeus, perched on his cloud, rains down lightning bolts onto the landscape as Bacchus and his followers flee. Weary after his endeavours, Zeus retires to sleep. Gradually, the clouds disperse, the sun shines, and life in Arcadia returns to normal. Iris draws a rainbow through the sky to show that the danger has passed. The sequence finishes with Helios driving his sun-chariot to the west and darkness descends after an eventful day. The mythological creatures retire to bed and the goddess Artemis shoots a comet through the night sky.

Aladdin (dir. Clements and Musker, 1992)
Although this film does not obviously engage with classical material, it does provide a useful example of the Disney formula in action. Directed by the same directors as *Hercules*, this film is based on the Arab folktales surrounding the figure of Aladdin, in particular the story of Aladdin and the magic lamp taken from the collection of tales in *The Book of a Thousand and One Nights*. As with *Hercules*, the Aladdin myth is freely adapted to suit the purposes of the storyline. The brutality of the original tale is erased. In *The Book of a Thousand and One Nights*, Aladdin is a killer who is happy to dispose of his magician opponents. He is far removed from the sweet, happy-go-lucky adolescent of the Disney film. The film shares a number of similarities with *Hercules*. Both feature slightly awkward young male protagonists. Both have comic sidekicks (the Genie and Philoctetes) and rely upon a musical score to enliven proceedings. Indeed, the films are so compatible that Disney even exploited their shared sensibility by staging a *Hercules* and *Aladdin* crossover in one of its television cartoons. In the episode 'Hercules and the Arabian Night' from *Hercules: The animated series*, we see Hades and Aladdin's nemesis, the

evil sorcerer Jaffar, combining to destroy the two heroes. Naturally, their plans come to naught as Hercules and Aladdin team up to defeat them. The episode is striking for the ease with which it was possible to combine the two storylines. *Hercules* and *Aladdin* clearly belong in the same universe.

Achilles (dir. Purves, 1995*)*

It is hard to imagine a film that differs further from the Disney take on Greek myth than this one. *Hercules* is feature length; *Achilles* is very short (11 minutes). Instead of line animation, *Achilles* uses stop-motion claymation. The budget for *Hercules* dwarfs *Achilles*, which was the product of a small independent production house. *Hercules* was seen in mainstream cinemas throughout the world, *Achilles* had limited release mainly confined to the film festival circuit. Yet in terms of serious engagement with the world of classical myth, *Achilles* has equal claim to significance. Barry Purves is one of the UK's leading animators and his services have been used on a number of big cinematic projects. *Achilles* was Purves' fifth animated film and came on the back of his critically-acclaimed claymation version of Verdi's *Rigoletto* (1993). In *Achilles*, Purves tells the story of the love affair between Achilles and Patroclus and the tragic deaths of the lovers before the walls of Troy. The story is told in the manner of a Greek tragedy with the use of masks and stage props. Like Disney's *Hercules,* Purves' short film derives its aesthetic from classical art. Statuary and vase painting are referenced throughout the film. Yet its strong homoerotic subject-matter, art-house style, and serious content about the dehumanising effects of war make it a very different film.

10

The Return of the Epic?: *Gladiator* (2000)

Introduction

In May 2000, *Gladiator* became the first successful ancient world epic film
to be released for over thirty years, to the surprise of both film critics and
students of the ancient world. The genre had been virtually written off,
with satirical re-visionings of epic films like *Carry on Cleo* and *Monty
Python's Life of Brian* all too happy to lampoon its faults. It was a genre
thought to be too pompous, too self-important, and no longer a suitable
vehicle for discussing modern concerns. In the light of this widely-held
critical judgement, some of the choices made by *Gladiator*'s creators
seemed at the time almost perverse. The film borrowed a large part of its
narrative from the last Hollywood epic film to be produced, the aptly-
named *The Fall of the Roman Empire* (1964), itself a box-office failure. It
avoided the glamorous and well-known world of early emperors like Nero
and Caligula, and instead chose to focus on the more sombre period around
the death of emperor and Stoic philosopher Marcus Aurelius in 180 AD and
the accession of his son Commodus. It advertised and presented itself without
irony as an old-fashioned epic, making no concessions to post-modern taste
or fashion with its posters showing monumental architecture, its corny
tagline ('a hero will rise') and references in its trailer to all the clichés of the
past: soldiers, slaves, gladiators, emperors – even tigers in the arena.

Gladiator was often described by critics as the spearhead for a return
of the ancient world to the big screen; for the re-animation of the 'dead
genre' of cine-antiquity. In fact, as previous chapters have shown, cine-
antiquity never did die, although it did stop appearing in the form of epic
film. Moreover while films such as *Fellini-Satyricon* and Disney's *Hercules*
continued to reimagine the ancient world for new audiences, old-fashioned
epic still remained reasonably fresh in people's memories. Responses to
Gladiator's release showed that, in the popular cultural imagination, the
ancient world on film (indeed, for many, the ancient world generally) had
become the ancient world in epic film. A number of questions arise from
this. Why, given this popularity, had there been no new ancient world epic
films released for over thirty years? How, in the absence of new releases,
did the ancient world epic film achieve the cultural dominance described
above? What were the factors that made *Gladiator* so successful? And can
the ancient world epic films that followed match its success?

The decline and subsequent absence of the ancient world epic film

10. The Return of the Epic?: Gladiator (2000)

between 1964 and 2000 has been explained by scholars and film critics as the result of a combination of factors, including changing audience tastes and demographics, the transformation of the Hollywood studio system, and the growth of television viewing. It is usually claimed that the death rattle was heard most clearly with the 1963 release of Joseph Mankiewicz's *Cleopatra*. This film was beset with problems. Its eventual release followed a two-year period of production which saw the scrapping of early shooting and sets in England, serious illness for its star Elizabeth Taylor, and much potentially disastrous publicity about her very public adulterous affair with her co-star Richard Burton (see Chapter 8 for further discussion). The film's final budget of $44 million (from an original estimate of about $2 million) placed it among the most expensive films ever produced. It was actually extremely successful with audiences, becoming the highest-grossing film of 1963 in the US. However, studios receive only a relatively small proportion of the box-office gross, and a truly immense audience would have been needed to recoup costs. The final nail in the coffin came with one more Roman epic film released the following year; directed by Anthony Mann, *The Fall of the Roman Empire* described the death of the philosopher emperor Marcus Aurelius (played by Alec Guinness) and the disastrous succession of his son Commodus (Christopher Plummer), challenged by the Roman general Livius (Stephen Boyd, previously seen as the villain Messala in *Ben-Hur*) and Marcus Aurelius' daughter Lucilla (Sophia Loren). Despite, or perhaps because of, an intelligent script and strong performances from most of the lead actors, the film was not popular with filmgoers, grossing only $4,750,000 in return for its production costs of over $18 million.

Though the critical and audience receptions for these films were quite different, both illustrate one of the major reasons Roman epics fell out of favour with filmmakers. The films had always been massively expensive to produce. Indeed (as discussed in previous chapters) the expense of their production had been regularly used by publicists as part of the extra-cinematic spectacle to promote the films. However, by the early 1960s, the studios were no longer all-powerful. In 1948, a long-standing anti-trust lawsuit brought by the US Government against the major studios (known as 'the Paramount case') forced them to surrender certain monopolies over the means of film production, distribution, and exhibition. This case has been widely seen as the beginning of the end of the studio system, although it was some years before its consequences were properly felt.

The Hollywood studio system had acquired its power by maintaining control. On the production side, writers, actors, producers and directors were kept on contract; the studios owned the sets films were made on, the equipment used to make them, and the laboratories that processed the prints. On the distribution and exhibition side, they also owned the theatres in which the films were screened. The 1948 ruling banned block and blind booking, and led over the following years to the five major

217

studios selling off their theatres, breaking the monopoly on all aspects of the filmmaking process, and drastically reducing the overall power of the studios. Over a period of time, studios also shed their production role, using independent production companies to spread the financial load with costly productions. In the case of *The Fall of the Roman Empire*, for example, the burden of financial failure was borne by producer Samuel Bronston's production company with Bronston himself filing for bankruptcy in 1965. Without the power and financial resources of the major studios, funding for expensive epic films became much more difficult to secure. However (as later expensive productions proved) it would not have been impossible had there been confidence that such films would continue to achieve box-office success. By the time of the release and box-office failure of *The Fall of the Roman Empire*, such confidence had vanished.

And yet, in the years between the disastrous release of *The Fall of the Roman Empire* and the successful release of *Gladiator*, Roman epic films continued to play a significant role in shaping the reception of the ancient world in popular culture. A major reason for this was the growth of television; paradoxically also nominated as a key reason for cinema's decline. There is no doubt that television played a significant part in changing audience habits in the early 1960s, with more people acquiring their own television sets, and seeing television viewing as their primary source of entertainment. However, television is also a medium for film exhibition, and Roman epic films proved to have certain advantages here. Their length makes them highly suitable to fill daytime television viewing slots on Sundays and public holidays (and, on commercial channels at least, advertisement breaks made viewing less of a feat of stamina). Their coy attitude to sexuality and largely off-screen violence make them inoffensive for family viewing, an important consideration with television's less regulated audience. This has been especially the case for television scheduling on public holidays, when whole families would replicate the films' original viewing contexts, sitting down together to watch. In particular, *Ben-Hur* (1959) has become a staple of Easter viewing with its depiction of Christ's Passion, appearing on at least one channel every year. This continual rescreening both reinforced the familiarity of existing viewers with the conventions of the epic – their spectacle, grandeur, and presentation of ancient Rome – and introduced them to new viewers. This interest extended beyond television viewing, with the broad and repeated exposure also cementing the films' status as cultural icons which could be used as short-cut representations in other media, including advertising. In addition, the successful theatrical re-release of *Spartacus* in 1991 (grossing more than $1,600,000) showed that there was still an audience for the ancient world epic on the big screen.

Such continuous dissemination has fixed an identity for Rome (and, by extension, the ancient world generally) in popular culture that is very largely associated with the iconic representations of epic films. Hence

Monty Python's Life of Brian can expect audiences to instantly recognise a reference to the monumental lettering of *Ben-Hur* in its credit sequence. In an example from television, the BBC's trailer for an 'Ancient Rome' week in 2006 screened a vox-pop montage of random people stopped on the street, announcing 'I'm Spartacus' to camera (the intended implication presumably being that we are all ancient Romans, rather than that we are all slaves). The maintenance of this iconography for Rome in epic films over the long period of its disappearance from new cinema releases was undoubtedly one of the factors that helped *Gladiator* to success on its release in 2000, providing a bedrock of familiarity on which it could build its revisionary Rome. Given this iconic continuity, the decision to borrow so many aspects of *The Fall of the Roman Empire* for its own narrative might be understood as a deliberate attempt to frame Ridley Scott's film as the natural heir to the long-slumbering giant of a genre that was the Roman epic film.

The next section will focus in more detail on how *Gladiator* succeeded in this genre revival. But was there ever a true revival, or was the film a unique success in its own right? It is true that *Gladiator*'s release in 2000 has been followed by a number of other epic-scaled films set in the ancient world: *Troy* (2004), *Alexander* (2004) and *300* (2007) were in the first wave, achieving mixed degrees of success. More recently there has been a mini-flurry of antiquity-themed films, including *Agora* (2009), *Clash of the Titans* (2010), *Percy Jackson and the Lightning Thief* (2010), *Centurion* (2010), *Immortals* (2011) and *The Eagle* (2011). A sequel to *Clash of the Titans,* titled *Wrath of the Titans* is in production at the time of writing, slated for release in 2012. *Percy Jackson and the Sea of Monsters* is also in the early stages of production. More films have been proposed but remain unmade, including three more Alexander films, a prequel to *Gladiator,* and a remake of *Jason and the Argonauts*. However, there is some evidence for anxiety about the audience's appetite for ancient world epics: Vin Diesel's *Hannibal the Conqueror* was first announced in 2002, and is currently scheduled for release in 2012; prospective viewers may not wish to hold their breath.

Are there any common themes in this apparent revival? Many of the new films have taken their inspiration from children's literature. The Percy Jackson films adapt the first two of a successful series of juvenile novels by Rick Riordan which see an ordinary boy discover his true identity as the son of the god Poseidon, and follow his friendships and adventures at a training camp for demi-gods, Camp Half-Blood. The similarities with the Harry Potter series are irresistible, and although the original manuscript for the first Percy Jackson book was completed before the first Harry Potter book, it was not finally published until 2005, some time after the success of the latter in both book and film form. The first Percy Jackson film was directed by Chris Columbus who also directed the first two Harry Potter films. It is reasonable to assume then that economic confidence in the Percy Jackson films has been built on the success of other films adapted from children's literature, and not on the success of *Gladiator* as an ancient world epic. Similarly, *Centurion* and *The Eagle* both took their inspiration from the classic children's historical novel, *The Eagle of the Ninth* by Rosemary Sutcliffe, first published in 1954.

There are a greater number of films inspired by Greece than Rome, a significant change from the earlier preference for Roman epic films. In the case of *Troy*, *Alexander* and *300*, all have been read as repeating the classical Hollywood epics' use of the ancient world to discuss modern political concerns, in particular conflicts between the western world and Islam. Unlike the post-Second World War and Cold War Roman epics though, these films do not always offer clear-cut heroes and villains, illustrating the complexity of the issues rather than offering us easy answers. But is this what audiences want from an epic film? The films' mixed box-office reception bears witness to their difficult nature, with audiences complaining, for instance, that they were not provided with a clear moral schema in *Troy*. In contrast, the most successful of the three, *300*, is (like *Gladiator*) unequivocal in its identification of heroes and villains.

In the films that have been read as epics, history still tends to prevail over myth. Oliver Stone's *Alexander* is the only survivor of a clutch of proposed films about Alexander the Great; *300* adapts the narrative of the Spartan defence of Thermopylae in 480 BC (see Chapter 5 for more on this event in history and in film). Even in the Greek-inspired films that do take mythology as their starting point, fantastic elements are defused. *Troy* takes a resolutely historicising approach to the Trojan War cycle, offering rational explanations for the actions of gods and heroes in Homeric epic. At one point, even the film's title was changed to the more historical-sounding *The Trojan War*, though negative audience response led to the reinstatement of its earlier title.

One film that does seek to combine epic filmmaking and mythical elements is *Clash of the Titans*. Described as a remake of the 1981 adventure film of the same title (with iconic special effects by Ray Harryhausen), the 2010 film takes the same set of characters and some of the same events, but creates a much more gung-ho narrative based around man's superiority to the gods. The emphasis is on action rather than fantasy, and although the filmmakers enlisted Ray Harryhausen's involvement, it is hard to see how this film could have met his earlier pleas for more fantasy in cinema (see Chapter 6 for a discussion of this). What *Clash* does appeal to is the videogames aesthetic, with its dense backgrounds, simple character motivations and accented metallic sound design. Dunstan Lowe has noted that the film shares common features with the *God of War* videogame franchise: 'both have a butch, vengeful anti-hero whose family's deaths were indirectly caused by a god; both feature climactic, scenery-smashing wrestling matches with Gorgons; and both portray a dysfunctional world in which mortals are innocent but weak, and gods are cruel but vulnerable'. Indeed, the videogame version of *Clash* was due for release a month before the film, although it was delayed due to technical problems. Lowe (2009: 72-4) has argued elsewhere that the concurrent growth in popularity of antiquity-themed films and antiquity-themed videogames has been a symbiotic process. Certainly there are popular videogames either directly based on, or inspired by the same narratives as all of the new films mentioned in this chapter. With an increasingly large proportion of an epic film's visual look governed by Computer Generated Imagery (CGI), and videogames being accessed on ever bigger screens by multiple concurrent users (as in Massively Multiplayer Online Role Playing Games), films and videogames seem to be growing ever closer in their modes of consumption.

In fact, the effect that the success of *Gladiator* has had has not simply been on the epic film genre. Rather it has raised general interest in the ancient world, and thus encouraged its representation in mass popular culture across a range of contexts: in advertising campaigns like the Pepsi gladiator advertisements that screened throughout the US and the UK in 2006 and 2007; in a reported increase in interest in university study; in the increasingly culturally important field of videogames; in the production of new television programmes including historical docudramas and prestigious series like HBO/BBC's *Rome*. The revival of the epic film genre may still be tentative, but popular culture's increasing interest in the reception of antiquity is more certain.

Background to case study

In fact, re-invention rather than revival was closer to the agenda of the film's director. Talking to Richard Corliss in an interview for *Time* magazine at the time of *Gladiator*'s release, Ridley Scott discussed his recollection of Roman epic films: 'I loved the costume drama of it all and remembered that world vividly ... But I also knew you can't bring that to bear today. You've got to re-invent it.' A closer look at *Gladiator* shows that it is very much the product of a postmodern sensibility: knowing, with regard to its cultural antecedents, and in open collusion with its audience over the techniques it uses to re-present the ancient world.

The decision to make gladiators the central theme of this attempted re-invention was an astute one. Gladiators and the arena have been persistent and popular features of cine-antiquity from early days; for instance, DeMille's *The Sign of the Cross* (1932) has an extended and influential arena sequence. Gladiators have been the focus of films set in Rome like *Demetrius and the Gladiators* (1954) and *Spartacus* (discussed in Chapter 4); have stood as a powerful symbol for the decadence of Rome in films like *Barabbas* (1962) and *The Fall of the Roman Empire*; and provided a vehicle for satire in *Monty Python's Life of Brian* (discussed in Chapter 8). Their cinematic appearances are not restricted to films set in

Rome. Gladiatorial-style combats feature in most films set in antiquity. In *Jason and the Argonauts*, for instance, Jason and his opponent Acastus battle it out on the deck of the Argo with trident, net, and short sword. In *Alexander the Great* (1955), the sequence marking the turning point for Alexander's ambitions begins with a gladiatorial-style combat between a (Macedonian) Greek and a Persian. Such one-on-one combats offer a perfect opportunity for the physical expression on-screen of more abstract narrative oppositions including good and evil, new and old, East and West, paganism and Christianity.

However, the modern notion of the cinematic gladiator as hero is at odds with the generally unsympathetic Roman attitudes towards his ancient counterpart (see discussion in Chapter 4). Although gladiators could achieve something akin to celebrity status, they were more usually regarded as degraded by the use of their bodies for public entertainment. In the ancient sources, the enthusiasm of emperors and other figures for taking part in such public entertainments as the games is used as a sign that they have crossed the line of acceptable behaviour. For example, there is little that is glamorous in Dio Cassius' description of the emperor Commodus shooting ostriches in the arena with a bow and arrow. Whatever the Romans thought of gladiators, they were never the moral exemplars found in Hollywood films.

Predictably (and understandably), the makers of *Gladiator* took a similar stance towards historical authenticity to that taken by all other epic filmmakers before them. They used the bits of antiquity that made the film attractive to its target audience and excised the rest. Maximus is fictional, but Marcus Aurelius, Commodus, and Lucilla are all genuine historical figures, although their stories are highly revised. Marcus Aurelius did not name another heir, though later historians argued that he might have done better to do so. Lucilla was married to Lucius Verus and did plot against Commodus, and lost her life as a result. Commodus was finally (after attempts at poisoning) killed by a young athlete, Narcissus, though Narcissus was more likely a wrestler than a gladiator. The most startling historical inaccuracy was the film's climactic ending: the implication that Commodus' death was followed by a restoration of the republic. In fact, Commodus was followed by a quick succession of five emperors in one year, starting with Pertinax, and the empire itself continued for almost 300 years. Professor Kathleen Coleman of Harvard University was employed as historical consultant to the film, but most of her comments were politely ignored. Coleman countered by asking for her name to be removed from the credits (her credit as consultant was removed but she is still thanked by name). She has subsequently published a response to her experience that queries the balance in the relationship between historian and historical filmmaker (Coleman 2004).

Maximus is drawn as a postmodern hero for an audience much more likely to be familiar with modern popular culture than ancient history.

Nineteenth-century history paintings, previous films from a variety of genres and popular literature are valued as equal sources to ancient authors for the film's representations. The original scriptwriter David Franzoni cited Daniel P. Mannix's book *Those About to Die* (1958) as his inspiration. This popular history book included fictionalised narrative sections showing life from the gladiator's own viewpoint, something not found in ancient sources. Little of Franzoni's first draft remained by the time the film was released though, with major successive rewrites by two more writers (John Logan and William Nicholson) and continuous revisions during shooting. One notable alteration may also have been inspired by popular literature, albeit from an earlier tradition. Initially, the hero was named Narcissus after Commodus' historical assassin, but this was changed to Maximus, also the name of a gladiator in Henryk Sienkiewicz's novel *Quo Vadis*. Other significant aspects of narrative may be traced to the particular interests of key stakeholders. For instance, Franzoni's reputation in the film industry had been made by his role as writer of Stephen Spielberg's epic *Amistad* (1997) which described a mutiny by (African) slaves, while Solomon (2004: 13) points out that the death of the film's hero in *Gladiator* is a device previously used to great effect by director Ridley Scott in *Thelma and Louise* (1991).

The influence of Scott's previous experience is further evidenced throughout the film. His film career began in set design, and he is notoriously obsessive about props. An interesting example of this in *Gladiator* is in the decoration on the succession of breastplates worn by Maximus through the film. In the battle in Germania, when Maximus is still a loyal soldier of the empire, his breastplate features the Wolf of Rome. After he becomes a slave and gladiator, his allegiances continue to be drawn on his breastplate. In the first combat, his two horses to symbolise home; in the second, his (now dead) wife and son are added; in the third and final combat, the figure of winged Victory appears. Throughout the combats, the central image on the breastplate is a cypress tree, signifying the death he longs for. The changes are deliberate, but so small that in the earlier epic tradition when video and DVD did not exist to allow repeated close viewings, they would be most unlikely to have been noticed by cinema viewers. With the more intense and informed viewing habits of a contemporary audience however, discussion of the breastplates began on online forums within days of the film's release. Scott has also had considerable experience directing commercials through the production company he set up in 1968 with his brother Tony. The rapid cross-cutting seen in the battle and arena scenes is often cited as originating in this experience of working in advertising where high impact was required from brief sequences. In *Gladiator*, it enables a great deal of explicit violence to be included without appearing overly exploitative. We can also see the influence of his previous cinematic work, most notably *Alien* (1979) and *Blade Runner* (1982), science-fiction films, driven by special effects. Although on the surface these may seem to have little in common with epic films set in antiquity, both necessitate the invention of a world simultaneously similar to, and quite different from, our own. The opportunity to 're-invent' a world was not such a new thing for *Gladiator*'s director.

Two particular iconographic sources were cited in interviews and pre-publicity for the film. In various interviews, Scott described how he was persuaded to take on the direction of the film after being shown a copy of Jean-Léon Gérôme's painting *Pollice Verso* (1872). Like other Academy painters of the nineteenth century, Gérôme often produced paintings inspired by ancient Greece and Rome, including a number set in the arena. This painting shows a triumphant gladiator, poised with his foot on the neck of his defeated opponent and awaiting the verdict of the watching emperor, seen in his box behind and to the left of the gladiator. The gladiator himself is looking at another section of the audience though, and his gaze draws ours to the same place: on the right of the picture, six Vestal Virgins stand at a ringside parapet, draped in white, protected from the cold stone by rich oriental tapestries, and unanimously gesturing for the victor to complete the kill. Their enthusiasm is repeated in the tiers of spectators shown behind them, but it is in this shocking lust for violence on the part of female spectators that the power of Gérôme's painting lies. The imagery of Academy painters has been the inspiration for many examples of cine-antiquity, and Gérôme's arena pictures, most notably both *Pollice Verso* and *The Christian Martyrs' Last Prayer* (1863-83), were among the key visual sources for art direction in other cinematic arenas as well as *Gladiator*. [Fig. 20] However, the visual iconography is less important here than the frenzied reactions of the crowd. A key narrative theme in *Gladiator* is the power of the mob, and Gérôme's painting viscerally conveys the terrifying potential of that force.

Another highly significant source was the propaganda films of Leni Riefenstahl, made in the 1930s to establish a heroic iconography for Adolf Hitler, his Nazi followers, and their vision of Aryan supremacy. One in particular is referenced, *Triumph of the Will* (1935). The film recorded the 1934 rally of the Nazi party at Nuremberg. There are extensive visual quotations to Riefenstahl's menacing and machine-like imagery in *Gladiator* in the sequence showing Commodus' triumphant entry into Rome following his accession. These include the opening swoop down through the clouds to reveal the city; in Riefenstahl's film, this shot reveals the massed followers of the Nazi party below. The final shots of the sequence have Commodus greeted on the steps of the Temple of Jupiter by a young girl bearing flowers (repeating a moment in Riefenstahl's film when a young girl gives flowers to Hitler). Two senators dominate the foreground of the shot, with their backs to the camera, while behind the young emperor are two powerful images of man's control over the world: the monumental architecture of Rome, with the Coliseum in the centre background, and the perfectly regular massed ranks of the Roman armies. This

10. *The Return of the Epic?: Gladiator* (2000)

20. The influence of Jean-Léon Gérôme, recreating the
Roman arena, *Gladiator* (2000).

shot mirrors the composition of one showing Hitler's arrival; in the central position occupied by the Coliseum are three pennant swastika flags. In these identifying strategies, power (in the storyworld of the film) is equated with control of the masses, and the symbol of that power is the place where the masses are entertained, the arena.

Such detailed quotation from a film made more than sixty years previously, which could hardly be described as mainstream audience viewing, indicates Scott's ambition for *Gladiator* as a film that could be appreciated on multiple critical levels. It further suggests the filmmakers' confidence in the film's entitlement to its own legacy, especially in the opportunities for multiple and detailed viewings afforded by home viewing on video and DVD. In fact, pre-publicity for the film actively recruited the prospective cinema audience as fans rather than just viewers, knowing conspirators in the film's re-presentation of a Rome that never did, and never could exist. Articles placed in film preview magazines described Scott's explicit instructions to Mill Films who produced the special effects for the film to use Riefenstahl's film as reference in the CGI used to create the spectacle of Rome, and these articles showed how CGI had been used to simulate a crowd of thousands in the Coliseum from just a few extras. Where in the old epics there would have been an opportunity for the studios to trumpet their power and wealth with literal casts of thousands and monumental sets, *Gladiator* celebrated the new technological capabilities that made spectacular displays possible without the kind of expense that the old films

225

necessitated. The effects here were not hidden in an attempt to suspend the audience's disbelief – separating consumer from producer. Rather filmmakers acknowledged the new sophistication of the audience by openly inviting scrutiny of technical practices and collusion in their effects, and thus devolved some of the power previously wielded by filmmakers and the studios to cinema's viewers. This intelligent recognition of changes in the audience demographic and viewing practices was one of the aspects that made it possible to present a film that, without irony, positioned itself as an example of an almost fatally unfashionable genre.

While *Gladiator* certainly earns its place in postmodern culture with its open borrowing of a range of other cultural texts, the biggest influence on the film's iconography remains previous epic films. *The Fall of the Roman Empire* is a major source of characters (Marcus Aurelius, Commodus, and Lucilla), setting (Germania and Rome) and narrative features (a fictional soldier who is about to be named imperial heir and who has had a relationship with the emperor's daughter Lucilla). One particular scene (showing Commodus undertaking gladiatorial training in the German forest) is replicated almost exactly. However, *Gladiator* focuses on more visceral elements of the story than the weighty political discussions of *The Fall of the Roman Empire*. This is a story about the arena, and the revenge of a wronged man. Interestingly, this puts the filmmakers in the same position with regard to the viewing public as the intra-diegetic Commodus: prioritising easy gratification and entertainment over more serious matters. As viewers, we are asked to simultaneously condemn Commodus for this and conversely to praise the filmmakers. But in this paradox is the point of *Gladiator*'s successful re-invention of the historical epic film. It is the job of politicians and emperors to govern and that is a serious undertaking – but the job of filmmakers is to entertain and the two should not be confused. Scott's recognition of this primary purpose of popular cinema both places *Gladiator* in the tradition of the epic films that immediately preceded it, and distinguishes it from the less successful films that followed it (in particular the all-too-portentous *Alexander*).

In addition to the specific parallels with *The Fall of the Roman Empire*, the film takes the narrative conventions of other examples of cinema's re-presentation of gladiators and the arena and rethinks them for a new critically and culturally aware audience. Particular features that recur in earlier films include the hero's African 'buddy' [Fig. 21]; the salacious spectator; a scene welcoming the new gladiator to the training school; and a strong belief system for those participating in the arena. Each of these features is revised to play a significant role in defining a new moral schema for the film, utilising audience familiarity with the existing vocabulary of the genre to interrogate new anxieties about identity, heroism, masculinity, and spectatorship.

In particular, no epic film is complete without a hero. On the surface,

21. Maximus and Juba fight the beast. Scene from the provincial arena,
Gladiator (2000).

Maximus embodies all of the features of the typical hero of a classical
Hollywood Roman epic. This hero is (in this case, very soon becomes)
single, leaving him free to develop a relationship with the heroine over the
course of the film. Indeed, rescuing the heroine from peril is a key feature
of most epic film narratives and *Gladiator* does not disappoint. The epic
hero is brave and self-sacrificing, a man looked to by other men for
leadership, and a skilful fighter. He is (if not at first, then certainly
eventually) shown to be naturally possessed of an upright and simple
code of morality. His temptation away from, and re-assumption of, this
code shapes the narrative. Visually he has a well-built but not overly-
muscular torso, distinguishing the epic heroes from those of the pepla,
where the heroes are defined by their extreme muscle development.
Aurally, he is distinguished from other, often weaker and more decadent Romans by his accent which is usually American to their British.
This last might alert us to the possibility of other revisions. In *Gladiator*, the hero retains a trace of the Antipodean in his speech, while
other major cast members have a variety of accents (Scandinavian,
English, Celtic) – but the villain is certainly American. This subtle
subversion of the usual aural scheme for epic films models the treatment

227

of other epic conventions used in the film, as will be shown in the closer textual analyses that follow.

The centrality of heroism in *Gladiator* is flagged up in one of the film's taglines: 'A hero will rise.' Yet as we will see, the precise nature of this heroism is complicated. Its definition will involve discussion of different versions of masculinity; the cult of celebrity and the dangers of worship by the crowd; questions about the legitimate use of violence; and the role of the family in establishing codes of morality.

Plot summary

On the far borders of the Roman empire in Germania, imperial troops fight a successful battle against the local tribes under the leadership of Maximus Decimus Meridianus (Russell Crowe). Following the battle, Maximus plans to return to his farm in Spain where his wife and son await. However, the aging emperor Marcus Aurelius (Richard Harris) tells Maximus that he will name him as successor instead of his own son Commodus (Joaquin Phoenix), in the hope that he will restore Rome to a republic. Meanwhile Commodus has arrived in Germania with his sister Lucilla (Connie Nielsen), an old flame of Maximus', expecting to be named as heir. When he is told that he will not succeed, he murders his father. Maximus refuses to declare his loyalty to Commodus as emperor and is taken away from the camp for execution by the new emperor's henchmen. He escapes, and despite being wounded sets out on a marathon dash back to Spain to protect his family, but on arrival discovers that both are already dead. Having buried them, he collapses from his wounds.

Maximus is found and taken by slave traders to Zucchabar, where he is bought by a gladiator trainer, Proximo (Oliver Reed), along with a young African, Juba (Djimon Hounsou). At first he refuses to fight, or even to speak. However, chained to Juba in his first combat, he rediscovers his instinct for self-preservation. Alongside the German, Hagen (Ralf Möller), they defeat their opponents, to the acclaim of the crowd. Maximus' skill in the arena makes him a local celebrity, nicknamed 'the Spaniard'. He continues to win, now fighting on his own against multiple opponents, but treats the crowd and their desire for blood with contempt. Proximo then tells him they are to fight in the Coliseum in Rome as part of Commodus' accession games, and Maximus sees his chance for revenge.

In Rome, the gladiators are sent into the arena as Carthaginians to fight a restaged 'Battle of Carthage'. Organised by Maximus to operate with military discipline, they succeed against the odds. Commodus asks to meet the gladiators, and Maximus prepares to attack him, but has to halt when Lucilla's young son, Lucius, joins his uncle. Maximus reveals his true identity and tells Commodus that he will have his revenge. That night Lucilla visits him and tries to recruit him to a plot to overthrow Commodus and restore the republic, but he refuses. His next combat is with a hitherto

228

undefeated gladiator, Tigris of Gaul. Commodus has arranged for tigers to be set against Maximus during the combat, but Maximus still triumphs, refusing to despatch his opponent and gaining the new nickname of 'Maximus the Merciful'.

Maximus encounters his former manservant Cicero, who tells him that the troops remain loyal to him. The former general agrees to conspire with Lucilla and the senator Gracchus, but the plot is discovered. Despite a brave fight by the gladiators, Hagen is killed and Maximus captured. Commodus tells Lucilla that she will bear his children or else he will kill Lucius. He arranges to take part himself in a final combat with Maximus, wounding him before they enter the arena to ensure his defeat. However, Maximus rouses himself for one final effort and kills the emperor. Having received the agreement of Gracchus that the republic will be restored, he dies in the expectation of a reunion with his family in the afterlife.

Key scenes and themes

Violence as entertainment

Any epic film featuring gladiators has a paradox at its heart. It needs to attract a large audience to recoup costs, so must take a conservative approach to moral issues; this includes condemning violence, and particularly the violence as public entertainment that takes place in the arena. However, the same violence forms part of the spectacle that attracts viewers to epic films. One of the ways that cinema sidesteps this dilemma is to use the violence inevitably present in arena combats to discuss broader issues. In *Gladiator* the arena combats link to other intra-cinematic events to present ideas about acceptable contexts for violence, military training, and the nature of celebrity.

'Are you not entertained?'

In his second combat in Zucchabar, Maximus is preparing to enter the provincial arena as a single combatant. Huge crowds chant, 'Spaniard, Spaniard', and young boys clamber onto the roof of the gladiators' cage to drop rose petals. As Maximus passes along the line of gladiators, they salute and acknowledge him as 'Spaniard'. Entering the arena to more falling petals, he is met by a number of gladiators to whom he bows before commencing the combat. All of the gladiators are despatched swiftly and brutally; the last one is decapitated with two swords. The combat takes less than a minute from bow to decapitation. Maximus hurls one of the swords into the balcony where the *editore* or promoter of the games would have sat, and demands of the crowd, 'Are you not entertained? Is this not why you are here?' He throws down his remaining sword and contemptuously spits on the ground of the arena. The crowd are at first silenced by his outburst, then begin chanting again: 'Spaniard, Spaniard, Spaniard.'

Like other gladiator films, *Gladiator* draws links between violence for entertainment purposes and violence for what are classed as more legiti-mate purposes such as the violence of war. In other films, gladiatorial training proves invaluable for the gladiators when they find themselves fighting as soldiers. In *Spartacus* (1960), for example, training methods used in the gladiatorial school are later borrowed to train the slave army in their conflict with the Roman army. In *Demetrius and the Gladiators* (1954) the disciplined fighting ability learnt as gladiators admits the freed slave Demetrius and the African Glycon into legitimate Roman society as Christian warriors, fighting the good fight with the support of the newly ascended emperor Claudius and his reformed empress, Messalina. In *Gladiator* this convention is subverted. It is Maximus' military training which saves him and the other gladiators in the arena. This interplay between military and arena violence is signalled at the opening of the arena sequence, when Maximus is saluted by the gladiators as 'Spaniard' as he passes them on his entry to the arena, a distorted mirror of the troops' acknowledgement of his identity as 'General' in the prelude to the battle against Germania. Other imagery from this opening battle sequence re-appears in the later arena sequences to emphasise the association of military and gladiatorial combat. For example, the 'minotaur' swinging a mace that greets the gladiators on their first entrance into the provincial arena corre-sponds to the giant German in the battle scene, also clad in animal skins and swinging a staff at the Roman soldiers. Later Maximus uses his military experience to unite and direct the gladiators, thus beating impossible odds in the 'Battle of Carthage' staged in the Coliseum. Commodus is also shown to be a skilful fighter, undertaking gladiatorial training in the forests of Germa-nia. However, having 'missed' the actual battle, his combat skills lack moral purpose, only being utilised in the final arena combat where the emperor is schematised as the 'evil' that threatens Maximus' 'good'.

Another kind of institutionalised violence is also referenced here, this time more modern: the bullfight. Maximus, already identified as 'the Spaniard', brings a matadorial flair to his fighting moves, bowing as he enters the arena, and twisting his body as if swerving a bull before stabbing behind his back. At one point he sticks two swords into a gladiator in an action reminiscent of the use of *banderillas* in bullfighting, small sharpened sticks stabbed into the bull's shoulders to weaken him before he is killed. This reference combines with the chaotic and emotive atmosphere of the provincial arena (quite different from the controlled Roman audiences more usually shown in cinema), to strip back ideas about the gladiator as hero and shock us into a recognition of the bloodlust (perhaps our own) at the heart of viewing violence.

Such forthright acknowledgement of violence as entertainment denies Maximus the gladiator the conventional cinematic status of hero, though he will regain it later when he rediscovers his moral purpose. His liminal state in this scene is signalled by the falling petals that greet his entry into

230

the arena, a classic symbol for lost innocence. Maximus' ability to deliver the brutality that the crowd demands makes him no longer a hero, but a celebrity. He is himself conscious of this status and accepts it, though not without bitterness, telling Lucilla that he has 'the power only to amuse the mob'. Lucilla's reply is that 'that *is* power'. The postmodern pragmatism of *Gladiator* suggests we should use power when it is offered, whatever the source. Power is no longer something that arises only from purity of motive, as suggested in *Spartacus*. Morality is found, not in how we acquire power, but in what we do with it.

Watching the spectators

Another familiar cinematic strategy for dealing with the problem of screening violence is to turn the camera from the action on the floor of the arena to the action in the stands. By taking the spectators in the arena to stand for society as a whole, violence and the desire to view it is shown as a symptom of more general societal decadence and perversion. However, such condemnation cannot be limited to the on-screen viewers; the cinema viewer must also question their own viewing habits, and what they might suggest about our own society and mores.

Re-enacting the Battle of Carthage

It is the first combat for Proximo's provincial gladiators before the Roman crowds in the Coliseum. As they enter the arena, a 360° pan gives the cinema viewer the same awe-inspiring viewpoint as the gladiators are experiencing for the first time. Like them, we marvel at the size of the Coliseum compared to the provincial arena and the vast numbers of spectators. A fanfare sounds as the emperor Commodus and his party take their seats. The crowds cheer and chant, 'Caesar! Caesar!' while Commodus acknowledges them. The gates open and the gladiators (representing the Carthaginians) are confronted by archers and spear-throwers (representing Rome), driven in chariots with bladed wheels. The point of view shifts to the stands. From among the spectators there is rising excitement and a chant of 'Kill! Kill! Kill!' As the 'Battle of Carthage' commences, the gladiators begin to work together under Maximus' command, successfully defending themselves against the odds. The camera turns towards the crowd in which both males and females shout their approval, applauding and shaking their fists. Now the gladiators begin to fight back, overturning a chariot. A woman covers her mouth in horror, while others cheer. In the imperial box, Commodus raises an eyebrow. As the chariots are one after another overturned (and one female archer sliced in half), the camera turns to show the crowd rushing forward, Commodus and Lucius included, to get a better view of the carnage. The crowd are cheering the 'Carthaginians' now, and the emperor is himself engrossed in the combat, leaning forward in his seat. As the last opponent falls, the gladiators receive the adulation of the crowd.

The explicit violence of the 'Battle of Carthage' sequence [see box: 'Re-enacting the Battle of Carthage'] is defused by fast cross-cutting between action on the floor of the arena and action in the stands, particularly in the imperial box. As film viewers, our point of view constantly changes; one moment we are amongst the gladiators, the next we are looking at the stands. At one point (and not for the first time) Scott borrows a trick from the arena sequence in *Spartacus*, giving the cinema audience a view of the action that mimics that of the arena audience of the story-world. The contrast between the dark of the stands, and the view into the light of the arena, brings to mind the voyeurism of film-viewing; as spectators, we are usually unseen onlookers. Such strategies persuasively posit an identification between spectators in the cinema and those in the arena.

For historical arena spectators in ancient Rome, such occasions would have been as much about seeing the emperor as seeing the gladiators. For the film viewer too, Commodus' appearance and actions are significant; the scene is a crucial one for the cinema audience's reading of Commodus, and particularly for his version of masculinity. It is, above all, Commodus' enthusiasm for violent combat that marks him as separate from Maximus, who avows his wish to return to a quiet home life and refuses to fight back when he first arrives at the gladiator school. In contrast, Commodus is shown treating violent combat as a leisure pastime, practising gladiatorial moves in the forests of Germania, though he has had no part in the real battle. Commodus is an especially keen spectator at the arena, shown to be highly involved and engaged with the action. At one point he makes a comedy gesture, saying 'Oooooh!' and waggling his head and hands; at another especially gruesome killing, he sticks his tongue out in a gesture of empathetic sensuality. There are no pretensions here to imperial dignity.

Commodus' undisciplined enthusiasm when viewing violent combat takes on new meaning when viewed through the filter of previous Roman epic films, where such spectator behaviour is typically focused on as a means of defining 'good' and 'bad' women. In *The Sign of the Cross*, DeMille used close-up shots of two contrasting types of female spectators in the arena, one salaciously bloodthirsty and the other piously weeping. In *Demetrius and the Gladiators*, the empress Messalina (Susan Hayward) is driven almost to an orgasmic ecstasy watching the combats, breathing increasingly heavily and running to the parapet to make sure she does not miss the denouement (actions restaged in *Gladiator* by Commodus). In *Spartacus*, the two Roman women who have demanded a 'to the death' private arena combat are transfixed by the violence, while the male spectators are uninterested, leaning back and discussing politics. The women's bloodlust and the men's disinterest are compared with the focused concern and anxiety of the watching slave Varinia – this is framed as proper behaviour for a woman, and evidenced in *Gladiator* by the actions of Lucilla. In these earlier gladiator films, enthusiasm for watching violence marks out a female as decadent and perverted. In *Gladiator*, Scott takes the existing conventions of the genre, and uses them to serve a linked, but different purpose. The emperor is simultaneously emasculated and defeminised. He cannot measure up to Maximus' defining performance of a man but, in addition, does not even pass muster as a good woman.

Family – the new religion?

In one important respect, *Gladiator* has been generally acknowledged to be quite different from the majority of Roman epic films that preceded it. It is an epic with a complete absence of Christianity. As we have seen in previous chapters, imperial Rome as a location for early Christianity has been a major motivating factor in the popularity of the ancient world for filmmakers. Even *Spartacus* – adapted from a novel written by a Communist, with a screenplay written by a Communist sympathiser and produced and starring a supporter of Zionism – ended with a crucifixion scene widely viewed as a coded Christian narrative. However, *Gladiator*'s narrative eschews religion as a force for morality, finding a substitute in our contemporary worship of the notion of family.

Family prayers

In his tent on the battlefields of Germania, Maximus is praying, following the news that Marcus Aurelius intends to name him as imperial heir. There are a number of figurines in his candlelit shrine. However it is not the gods, but his parents that he prays to. 'Ancestors, I ask for your guidance. Blessed mother, come to me with the Gods' desire for my future.' At the front of the shrine are two smaller and more rustic clay figures: his wife and son, explicitly identified here by an overlay on the screen of their 'live' images. 'Blessed father, watch over my wife and son with a ready sword. Whisper to them that I live only to hold them again.' Maximus ends his prayers, saying, 'Ancestors, I honour you. I will try to live with the dignity you have taught me.' He takes the figurine of his wife and kisses it tenderly before replacing it. It is clear that his prayers for guidance have been answered, and not entirely to his satisfaction, when he asks his manservant Cicero, 'Do you ever find it hard to do your duty?' Cicero replies, 'Sometimes I do what I want to do, and sometimes I do what I have to do', before extinguishing the candles and closing the doors of the portable shrine.

In *Gladiator*, being a hero is defined by being a good husband and father. The film uses nominal identities to build this notion. Maximus is identified by others as 'General', 'Spaniard', 'Maximus the Merciful'. His identity is even fixed by the title of the film, 'Gladiator'. But when he is called on to identify himself, he does so in terms of his family: 'husband to a murdered wife, father to a murdered son'. From beginning to end of the film, Maximus longs to be reunited with his wife and son, first in life, and then in death. This unvarying attachment ultimately makes the resumption of his previous relationship with Lucilla (Marcus Aurelius' daughter) impossible. The film's inevitable rescue mission is not for the heroine but for her son, confirmed in Maximus' dying declaration that 'Lucius is safe now'.

Maximus' prayers to and for his mother, father, wife and son draw family as the focus for duty, loyalty, respect, and protection. The clay figurines of Maximus' wife and son play an important structural role in the film's narrative. In addition to marking the end of the film when they are buried in the sand of the arena by Juba, the surviving gladiator, they are restored to Maximus by his manservant Cicero following his second combat in Rome against Tigris the Gaul. Cicero is first seen as a spectator in the arena, seeking out Maximus as he is returned under guard to the gladiators' quarters and pressing the bag containing the figurines into his hands. This marks the turning point in Maximus' journey of moral recovery: from his despair at his family's murder and resignation to death in the arena; through the return of his instinct to fight, despite his disgust at the bloodlust of the crowd; until finally he regains purpose in his desire for revenge on Commodus. The figurines of family recall him to the notions of duty.

Counterpoints to Maximus' good husband and father are found in both Marcus Aurelius and his son Commodus. The former bemoans his 'failure as a father', the immediate narrative reward for this regret being his death at the hands of the son he has failed. Commodus sees the ties of family as a tool for power, attempting to recruit Maximus by calling him 'brother' and asking him to mourn 'our great father'. Having failed in this endeavour, he then extends the family metaphor to his relationship as emperor with the Roman people, telling the Senate that 'the people are my children, I am their father', before putting the weaknesses of a child-centred, instant gratification and discipline-averse society on display by giving his 'children' entertainment when they need governance. Worse still, Commodus plans to become a perverted husband, taking his own sister to his bed and even appearing to predate on his young nephew Lucius. Incest and paedophilia are modern society's particular fears; the film plays on these to promote our strong moral distaste for the villain.

The African gladiator Juba reinforces Maximus' strong drive to be reunited with his family with stories about his own family and his own desire to return to them. After Maximus regains the figurines, Juba asks him, 'Can they hear you? Your family ... in the afterlife?' And herein lies the hero's reward: reunion in death. Finally, even this resolutely religion-free film cannot completely escape a Christian reading, as Maximus the merciful sacrifices himself for the greater good, going joyously as a martyr to an afterlife where his true family awaits him.

Suggested further viewing

Troy (dir. Petersen, 2004)
Menelaus' wife Helen (Diane Kruger) falls in love and elopes with Paris (Orlando Bloom), prince of Troy, while he and his brother Hector are on a peace mission. This conveniently provides the excuse her brother-in-law Agamemnon (Brian Cox), king of Mycenae, needs to invade Troy. As the expedition commences, Achilles (Brad Pitt) and his Myrmidons sack the temple of Apollo and seize its priestess Briseis (Rose Byrne). Agamemnon claims Briseis for himself, and Achilles withdraws from further combat. Paris meets Menelaus (Brendan Gleeson) in single combat but has to be rescued by Hector (Eric Bana) who kills Menelaus. In the ensuing battle, the Trojans prevail. Agamemnon returns Briseis to Achilles, but he still refuses to fight. In the next attack, Patroclus (Garrett Hedlund), Achilles' young cousin, leads the Greek defence wearing Achilles' armour, but is killed by Hector. Outraged at the death of Patroclus, Achilles kills Hector in single combat, dragging his corpse away. Priam (Peter O'Toole) goes to plead for Hector's body, returning with the corpse, Briseis and a truce. The Greeks disappear, leaving a wooden horse as an offering. After dark, Greeks hidden in the horse open the city gates and Troy is sacked. Hector's widow Andromache (Saffron Burrows) and his baby son, with Helen and Paris, escape the city via a secret passage. Achilles dies trying to save Briseis from Agamemnon whom she kills.

Troy took a rationalising approach to mythology and the gods, offering explanations for the supernatural. It positioned itself as an old-fashioned epic, but missed its mark in several places: its leading man was too beefy, its leading woman too insubstantial, its heroes and villains not always clearly fixed in a simple moral schema. In its promotional strategies it failed to understand *Gladiator*'s success in recruiting the audience, staying silent about its use of CGI and having to reinstate the original title after an unpopular change to *The Trojan War*. However, *Gladiator* resonated throughout the film in visual and verbal instances, including blazing balls of straw in the opening battle, Achilles' repeated cry to the Thessalians, 'Is there no one else? Is there no one else?' and, in particular, the opening narration when Odysseus asks, 'Will our actions echo across the centuries?'

Alexander (dir. Stone, 2004)
The film opens on the narrator, Ptolemy (Anthony Hopkins), declaring his intention to write a biography of Alexander of Macedon (Colin Farrell). Alexander's own story then begins with his boyhood, showing his education by his tutor Aristotle and the early friendships that developed with those who later became his Companions. As he grows into a young man, his relationships with his father, King Philip of Macedon (Val Kilmer) and his mother Olympias (Angelina Jolie) become increasingly complex. When

Philip is murdered by one of Alexander's Companions, Alexander becomes king of Macedon, and embarks on a successful campaign against the Persians and their king, Darius (Raz Degan). He meets and marries Roxana (Rosario Dawson), but their relationship is complicated by his continuing love for his boyhood friend Hephaestion (Jared Leto). Alexander continues his military campaign into India, but Hephaestion dies of a fever and, after receiving a wound in battle, Alexander also succumbs.

The film did not do well at the box-office in the US, though it was better received in Europe. The poor audience response in America was blamed on the moral uproar in the press and among religious and Greek nationalist groups before the film's release about its depiction of Alexander's sexuality. However, the film itself is seriously flawed, with a sprawling and not always cohesive narrative and overly large central cast. The use of broad Celtic accents by Colin Farrell playing Alexander and other key actors playing Macedonians was probably a new version of the aural paradigm mentioned previously, marking the Macedonians as outsiders, but was the source of unintentional humour for audiences and critics. At the same time, the film misses the deliberate humour that functioned in the classical Hollywood epics to defuse any pomposity. Its director, Oliver Stone, blamed the film's failure on inappropriate editing decisions, forced by anxious backers. He produced two subsequent Director's Cuts for release on DVD, the second three and a half hours long and including an intermission.

300 (dir: Snyder, 2007)
King Leonidas of Sparta (Gerard Butler) receives an emissary from the Persian king Xerxes (Rodrigo Santoro), demanding his obeisance. In return, Leonidas murders the messenger, and sets off to gain the approval of the Spartan elders for war against Persia. The ephors declare that this cannot happen until after the imminent religious festival. Knowing that a delay would be disastrous, Leonidas sets out anyway with only his personal bodyguard of 300 men. He plans to confront the Persians at the narrow pass of Thermopylae, and the Spartans prove successful at holding the massive army back against the odds. However they are betrayed by Ephialtes (Andrew Tiernan), a deformed Spartan rejected by Leonidas for his guard. Knowing that they face certain death, Leonidas sends the Spartan Dilios (David Wenham) back to Sparta to appeal to the Spartan council. Meanwhile Leonidas' wife, Queen Gorgo (Lena Headey), has responded to an attempt at blackmail by the corrupt councillor Theron (Dominic West) by killing him, revealing that he has been in the pay of the Persians. The 300 Spartans die in a shower of Persian arrows, but a postscript by Dilios shows that their actions had delayed and depleted the Persians long enough to allow the Greek city-states to unite and ultimately defeat them.

'The hit film *300* is pretty much what you'd hear from a history teacher

– if your history teacher was a pro-wrestler' (Fallow 2007: 1). As a child, Frank Miller was deeply moved by watching *The 300 Spartans* with his father. The idea of a film where all the heroes died altered his notion of heroism. Years later he returned to the theme in his graphic novel *300* (1998) which retold the life story of Leonidas from his birth to his death at Thermopylae. The film is a faithful adaptation of Miller's comic. As such it preserves the work's raw brutality and dark humour. These Spartans fight for freedom, but they hit below the belt. Miller took their buff bodies straight from the French history-painting tradition (most notably David's *Leonidas before the Battle of Thermopylae*, 1814), but their dialogue is more *Apocalypse Now* (1979).

The film aped the look of the graphic novel by using pages from the book for storyboarding, filming almost exclusively against blue screen and adding dramatically coloured backgrounds later. Extremely popular with audiences (setting several box-office records), the film was generally disliked by critics for its senseless violence and tendency to fall into cliché. It was even more unpopular with the Iranian government who took the film as a personal insult to Iranian culture. However, a few critics dared to suggest that it was the vast and powerful Persian army rather than the guerrilla-like Spartans that might best stand as a metaphor for the USA in current global conflicts.

Notes

Introduction

Fantasies about Rome: Orgies, see Blanshard (2010): 48-64; Roman salute, see Winkler (2009a).

Classical art, the Renaissance, and the artistic tradition: Bober and Rubinstein (1986); Haskell and Penny (1981); Coltman (2009). History painting: Rosenblum (1967) contains an excellent introduction to neo-classical history painting.

Julius Caesar as model commander: Wintjes (2006). For Caesar more generally, see Wyke (2006a).

Pompeii and its impact: Hales and Paul (2011).

Leighton and Alma-Tadema: Dunant (1994) and Becker et al. (1997): esp. essays by Prettejohn, Morris, and Whiteley.

Impact of *Hercules Furens*: Riley (2008).

Shakespeare and the Roman world: Martindale and Taylor (2004): esp. essays by Roe and Braden; Miles (1996); Chernaik (2011).

Cambridge Greek Play: Easterling (1999). Rome in popular entertainments: Malamud (2001a).

Gérôme in the cinema: Gotlieb (2010) cf. Beeny (2010).

1. Establishing the Conventions: *Cleopatra* (1934)

Cleopatra in film: Wyke (1997a): 73-109; Cyrino (2005): 121-58; Hughes-Hallett (1990): 329-64; Hamer (1993): 117-32; Winkler (2009b): 264-81; Llewellyn-Jones (2002); Solomon (2001a): 62-78.

Early film industry: Monaco (2009): 256-70. Cultural status of early cinema: Perkins (1972): 9-27.

Ancient world in silent cinema: Solomon (2001a): 3-10.

Pyrodramas: Mayer (1994): 90. Strongmen and *tableaux vivants*: Dutton (1995): 119-22.

Early Italian historical epics: Bondanella (2009): 8-11; Brunetta (2009): 34-8.

Cabiria (1941): Winkler (2009a): 94-121; Landy (2000): 33-9.

Socio-historical influences on Italian cine-antiquity: Wyke (2006b): 171-9 (for a case study on Julius Caesar's role in this).

Synecdoche and historiophoty: White (1988): 1193-99.

Cine-antiquity as education: Wyke (1997a): 92, 94 (on the Paramount Study Guide for *Cleopatra*).

Moral coding through accents: Wood (1975): 184; Joshel et al. (2001): 8-9. Cf. Levene (2007): 389-94.

Music in cine-antiquity: Solomon (2001b): 319-37, esp. 324-6.

Primary sources for Cleopatra: The most influential accounts are those found in Plutarch, *Life of Antony*. Cf. Plutarch, *Life of Caesar* 48-9 and Suetonius, *Life of Julius Caesar* 35, 52 and *Life of Augustus* 17 as well as the accounts of Dio Cassius and Appian.

Cultural reception of Cleopatra: Hughes-Hallett (1990); Hamer (1993).

The Production Code and Pre-Code Hollywood films: Leff and Simmons (2001); Doherty (1999); Higham (1973).

Influence of nineteenth-century paintings: Dunant (1994): 82-93; Wyke (1997a): 120-3.

Art Deco cinema architecture: Curl (1994): 212-20; Montserrat (2000): 89.

Cinema viewing as voyeurism: (in *Cleopatra*) Wyke (1997a): 95; (more generally) Mulvey (1975) 6-18.

The 'New Woman' and merchandising: Wyke (1997a): 90-9; Stacey (1994): 177-223; Hamer (1993): 121-3; Hartigan (2002) on the uses of antiquity in advertising more generally.

Denying her a 'maternal' dimension: Hamer (1993): 120.

2. The Roman Epics of Classical Hollywood: *Quo Vadis* (1951)

Quo Vadis (1951): Wyke (1997a): 138-46; Cyrino (2005): 7-33; Scodel and Bettenworth (2009); Morey (2008): 43-52; Winkler (2001b): 55-62; Babington and Evans (2003): 177-205; Solomon (2001a): 217-21.

Roman historical epic films: Wyke (1997a); Elley (1984): 76-135; Cyrino (2005); Solomon (2001a): 47-99; Fitzgerald (2001): 23-49; Babington and Evans (2003).

Film as commercial enterprise: Maltby (2003): 113-87; Eldridge (2006): 37-42.

Showcasing the power of the studio system: Wood (1975): 184; Sobchack (1990): 24-49.

Epic as film genre: Maltby (2003): 74; Neale (2000): 85. Toga dramas: Mayer (1994).

Ancient epic and epic films: Elley (1984): 13-24; Winkler (2007a): especially 43-57; Price (2008): 117-32.

Predominance of Rome over Greece: Elley (1984): 52; Nisbet (2006): vii-x, 2-44.

Alexander and *300*: Cartledge and Greenland (2010); Cyrino (2011).

Political sub-texts in epic films: Wyke (1997a); Winkler (2001b): 50-76 and (2009a): 141-50.

Quo Vadis? as metaphor for Polish oppression: Wyke (1997a): 117.

Quo Vadis (1913) and (1924): Wyke (1997a): 118-30.

Mixed critical reception for *Quo Vadis*: Morey (2008): 47.

Primary sources for *Quo Vadis*: Sienkiewicz (1997, first published in book form, 1896); Tacitus, *Annals*; Suetonius, *Life of Nero*; Petronius, *Satyricon*.

Quo Vadis in reception: Scodel and Bettenworth (2009); Wyke (1997a): 110-46.

Religious films: Babington and Evans (1993): 177-205; Elley (1984): 115-35; Fitzgerald (2001): 25-6.

Hollywood narrative: Bordwell et al. (1985): 1-84.

Economic advantages of filming in Europe: Wyke (1997a): 145; Hall and Neale (2010): 137.

Validating cine-antiquity through research: Eldridge (2006): 127-51; Wyke (1997a): 139.

Merchandising and box-office: Hall and Neale (2010): 137-9; Wyke (1997a): 145-6.

Rossen *Alexander* (1956): Shahabudin (2010).

3. Peplum Traditions: *Hercules* (1958)

Hercules: Solomon (2001a): 119-22; Elley (1984): 21-2; Blanshard (2005): 149-63; Spina (2008).

Italian peplum films: Bondanella (2001): 158-60; Brunetta (1994); Dyer (1997):

145-83 ('White Men's Muscles'); Lagny (1992); Lucanio (1994): esp. 12-56; Frayling (2004).

Hit and run cycles: Frayling (2004): 163-4

Financing of peplum films and production arrangements: Wagstaff (1995) and (1998). cf. 'Nine British Films Earn £2,400,000', *The Times* (27/4/1961): 18.

Contemporary reaction to *Hercules*' 1959 US release: Nason (1959)

Later reaction to peplum: Bosley Crowther, 'Spears and sandals: flood of cheap costume films causes dismay', *New York Times* (12/3/1961): X1; Richard Nason, '"Hercules" starts flood of movies', *New York Times* (24/10/1959): 13; Charlton Heston, 'The epic fever', *Chicago Daily Tribune* (17/12/1961); Bosley Crowther, 'Sweet life in Italy', *New York Times* (8/5/1960): X1; Thomas Meehan, 'It's not good taste, not bad taste – it's camp', *New York Times* (21/3/1965).

Times review: 'Review: Thriller and social study: an awkward film mixture', *The Times* (8/5/1959): 6.

Hercules and the Olympics: 'New movie "Hercules" shows Greek Olympics', *Chicago Daily Tribune* (28/6/1959): J12.

Hercules Unchained (1960): 'Most successful film in Britain', *The Times* (8/12/1960): 18; Howard Thompson, '"Hercules Unchained" heads twin bill', *New York Times* (14/7/1960): 23.

Joseph E. Levine: N. Robertson, 'Joseph E. Levine, a towering figure in movie making is dead', *New York Times* (1/8/1987); Douglas Gomery (2000) 'Levine, Joseph E', *International Dictionary of Film and Filmmakers*.

On Levine's marketing campaign: Hedda Hopper, 'Looking at Hollywood', *Chicago Daily Tribune* (11/3/1959): B5 and (13/7/1959): B6. Promotion of peplum films: Chapman (2002).

Hercules and Macy's advertisement: *New York Times* (22/7/1959): 7.

Cicero: *De Officiis* 3.5.25.

Staging Greece: Nisbet (2006): esp. 7-9. Importance of landscape: García (2008).

Fascism and antiquity: Fleming (2007). Fascism in film: Landy (1986).

Farnese Heracles: Haskell and Penny (1981); Beard and Henderson (2001): 199-202; Beard (1996).

On demand for bodybuilders after *Hercules*: 'Nice work if you can get it', *Chicago Daily Tribune* (23/7/1961): C16.

On the decline of Hercules in the twentieth century: Galinsky (1972).

Bodybuilding: Dutton (1995): 119-29; Webster (1979): 29-35.

Classics and bodybuilding: Wyke (1997b).

On peplum and the crisis of masculinity: Kasson (2001); Faludi (1999).

Women in *Hercules* advertising: 'Display advertisement', *New York Times* (22/7/1959): 7.

Lemnian women: Apollonius of Rhodes, *Argonautica* 1.610-39. Amazons: Dowden (1997); Henderson (1994); von Bothmer (1957); Blondell (2005).

Hercules Conquers Atlantis: Shahabudin (2009).

4. Roman History on Screen: *Spartacus* (1960)

Spartacus (1960): Wyke (1997a): 34-72; Solomon (2001a): 50-8; Winkler (2007b); Theodorakopoulos (2010): 51-76.

The rape of Lucretia: Camino (1995); Donaldson (1982).

Horatii: Livy, *History of Rome* 1.24-6. David, *Oath of the Horatii*: Crow (1985): esp. 211-20, 235-41; Lee (1999): 81-95; Wind (1941-42).

Lictors Bringing Brutus the Bodies of his Sons (1789): Crow (1985): 247-54, (1995): 102-11; Lee (1999): 119-27; Herbert (1972); Korshak (1987): 113-15.

Romulus and Remus: For an introduction to the mythic background, see Wiseman (1995). *Duel of the Titans*: Solomon (2001a): 129-30 (oddly sees the film as faithful to the sources).

HBO's *Rome*: Cyrino (2008).

Historical Spartacus: A selection of the main historical sources for Spartacus are translated in Winkler (2007b): 234-47.

Fast: One of the best sources for Fast is his autobiography *Being Red* (1990). Fast and Spartacus: Fast (1990): 275-7, 285-95. C. Osborne Ward: Obituary 'C. Osborne Ward', *New York Times* (21/3/1902).

J. Edgar Hoover: Fast (1990): 288.

Fast claim for screenwriting credit: 'Credit to Trumbo disputed by Fast: author of Spartacus says that he wrote half the script', *New York Times* (23/2/1960): 36; M. Schumach, 'Trumbo will get credit for script: Spartacus' authorship to be attributed to blacklisted writer by U-I studio', *New York Times* (8/8/1960): 25.

Trumbo: For an account of the persecution of Trumbo, see Cook (1977); Hanson (2001); Trumbo (1982).

Kubrick as director: Naremore (2007). Kubrick claims *Spartacus*: E. Archer, 'Hailed in Farewell: "Spartacus" gets praise of pleased director', *New York Times* (2/10/1960): X9.

Deleted scenes: Cooper (2007).

Protests: M. Schumach, 'Hollywood eyes Legion policy. Industry is expecting action over blacklisted writers at coming convention', *New York Times* (14/10/1960): 24; Wyke (1997a): 71. Kennedy attendance: 'Kennedy sees Spartacus', *New York Times* (4/2/1961): 17; 'Kennedy attends movie in capital: slips out of White House to see "Spartacus" with sub-cabinet official', *New York Times* (5/2/1961): 39.

Script credit for Trumbo and end of blacklist: M. Schumach, 'U.-I. is pondering credit to Trumbo: Spartacus may be first test case of blacklisting involving major studio', *New York Times* (22/2/1960): 12; 'Trumbo will get credit for script: Spartacus' authorship to be attributed to blacklisted writer by U-I studio', *New York Times* (8/8/1960): 25; 'Hollywood test: hiring of banned writers indicates challenge to industry blacklist', *New York Times* (11/9/1960): X15.

Gladiators: Wiedemann (1992); Barton (1993); Gunderson (1996); Futrell (1997); Kyle (1998). Town refusal to allow burial: Suetonius, *Tiberius* 37. Legal and social status: Kyle (1998): 79-90.

Bodybuilding: Dutton (1995).

Objectification of Spartacus: Hark (1993).

Theme of freedom: M.M. Winkler, 'The holy cause of freedom: American ideals in *Spartacus*', in Winkler (2007b): 154-88.

Bird's *Spartacus*: Wyke (1997a): 57-60.

Strode: On the tradition of the black gladiator and Strode's fight, see Girgus (2002): 89-95. Cf. Winkler 'Holy cause of freedom': 168-75. On depiction of race in cinema, see Benshoff and Griffin (2004): esp. 75-95.

Debate about the leftist nature of *Spartacus*: Smith (1989); Futrell (2001). The debate is neatly summed up in Winkler (2007b): 168, esp. n. 29.

Homosexuality in cinema: The classic study is Russo (1987); cf. Barrios (2002); Benshoff and Griffin (2004): 297-317; Davies (2008). Western deployment of classical homosexuality: Blanshard (2010): 124-63. Homosexuality in Alexander films: E. Eakin, 'Ancient conqueror, modern devotees', *New York Times*

(26/11/04). See also S. Waxman, 'Breaking ground with a gay movie hero', *New York Times* (20/11/04) and 'Alexander faces law suit', *Sydney Morning Herald* (21/11/04); cf. Nisbet (2006): 97-8, 109-11, 119-24 and Cyrino (2010): 174-9.
Ancient homosexuality: Williams (2010); Skinner (2010) with bibliography.

5. Greek History on Screen: *The 300 Spartans* (1962)

The 300 Spartans: Levene (2007) and Redonet (2008). For a discussion of the battle of Thermopylae: Cartledge (2006).
Bones of Theseus: Plutarch, *Cimon* 8.3-6; *Theseus* 36.1-2.
Rationalism of *Troy* (2004): Rabel (2007).
The Giant of Marathon: Solomon (2001a): 39. *Damon and Pythias*: Berti (2008).
Rossen's *Alexander the Great* (1955): Solomon (2001a): 42-5; Shahabudin (2010). Stone's *Alexander*: Berti and Morcillo (2008): esp. articles by Wieber, Petrovic, and Chaniotis; Cartledge and Greenland (2010). Critical reaction to Stone's *Alexander*: Solomon (2010).
Decree of Themistocles: Knox (1960) cf. 'How Athens was prepared for Salamis: Themistocles's orders found', *Times* (6/6/1960); 'How Athens was evacuated and prepared for Salamis: foresight and genius of Themistocles', *Times* (14/6/1960).
Cold War rhetoric in *The 300 Spartans*: Levene (2007): esp. 383-5. Submarine *Thermopylae*: 'Thermopylae visit by British crew', *Times* (8/10/1962): 11.
Reviews of *The 300 Spartans*: 'Rialto: *The 300 Spartans*', *Times* (26/10/1962): 14; A.H. Weiler, 'Richard Egan and Ralph Richardson star in "300 Spartans"', *New York Times* (20/9/1962): 29; M. Tinee, 'Actor's skill can't save "Spartans"', *Chicago Daily Tribune* (12/9/1962): B6. Ralph Richardson: O'Connor (1986): 40-1 (as Mark Antony).
Life of the Spartans: Xenophon, *Constitution of the Lacedaimonians*. Cf. Forrest (1968); Powell (1988).
Sparta in children's books: See, for example, the story of the 'brave Spartan boy' in Guerber (1896). Fox and boy: Plutarch, *Life of Lycurgus* 18. 'With this or on this': Plutarch, *Sayings of Spartan Women* (*Moralia* 241f.).
Admiration of Spartan constitution: Rawson (1969). Polybius on the Spartan constitution: Polybius, *Histories* 6.3.5-8. Cf. Von Fritz (1954).
Making Sparta democratic: Levene (2007): 386-8.
Treatment of helots: Plutarch, *Life of Lycurgus* 28.
Spartan women: Pomeroy (2002).
Night expedition: Diodorus Siculus 11.10; Justin 2.11.11-8; Plutarch, *Malice of Herodotus* 866a-b. Cf. Levene (2007): 395-6.
Manliest film of all time: G. Kane, 'Movies for men', *Austin American Statesman* (4/9/1997): 55.

6. Myth and the Fantastic: *Jason and the Argonauts* (1963)

Jason and the Argonauts on film: Elley (1984): 60; Solomon (2001a): 113-15; Nisbet (2006): 61-2; Wells (2002): 53-4; Jackson and Harryhausen (2005): 96-115; Harryhausen and Dalton (2003): 149-74; Harryhausen (1972): 85-91; Rickitt (2006): 190. On the difference between CGI and model animation: Purves (1998).
Myth on film: Elley (1984): 52-66; Solomon (2001a): 101-31; Winkler (2007a): 43-68.
Fantasy films: Fowkes (2010); Butler (2009). The fantastic in literature: Todorov (1975).

Georges Méliès: Ezra (2000).
Gods on film: Winkler (2009b): 70-121; Shahabudin (2007): 114-16.
Special effects and animation: North (2008); Rickitt (2006); Wells (1998) and (2002): 1-29.
Ray Harryhausen – career and films: Harryhausen and Dalton (2004): esp. 286-7 (Harryhausen and ancient myth); Harryhausen (1972): 85 (Harryhausen on peplum films), 141 (on fantasy); Harryhausen et al. (2006): 96-127; Wells (2002): 90-101.
Primary sources for Jason and the Argonauts: Apollonius, *Argonautica*; Pindar, *Fourth Pythian Ode*; Apollodorus, *Library* 1.9.16-28; Diodorus Siculus 4.40-52.
Medea on film: Christie (2000): 144-65; McDonald (1983): 3-88; MacKinnon (1986): 146-54, 156-60.

7. Art Cinema: *Fellini-Satyricon* (1969)

Fellini-Satyricon: For an introduction to the film and the issues that it raises, see Paul (2009); Solomon (2001a): 274-80; Sullivan (2001); Theodorakopoulos (2010): 122-44; Wyke (1997a): 188-91. Zanelli (1970) collects a lot of useful material including interviews, film treatments, and a draft screenplay. Hughes (1971) provides a useful diary detailing numerous production details.
Art cinema: For an introduction to 'art cinema' and its features, see Bordwell (1999). See also the discussion of the terms 'art cinema' and 'auteur' in R. Stam, *Film Theory: An Introduction* (Malden and Oxford): 83-92; Susan Hayward, *Cinema Studies: The Key Concepts*, 3rd edn (Abingdon and New York).
Cacoyannis: Although a little dated, the best discussion is still McDonald (1983). See also the discussion in Karalis (2012) and García (2008): 27-8.
Cocteau: For Cocteau's own vision of cinema, including a chapter on Orpheus, see Cocteau (1992), cf. Klawans (2011). Orpheus in the Underworld scene: Smith (1996).
Initial announcement: 'Fellini casts Mae West in film on debauchery', *New York Times* (10/8/1968).
Attribution of *Satyricon* to Petronius: For discussion, see Prag and Repath (2009): 5-10. Fragmentary nature of the text: Slater (2009).
Arms for Venus: 'Obituary: Randolph Carter', *New York Times* (26/10/1998): A19. Maderna's *Satyricon*: D. Henahan, 'Music: New "Satyricon" at Tanglewood', *New York Times* (7/8/1973): 29.
Terence Stamp, Mickey Mouse and extended cast: Mark Shivas, 'Fellini's back and Mae West's got him', *New York Times* (13/10/1968): D21; Hughes (1971): 8. Opening night: 'Fellini Satyricon to open', *New York Times* (13/2/1970).
Mae West: George Eels and Stanley Musgrove, *Mae West: A Biography* (New York): 270. Stamp and financial constraints: Zanelli (1970): 5.
Musical *Satyricon* in 1939 and early exposure to gladiator films: Shivas (1968): D21.
Fellini's autobiographical works: Bondanella (2001): 124-30, 241-5.
Luca Canali and Ettore Paratore: Highet (1983): 347.
On using unknown actors: Burke (1970); Zanelli (1970): 5. Beautiful boys: Shivas (1968). Max Born and Hiram Keller: Zanelli (1970): 5.
On the filming of the *Fellini Satyricon*: Zanelli (1970): 3-20 and Hughes (1971). Cinecittà: Bondanella (2001). Donati: Zanelli (1970): 14.
Poliodoro and Bini: A. Friendly, 'The "other" Italian "Satyricon" is out of court and on screen', *New York Times* (12/3/1970): 47.

Notes

Best of 1970 list: V. Canby, 'Critic's choice: ten best films of 1970', *New York Times* (27/12/1970): 61; cf. 'Notables name bests', *New York Times* (27/12/1970): 77; A.H. Weiler, 'Critics vote "5 Easy Pieces" best film', *New York Times* (29/12/1970): 31. For a contemporary cinematic defence, see A.O. Scott, 'Fellini's fever dream of Ancient Rome', *New York Times* (26/1/2001): E20.

Critical reception: Highet's essay was originally printed in *Horizon* (1970) 12: 42-7 and is reprinted in Highet (1983). On intertextuality in *Fellini-Satyricon*, see especially Sullivan (2001). Simon's criticism: Simon (1970). Defence of intertextuality: See Pandiri and Baxter's letter in 'Move mailbag: "Airport", "Satyricon", Women's Lib', *New York Times* (7/6/1970): 94; cf. John Simon's response in 'Movie mailbag: from "Patton" to "Satyricon" to "Chaplin"', *New York Times* (28/6/1970): 80.

Gallery scene: Hughes (1971): 119-21.

Suburra Scene: Hughes (1971): 79-87; Zanelli (1970): 11-14. Non-grammatical Latin inscriptions: Zanelli (1970): 12; Hughes (1971): 80. Head of Vitellius: Sullivan (2001): 264. Use of *Roma Amor*: Zanelli (1970): 4.

Filming of hermaphrodite scene: Hughes (1971): 44-66. Influence of Lourdes: Hughes (1971): 45; Zanelli (1970): 80. Post-Christian world: Zanelli (1970): 13.

Cledonomancy: Halliday (1903): 47-53. Sporus: Suetonius, *Nero* 27-9. Mirth ritual: Apuleius, *Golden Ass* 2.31-311. Mythological executions: Coleman (1990).

8. Satirising Cine-Antiquity: *Monty Python's Life of Brian* (1979)

Monty Python's Life of Brian: Cyrino (2005): 176-93; Cleese, Gilliam, Palin, Idle, Jones and the Estate of Graham Chapman (2005): 349-87; Elley (1984): 147; Solomon (2001a): 301-3; Sellers (2003): 1-24; Hewison (1981): 59-93, especially good on the blasphemy and censorship issues; Johnson (2008): a journal on the making of the film.

The ancient world in comic films: Solomon (2001a): 283-305; Cull (2001): 162-90; Malamud (2001b): 191-208.

Satire: Guilhamet (1987); Carpenter (2000).

Decline of cine-antiquity: Wyke (1997a): 183-8; Winkler (1995); Solomon (2001a): 15.

Cleopatra (1963) and *Carry on Cleo*: Wyke (1997a): 100-9; Cyrino (2005): 121-58; Elley (1984): 93-5; Cull (2001): 162-90.

Mystery Science Theatre 3000: Beaulieu et al. (1996).

Monty Python: Cleese et al. (2005); Perry (2006); McCall (1991); Hewison (1981).

Monty Python and the Holy Grail: Cleese et al. (2005): 307-48; Elley (1984): 147; Hewison (1981): 38-9.

9. The Disney Version: *Hercules* (1997)

Disney and the Disney corporation: Maltin (1987): 29-82; Byrne and McQuillan (1999); Bell et al. (1995); Watts (2002); Sammond (2005). Financial statements: Information about the size and composition of the Disney corporation is provided by Disney Investor relations. Key documents include the 2010 Disney Fact Book and the 2010 Annual Report.

Disney and family therapy: Towbin et al. (2003).

René Clair: Finch (1995): 85.

Production history of *Hercules*: Thomas (1997): 164-99.

On the age suitability for the film: J. Benzel, 'Taking the children: you're a celebrity hero now, Herc, ya big lug', *New York Times* (29/6/1997): 22.

245

Menken: J. Bergernorth, 'Making Disney's world go round', *New York Times* (13/7/1997): 30.

Tie-in with McDonalds: 'Disney, McDonald's plan joint campaign', *New York Times* (9/6/1997): 31.

Hercules on Ice: See Van Gelder, L. 'Mythology for the young and light-hearted', *New York Times* (15/11/1997): 13.

Hercules parade in New York: B. Weber, 'Disney unveils restored New Amsterdam theater', *New York Times* (3/4/1997): B3; M. Purdy, 'Disney parade about to turn Midtown Goofy', *New York Times* (13/6/1997): B1; D. Martin, 'Its Greeks bearing glitz, Disney parades a hero', *New York Times* (15/6/1997): 27. Letters to the Editor: Reckler, 'Disney parade madness', *New York Times* (17/6/1997); J. Duban, 'Who doesn't love a parade? Some of us', *New York Times* (3/7/1997).

Box-office: G. Fabrikant, 'Marketplace: Hercules is too weak to lift Disney stock', *New York Times* (10/7/1997).

Greek heroism: Nagy (1999); Kearns (1989); Larson (2007). Sacrifice: Ekroth (2002). Child heroes: Pache (2004). Hercules: Galinsky (1972); Blanshard (2005); Riley (2008). Hercules and the King of Troy: Apollodorus, *Library* 2.5.9; Diodorus Siculus 4.42; Ovid, *Metamorphoses* 11.215-19.

Sanitising myth. 'Don't look for this plot in Bulfinch': R. Corliss, 'A hit from a myth', *Time* vol. 149 issue 25 (23/6/1997): 76. See also J. Maslin, 'Oh, Heavens! What a hero!', *New York Times* (13/6/1997): C1. Disney's conservative values: Towbin et al. (2003). A more nuanced and slightly more positive view is presented in Davis (2006).

Changing representation of women in US media: Davis (2006): 169.

Altering of Pocahontas: Ward (2002): 35-8.

Hercules and Deianeira: Apollodorus, *Library* 2.7.5-7. Cf. Sophocles, *Women of Trachis*.

On the 'tough gal' figure in Disney films, see Davis (2006): 206-9.

Daughters of Thespius: Athenaeus, *Deipnosophistae* 13.4; Apollodorus, *Library* 2.4.11; Diodorus Siculus 4.29.2-3; Pausanias 9.27.6-7. Auge: Apollodorus, *Library* 2.7.4; Diodorus Siculus 4.33.7-12.

Clements on the Hercules myth: Thomas (1997): 165 (the first superhero) and 166 (the problem of illegitimacy).

10. The Return of the Epic? *Gladiator* (2000)

Gladiator: Winkler (2004); Cyrino (2005): 207-56; Burgoyne (2011): 82-98; Albu (2008): 185-204 on the political sub-texts of the film.

Decline of cine-antiquity: Wyke (1997a): 183-8; Winkler (1995): 135-54; Solomon (2001a): 15.

Cleopatra (1963): Wyke (1997a): 100-9; Cyrino (2005): 121-58; Elley (1984): 93-5.

The Fall of the Roman Empire (1964): Wyke (1997a): 185-8; Winkler (1995): 135-54.

The studio system and the Paramount Case: Monaco (2009): 270-80; Gil (2010): 171-83.

Troy (2004): Winkler (2007a).

Alexander (2004): Cartledge and Greenland (2010); Pomeroy (2008): 100-3.

300 (2006): Cyrino (2011).

Political sub-texts in epic films: Wyke (1997a); Winkler (2001b): 50-76 and (2009a): 141-50.

Predominance of Rome over Greece: Elley (1984): 52; Nisbet (2006): vii-x, 2-44.

Notes

Troy as historical epic: Shahabudin (2007): 107-18.

Videogames inspired by antiquity: Lowe (2009): 64-90. Ancient world in mass popular culture: Lowe and Shahabudin (2009); Hartigan (2002).

Primary sources for *Gladiator*: *Historia Augusta*: *The Life of Commodus*; Dio Cassius, *Roman History*; Herodian, *History of the Empire After Marcus Aurelius*.

Historical gladiators: Wiedemann (1992); Barton (1993): 11-81.

Gérôme, gladiators, and cinema: Gotlieb (2010); Beeny (2010).

Role of historical consultant: Coleman (2004): 45-52.

Script revisions on *Gladiator*: Lowe (June 2004): 18-19; Solomon (2004): 1-15.

Ridley Scott: Schwartz (2001).

Fascist imagery in *Gladiator*: Pomeroy (2004).

Computer Generated Imagery in large-scale films: Hall and Neale (2010): 253-5.

Bibliography

Albu, E. (2008) 'Gladiator at the Millennium', *Arethusa* 41: 185-204.

Babington, B. and Evans, P.W. (1993) *Biblical Epics: Sacred Narrative in the Hollywood Cinema*. Manchester.

Barr, S. (1961) *The Will of Zeus: A History of Greece from the Origins of Hellenic Culture to the Death of Alexander*. Philadelphia.

Barrios, R. (2002) *Screened Out: Playing Gay in Hollywood from Edison to Stonewall*. New York.

Barton, C.A. (1993) *The Sorrows of the Ancient Romans: The Gladiator and the Monster*. Princeton, NJ.

Beard, M. (1996) 'Le mythe (grec) à Rome: Hercule aux bains', in Georgoudi, S. and Vernant, J.-P. (eds) *Mythes grecs au figuré de l'antiquité au baroque*. Paris: 81-104.

Beard, M. (2005) 'Apart from vomitoriums and orgies, what did the Romans do for us?' *The Guardian* (29/10/2005).

Beard, M. and Henderson, J. (2001) *Classical Art: From Greece to Rome*. Oxford.

Beaulieu, T. et al. (1996) *The Mystery Science Theater 3000 Amazing Colossal Episode Guide*. New York.

Becker, E. et al. (eds) (1997) *Sir Lawrence Alma-Tadema*. New York.

Beeny, E. (2010) 'Blood Spectacle: Gérôme in the arena', in Allan, S. and Morton, M. (eds) *Reconsidering Gérôme*. Los Angeles: 40-53.

Bell, E. et al. (eds) (1995) *From Mouse to Mermaid: The Politics of Film, Gender, and Culture*, Bloomington.

Benshoff, H.M. and Griffin, S. (2004) *America on Film: Representing Race, Class, Gender, and Sexuality at the Movies*. Malden, MA.

Berti, I. (2008) ' "A rare example of Friendship true": the story of *Damon and Pythias*', in Berti, I. and Morcillo, M.G. (eds) *Hellas on Screen: Cinematic Receptions of Ancient History, Literature, and Myth*. Stuttgart: 131-46.

Berti, I. and Morcillo, M.G. (eds) (2008) *Hellas on Screen: Cinematic Receptions of Ancient History, Literature, and Myth*. Stuttgart.

Blanshard, A.J.L. (2005) *Hercules: A Heroic Life*. London.

Blanshard, A.J.L. (2010) *Sex: Vice and Love from Antiquity to Modernity*. Malden, MA.

Blondell, R. (2005) 'How to kill an Amazon', *Helios* 32: 182-213.

Bober, P.P. and Rubinstein, R. (1986) *Renaissance Artists and Antique Sculpture*. Oxford.

Bondanella, P.E. (2001) *Italian Cinema: From Neorealism to the Present*. New York.

Bondanella, P.E. (2009) *A History of Italian Cinema*. New York.

Bordwell, D. (1999) 'The art cinema as a mode of film practice', in Braudy, L. and Cohen, M. (eds) *Film Theory and Criticism: Introductory Readings*. Oxford: 716-29.

Bibliography

Bordwell, D. et al. (1985) *The Classical Hollywood Cinema: Film Style and Mode of Production to 1960.* New York.

Brunetta, G.P. (1994) 'The Long March of American Cinema in Italy: From Fascism to the Cold War', in Ellwood, D.W. and Kroes, R. (eds) *Hollywood in Europe: Experiences of Cultural Hegemony.* Amsterdam: 139-54.

Brunetta, G.P. (2009) *The History of Italian Cinema: A Guide to Italian Film from its Origins to the Twenty-first Century.* Princeton, NJ.

Burgoyne, R. (2011) 'Bare life and sovereignty in *Gladiator*', in Burgoyne, R. (ed.) *The Epic Film in World Culture.* Hoboken: 82-98.

Burgoyne, R. (2011) *The Epic Film in World Culture.* Hoboken.

Burke, T. (1970) 'Fellini finds "an unknown planet for me to populate!"', *New York Times* (8/2/1970): 99.

Butler, D. (2009) *Fantasy Cinema: Impossible Worlds on Screen.* London.

Byrne, E. and McQuillan, M. (1999) *Deconstructing Disney.* London.

Camino, M.M. (1995) *'The Stage Am I': Raping Lucrece in Early Modern England.* Lewiston and Salzburg.

Canby, V. (1984) 'Fellini charts his latest magical mystery tour', *New York Times* (5/2/1984): 15.

Canby, V. (1993) 'Tracing the splendid arc of Fellini's sweeping vision', *New York Times* (29/10/1993): C15.

Carpenter, H. (2000) *That Was Satire That Was: Beyond the Fringe, The Establishment Club, Private Eye, That Was The Week That Was.* London.

Cartledge, P.A. (2006) *Thermopylae: The Battle that Changed the World.* London.

Cartledge, P.A. and Greenland, F.R. (eds) (2010) *Responses to Oliver Stone's Alexander: Film, History, and Cultural Studies.* Madison.

Chapman, D. (2002) *Retro Stud: Muscle Movie Posters from Around the World.* Portland.

Chernaik, W.L. (2011) *The Myth of Rome in Shakespeare and his Contemporaries.* Cambridge.

Christie, I. (2002) 'Between magic and realism: Medea on film' in Taplin, O. et al. (eds) *Medea in Performance, 1500-2000.* Oxford: 1500-2000.

Cleese, J. et al. (2005) *The Pythons: Autobiography by the Pythons.* London.

Cocteau, J. (1992) *The Art of Cinema.* London.

Coleman, K.M. (1990) 'Fatal charades: Roman executions staged as mythological enactments', *Journal of Roman Studies* 80: 44-73.

Coleman, K.M. (2004) 'The pedant goes to Hollywood: the role of the academic consultant', in Winkler, M.M. (ed.) *Gladiator: Film and History.* Malden: 45-52.

Coltman, V. (2009) *Classical Sculpture and the Culture of Collecting in Britain since 1760.* Oxford.

Cook, B. (1977) *Dalton Trumbo.* New York.

Cooper, D. (2007) 'Who killed the legend of Spartacus? Production, censorship, and reconstruction of Stanley Kubrick's epic film', in Winkler, M.M. (ed.) *Spartacus: Film and History.* Oxford: 14-55.

Crow, T. (1985) *Painters and Public Life in Eighteenth-Century Paris.* New Haven.

Crow, T. (1995) *Emulation: Making Artists for Revolutionary France.* New Haven.

Cull, N. J. (2001) '"Infamy! Infamy! They've all got it in for me!": *Carry on Cleo* and the British camp comedies of ancient Rome', in Joshel, S.R. et al. (eds) *Imperial Projections: Ancient Rome in Modern Popular Culture.* Baltimore and London: 162-90.

Curl, J.S. (1994) *Egyptomania. The Egyptian Revival: A Recurring Theme in the History of Taste.* Manchester.

Bibliography

Cyrino, M.S. (2005) *Big Screen Rome*. Malden, MA.

Cyrino, M.S. (ed.) (2008) *Rome, Season One: History makes Television*. Malden, MA.

Cyrino, M.S. (2010) 'Fortune favours the blond: Colin Farrel in *Alexander*', in Cartledge, P.A. and Greenland, F.R. (eds) *Responses to Oliver Stone's Alexander: Film, History, and Cultural Studies*. Madison: 168-82.

Cyrino, M.S. (2011) '"This is Sparta!": the reinvention of the epic in Zack Snyder's *300*', in Burgoyne, R. (ed.) *The Epic Film in World Culture*. Hoboken: 19-38.

Davies, S.P. (2008) *Out at the Movies: A History of Gay Cinema*. Harpenden.

Davis, A.M. (2006) *Good Girls and Wicked Witches: Women in Disney's Feature Animation*. Bloomington.

Doherty, T.P. (1999) *Pre-code Hollywood: Sex, Immorality, and Insurrection in American Cinema, 1930-1934*. New York.

Donaldson, I. (1982) *The Rapes of Lucretia: A Myth and its Transformations*. Oxford.

Dowden, K. (1997) 'The Amazons: development and function', *Rheinisches Museum für Papyrologie* 140: 97-128.

Dunant, C. (1994) 'Olympian dreamscapes: the photographic canvas. The widescreen paintings of Leighton, Poynter and Alma-Tadema', in Bratton, J., et al. (eds) *Melodrama: Stage Picture Screen*. London: 82-93.

Dutton, K. (1995) *The Perfectible Body: The Western Ideal of Physical Development*. London.

Dyer, R. (1997) *White*. London and New York.

Easterling, P.E. (1999) 'The early years of the Cambridge Greek Play: 1883-1912', in Stray, C.A. (ed.) *Classics in Nineteenth- and Twentieth-Century Cambridge: Curriculum, Culture, and Community* (PCPS Suppl. no. 24). Cambridge: 27-47.

Eisenstein, S. (1988) *Eisenstein on Disney*. London.

Ekroth, G. (2002) *The Sacrificial Rituals of Greek Hero-cults in the Archaic to the Early Hellenistic Periods*. Liège.

Eldridge, D. (2006) *Hollywood's History Films*. London.

Elley, D. (1984) *The Epic Film: Myth and History*. London.

Ezra, E. (2000) *Georges Méliès: The Birth of the Auteur*. Manchester.

Fallow, M. (2007) 'Hollywood at the Hot Gates', *The Southland Times* (7/4/2007): 1.

Faludi, S. (1999) *Stiffed: The Betrayal of the American Man*. New York.

Fast, H. (1990) *Being Red*. Boston.

Finch, C. (1995) *The Art of Walt Disney: From Mickey Mouse to the Magical Kingdom*. New York.

Fitzgerald, W. (2001) 'Oppositions, anxieties, and ambiguities in the Toga Movie', in Joshel, S.R. et al. (eds) *Imperial Projections: Ancient Rome in Modern Popular Culture*. London and Baltimore: 23-49.

Fleming, K. (2007) 'Fascism', in Kallendorf, K. (ed.) *A Companion to the Classical Tradition*. Oxford: 342-54.

Forrest, W.G.G. (1968) *A History of Sparta, 950-192 BC*. London.

Fowkes, K.A. (2010) *The Fantasy Film*. Chichester.

Frayling, C. (2004) 'Per un pugno di dollari/A fist full of dollars', in Bertellini, G. (ed.) *The Cinema of Italy*. London: 163-72.

Futrell, A. (1997) *Blood in the Arena: The Spectacle of Roman Power*. Austin.

Futrell, A. (2001) 'Seeing red: Spartacus as domestic economist', in Joshel, S.R. et al. (eds) *Imperial Projections: Ancient Rome in Modern Popular Culture*. Baltimore: 77-118.

Bibliography

Galinsky, K. (1972) *The Herakles Theme: The Adaptations of the Hero in Literature from Homer to the Twentieth Century.* Oxford.

García, N. (2008) 'Classic sceneries: setting ancient Greece in film architecture', in Berti, I. and Morcillo, M.G. (eds) *Hellas on Screen: Cinematic Receptions of Ancient History, Literature, and Myth.* Stuttgart: 21-38.

Gil, R. (2010) 'An empirical investigation of the Paramount antitrust case', *Applied Economics* 42: 171-83.

Girgus, S.B. (2002) *America on Film: Modernism, Documentary, and a Changing America.* Cambridge.

Golding, W. (1965) *The Hot Gates and Other Occasional Pieces.* London.

Gotlieb, M. (2010) 'Gérôme's cinematic imagination', in Allan, S. and Morton, M. (eds) *Reconsidering Gérôme.* Los Angeles: 54-64.

Guerber, H.A. (1896) *The Story of the Greeks.* New York.

Guilhamet, L. (1987) *Satire and the Transformation of Genre.* Philadelphia.

Gunderson, E. (1996) 'The ideology of the Arena', *Classical Antiquity* 15: 113-51.

Hales, S. and Paul, J. (eds) (2011) *Pompeii in the Public Imagination from its Rediscovery to Today.* Oxford.

Hall, S. and Neale, S. (2010) *Epics, Spectacles, and Blockbusters: A Hollywood history.* Detroit.

Halliday, W.R. (1953) *Greek Divination.* London.

Halperin, D.M. (1990) *One Hundred Years of Homosexuality and Other Essays on Greek Love.* London.

Hamer, M. (1993) *Signs of Cleopatra: History, Politics, Representation.* London and New York.

Hanson, P. (2001) *Dalton Trumbo, Hollywood Rebel: A Critical Survey and Filmography.* London.

Hark, I.R. (1993) 'Animals or Romans: looking at masculinity in Spartacus', in Cohan, S. and Hark, I.R. (eds) *Screening the Male: Exploring Masculinities in Hollywood Cinema.* London: 151-72.

Harryhausen, R. (1972) *Film Fantasy Scrapbook.* London.

Harryhausen, R. and Dalton, T. (2004) *Ray Harryhausen: An Animated Life.* New York.

Harryhausen, R. et al. (2006) *The Art of Ray Harryhausen.* London.

Hartigan, K. (2002) *Muse on Madison Avenue: Classical Mythology in Contemporary Advertising.* Frankfurt am Main and New York.

Haskell, F. and Penny, N. (1981) *Taste and the Antique: The Lure of Classical Sculpture, 1500-1900.* New Haven.

Heath, M. (1952) 'War of the gladiators: Spartacus by Howard Fast', *New York Times* (3/2/1952): BR22.

Henderson, J. (1994) 'Timeo Danaos: Amazons in early Greek art and pottery', in Goldhill, S. and Osborne, R. (eds) *Art and Text in Ancient Greek Culture.* Cambridge: 83-157.

Herbert, R.L. (1972) *David, Voltaire, "Brutus", and the French Revolution: An Essay in Art and Politics.* London.

Hewison, R. (1981) *Monty Python, The Case Against: Irreverence, Scurrility, Profanity, Vilification and Licentious Abuse.* London.

Higham, C. (1973) *Cecil B. DeMille.* New York.

Highet, G. (1983) 'Whose *Satyricon* – Petronius's or Fellini's?' in Ball, R.J. (ed.) *The Classical Papers of Gilbert Highet.* New York: 339-48.

Hughes, E.L. (1971) *On the Set of Fellini Satyricon: A Behind-the-scenes Diary.* New York.

Bibliography

Hughes-Hallett, L. (1990) *Cleopatra: Histories, Dreams and Distortions*. New York.

Johnson, K. (2008) *Monty Python's Tunisian Holiday: My Life with Brian*. New York.

Joshel, S.R. et al. (2001) *Imperial Projections: Ancient Rome in Modern Popular Culture*. Baltimore and London.

Kanfer, S. (1997) 'Air Hercules joins Disney's pantheon of pitchmen', *New York Times* (22/6/1997): 17.

Karalis, V. (2012) *A History of Greek Cinema*. London.

Kasson, J.F. (2001) *Houdini, Tarzan, and the Perfect Man: The White Male Body and the Challenge of Modernity in America*. New York.

Kearns, E. (1989) *The Heroes of Attica*. London.

Klawans, S. (2011) 'Narcissus sees through himself: On Jean Cocteau and the invention of the film poet', *Parnassus: Poetry in Review* 32: 321-33.

Knox, S. (1960) 'Ancient Greek tablet may rewrite history', *New York Times* (5/6/1960): 1 and 70.

Korshak, Y. (1987) 'Paris and Helen by Jacques Louis David: choice and judgment on the eve of the French Revolution', *The Art Bulletin* 69: 102-16.

Kyle, D. (1998) *Spectacles of Death in Ancient Rome*. New York.

Lagny, M. (1992) 'Popular taste: the peplum', in Dyer, R. and Vincendeau, G. (eds) *Popular European Cinema*. London: 163-80.

Landy, M. (1986) *Fascism in Film: Italian Commercial Cinema 1931-43*. Princeton.

Landy, M. (2000) *Italian Film*. Cambridge.

Larson, J. (2007) *Ancient Greek Cults: A Guide*. Abingdon.

Lee, S. (1999) *David*. London.

Leff, L.J. and Simmons, J. (2001) *The Dame in the Kimono: Hollywood, Censorship, and the Production Code*. Lexington.

Levene, D.S. (2007) 'Xerxes goes to Hollywood', in Bridges, E. et al. (eds) *Cultural Responses to the Persian Wars: Antiquity to the Third Millennium*. Oxford: 383-403.

Llewellyn-Jones, L. (2002) 'Celluloid Cleopatras or Did the Greeks ever get to Egypt?', in Ogden, D. (ed.) *The Hellenistic World: New Perspectives*. London: 275-304.

Lowe, D. (2009) 'Playing with antiquity: videogame receptions of the classical world', in Lowe, D. and Shahabudin, K (eds) *Classics for All: Reworking Antiquity in Mass Culture*. Newcastle upon Tyne: 64-90.

Lowe, D. and Shahabudin, K. (eds) (2007) *Classics for All: Reworking Antiquity in Mass Culture*, Newcastle upon Tyne.

Lowe, N. (2004) 'Beware Geeks bearing scripts', *Times Literary Supplement* (4/6/2004): 18-19.

Lucanio, P. (1994) *With Fire and Sword: Italian Spectacles on American Screens, 1958-1968*. Munich.

MacKinnon, K. (1986) *Greek Tragedy into Film*. London.

McCall, D.L. (1991) *Monty Python: A Chronological Listing of the Troupe's Creative Output, and Articles and Reviews about them, 1969-1989*. Jefferson, NC.

McDonald, M. (1983) *Euripides in Cinema: The Heart made Visible*. Philadelphia.

Malamud, M. (2001a) 'Roman entertainments for the masses in turn-of-the-century New York', *Classical World* 95: 49-57.

Malamud, M. (2001b) 'Brooklyn-on-the-Tiber: Roman comedy on Broadway and in

Bibliography

film', in Joshel, S.R. et al. (eds) *Imperial Projections: Ancient Rome in Modern Popular Culture*. Baltimore and London: 191-208.

Maltby, R. (2003) *Hollywood Cinema*. Malden, MA.

Maltin, L. (1987) *Of Mice and Magic: A History of American Animated Cartoons*. New York.

Martindale, C. and Taylor, A.B. (eds.) (2004) *Shakespeare and the Classics*. Cambridge.

Mayer, D. (1994) *Playing Out the Empire: Ben-Hur and other Toga Plays and Films, 1883-1908; A Critical Anthology*. Oxford, New York.

Miles, G. (1996) *Shakespeare and the Constant Romans*. Oxford.

Monaco, J. (2009) *How to Read a Film: Movies, Media, and Beyond*. Oxford.

Montserrat, D. (2000) *Akhenaten: History, Fantasy, and Ancient Egypt*. London.

Morey, A. (2008) 'Home or away? Words and things in Quo Vadis', in Wrigley, R. (ed.) *Cinematic Rome*. Leicester: 43-52.

Mulvey, L. (1975) 'Visual pleasure and narrative cinema', *Screen* 16: 6-18.

Nagy, G. (1999) *Best of the Achaeans: Concepts of the Hero in Archaic Greek Poetry*. Baltimore.

Naremore, J. (2007) *On Kubrick*. London.

Nason, R. (1959) 'Weak "Hercules": Italian-made spectacle opens at 135 theatres', *New York Times* (23/7/1959): 32.

Neale, S. (2000) *Genre and Hollywood*. London.

Nisbet, G. (2006) *Ancient Greece in Film and Popular Culture*. Exeter.

North, D. (2008) *Performing Illusions: Cinema, Special Effects and the Virtual Actor*. London.

O'Connor, G. (1986) *Ralph Richardson: An Actor's Life*. London.

Pache, C.O. (2004) *Baby and Child Heroes in Ancient Greece*. Urbana.

Paul, J. (2009) 'Fellini-Satyricon: Petronius and film', in Prag, J. and Repath, I. (eds) *Petronius: A Handbook*. Oxford: 198-217.

Perkins, V.F. (1972) *Film as Film*. Harmondsworth.

Perry, G.C. (2006) *Life of Python*. London.

Pomeroy, A.J. (2004) 'The vision of a fascist Rome in *Gladiator*', in Winkler, M.M. (ed.) *Gladiator: Film and History*. Malden: 150-72.

Pomeroy, A.J. (2008) *Then It Was Destroyed by the Volcano: The Ancient World in Film and on Television*. London.

Pomeroy, S.B. (2002) *Spartan Women*. Oxford.

Powell, A. (1988) *Athens and Sparta: Constructing Greek Political and Social History from 478 BC*. London.

Prag, J. and Repath, I. (eds) (2009) *Petronius: A Handbook*. Oxford.

Prescott, O. (1961) 'Books of the Times', *New York Times* (13/12/1961): 41.

Price, S. (2008) 'Displacing the gods? Agency and power in adaptations of ancient history and myth', *Journal of Adaptation in Film & Performance* 1: 117-32.

Purves, B. (1998) 'Boldly throwing down the gauntlet', *Animation World Magazine* 2.11.

Rabel, R.J. (2007) 'The realist politics of *Troy*', in Winkler, M.M. (ed.) *Troy: From Homer's Iliad to Hollywood Epic*. Malden, MA: 186-201.

Rawson, E. (1969) *The Spartan Tradition in European Thought*. Oxford.

Redonet, F.L. (2008) 'Sparta and Ancient Greece in *The 300 Spartans*', in Berti, I. and Morcillo, M.G. (eds) *Hellas on Screen: Cinematic Receptions of Ancient History, Literature, and myth*. Stuttgart: 117-30.

Rickitt, R. (2000) *Special Effects: The History and Technique*. New York.

Bibliography

Riley, K. (2008) *The Reception and Performance of Euripides' Herakles: Reasoning Madness*. Oxford.

Rosenblum, R. (1967) *Transformations in Late Eighteenth-Century Art*. Princeton.

Russo, V. (1987) *The Celluloid Closet: Homosexuality in the Movies*. New York.

Sammond, N. (2005) *Babes in Tomorrowland: Walt Disney and the Making of the American Child, 1930-1960*. Durham, NC.

Schwartz, R.A. (2001) *The Films of Ridley Scott*. Westport, CT.

Scodel, R. and Bettenworth, A. (2009) *Whither Quo Vadis?: Sienkiewicz's Novel in Film and Television*. Malden, MA.

Segal, E. (1971) 'Arbitrary *Satyricon*: Petronius and Fellini', *Diacritics* 1: 54-7.

Sellers, R. and Palin, M. (2003) *Always Look on the Bright Side of Life: The Inside Story of HandMade Films*. London.

Shahabudin, K. (2007) 'From Greek Myth to Hollywood Story: Explanatory Narrative in Troy', in Winkler, M.M. (ed.) *Troy: From Homer's Iliad to Hollywood Epic*. Malden: 107-18.

Shahabudin, K. (2009) 'Ancient mythology and modern myths: *Hercules Conquers Atlantis* (1961)', in Lowe, D. and Shahabudin, K. (eds) *Classics for All: Reworking Antiquity in Mass Culture*. Newcastle upon Tyne: 196-216.

Shahabudin, K. (2010) 'The Appearance of History: Robert Rossen's *Alexander the Great*', in Cartledge, P.A. and Greenland, F.R. (eds) *Responses to Oliver Stone's Alexander: Film, History, and Cultural Studies*. Madison: 92-116.

Shivas, M. (1968) 'Fellini's back and Mae West's got him', *New York Times* (13/10/1968): D21.

Sienkiewicz, H. (1955) *Quo Vadis*. New York.

Skinner, M. (2010) '*Alexander* and ancient Greek sexuality: some theoretical considerations', in Cartledge, P. and Greenland, F.R. (eds) *Responses to Oliver Stone's Alexander: Film, History, and Cultural Studies*. Madison: 119-34.

Slater, N. (2009) 'Reading the Satyrica', in Prag, J. and Repath, I. (eds) *Petronius: A Handbook*. Oxford: 16-31.

Smith, E.L. (1996) 'Framing the Underworld: threshold imagery in Murnau, Cocteau and Bergman', *Literature/Film Quarterly* 24: 241-54.

Smith, J.P. (1989) '"A good business proposition": Dalton Trumbo, *Spartacus*, and the end of the blacklist', *The Velvet Light Trap* 23: 75-100.

Sobchack, V. (1990) '"Surge and Splendor": a phenomenology of the Hollywood historical epic', *Representations* 29: 24-49.

Solomon, J. (2001a) *The Ancient World in the Cinema*. New Haven.

Solomon, J. (2001b) 'The sounds of cinematic antiquity', in Winkler, M.M. (ed.) *Classical Myth and Culture in the Cinema*. Oxford: 319-39.

Solomon, J. (2004) 'Gladiator from screenplay to screen', in Winkler, M.M. (ed.) *Gladiator: Film and History*. Malden: 1-15.

Solomon, J. (2010) 'The popular reception of *Alexander*', in Cartledge, P.A. and Greenland, F.R. (eds) *Responses to Oliver Stone's Alexander: Film, History, and Cultural Studies*. Madison: 36-51.

Spina, L. (2008) 'By Heracles! From satyr-play to *peplum*' in Berti, I. and Morcillo, M.G. (eds) *Hellas on Screen: Cinematic Receptions of Ancient History, Literature, and Myth*. Stuttgart: 57-64.

Stacey, J. (1994) *Star Gazing: Hollywood Cinema and Female Spectatorship*. London.

Sullivan, J.P. (2001) 'The social ambience of Petronius' *Satyricon* and *Fellini-Satyricon*', in Winkler, M.M. (ed.) *Classical Myth and Culture in the Cinema*. Oxford: 258-71.

Bibliography

Taplin, O. et al. (2000) *Medea in Performance 1500-2000*. Oxford.

Theodorakopoulos, E. (2010) *Ancient Rome at the Cinema: Story and Spectacle in Hollywood and Rome*. Exeter.

Thomas, B. (1997) *Disney's Art of Animation: From Mickey Mouse to Hercules*. New York.

Todorov, T. (1975) *The Fantastic: A Structural Approach to a Literary Genre*. Ithaca.

Towbin, M.A. et al. (2003) 'Images of gender, race, age, and sexual orientation in Disney feature-length animated films', *Journal of Feminist Family Therapy* 15: 19-44.

Trumbo, D. (1982) *The Time of the Toad: A Study of Inquisition in America*. London.

Tucker, E. (1997) 'Herc goes to Hollywood: but movie's animated "stew" had local flavour', *Chicago Sun-Times* (27/6/1997): 38.

Turner, G. (2006) *Film as Social Practice*. London.

Van Dyke, W. (1970) 'Movie mailbag: from "Patton" to "Satyricon" to Chaplin', *New York Times* (28/6/1970): 80.

Von Bothmer, D. (1957) *Amazons in Greek Art*. Oxford.

Von Fritz, K. (1954) *The Theory of the Mixed Constitution in Antiquity: A Critical Analysis of Polybius' Political Ideas*. New York.

Wagstaff, C. (1995) 'Italy in the Post-War International Cinema Market', in Duggan, C. and Wagstaff, C. (eds) *Italy in the Cold War: Politics, Culture, and Society 1948-58*. Oxford: 89-116.

Wagstaff, C. (1998) 'Italian genre films in the world market', in Nowell-Smith, G. and Ricci, S. (eds) *Hollywood and Europe: Economics, Culture, National Identity, 1945-95*. London: 74-85.

Ward, A.R. (2002) *Mouse Morality: The Rhetoric of Disney Animated Film*. Austin.

Ward, C.O. (1889) *The Ancient Lowly: A History of the Ancient Working People from the Earliest Known Period to the Adoption of Christianity by Constantine*. Chicago.

Watts, S. (2002) *The Magic Kingdom: Walt Disney and the American Way of Life*. Columbia, MO.

Webster, D. (1979) *Barbells and Beefcake*. Irvine.

Wells, P. (1998) *Understanding Animation*. London.

Wells, P. (2002) *Animation: Genre and Authorship*. London.

White, H. (1988) 'Historiography and historiophoty', *American Historical Review* 93: 1193-9.

Wiedemann, T.E.J. (1992) *Emperors and Gladiators*. London.

Williams, C. (2010) *Roman Homosexuality*. Oxford.

Wind, E. (1941-42) 'The sources of David's Horaces', *Journal of the Warburg and Courtauld Institutes* 4.3/4: 124-38.

Winkler, M.M. (1995) 'Cinema and the Fall of Rome', *Transactions of the American Philological Association* 125: 135-54.

Winkler, M.M. (ed.) (2001a) *Classical Myth and Culture in the Cinema*. Oxford.

Winkler, M.M. (2001b) 'The Roman empire in American cinema after 1945', in Joshel, S.R. et al. (eds) *Imperial Projections: Ancient Rome in Modern Popular Culture*. Baltimore and London: 50-76.

Winkler, M.M. (ed.) (2004) *Gladiator: Film and History*. Malden, MA.

Winkler, M.M. (ed.) (2007a) *Troy: From Homer's Iliad to Hollywood Epic*. Malden, MA.

Winkler, M.M. (ed.) (2007b) *Spartacus: Film and History*. Oxford.

Bibliography

Winkler, M.M. (2009a) *The Roman Salute: Cinema, History, Ideology*. Columbus.

Winkler, M.M. (2009b) *Cinema and Classical Texts: Apollo's New Light*. Cambridge.

Wintjes, J. (2006) 'From "Capitano" to "Great Commander": the military reception of Caesar from the sixteenth to the twentieth centuries', in Wyke, M. (ed.) *Julius Caesar in Western Culture*. Malden, MA: 269-84.

Wiseman, T.P. (1995) *Remus: A Roman Myth*. Cambridge.

Wood, M. (1975) *America in the Movies, or 'Santa Maria it had slipped my mind'*. London.

Wrigley, R. (2008) *Cinematic Rome*. Leicester.

Wyke, M. (1997a) *Projecting the Past: Ancient Rome, Cinema, and History*. London.

Wyke, M. (1997b) 'Herculean muscle!: the classicizing rhetoric of bodybuilding', *Arion* 4.3: 51-79.

Wyke, M. (ed.) (2006a) *Julius Caesar in Western Culture*. Malden, MA.

Wyke, M. (2006b) 'Caesar, cinema, and national identity in the 1910s', in Wyke, M. (ed.) *Julius Caesar in Western Culture*. Malden, MA: 170-89.

Zanelli, D. (ed.) (1970) *Fellini's Satyricon*. New York.

Index

257

Index

Dionysus 162, 214
Disney Corporation 195, 200
Disney, Roy E. 197
Disney, Walt 194-5, 213-14
Do Not Adjust Your Set (television series) 177
Dolce Vita, La (1960) 153, 155, 163, 165
Don't Change Your Husband (1919) 23
Donati, Danilo 156
Donovan, Tate 202
dormouse test 185-6
Double Take Meets Hercules (stage show) 192
Douglas, Kirk 39, 83-5, 86, 94
Douglas, Lloyd C. 38, 56
Duel of the Titans (1961) 78
Dungeons and Dragons (role-playing game) 140
Dynamation 129, 130; see also animation

Eagle of the Ninth (children's novel) 219
Eagle, The (2011) 219-20
Earth vs the Flying Saucers (1956) 130
Edward Scissorhands (1990) 126
Egan, Richard 108, 110
Egyptomania 24
Eisenstein, Sergei 194-5
Eisner, Michael 196
Electra (1962) 149
EMI Films 179
Encolpio (Encolpius) 151, 155, 158-60, 163, 165, 169, Fig. 15
epic film 36-40, 102, 164, 207, 209; as metaphor for Hollywood studios 37, 50; cost 36, 174, 217; decline in popularity 174, 216-18; extravagance 36, 45, 185-6; narrative themes 39-40, 43, 50-3, 56, 184; on television 40, 46, 218; revival 216, 219-21; satirized 181, 183-6, 216
Eumolpo (Eumolpus) 151, 158-60, 161, Fig. 15
Euripides 149, 170

Fall of the Roman Empire, The (1964) 36, 40, 57, 216-19, 217, 221, 226
Fall of Troy, The (It: *La caduta di Troia*, 1911) 18, 125
Fantasia (1940) 213-14
fantasy films 37, 125-8, 133
Farnese Heracles 2, 70-2
Fascism 40, 42, 50, 69, 184; see also Nazism
Fast, Howard 81
Fawlty Towers (television series) 179
Fellini, Federico 59, 152-3, 163, 166-7, 168
Fellini-Satyricon (1969) 146-71, 184, 216, Figs 15 and 16; budget 4, 156; casting

151-2, 154-5; fragmentary nature 160-3; marketing 9; naming of film 156-7; reception 157-8
Fifth Element, The (1997) 125
film, as art 16; audience 11, 15-16, 39, 232; casting 9, 154-5; censorship 22-3, 54, 140, 181; distribution and exhibition 217-18; finance and commercial pressures 9, 15, 37, 60, 134, 147, 156, 174, 217; how to watch 7-12; marketing 9-10, 11, 156, 157, 199; realism 39, 44, 173; silent 16; sound 19-20, 140, 173; studio system 36, 217-18; technology and special effects 11, 18, 35, 37, 62, 147, 155, 225-6
Flying Wedge 107-8, Fig.10
Flynn, Errol 178
Four Frightened People (1934) 23
Franzoni, David 223
French Revolution 4
Friday Night, Saturday Morning (television series) 181-2
Frost Report, The (television series) 177

gangster film 34
Gardner, Helen 22
Gérôme, Jean-Léon 3, 24, 185, 224, Fig. 20
Giant of Marathon (It.: *La battaglia di Maratona*, 1959) 68, 103-4, 123-4
Gibbon, Edward 57
Gilliam, Terry 176-9
Gitone (Giton) 151, 155, 158-60, 161, 165, 177
Gladiator (2000) 8, 11, 216, 218-35, Figs 20 and 21; accents in 227-8; as postmodern epic film 221, 222-3, 226, 231; family as new religion 228, 233-4; heroism 226-8; history painting as inspiration 185, 224, Fig. 20; Leni Riefenstahl, influence of 224-5; reception 3-4; set-design 7; violence as entertainment 229-33
gladiators (Roman) 88-92, in film 184-5, 221-2, 226, 230, 231-3
Gladiator, The (play) 92-3
God of War (videogame series) 220-1
gods, Greek 39, 125, 127-8, analogy with animator 133, 143; problem of representation on film 127-8, 141; relationship with man 132, 135, 140-3, 145, Fig. 14
Godzilla (1956) 62
Golden Voyage of Sinbad, The (1974) 130
Golding, William 106
Goldstone, John 179
Gorgo 113, 118-20, Fig. 11
Gray, Hugh 39, 45
Great Mouse Detective, The (1986) 197

259

Index

Greece, conventions in depiction 65-9, 107; depictions of history 101-5
Greek chorus 172-3
Greek pottery, use of 68, 161-2, 209
Green, Nigel 131
Greenland, Fiona 104
Guinness, Alec 217

Hades 202, 203, 204
Half a Sixpence (stage play) 132
Handmade Films 179
Hanks, Tom 135
Hannibal the Conqueror (in development 2011) 219
Harpies 135, 136, 139, 140
Harris, Richard 228
Harrison, George 179
Harry Potter films 145, 219
Harryhausen Chronicles, The (1997) (television film) 133
Harryhausen, Ray 35, 129-35, 136-43, 144, 220
haruspicy 169
Hays, Will 22
Haywood, Susan 232
Hecht, Ben 39
Hector 204
Helen of Troy (1956) 39, 45, 76, 128, 155
helots 117-18
Hephaestion 97-8
Hephaestus 75, 214
Hera 132, 135, 141, 143, 201, 213
Herculaneum 2
Hercules (1958) 58-76, 132, 192, Fig. 8; depiction of Greece 65-9; gender roles 73-5; male bodies 70-2; marketing 12, 62-3; reception 12, 62, 64; satirized 175
Hercules (1997) 128, 141, 194-215, 216, Fig. 19; depiction of heroism 203-7; distance from epic film 207-10; marketing 199-201; production history 197-8; treatment of myth 210-13
Hercules (Disney TV series) 199
Hercules against the Barbarians (It.: *Maciste nell'inferno di Gengis Khan*, 1964) 61
Hercules against the Mongols (It.: *Maciste contro i Mongoli*, 1963) 61, 133
Hercules against the Moon Men (It.: *Maciste e la regina di Samar*, 1964) 61, 174, 175
Hercules against the Sons of the Sun (It: *Ercole contro i figli del sole*, 1964) 61
Hercules and the Captive Women (It.: *Ercole alla conquista di Atlantide*, 1961) 76, 175

Hercules in New York (1970) 61, 126, 128, 143-4
Hercules in the Haunted World (It.: *Ercole al centro della terra*, 1962) 61
Hercules in the Valley of Woe (It.: *Maciste contro Ercole nella valle dei guai*, 1961) 61
Hercules myth 17, 72, 204
Hercules on ice (Disney skating spectacular) 199-200
Hercules Returns (1993) 61, 174, 192-3
Hercules Unchained (It: *Ercole e la regina di Lidia*, 1959) 61-2, 63
Hercules, Samson, Maciste and Ursus (It: *Ercole, Sansone, Maciste e Ursus gli invincibili*, 1964) 61, 174, 192
hermaphrodite 167-8
Herod the Great (It.: *Erode il Grande*, 1958, US release 1960) 5-6, Fig. 1
Herodotus 6, 104, 107, 114, 118-19, 120, 121-3
heroes and heroines 38, 128, 203-7, 226
Heston, Charlton 208, 209
Highet, Gilbert 157
historical consultants 4, 222
historical fiction 18, 19, 38, 40
history painting 2, 24, 185, 223, 237
Hitler, Adolf 43, 51, 224-5
Hollywood Ten 53, 84; see also blacklist
Homer 39, 125, 220, *Iliad* 38-9, 68, 125, 204; *Odyssey* 38-9, 84, 197
homosexuality 95-8, 103, 109, 163, 169, 215
Hoover, J. Edgar 83
Hopkins, Anthony 20, 95, 235
Horace 158
horror films 125
Hounsou, Djimon 228
House of the Flying Daggers (2004) 126
House Un-American Activities Committee (HUAC) 53-4, 81, 84, 94-5, 124
Hunchback of Notre Dame (1996) 197
Huston, John 43, 45, 54
Hydra 128, 134, 136, 202

I'm No Angel (1933) 23
Idle, Eric 176-9, 182, 188
Iphigenia (1977) 149
Iron Crown, The (It.: *La corona di ferro*, 1941) 69
Island of the Lost Women (1959) 75
It Came From Beneath the Sea (1955) 130
It's a Wonderful Life (1946) 126
Italian film industry 17, 59-61
Izzard, Eddie 177

Jabberwocky (1977) 179
Jason 131-2, 135-6

260

Index

CPSIA information can be obtained
at www.ICGtesting.com
Printed in the USA
LVOW04s1923190416
484356LV00003B/57/P